Wild Things Are Happening

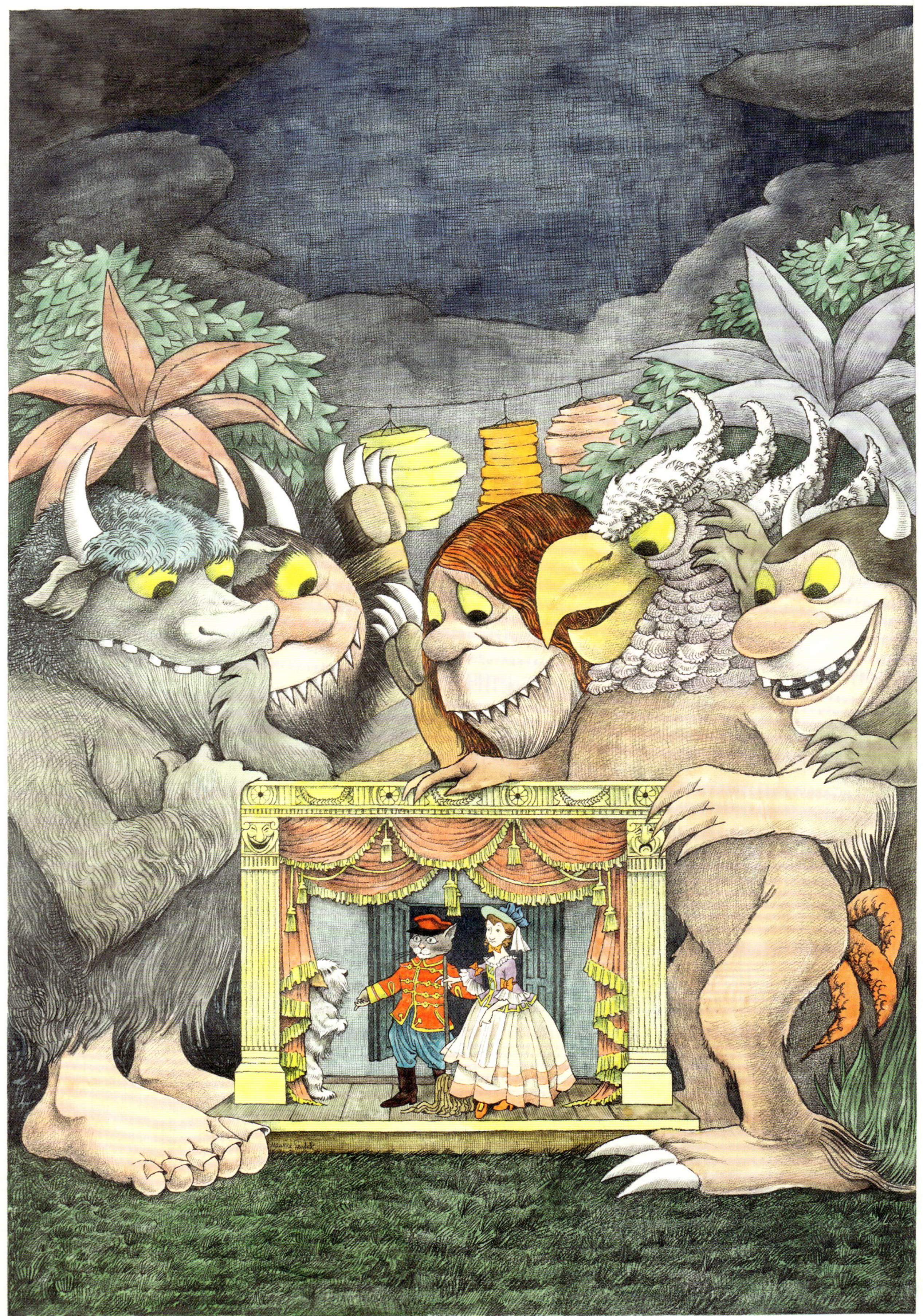

Wild Things Are Happening
The Art of Maurice Sendak

Edited by Jonathan Weinberg

With an analysis by Thomas Crow

Columbus Museum of Art

DelMonico Books • D.A.P.
New York

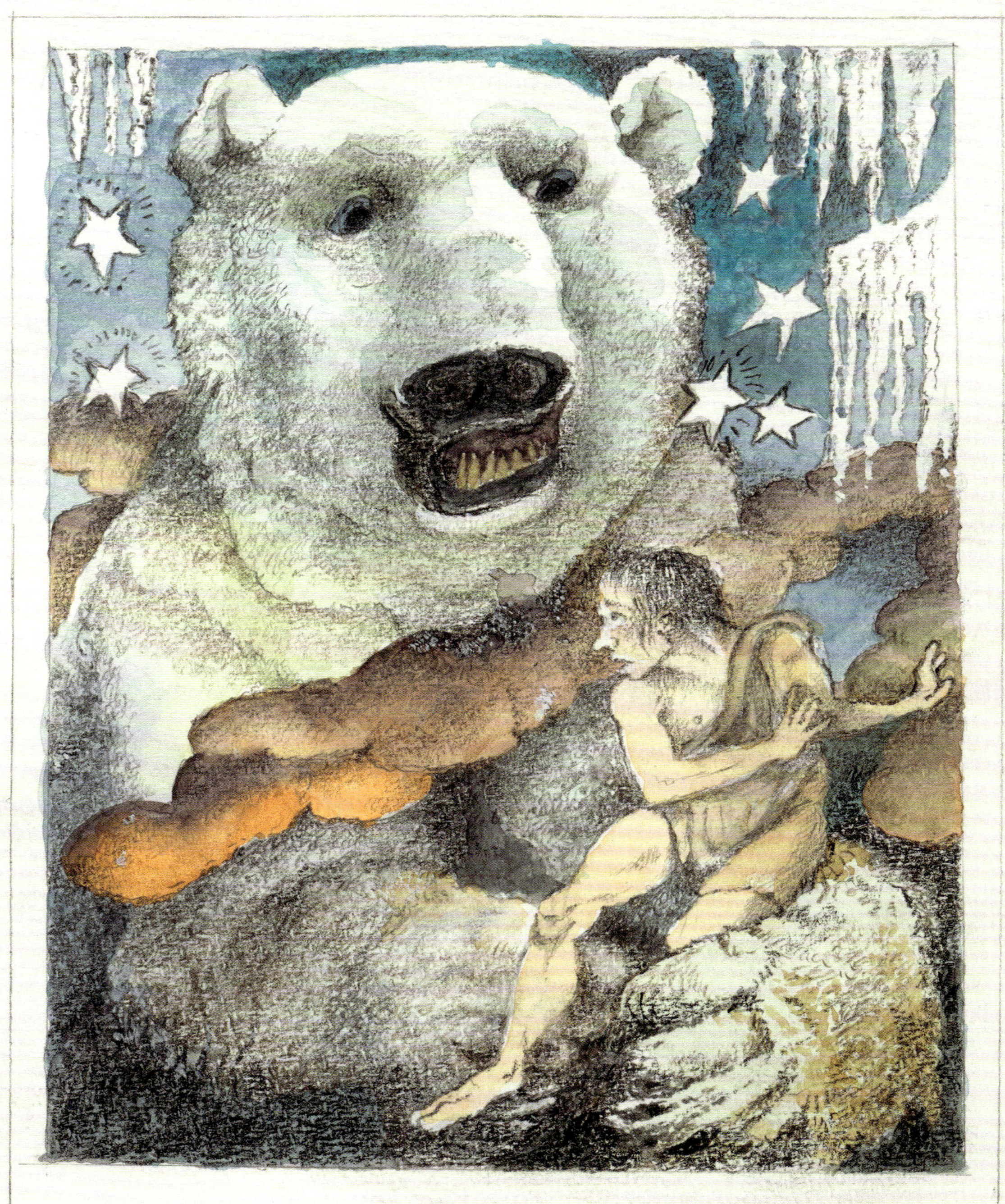
AUG. 20, 2010

TABLE OF CONTENTS

Director's Foreword

Wild Things Are Happening, The Art of Maurice Sendak is the first major retrospective of the artist since his death in 2012. Its title is taken from an advertising campaign Sendak designed for the Bell Atlantic telecom company in the 1990s in which he recreated some of the loveable monsters he first painted in 1963. Here the title signals not only the magnetic effect of Sendak's most famous work, *Where the Wild Things Are*, but all the beauty and mischief-making his art has generated over his sixty-year career.

Comprised of over 150 objects, the exhibition features sketches, story boards and paintings by Sendak drawn from the collection of the Maurice Sendak Foundation. The Foundation owns most of Sendak's major works including the original paintings and sketches for his books, as well as designs for many of his opera, theatre, film, and television productions. This exhibition and catalog are notable not only for their scope, but for the way they focus on Sendak's emulation of other artists, and the role art history plays in his creative process by including works Sendak owned, by such artists as William Blake, George Stubbs, Philipp Otto Runge, and Winsor McCay.

Maurice Sendak (1928–2012) was born in Brooklyn, New York, to Polish Jewish immigrant parents. A largely self-taught artist, his career was jumpstarted in 1952, when he created the delightful pictures for Ruth Krauss's acclaimed *A Hole Is to Dig*. His *Little Bear* series of books begun in 1957, with text by Else Holmelund Minarik, became instant classics. *Kenny's Window*, the first children's book that he both wrote and illustrated, was published in 1956. In 1962, the four tiny volumes of *The Nutshell Library* (with its boy Pierre who keeps saying "I Don't Care!") were an instant hit. But it was in 1963, with the acclaim and controversy surrounding the monsters of *Where the Wild Things Are* that Sendak's work became a cultural touchstone. Sendak continued to expand on the boundaries of the picture book medium in terms of both form and content with such works as *In the Night Kitchen* (1970), *Outside Over There* (1981), *We are All in the Dumps with Jack and Guy* (1993), and, with Tony Kushner, *Brundibar* (2003).

Sendak remains the most honored picture book artist in history. His numerous awards include the Caldecott Medal, The Hans Christian Andersen Award, and the National Medal of Arts. In the 1970s Sendak began a second career designing productions for the stage including *The Magic Flute*, *The Cunning Little Vixen*, and the *Nutcracker*. Sendak has collaborated with some of the greatest writers and directors of his time, including Carroll Ballard, Frank Corsaro, Randall Jarrell, Spike Jonze, Tony Kushner, Isaac Bashevis Singer, and Arthur Yorinks.

Jonathan Weinberg, guest curator of the exhibition, is an artist and art historian. A close friend of Sendak, he is Curator of The Maurice Sendak Foundation. He has brought together for this book a diversity of perspectives on the artist, with an introduction by Lynn Caponera, Sendak's longtime friend, assistant and now Executive Director of his Foundation and President of its Board; and leading essays by Thomas Crow, Rosalie Solow Professor of Modern Art, Institute of Fine Arts, New York University; and John Bell, Director, of the University of Connecticut's Ballard Institute and Museum of Puppetry. In 2022 Bell curated an exhibition at The Ballard, on Sendak's relationship to puppetry and to performing objects. Sendak's eloquence in speaking about the sources and meanings of his art is apparent in two interviews with the artist and numerous quotes from previously published writings and interviews. His charisma is also conveyed through extracts from oral histories with Sendak's collaborators and friends.

This project would not have been possible without the generous collaboration of The Maurice Sendak Foundation. Specific thanks go to Lynn Caponera and Jonathan Weinberg. We are also grateful to John Monaco for his exhibition design and advice.

Preliminary planning for the exhibition was aided significantly by the faculty and staff of the University of Connecticut and in particular Anne D'Alleva, Amanda Douberley, Clara Nguyen, Rebecca Palmer, Kerry Smith, Mollie Sixsmith, Karen Sommer, Nancy Stula, and Rachel Zilinski. Thanks also go to Susan Bahr, Christina and Carroll Ballard, Nicholas Boshnack, Virginia Caponera, Michael di Capua, Nina and Larry Chertoff, Brother Christopher, Dennis David, Tyler Fallas, Jorie Feldman, Rachel Federman, John Firestone , Mark Greenhalgh, Paul Gulla, Melissa Hagar, Luke Ingram, Bill Jersey, Spike Jonze, Shirley Kessler, Jaqueline Ko, Swietlan Kraczyna, Tony Kushner, Toni Markiet, Leah McCloskey, Marilyn Palmeri, Elvira Piedra, Doug Salati and Justin Schiller, David Shevlin, Matthew Sorensen, Stephen Stinehour, Maura Whelan, Emily Wicks, Andrew Wylie, Arthur Yorinks, and Beth Ziemacki.

We would like to thank our distribution partner, DelMonico Books, especially Mary DelMonico. This exhibition and catalog have benefited immeasurably from the design skills of Miko McGinty and Rita Jules. Their contribution to the book goes far beyond laying out its pictures and type—they were crucial collaborators in crafting both its form and content. Thanks too go to Tina Henderson for expert typesetting and editor Sally Salvesen.

At the Columbus Museum of Art we would like to thank the entire staff, including David Stark, chief curator emeritus, who oversaw the exhibition in Columbus; in curatorial, Tyler Cann, Nicole Rome, and Elizabeth Hopkin; Greg Jones, exhibition design and production manager and his team, David Holm and Cameron Sharp; Lucy Ackley, director of advancement and her team, Maureen Carroll, Tiffany Duncan, and James Allen, Betsy Meacham and Amber Wacker; Cindy Foley, executive deputy director for learning and experience and her team Hannah Mason-Macklin, Jennifer Lehe, Amanda Kepner, Caitlin Lynch, Lauren Emond, Mark Zuzik, and Megan Green; and Tricia Mitchell, director's office.

It is no small matter that the current exhibition is organized by The Columbus Museum of Art, whose collections and exhibition history encompass the entire gamut of world art. Often remembered as America's greatest illustrator, Sendak deserves to be known simply as a great artist whose work shines both on the page and on the walls of museums alongside the wonderful painters and printmakers he revered.

Nannette V. Maciejunes
Executive Director and CEO
COLUMBUS MUSEUM OF ART

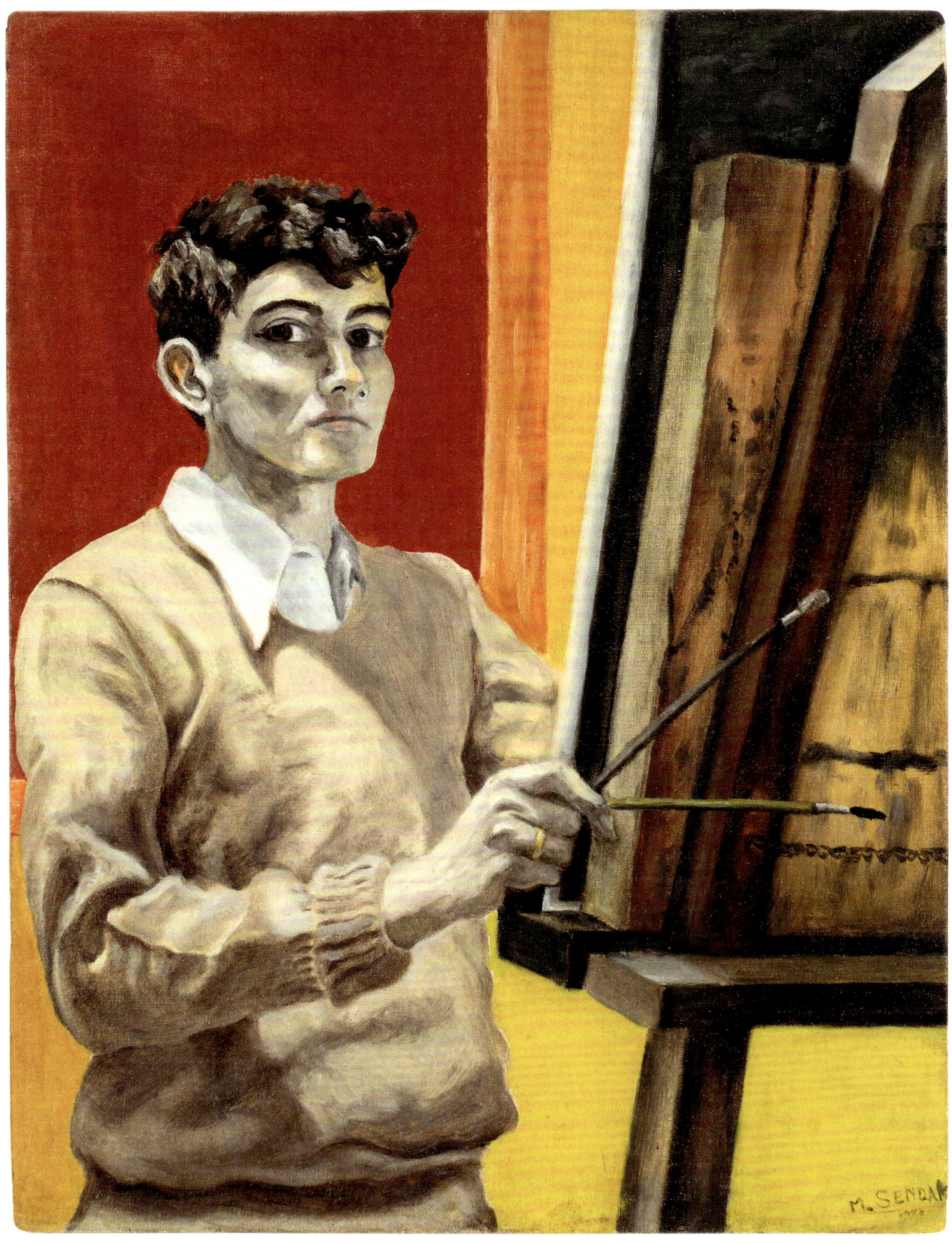

Maurice Sendak, *Self-Portrait*, 1948, oil on board, 17½ × 24 in.

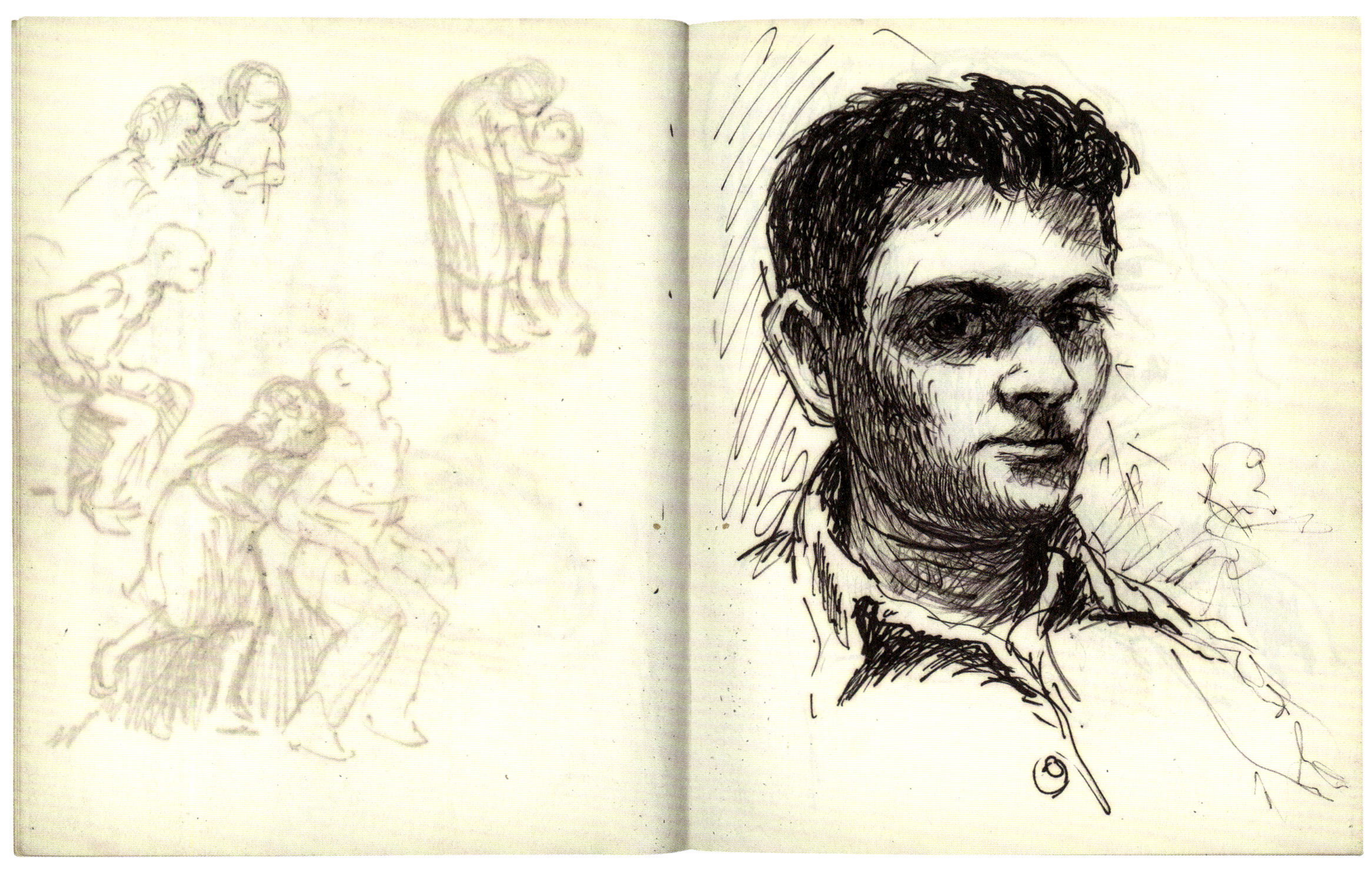

Maurice Sendak, *Self-Portrait*, 1950, ink on paper, 10¾ × 16½ in.

page 10: Maurice Sendak, *Self-Portrait*, 1968, pencil on paper, 11 × 8½ in.

page 11: Maurice Sendak, *Self-Portrait*, 1971, pencil on paper, 11 × 8½ in.

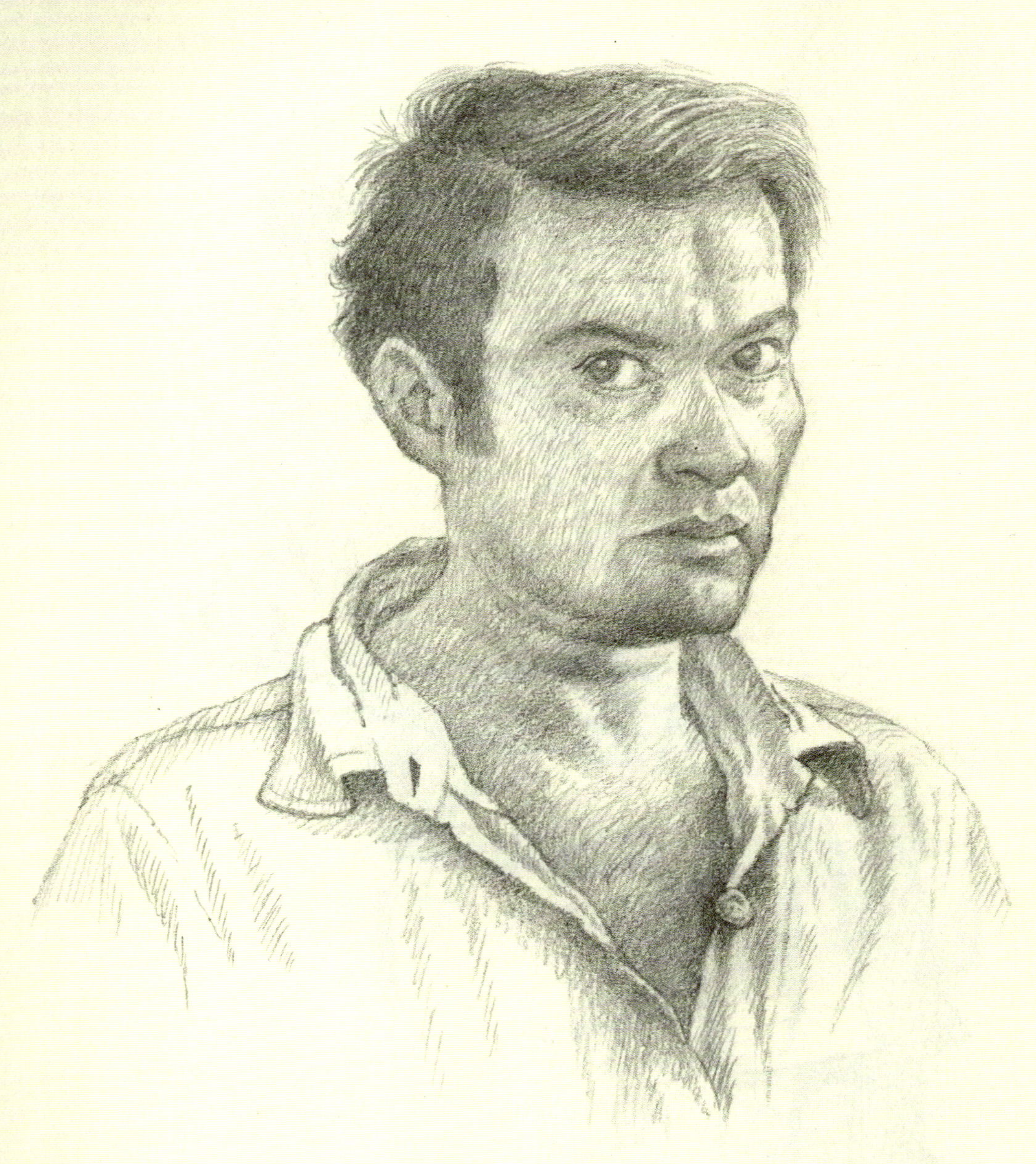
Sept. 12, 68
Fire Island

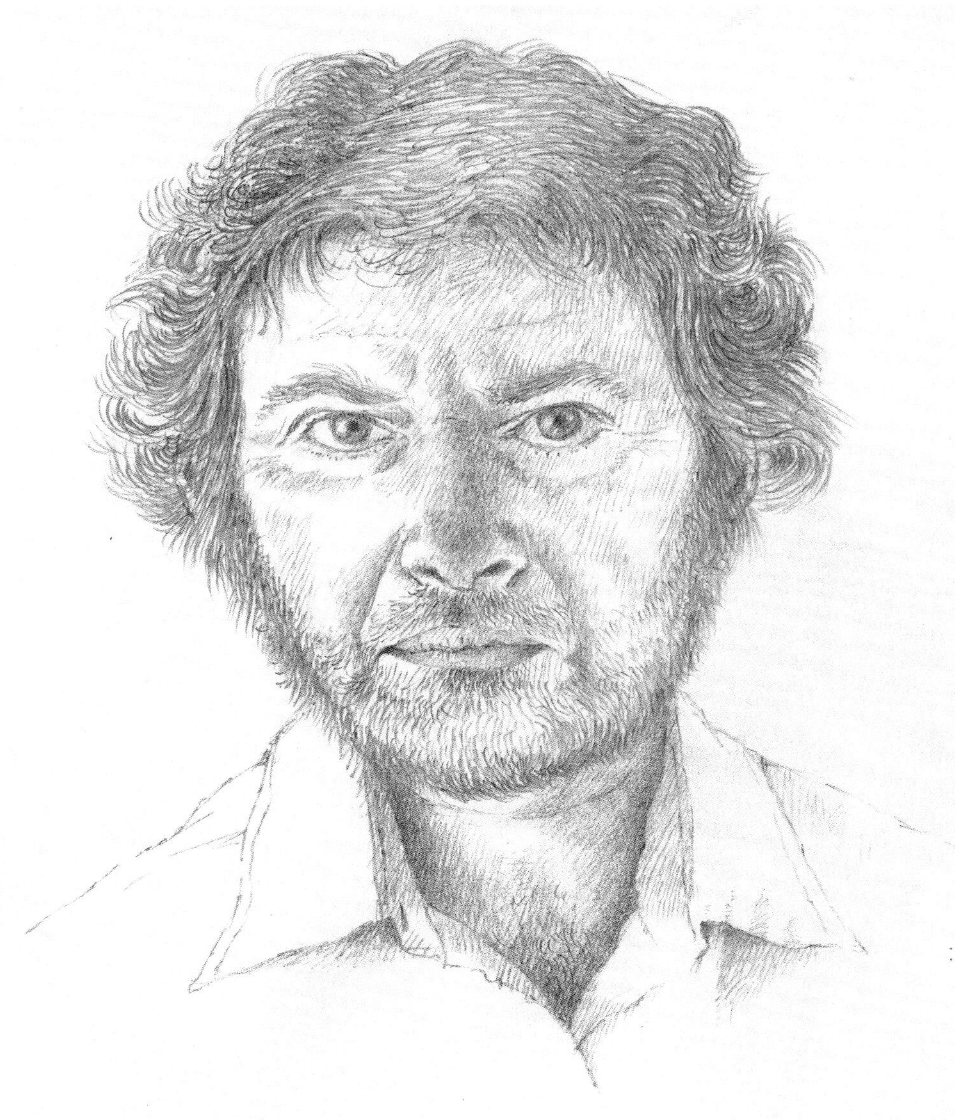
July 15, 71
Wales

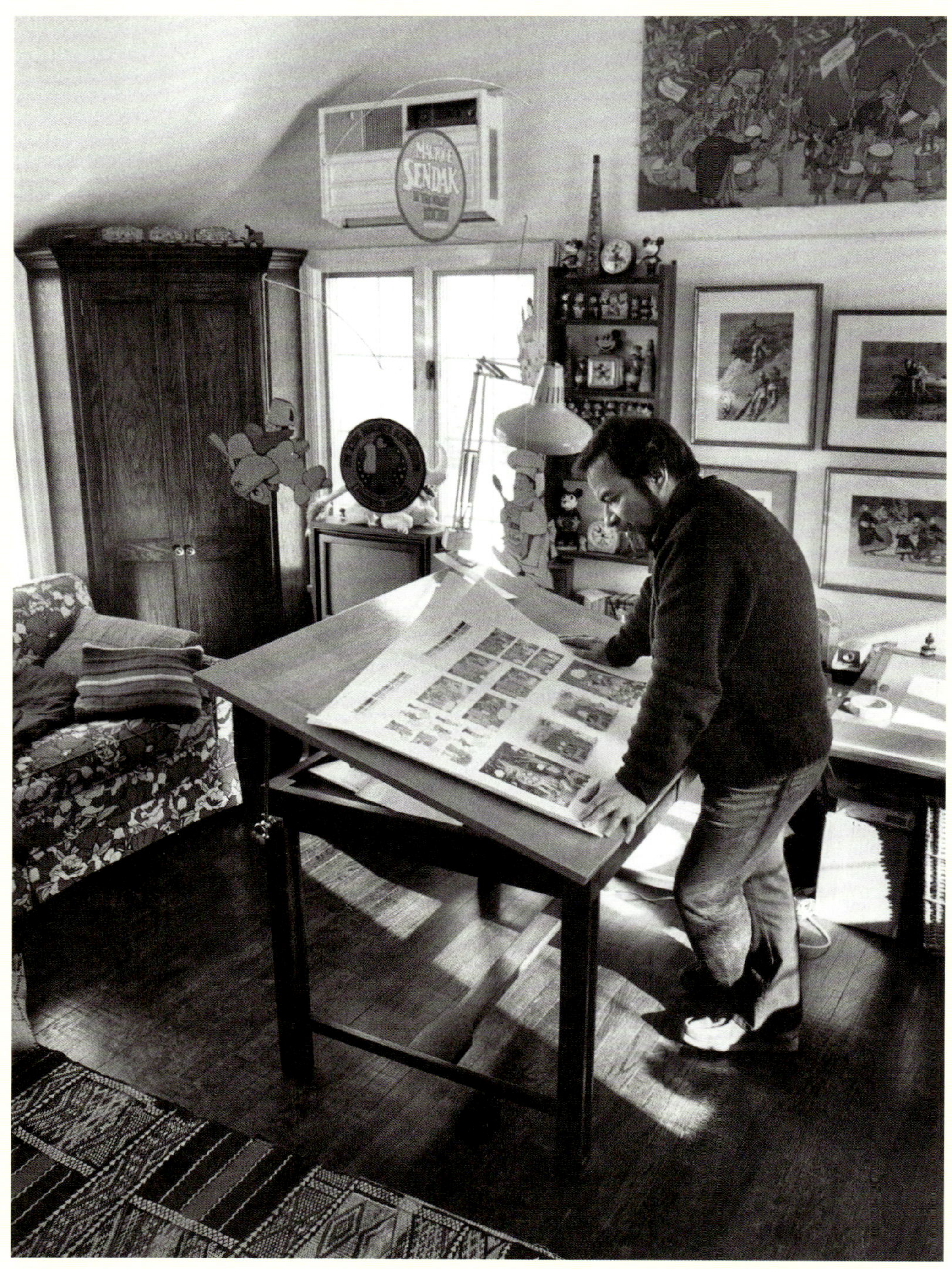

Maurice Sendak in his Studio, 1976 © copyright Nancy Crampton.

"As a child I felt that books were holy objects,
to be caressed, rapturously sniffed, and devotedly
provided for. I gave my life to them . . ."

Maurice Sendak Works

LYNN CAPONERA

The typical question when calling the Sendak house was "Is he working?"

And the typical answer was "Yes!"

Friends knew that for Maurice work was a sort of life support. And those in his circle, we who loved him, strove to create an atmosphere conducive to that work that kept him alive.

Maurice found comfort in a rigorous schedule: up at 9:00 am, green tea and English muffin spread with just the right amount of orange marmalade, freshly squeezed orange juice and two hours of reading the *New York Times*, sprinkled with the hilarious, ridiculous commentary that he swore, of course, he was reading in the paper. 11:00 am answer or return phone calls; 12 noon shower and dress, then an hour walk with one of his beloved dogs.

It was during his walk time that guests could visit if they liked. But it was walk and talk and a quick bite for lunch then off you go. If you weren't too demanding of his time, you might be asked to sit in the studio while he worked.

He had this uncanny ability to draw and paint while having a conversation, listening to the TV or music on the stereo or radio. It was almost as if he needed to occupy one side of his brain to let the other side create. While working, the only time he needed complete silence was when writing, which he said didn't come as easily as drawing.

5 pm was news on the TV time and cake, most likely a piece he saved after having a piece with lunch. 7 pm was nap time, then, after waking, dinner while watching old movies or anything to do with nature. 9 pm it was back at work in the studio until the 11 o'clock news came on. Then more cake and . . . yes, more work till 2 or 3 in the morning.

Maurice followed this routine just about every day. He didn't like going to parties or doing anything that would disrupt his work time. His friends understood that if you wanted him in your life you had to fit into his schedule, which they gladly did, since it's not often you can witness a genius at work.

He didn't have any formal education in art. He chose from an early age to educate himself, to study and draw on his own. While most kids would pin up athletes and movie stars on their bedroom walls, Maurice would pin magazine clippings of Titian and El Greco paintings. He would spend countless hours sketching his family and the children playing in the streets outside his apartment window.

Even after becoming a successful artist, he kept up his studies throughout his life. His immense knowledge of art and literature made it possible for him to seemingly shape shift between different styles of illustration. His work had the magical ability to be different and still be essentially Sendak all at the same time.

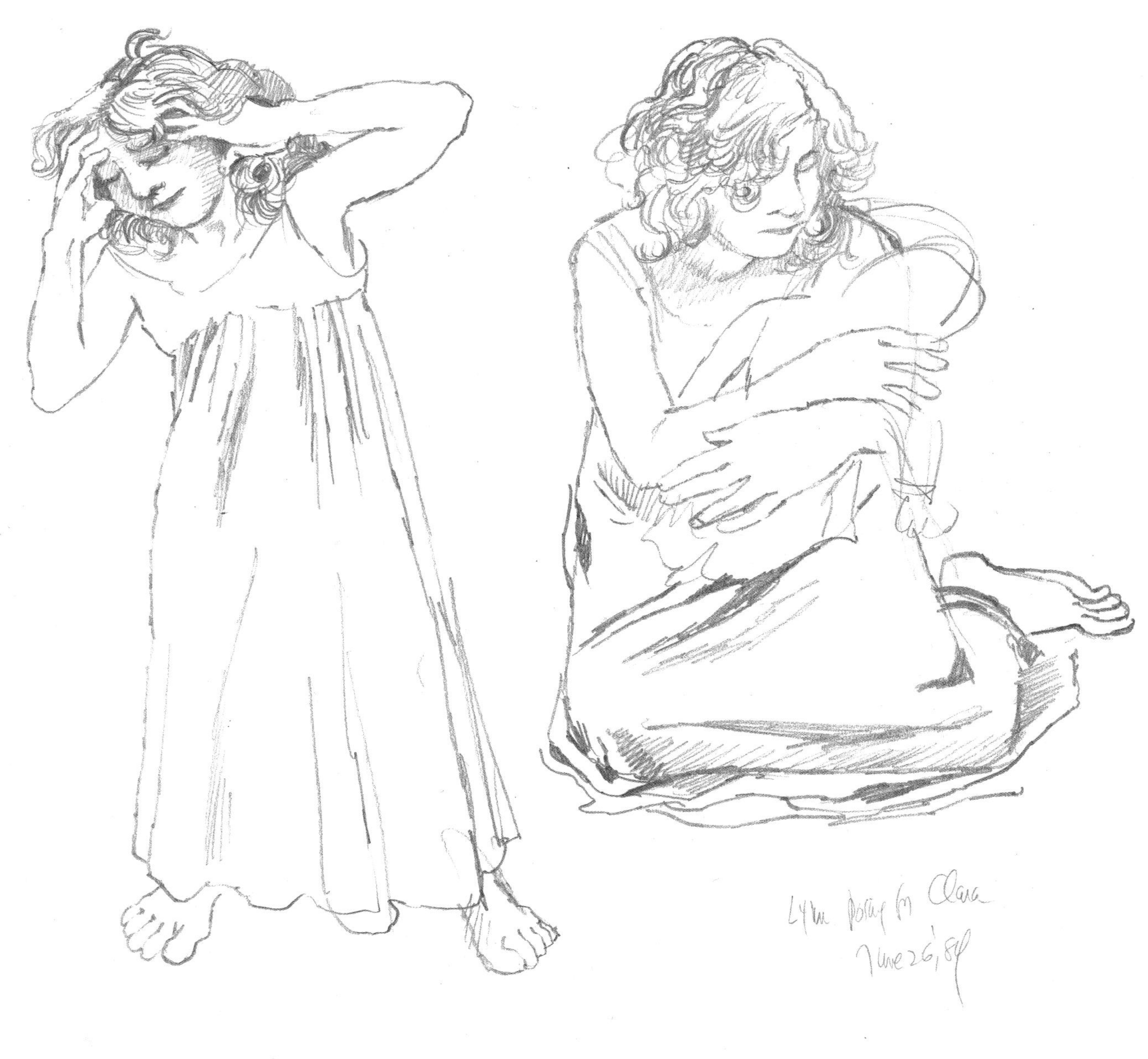

Maurice Sendak, Study for *Nutcracker*: Lynn Caponera posing for Clara, 1984, pencil on paper, 11 × 14 in.

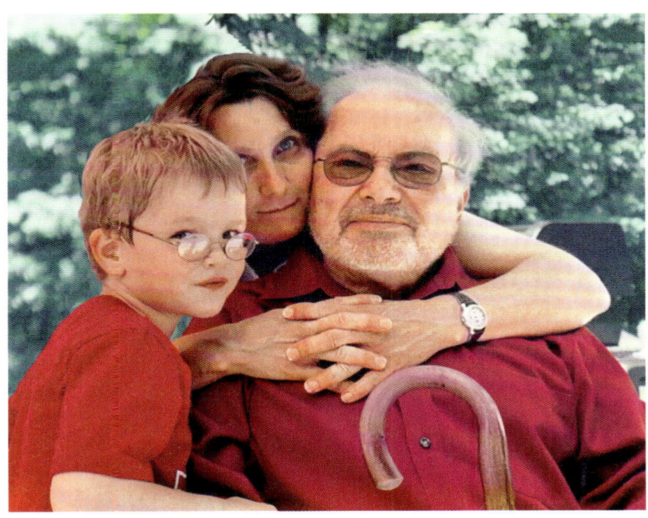

Maurice Sendak with Lynn Caponera and her son Nick Frost, 2005

When Jonathan Weinberg suggested the foundation should mount a retrospective of Maurice's work it was an enthusiastic "Yes!" Afterall, Jonathan and I spent more than forty years peering over his shoulder at his drawing table. We witnessed how he would draw on his deep knowledge of artists from the past to weave their way into whatever his current book or opera project was.

The life of an artist can be a lonely business, but having his old friends, the long-gone artists and composers whom he revered, helped him persevere through his long work hours and his bouts of depression. It was simple. Work was his salvation.

Those of us who knew him—well, we are fortunate to have been mentored by Maurice in how to make a picture book. Watching him journey from a single note, idea, sketch all the way to a full-blown finished book was a master class. I think while you're here flipping through this book or experiencing the exhibition in person you will no doubt come away feeling the need to look deeper into Maurice's work and the artistic gods who inspired him.

Maurice liked to quote one of his heroes, Herman Melville, who said

> Artists have to take a dive, and either you hit your head on a rock and it splits your skull, and you die, or that blow to your head is so inspiring that you come back up and you do the best work you ever did. But—you have to take the dive.

We invite you to take a dive! Wild things are happening here. Indeed.

following pages: Maurice Sendak, *The Moon Jumpers*, 1959, watercolor on board, 10 × 14¼ in.

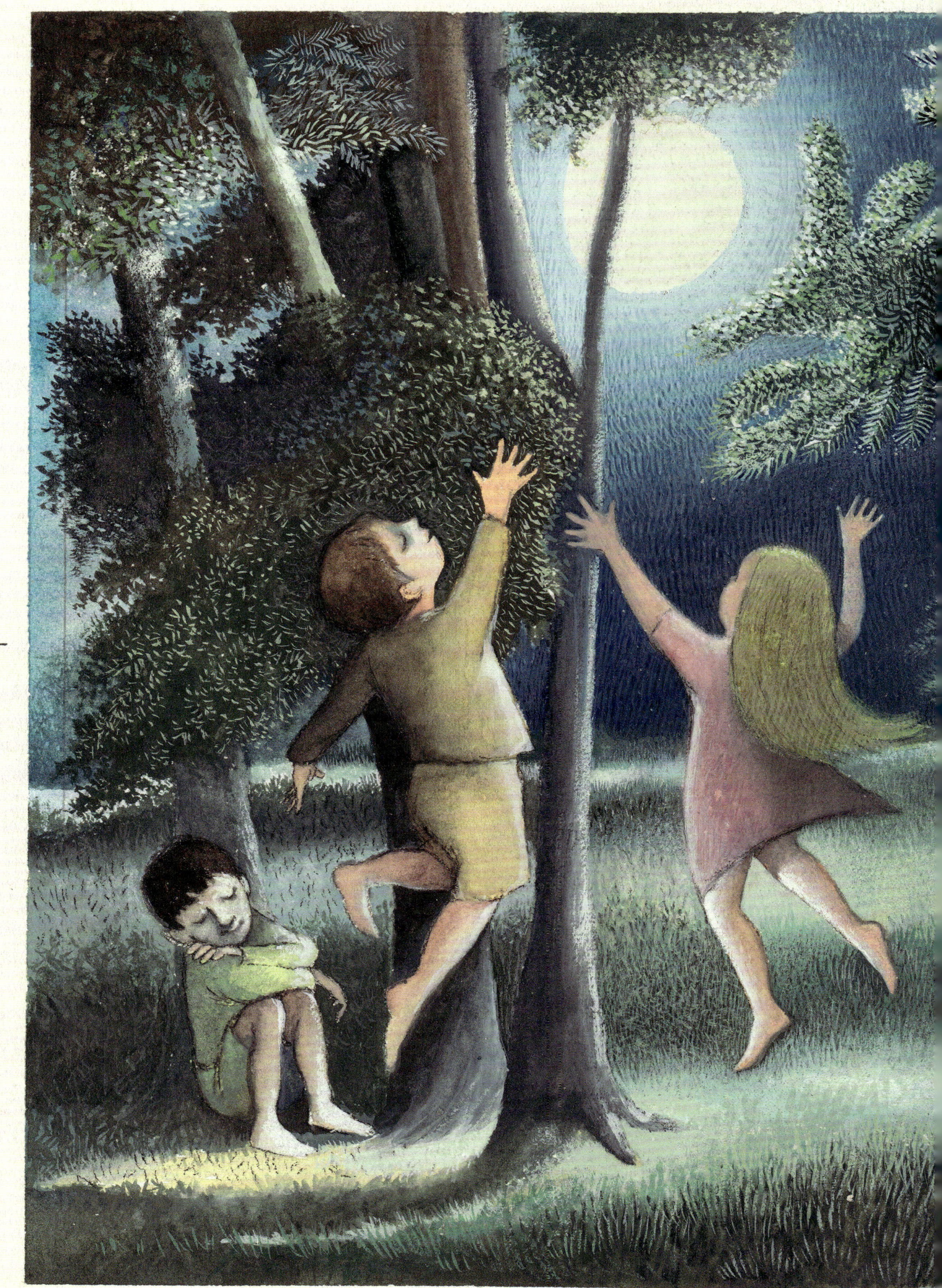

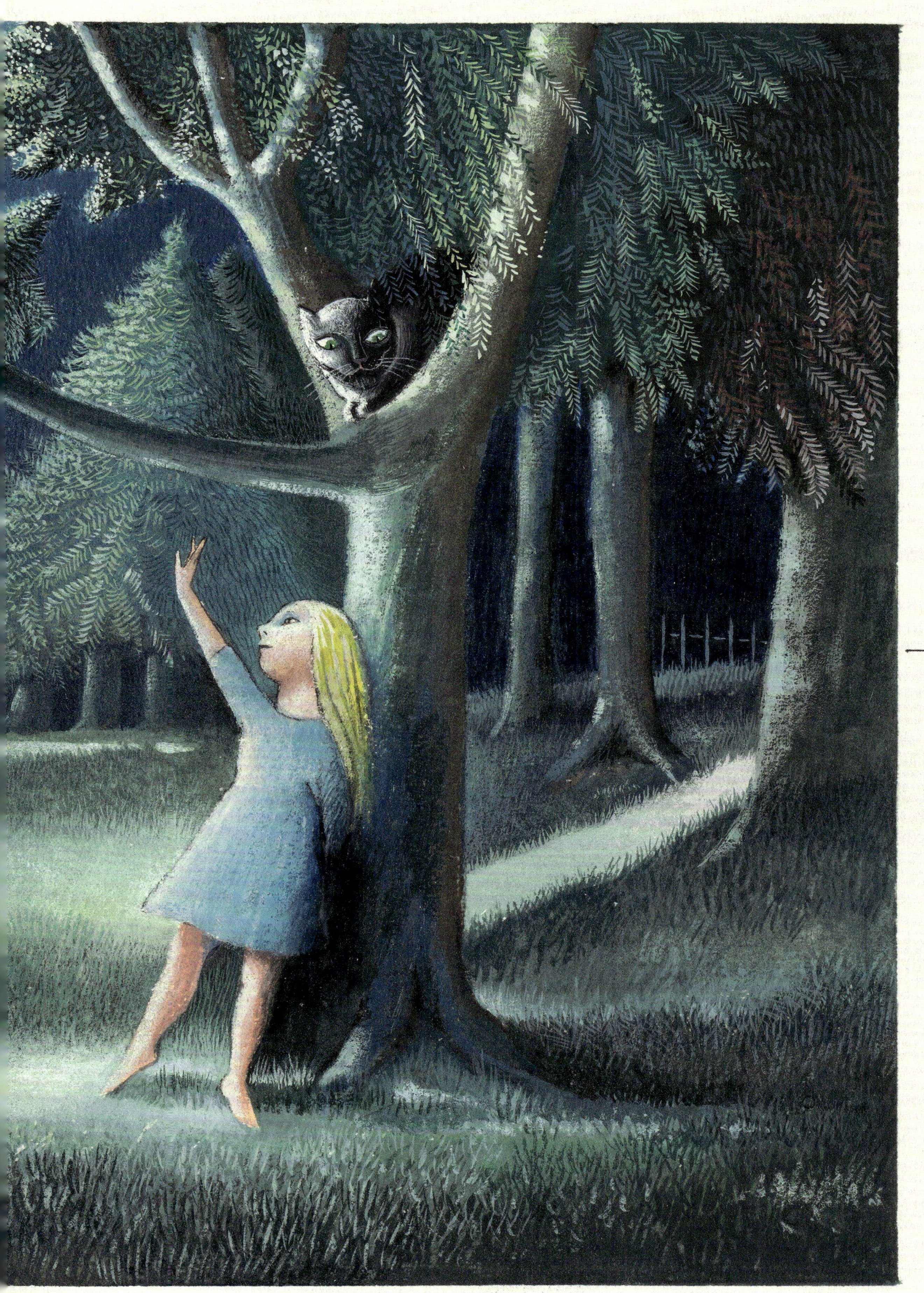

Sendak's Salvation

JONATHAN WEINBERG

Jonathan Cott begins his book *There's a Mystery There: The Primal Vision of Maurice Sendak*, by invoking Charles Baudelaire's declaration that "genius is no more than *childhood recovered* at will." Like many other critics and scholars, Cott claims that what makes Maurice Sendak's art so compelling is its instinctual connection to childhood fantasies and feelings.[1] However, Cott leaves out the second, and I think equally crucial aspect of Baudelaire's assertion, the way that the great artist must be equipped with "manhood's capacities and a power of analysis."[2] A central focus of *Wild Things Are Happening* is the second half of Baudelaire's concept and in particular, how Sendak, consciously utilized art history in his work. Crucial to his creative development has been the way he emulates artists of the past, ranging from William Blake to Vincent van Gogh, from Philipp Otto Runge to Winsor McCay. He weaves these often highly disparate sources into a constantly evolving practice so that no matter how derived from other styles, his work remains distinctly Sendakian.

Before launching into my main topic, I must admit that in writing about Sendak, I cannot be objective. He and his long-time companion, Dr. Eugene Glynn, a psychiatrist and art critic, were part of my extended family and I grew up in the late 60s and 70s watching Sendak draw and paint. In 2003 I had the privilege to publicly interview Sendak on the relationship of his work to the art of the past.[3] That interview, excerpts of which are included in this book (see pp. 216–19), was an attempt to distill the countless conversations we had over the years on long walks and when he was working at his drawing table. Sendak's studios, first in New York City's Greenwich Village in the 1960s, and then in Ridgefield, Connecticut after 1972, were magical places filled with images and objects that inspired him. Sendak talked of these things as "talismans," helping him guide whatever was his latest project.[4]

To follow the history of the paintings, toys, and figurines with which Sendak surrounded himself, is to chart his transformations as an artist. In the 1960s reproductions of paintings by William Blake, Pieter Bruegel the Elder, and Edouard Vuillard shared the walls with prints by Winslow Homer, and the illustrator Hans Fischer. When he moved to Ridgefield, several more Homer prints went up, along with a rare hand-colored engraving by Blake, a Maxfield Parrish painting, and landscape etchings by the British Romantic artist, Samuel Palmer. Mickey Mouse figurines and other memorabilia that were current in the 1930s when Sendak was a child, shared the same space with a set of exquisite watercolors by Beatrix Potter of bats, and photographs by Lewis Carroll. And of course, there was always at least one portrait of his beloved Mozart. In essence, he was creating an artistic genealogy. But there was room

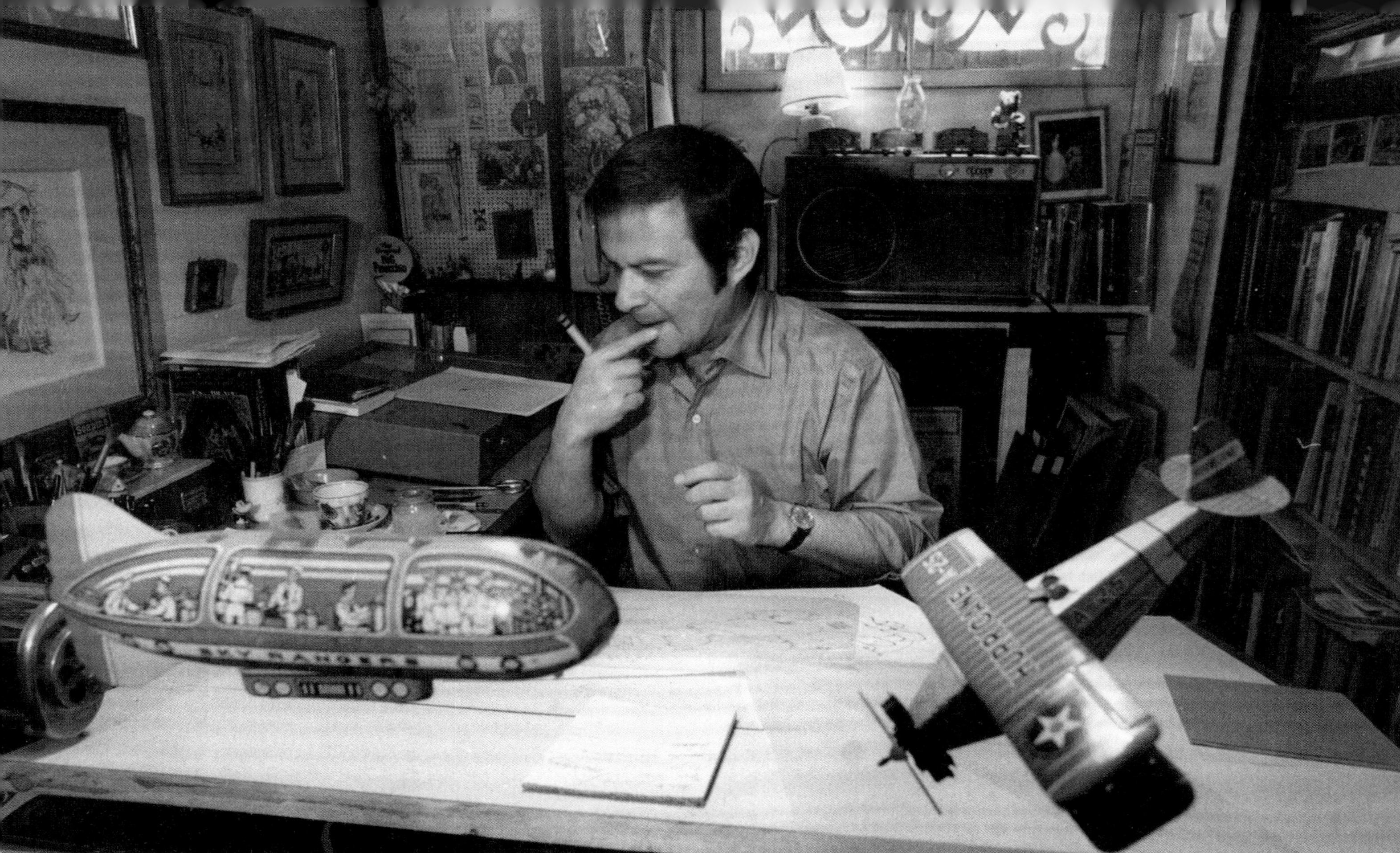

Maurice Sendak in his New York City 9th Street Studio, 1970 © copyright Kurt Ammann

too for photographs of his real family: his parents and grandparents, as well as pictures of his beloved dogs and of Glynn. Pride of place above his light table was given to a picture from Sendak's own *Higglety Pigglety Pop! Or There Must Be More to Life* of Jennie, Sendak's beloved Sealyham terrier. It was the only one of his own pictures that he consistently kept up in his Ridgefield studio until he died, and he insisted that it was his favorite book.[5]

There was nothing childlike about Sendak's work habits, as his long-time assistant, Lynn Caponera—now Executive Director and President of the Board of The Maurice Sendak Foundation—can attest (see pp. 13–15). Whenever possible, Sendak kept to a rigid schedule, drawing and painting through the day and long past midnight. He may have complained about the pressure, but the truth was he was always happiest when he was working (as he worked he whistled in perfect pitch to classical composers such as Mozart, Mahler, Schubert, or Verdi). This dedication to his art allowed him to complete pictures for over 150 books during his lifetime as well as more than a dozen set designs for operas and theater productions, animations, and numerous advertising campaigns.

> "Up in the corner over my light table is a peg board which I have had for many years, and it acts as a kind of talisman or good luck charm. There are specific objects on it which I never change, some of them I've had for many many years."

As remarkable as the high quality and sheer volume of work that Sendak accomplished in his career were his shifts in style. I can think of no other artist—illustrator or otherwise—who has employed so many

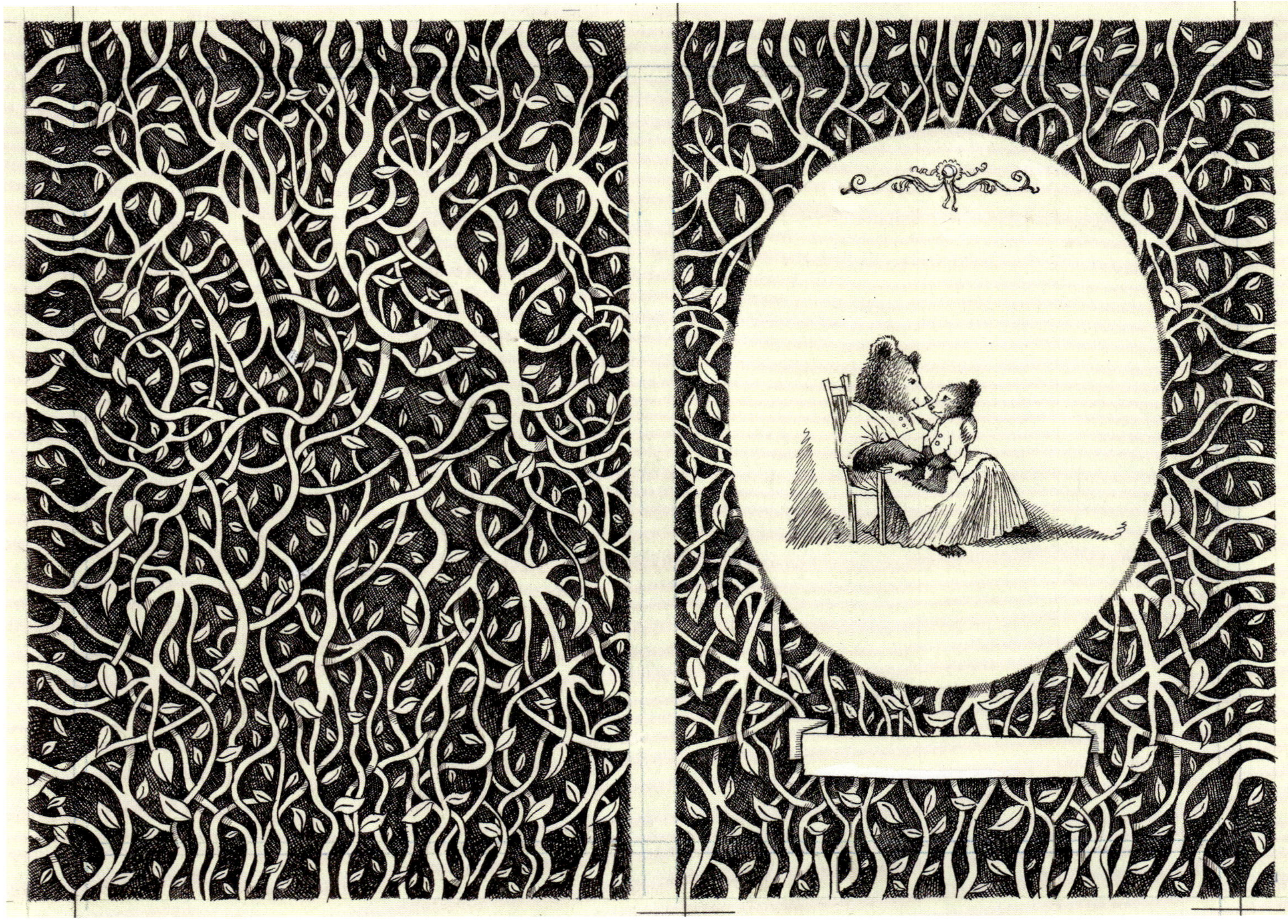

Maurice Sendak, Cover design for *Little Bear*, 1957, ink and white corrections on paper, 12¼ × 15⅜ in.

different forms of expression, not only over time, but often on projects that were in production simultaneously. In the very same five years, 1979–84, he not only did the designs for five operas including *The Magic Flute* and the ballet of *Nutcracker*, but he also designed and wrote the off-Broadway musical production of *Really Rosie*, and completed his acclaimed picture book, *Outside Over There.* This chameleon-like ability was most magically in evidence when, for the delight of his admirers, he would sometimes draw a little sketch in their books. Depending on the book, he would effortlessly change "voices" from the Victorian line of *Little Bear*, to the comic-strip style of *In the Night Kitchen*, to the neo-classic look of *Outside Over There.* Sendak attributed his very success as a collaborator who was often illustrating someone else's text to his flexibility and range:

> Style, to me, is purely a means to an end, and the more styles you have, the better . . . I worked up a very elaborate pen and ink style in *Higglety*, which is very finely crosshatched. But I can abandon that for a magic marker, as I did in *Night Kitchen*, and just go back to very simple, outlined, broad drawings with flat, or flatter, colors.[6]

The roots of Sendak's style shifts go back to a class he took just out of high school at the Arts Student

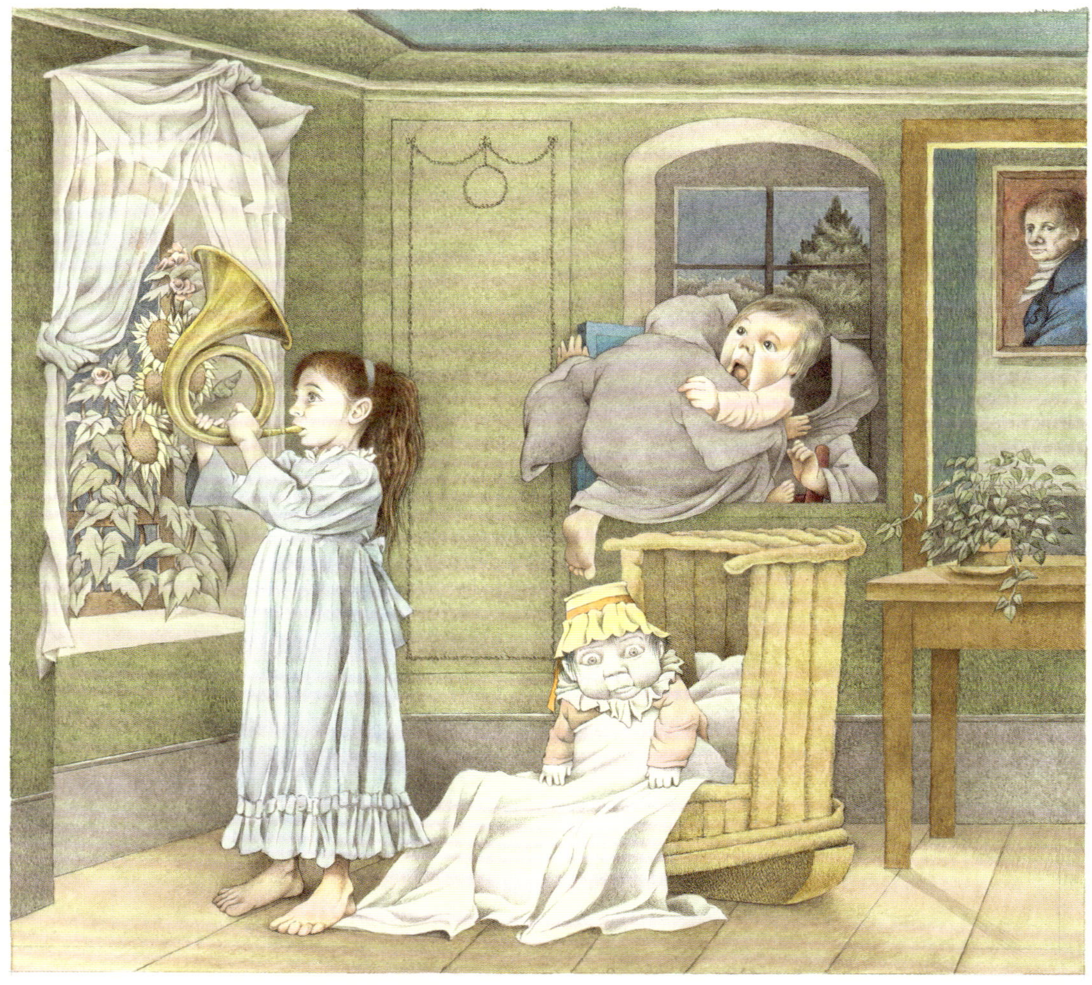

Maurice Sendak, *Outside Over There*, 1980, watercolor on paper, 13⅜ × 13¼ in.

League with the illustrator John Groth, who asked the students to draw scenes from a popular play or movie in the styles of different artists, such as Goya or Daumier.[7] Significantly, Sendak illustrated for Groth's class a scene from *Streetcar Named Desire*, whose director, Elia Kazan, and star, Marlon Brando, were leading proponents of method acting, a process where the actor is supposed to forego ego, and immerse himself totally in the character, researching the sources of the character's motivations. Likewise, Sendak began almost every project he took with research into the origins of a text and the background of its heroes. Tellingly, Sendak referred to his different styles, as "fine, thin, fat, and stout," as if he were describing people. Such shifts might lead to superficiality and pastiche. But Sendak, following the dictum of his hero Herman Melville, took a "deep dive," paradoxically by zeroing in on the inspiration of a key artist that he researched and emulated or as he would put it, stole from. And yet, as he liked to say, all his work "looks like me."[8]

But what are these qualities that make all his styles Sendakian? Notice that so many of his key figures share similar proportions, with big heads, almost no neck, and very large feet (this is also true of two of his favorites, Mickey Mouse and King Kong). Whether Sendak uses a *thin* pen point to define Little Bear's fur, or a *stout* magic marker stroke to describe Mickey's dough suit, or a *fine* pencil mark to sketch out Ida's billowing dress, Sendak's line emphatically outlines and contains his character's form. It gets wider when it moves into the shadowy crevices of the body, such as under the armpits or groin, and narrower when it describes those elements that are turned toward the light. Sendak's characteristic undulating line is probably most in evidence in the pictures for *In the Night Kitchen*. Although Sendak's debt to McCay's graphic style is obvious, Sendak's outlines are more emphatic, the color is richer, and the overall composition is far less busy. Sendak avoids McCay's vertiginous perspectives. Even when Mickey takes flight in his airplane, he always stays in the foreground, almost as if the plane hung from the ceiling on a string in front of a sky backdrop, rather than in the clouds. In general, Sendak's spaces are more contained, rectilinear and flatter—locked into the picture plane—than the artists like McCay and Blake that he emulated.

Sendak developed his distinctive style of cross hatching, so evident in *Where the Wild Things Are* and *Higglety Pigglety Pop!*, by studying such Victorian illustrators as George Cruikshank and Arthur Hughes. However, where their black-and-white engravings have a consistency of line and contrast that was geared to the black-and-white reproductive capabilities of nineteenth-century mass-market printing, Sendak used a metal nib to perfect a mode of crosshatching that subtly shifts in gradation and weight. Less a stand-in for color and light effects than a means of animating the page, while its grid-like regularity stitches everything together. Even when Sendak isn't crosshatching, he tends to stipple the color, or apply it in parallel strokes. This is particularly noticeable in his stage-drop designs.

Sendak used tracing paper as an essential aspect of his drawing process. With the aid of a light box that was placed next to his drafting table, he would often trace and retrace his own images to perfect the line and the composition. He had no compunction about tracing details from photographs and even from some of the pictures he was emulating, "stealing" whatever he needed for a particular scene. Given this process of literally seeing images through others, it is no wonder that Sendak took so quickly to set design, not only in the layering of drops, but in how lighting and transparency are used to make painted scrims suddenly appear, and just as magically disappear. Sendak's scavenger-like tracing was not about slavishly copying sources—he always re-forged what he traced, whether it was a nineteenth-century photograph of an Egyptian temple, or one of his own sketches. Yet, I would argue that Sendak's process of form-making was additive. He tended to stitch together pieces to create compositions in which you can feel the elements come together in tension.

In our current Post-Post-Modern moment, when sampling is a common element of popular music and visual artists brazenly re-represent and appropriate the art of the past, Sendak's copying and quoting might not seem so unusual, but in the 1950s, the emphasis in art criticism was on originality, and above all for artists to produce a signature style. However, because Sendak worked in a field most art critics

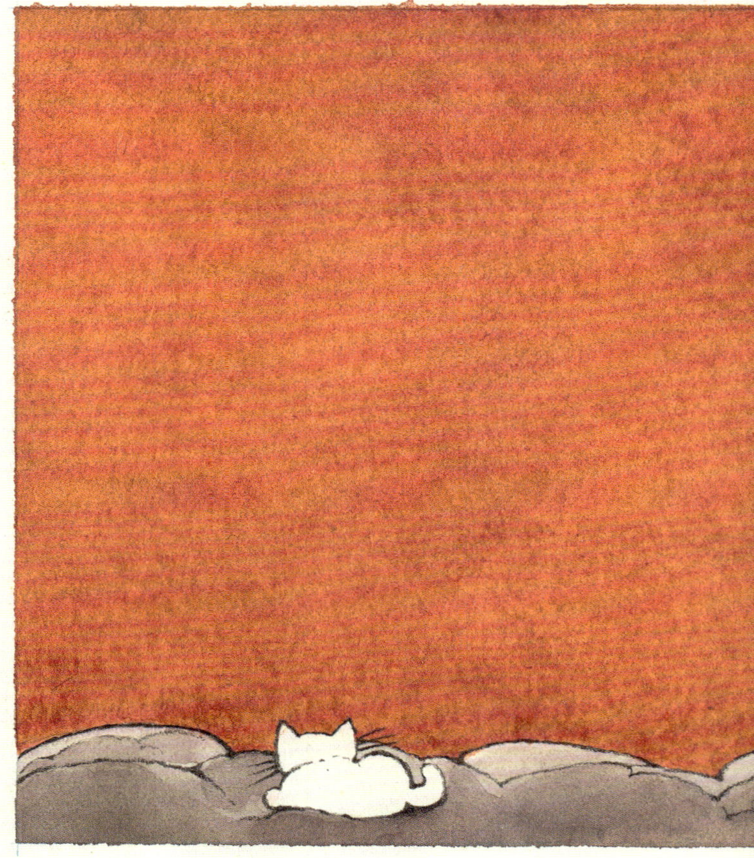

ignored, or considered minor, he had the freedom to follow his influences wherever they took him, creating complex figurative narratives in a realist style that was discouraged in so-called "fine art" painting.

Too often influence in art is conceived as a process in which a younger, inexperienced artist comes under the sway of a powerful precursor. In this model, influence is like an infection (the word influence and influenza have the same root). Yet in fact this is exactly the opposite of Sendak's method, in which he actively chose aspects of another artist's practice and fused them with other sources to make something new. Significantly, when Sendak was asked to talk about his creative process, he cited a painting, Andrea Mantegna's *Christ's Descent into Limbo*, in which Christ, his back turned to the viewer, reaches into an abyss to pull the prophets from an eternity of despair.[9] For Sendak, the challenge of an enormous project like the design for *The Magic Flute* or the

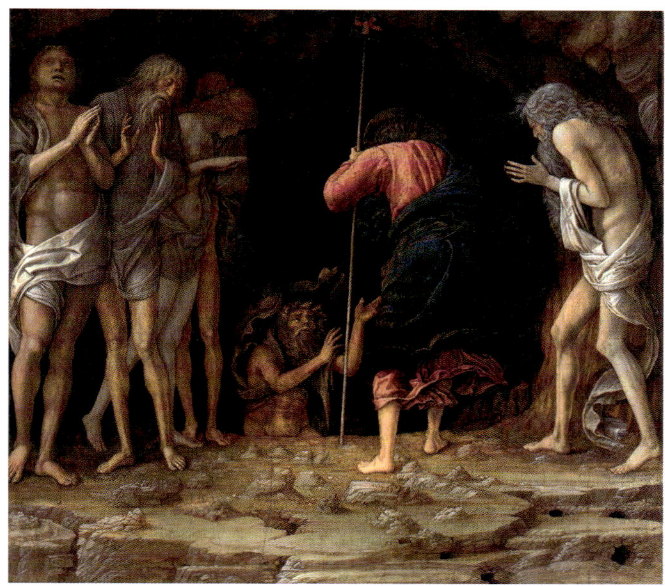

Andrea Mantegna, *Christ's Descent into Limbo*, 1470–75, oil on panel, 15 × 16 in., private collection

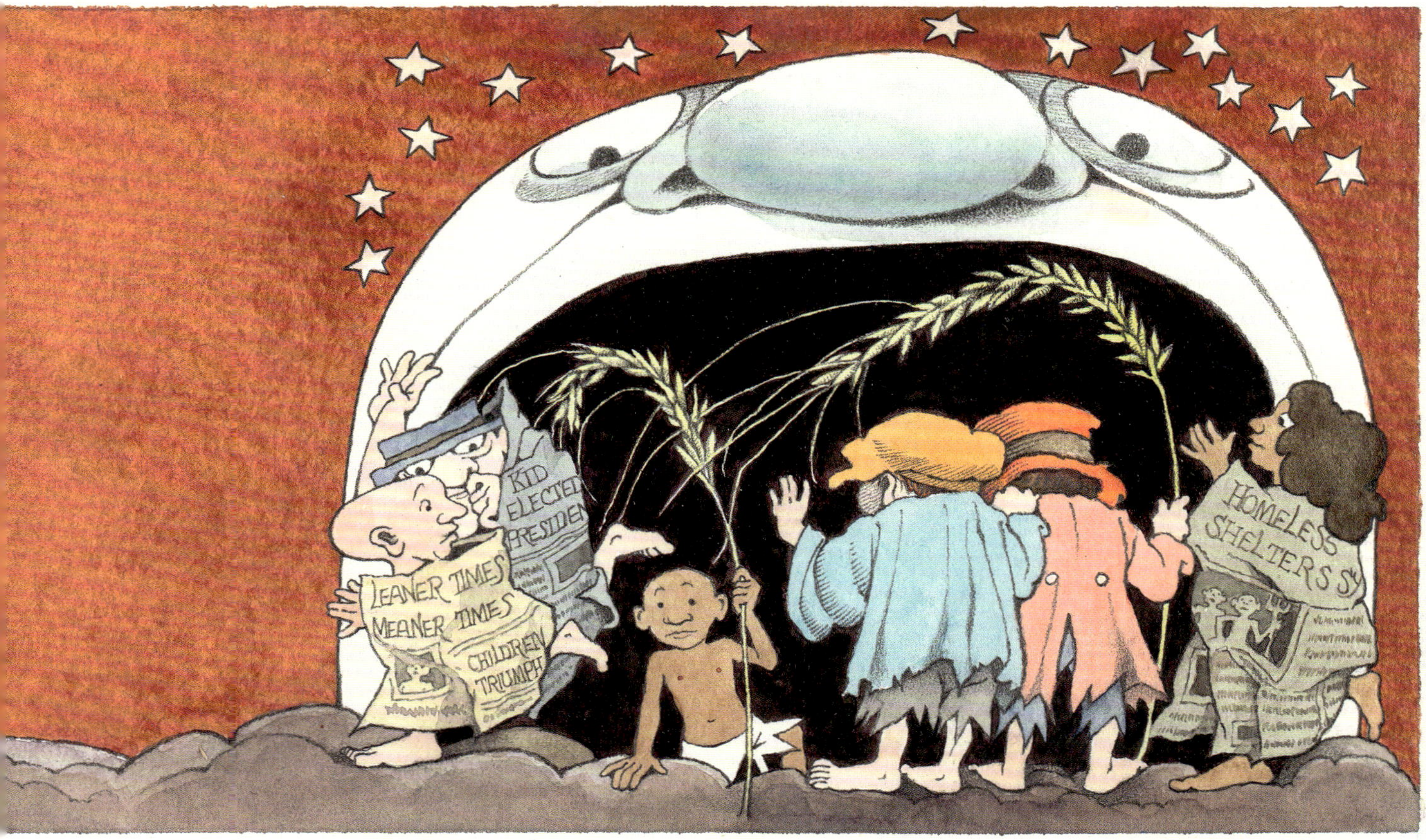

Maurice Sendak, *We Are All in the Dumps with Jack and Guy*, 1993, watercolor on paper, 5⅝ × 14¾ in.

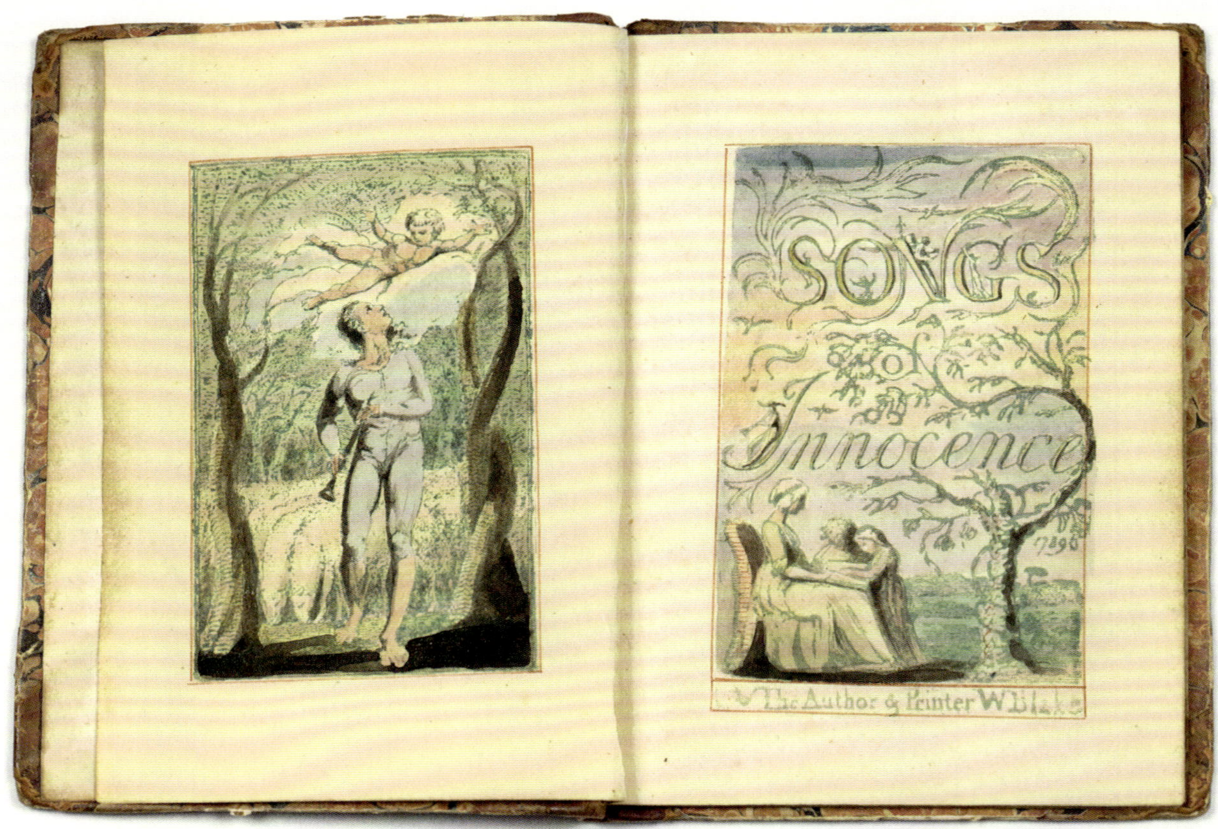

William Blake, *Songs of Innocence*, 1789, frontispiece and title page, hand-colored printed relief etching with watercolor, each plate 4½ × 2⅞ in.

book *Outside Over There* was equivalent to being cast into a similar state of limbo. Inspiration, or grace, comes, not from a god, but from works of art. Paintings and prints, and music and writing too: Mozart's music was a kind of religion for him, as was the poetry of John Keats and the novels of Henry James and Melville.

If Sendak identified with the old prophet in the painting, with the power of art standing in for Christ's offer of salvation, he also was inspired by Mantegna's theme of reconciliation of the past and the present. The painting's gesture of one man offering his hand to another also spoke to Sendak's success as an artist whose work so often takes hold of a text or score written by another artist. The key was not to just echo the original source but to heighten it. He insisted that the good illustrator never upstages the text but "enriches" it. He loved the opportunity to work with authors of the caliber of a Randall Jarrell or an Arthur Yorinks, but also the chance to be part of a community of crafts people, often unheralded, who brought his characters to life in an opera or in film.

Sendak talked about the opportunity to do the sets of *The Magic Flute* as a similar act of salvation that jump-started his second career designing for the stage. Even before he got the call from the director Frank Corsaro to do *The Magic Flute* he was immersing himself in the art and architecture of Mozart's age as part of the process of creating the picture book *Outside Over There.* A key inspiration was seeing Eric Rohmer's 1976 film *The Marquise of O.* Sendak told Cott, how he needed "a color clue," and how all "the greens and mauves of the film" excited him.[10] Based on a story by Heinrich von

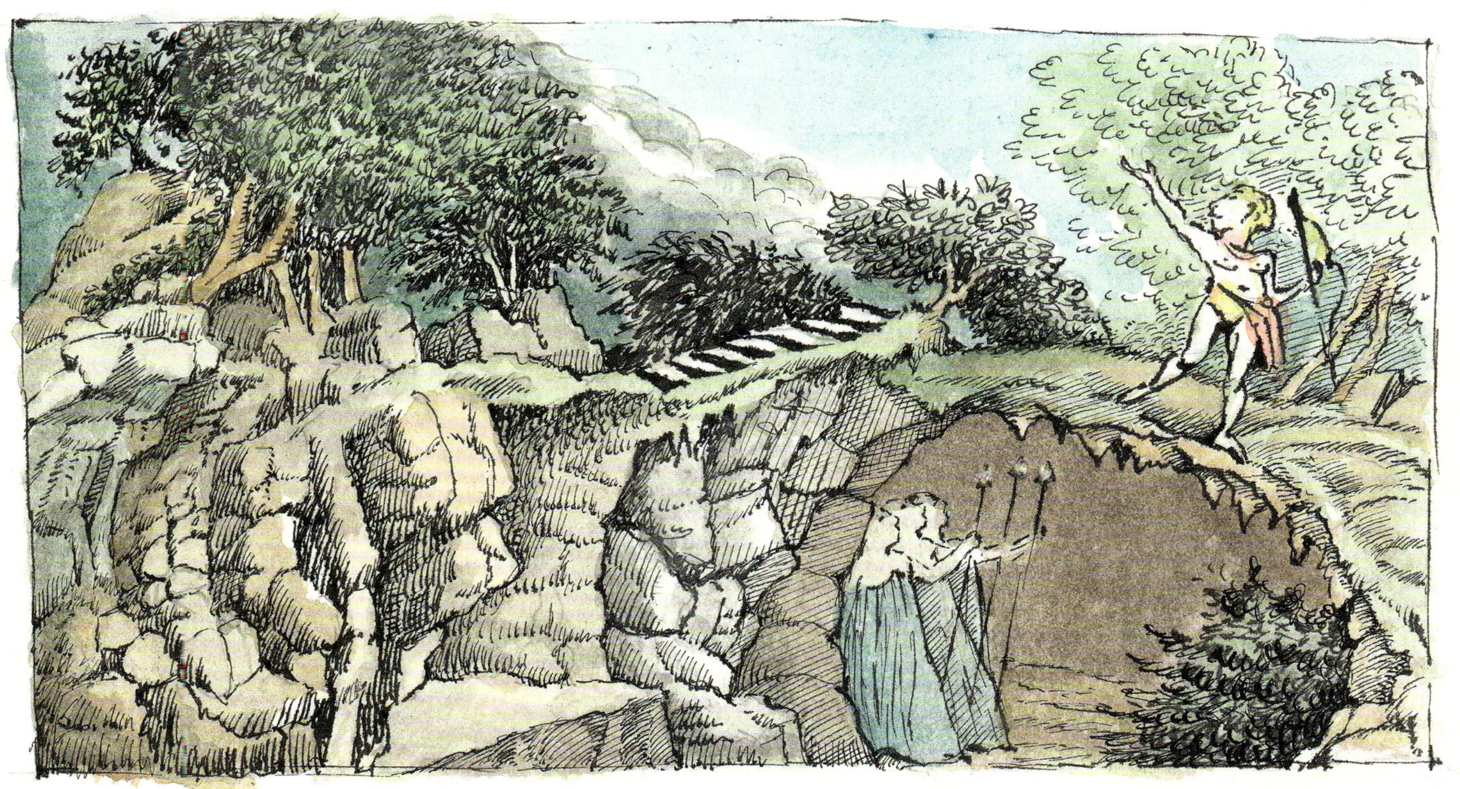

Maurice Sendak, Storyboard for *The Magic Flute*, 1979, watercolor, pen and ink, and graphite pencil, 8½ × 7 in., The Morgan Library & Museum

Kleist, the film is set in 1798–9. Its Napoleonic-era costumes and pastel tonalities became a model for the style and palette of *Outside Over There.* Early in the film Rohmer poses the protagonist like the woman in Henry Fuseli's *Nightmare*, a favorite of Sendak's and he owned an engraving of it. The interiors evoke the style of the German painters Caspar David Friedrich and Philipp Otto Runge. Like Rohmer, Sendak was drawn to these early-Romantic artists who came to maturity just after Mozart's untimely death. It is as if Sendak could not quite imagine living in the exact time when Mozart walked the earth. His relationship to Mozart was always belated, always from a distance, even when he is in closest communion with him. Fittingly, Mozart appears in the opening curtain of Sendak's *Magic Flute* as a shadowy silhouette, composing in a forest hut; he is both present, and not-present; alive through his music, and mourned. In the background of *Dear Mili*, Sendak imagines Mozart conducting a group of Jewish children destined for Auschwitz, reminding us of the terrible things we do to children, while consoling us for their loss.

If Mozart was Sendak's musical god, Blake was his visual and literary deity. Sendak emulated Blake's work almost from the beginning in such early picture books as *Kenny's Window*, and to the end with his final finished work, *My Brother's Book.* In his

following pages: Maurice Sendak, Design for Show Scrim for *The Magic Flute*, 1980, watercolor and graphite pencil on paper mounted to laminated paperboard, 21½ × 32 in., The Morgan Library & Museum

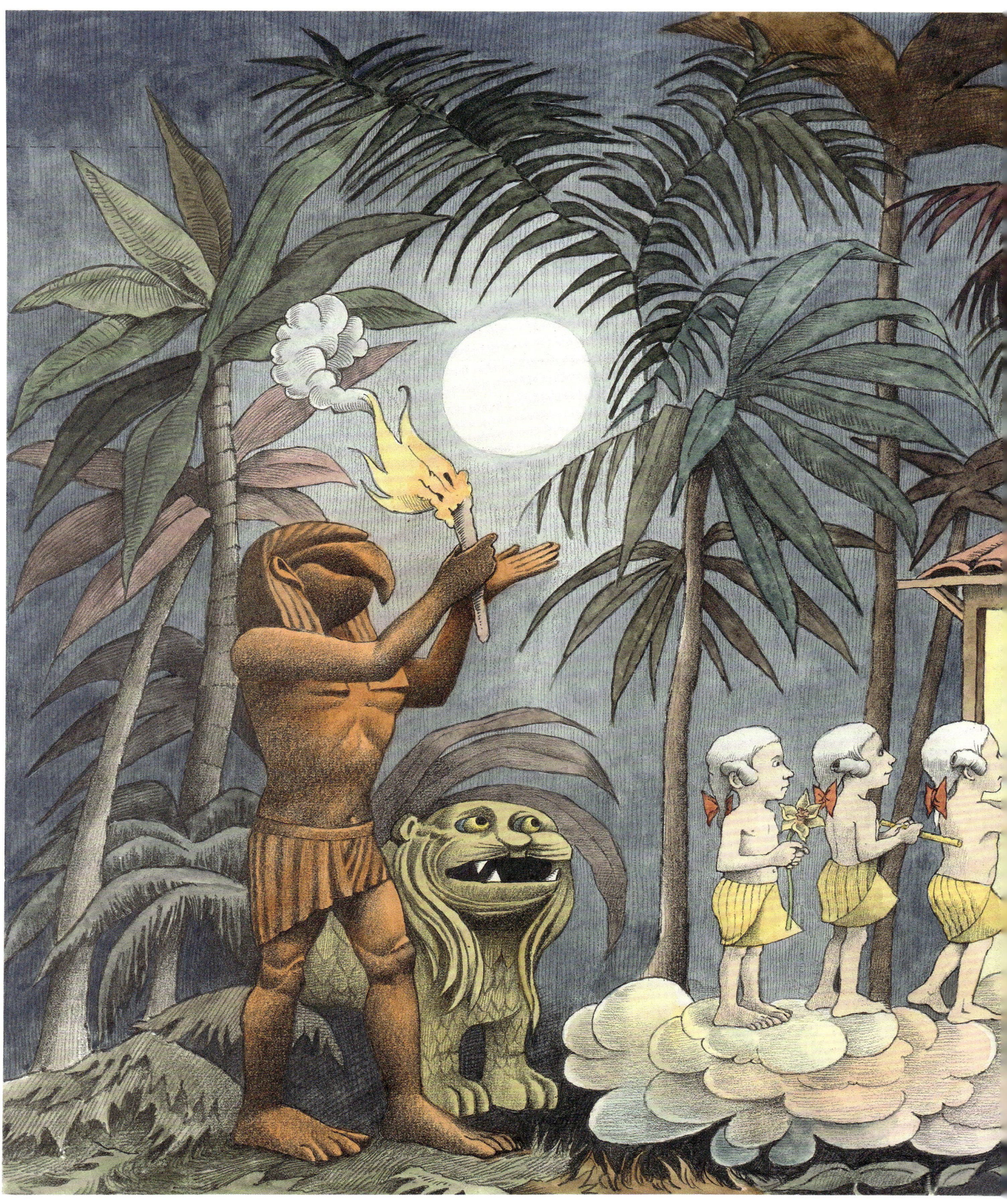

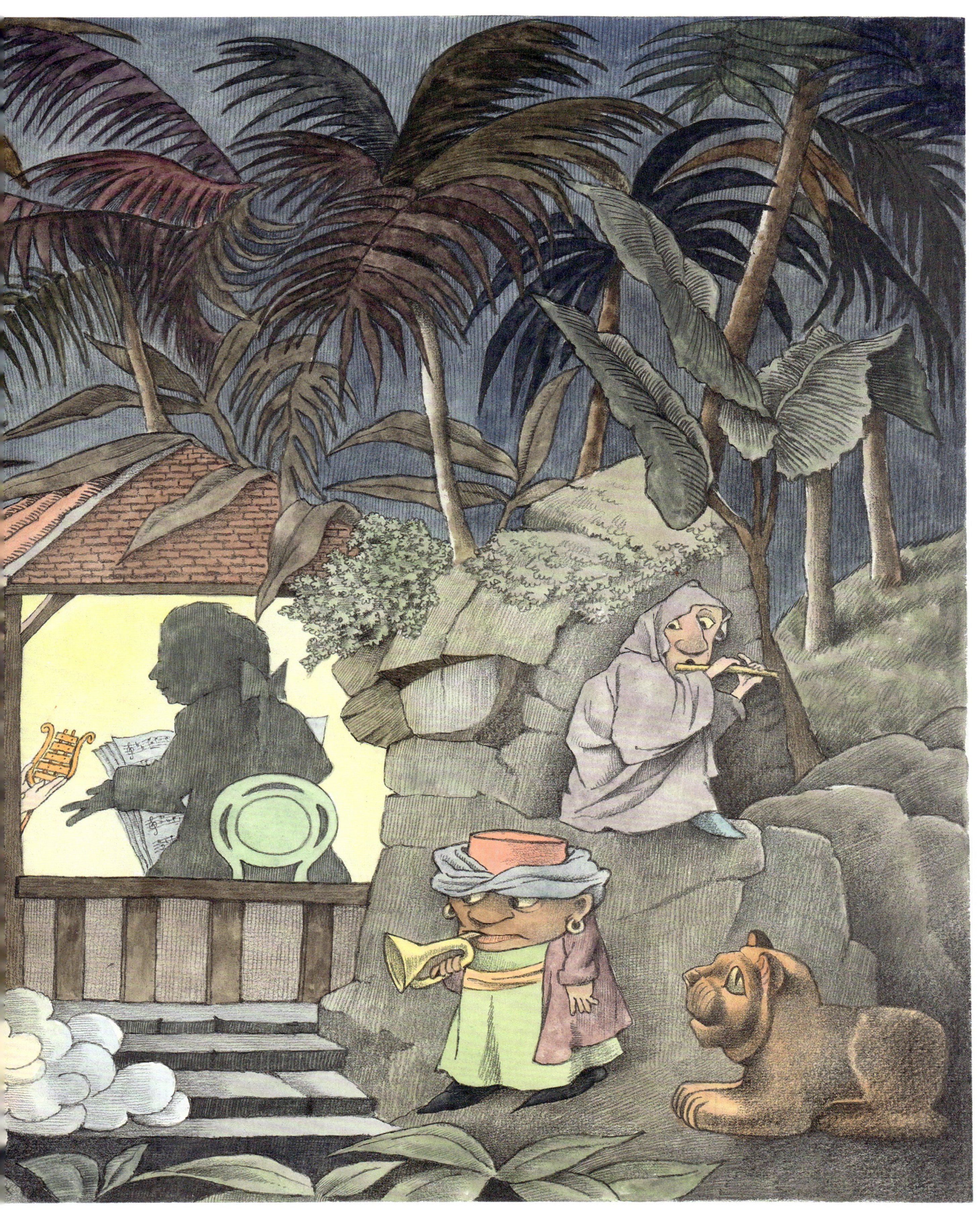

"From the first, my great and abiding love was William Blake, my teacher in all things."

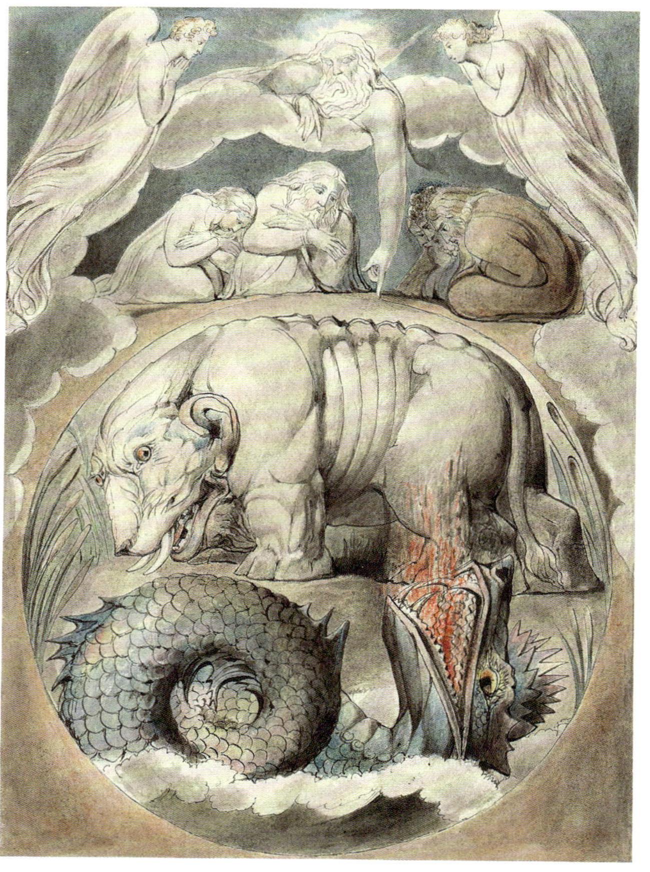

William Blake, *Behemoth and Leviathan*, 1805–10, pen and black ink and wash, and watercolor, over graphite, 10¾ × 7¾ in., The Morgan Library & Museum, purchased by Pierpont Morgan

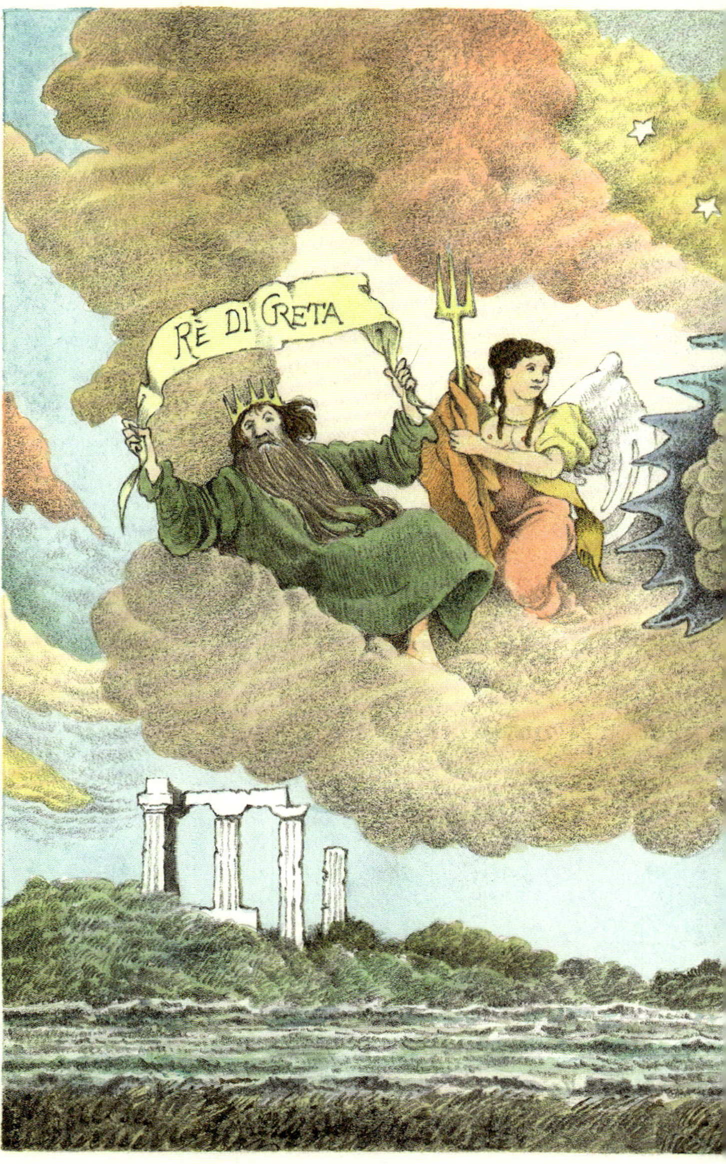

dual roles as poet and illustrator, Blake stands out among the artists that Sendak revered in his fusion of text and painting. The original storyboards for *The Magic Flute*'s design recall in coloring and line the style of Blake's illustrations for *The Songs of Innocence* and *The Songs of Experience*, which Sendak revered so much he purchased the rare original hand-colored albums for his own private collection. The serpent that attacks Tamino in the very first scene of *The Magic Flute* is derived from the spectacular Blake watercolor *Behemoth and Leviathan* which Sendak studied in the Morgan Library's collection. Sendak cribbed from the same picture for the monster that appears in the show

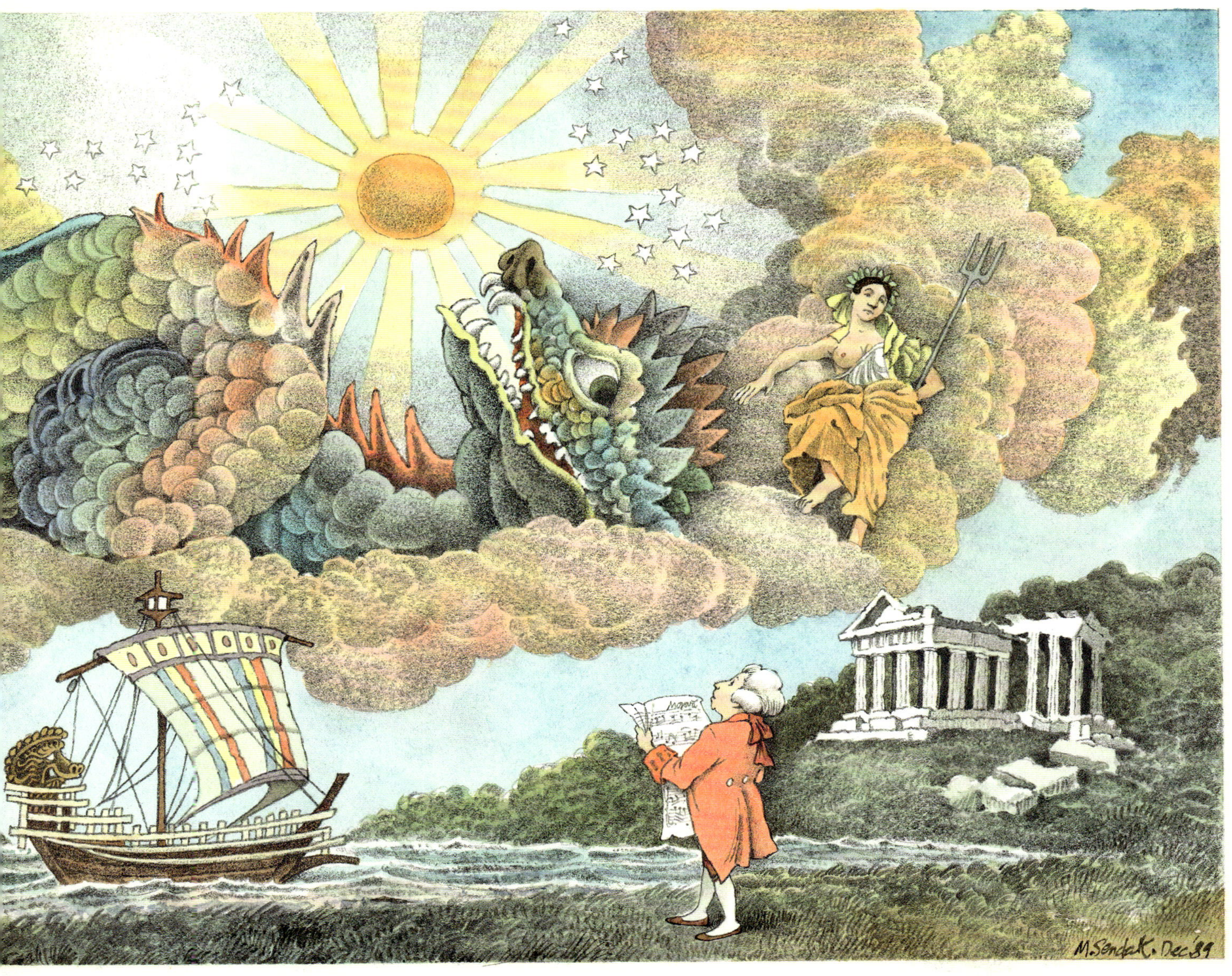

Maurice Sendak, Design for the show curtain for *Idomeneo*, 1988, watercolor on paper, 10 × 18 in.

curtain for Mozart's opera *Idomeneo.* And certainly, Blake's fabulous creatures were the inspiration for the sea monster who pops up to challenge Max on the high seas in *Where the Wild Things Are.*

Another romantic visionary, Carl Wilhelm Kolbe, was an inspiration for one of the most important drops in the *Magic Flute*, Pamina's garden, as well as the extraordinary plant life in the pages of *Dear Mili.* Kolbe created a series of finely cross-hatched etchings of gigantic vegetation that dwarfs the animals and people of his arcadias (p. 161). Kolbe claimed they came "completely out of my head, both as a whole and in details; and I acknowledge that I was wrong—very wrong—to do so."[11] It was precisely their "wrongness," or weirdness, that made Kolbe's prints so appealing to Sendak. They have a primeval quality, suggesting a lost world, like the jungles of the film *King Kong* or Sendak's own *Where the Wild Things Are.* Unlike Kolbe, however, Sendak, worked directly from life, basing the over-sized clivias of his *Magic Flute* sets and the *Dear Mili* book on real-life plants grown by Glynn and the gardener Peter Caponera.

Sendak probably discovered the work of Kolbe in the 1970s when he became obsessed with Kolbe's contemporary, Runge, and his most famous painting, *The Hülsenbeck Children* (see p. 156), which owes a debt to Kolbe. It is typical of Sendak's creative process that his love for one artist led him to that artist's inspirations. However, in Runge's strange portrait, it is the children, and not plants who have become giants. A boy and girl, who are almost as tall as the mammoth sunflowers that surround them, pull their fat-cheeked baby brother in a cart, with all the seriousness and élan of heroic soldiers. Sendak's friend, the art historian Robert Rosenblum, describes the picture as embodying "a kind of Romantic vitalism in which children are at one with the magical energies of sunlight and burgeoning landscape."[12] It is precisely this idea of vitalism—the life force that is everywhere in the cycle of nature—that Sendak instilled not only in Pamina's garden, but also in the opening sequences of Leoš Janáček's opera *The Cunning Little Vixen* in which bugs, plants, and animals are represented wildly out of scale. The enormous insects that end up devouring the body of the Vixen's mother, were a conceit of Corsaro and Sendak,

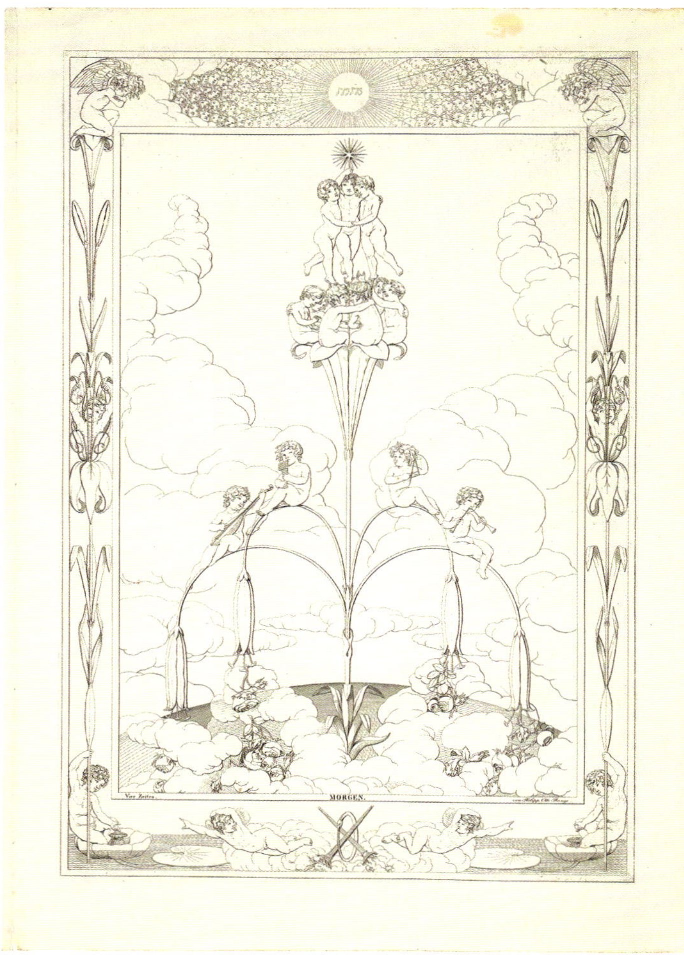

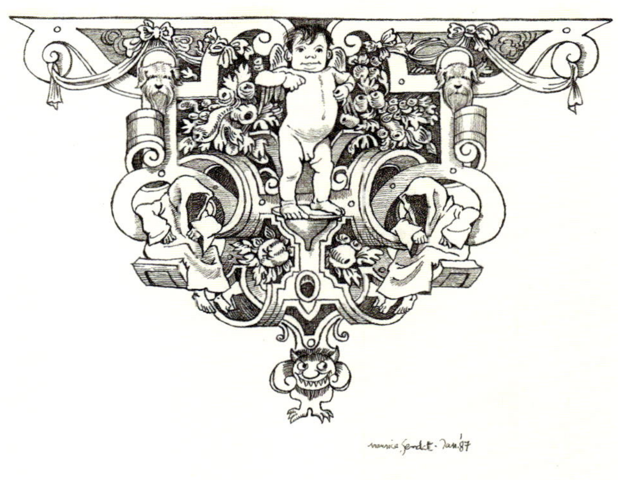

left: Philipp Otto Runge, *Morning*, 1807, engraving, 30⅞ × 21$^{3}/_{16}$ in.

above: Maurice Sendak, Cover Drawing for *Caldecott & Co.*, 1987, ink on paper, 8 × 7½ in.

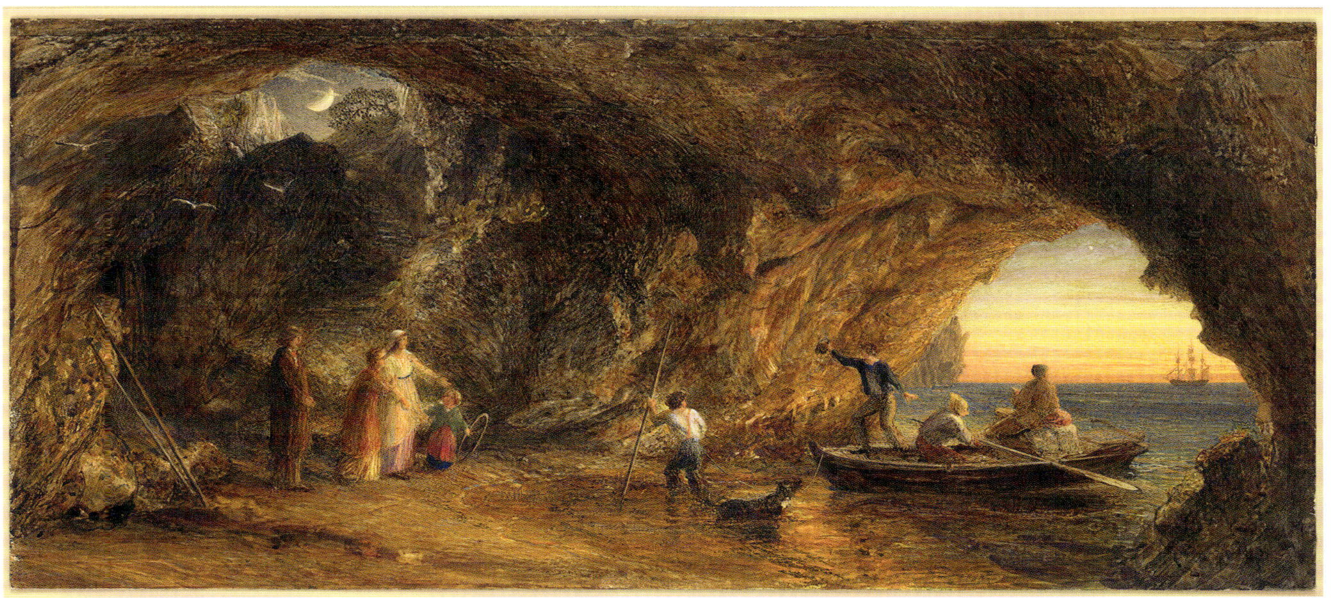

Samuel Palmer, *Returned from India*, 1858, watercolor on paper, 12 × 27⅜

who wanted to emphasize Janáček's theme of the natural cycles of birth, death, and rebirth, while announcing right from the start that this opera was no sweet fairytale.

As Sendak became increasingly successful, a key aspect of his creative process involved his art collecting. Sendak could not afford oil paintings by the likes of Mantegna and Runge, but he was able to purchase wonderful prints and watercolors by Blake, Palmer, Homer, and Stubbs. It was important to Sendak to see these artists' work every day. (These pictures meant so much to him that when he was asked by Bill Jersey what he would do if there was a fire and they were all destroyed, he only half-jokingly replied he would put his head in an oven.)[13]

Given the enormous impact of Palmer's etchings with their extraordinary cross-hatched moonlit night scenes on Sendak books like *Higglety Pigglety Pop!*, it is little surprise that Palmer's prints and paintings occupied pride of place not only in his studio, above his light box, but in his living room, alongside prints by Stubbs and Pierre Bonnard, and shelves of first-edition Beatrix Potter books. A key painting by Palmer for Sendak hung in his dining room: *Returned from India*. It depicts a sailor returning home from war, arriving in a small boat to a cave-like cove. The panoramic format of the painting is very much like the form of a Sendak picture book, as is the moment of the day, in which the sky is illuminated by both the sunset and a magical crescent moon. This scene of reunion is psychically connected to another work of art that Sendak owned, Homer's *Dad's Coming!*, in which a mother and children wait for their sailor to return, with the uneasy sense that perhaps this time he will not be so lucky. Homer's image was a model for the opening of *Outside Over There*.

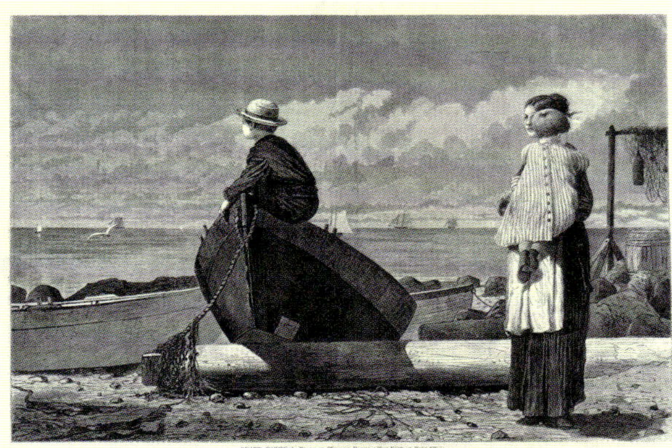

Winslow Homer, *Dad's Coming!*, 1873, wood engraving, 9¼ × 13 in.

following pages: Maurice Sendak, *Outside Over There*, 1977, watercolor on paper, 22⅛ × 28 in.

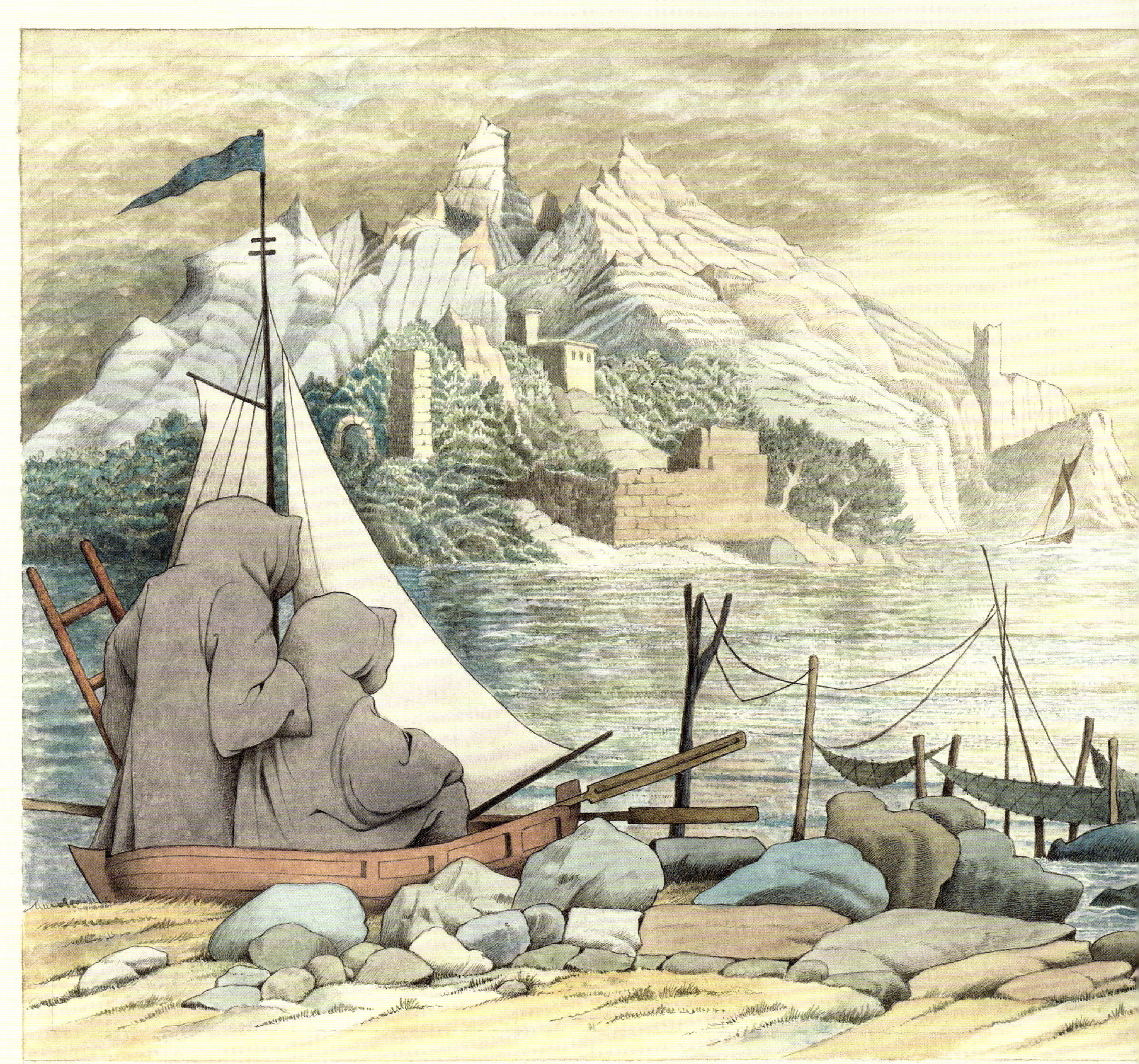

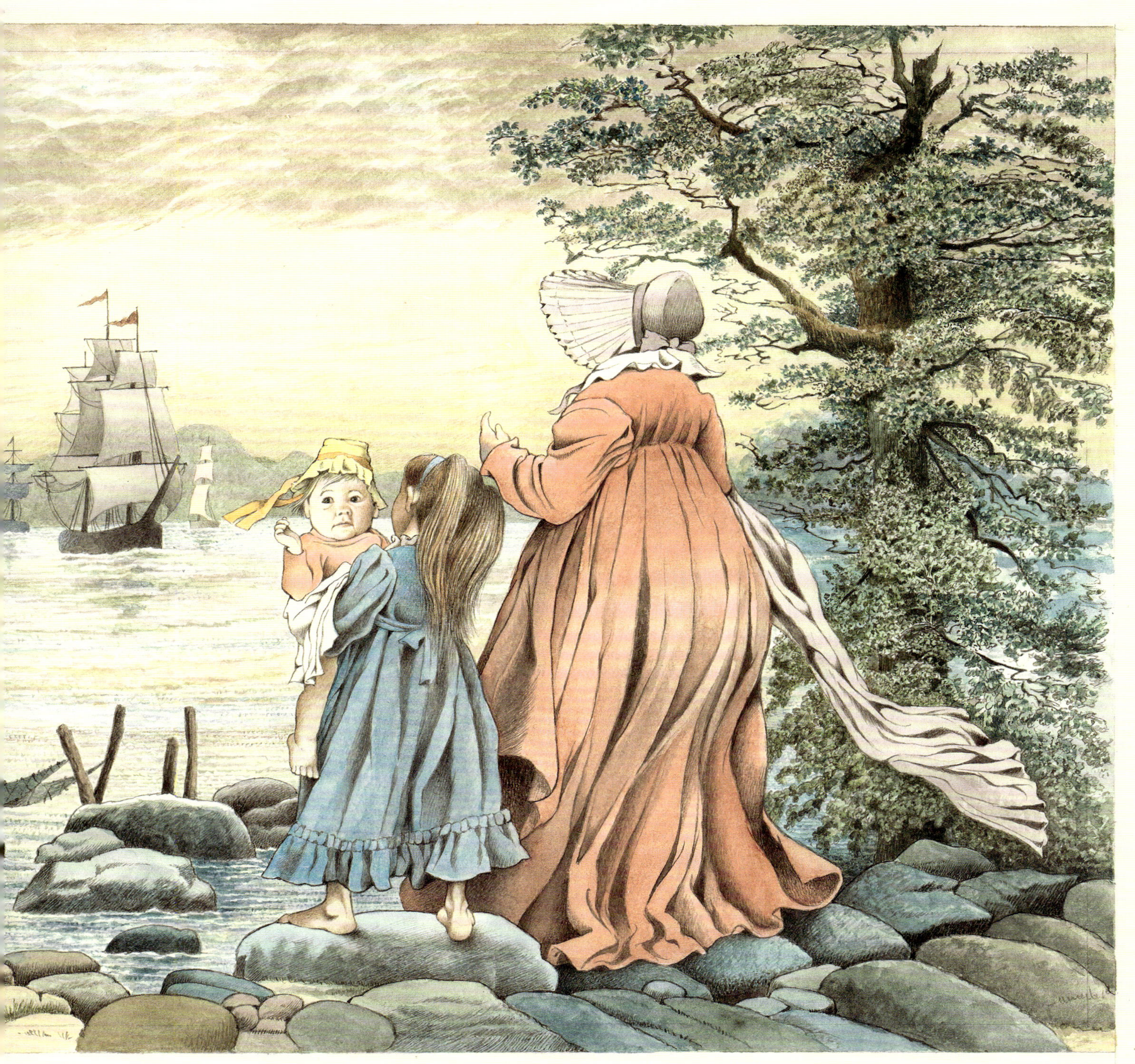

OCT. 18, 77 - NOV. 6, 77

As Thomas Crow reminds us in this book (pp. 54–79), the sense of longing and expectation in relation to a journey or quest is a constant of Sendak's art, driven by the question that begins one of his earliest books, *Very Far Away*: "Where is Far Away?" The heroes must make some sort of journey, sailing across the ocean in *Wild Things*, or flying across a giant moonlit sky in *In the Dumps*, or floating amidst the verdant landscape of *My Brother's Book*. But there is always the return home, and the sense of reconciliation and love, symbolized in so many Sendak images by the cave or the womblike arbor. Fundamentally, Sendak's journeys are usually not about physically leaving home, but about being safe in the bedroom, or waiting by the shore, fantasizing about escape.

Many of Sendak's best known books suggest that their characters are dreaming. Did Max fall asleep when his mother banished him to his room? Are goblins stealing Ida's little brother, or is she experiencing a nightmare? Is Mickey, like Little Nemo, asleep when he falls into the Night Kitchen? Certainly, it is no mistake to understand Sendak's world as dreamscapes and in some way an attempt to represent the unconscious. Afterall, he spent a lifetime in and out of psychoanalytic therapy and his partner of fifty years was a psychiatrist who wrote brilliantly about the relationship of psychoanalysis to art. But when Sendak was asked whether a work like *In the Night Kitchen*, with its narrative of a boy who begins and ends his night quest in bed, was based on actual dreams or nightmares, Sendak said absolutely not. The dreamscapes of Sendak's books are not a matter of him representing some flash of inspiration that struck at night, rather they were constructed in a long process of writing and re-writing, sketching and re-sketching. Sendak's "deep dive" into the unconscious, at the typewriter, or at the drawing table was hard work. His most celebrated book, *Where the Wild Things Are*, took a decade and many reiterations including the crucial change of title and subject from *Where the Wild Horses Are.* Sendak claimed he had to change the story because he couldn't draw horses, but let the truth be known here—Sendak drew horses quite well, as he proved in *Kenny's Window* and in Ruth Krauss's *Charlotte and the White Horse.* Indeed, it is one of the outstanding aspects of Sendak's craft that he would teach himself whatever skill his inspiration needed.

Sendak also claimed that the Wild Things characters were based on his Jewish relatives who pinched his cheeks when they came to visit on holidays and said he was so cute, they could eat him up.[14] Wild thing is close to the Yiddish "Vilde Chayes" or "wild animal" or "wild beast" that Maurice's parents called him when he was being unruly.[15] This origin myth has encouraged interpreters to connect the story to Sendak's immigrant Jewish heritage and his feelings of terror and guilt growing up in the 1930s and 40s while so many of his relatives were exterminated in the Holocaust. Other interpreters, ignoring the implications of the Wild Things being repulsive grownups, see their exuberant behavior as a celebration of the erotic, or of gay identity, or of non-conformist tendencies in general.[16]

Rarely mentioned in these interpretive leaps is that Sendak's story was derived, consciously or unconsciously, from Colette's libretto for Ravel's 1925 opera *L'Enfant et les Sortilèges.*[17] Colette's story, like Sendak's *Where the Wild Things Are*, is about a little boy who has a tantrum, wreaking havoc in his bedroom and infuriating his mother. The objects in the room magically turn against him and it becomes a garden. The crucial difference, however, is that in the garden, Colette's child comes to regret his behavior, saving a squirrel, and through that act of kindness winning his mother's forgiveness and love. Max never repents his bad behavior—we and the Wild Things may admire his panache, but he performs no similar act of goodness to that in Colette's moralistic tale. Yet in the end Max's mother welcomes him home anyway with hot soup. In Sendak's fantasy, the parent's love is non-conditional. Indeed, it is precisely when children go their own way and express themselves that parents should love them. Likewise, it is when children escape the confines of the home and become free that they still need their parents' love.

A less obvious source is the writings of Sendak's beloved author, Henry James. Sendak loved James so much that he collected his first editions, and he owned examples of his signature. One of James's favorite words was "thing," which he used in several key stories to signal emotions, desires, and forbidden

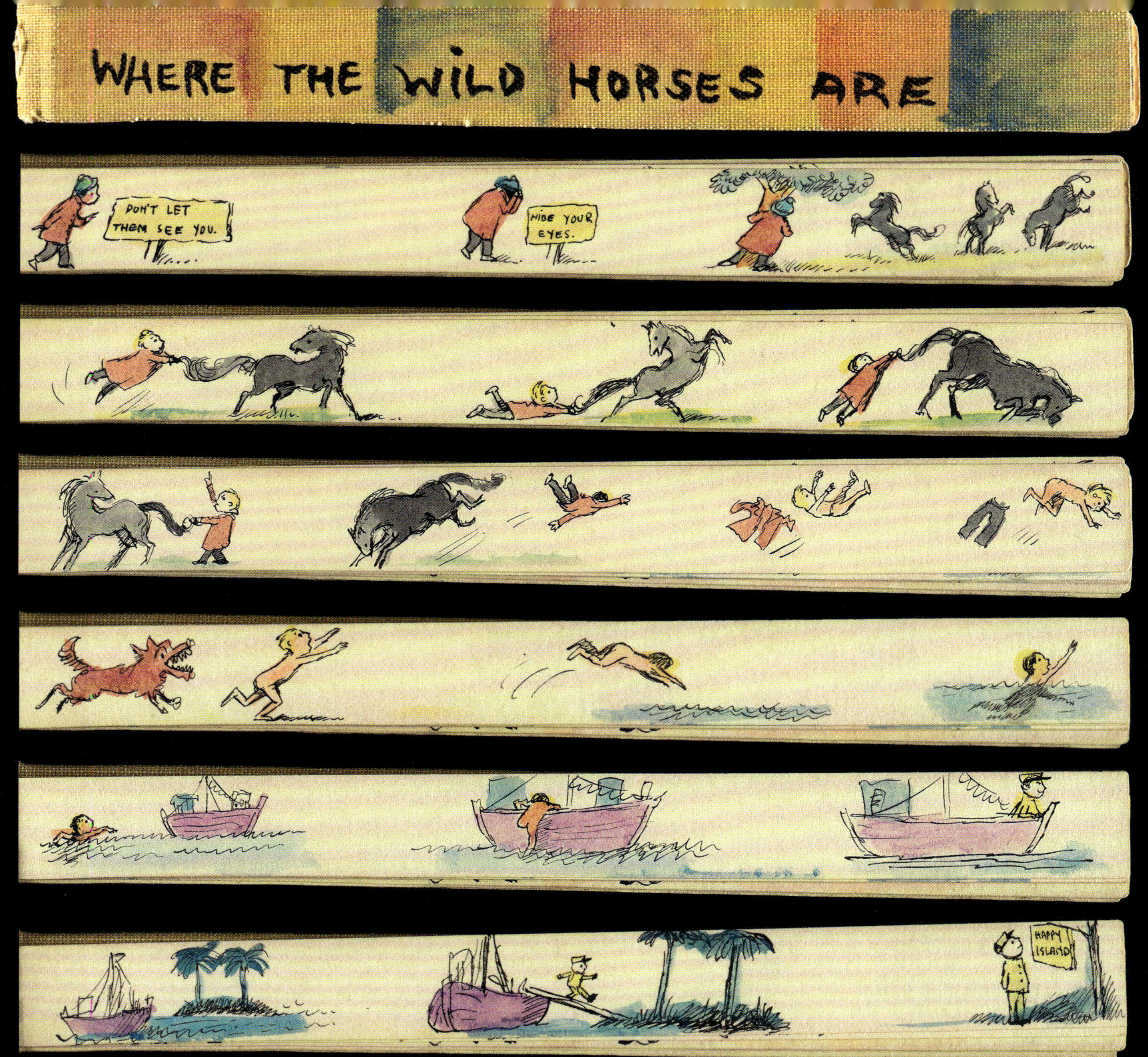

Maurice Sendak, *Where the Wild Horses Are*, 1955, watercolor and ink on paper, each strip approximately ⅞ × 6⅝ in.

acts without actually defining them, allowing the reader to imagine what these *things* might be. In James's *Beast in the Jungle* (a title that could almost be an alternative to *Where the Wild Things Are*), the hero spends his whole life waiting for the beast to spring, not some real animal but an extraordinary *something* to happen to him. In *The Turn of the Screw*, the little boy Miles has done some terrible *thing* at school that is never disclosed. And fittingly, James at the end of his life supposedly heard a disembodied voice say to him, "So here it is at last, the distinguished thing!" leaving the world to imagine what death might be.[18] What I am suggesting is that Sendak's shift from "Where the Wild Horses Are" to "Where the Wild Things Are," is a Jamesian move, crafted so that the reader could project a myriad of fantasies onto Sendak's creatures. The banality of horses as symbols of frustrated erotic desire made

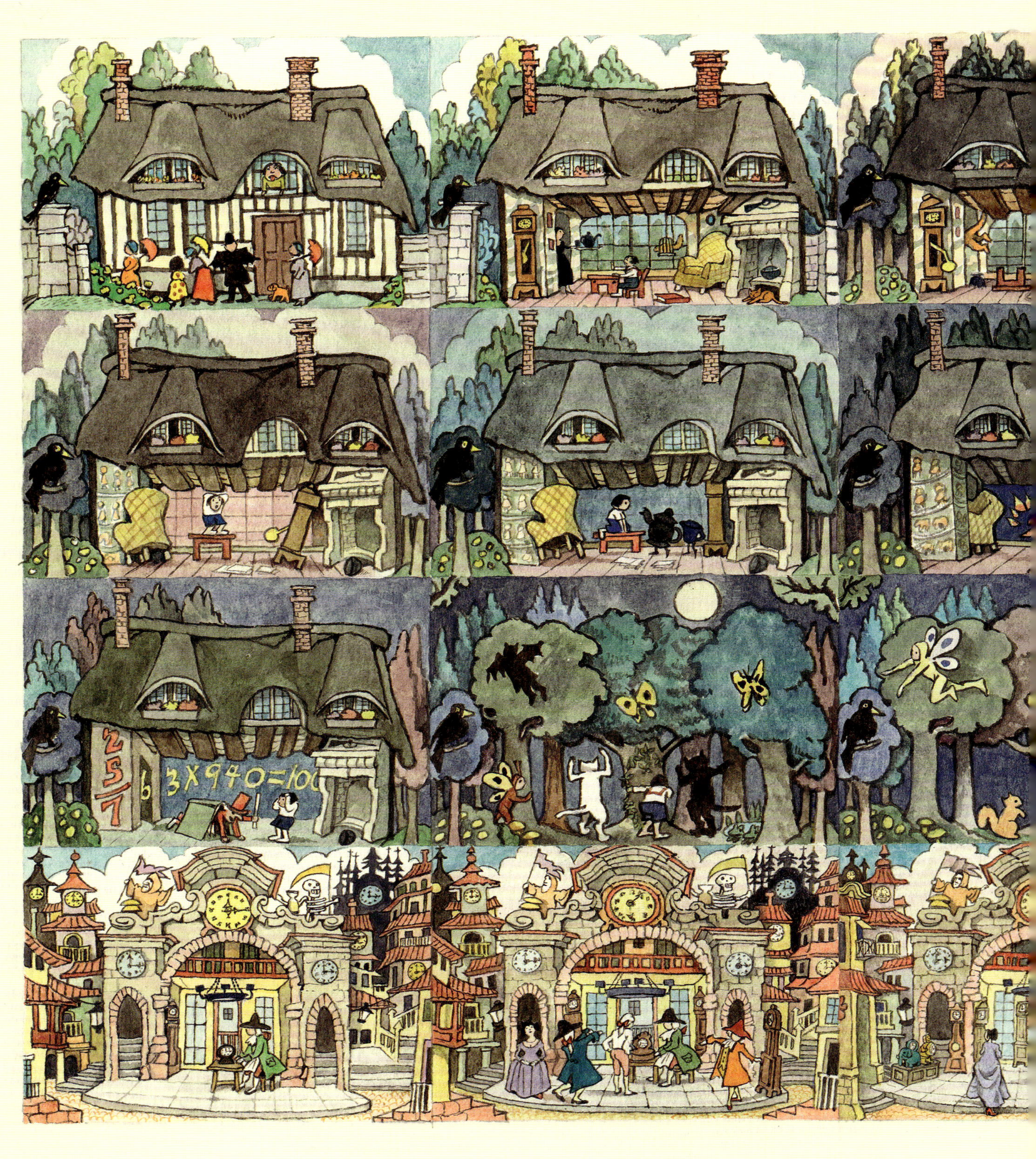

Maurice Sendak, *L'Enfant et les Sortilèges: Storyboard*, 1986, watercolor and ink on paper, 11½ × 20 in.

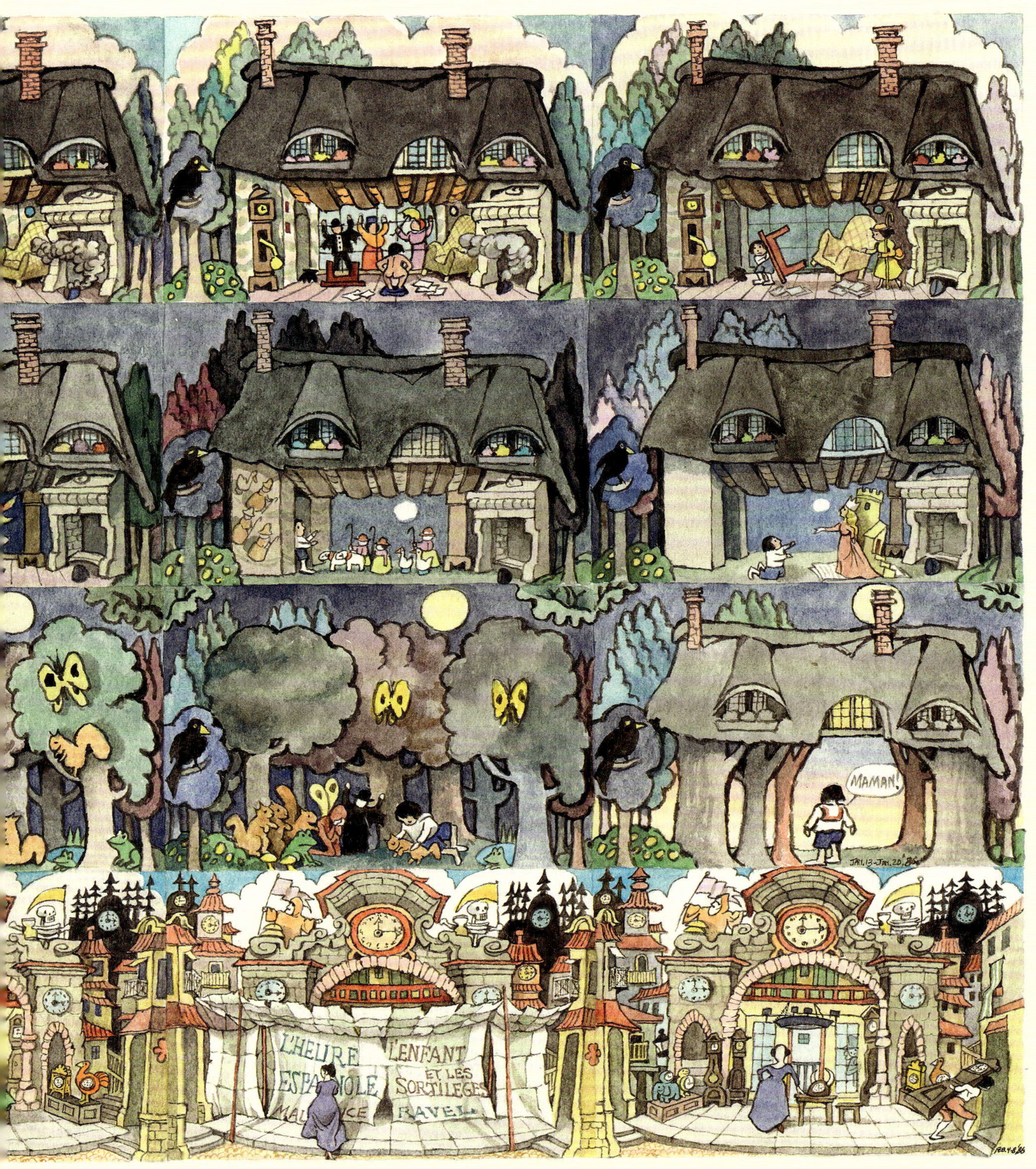
MAMAN!
L'HEURE
ESPA NOLE
MAU ICE
L'ENFANT
ET LES
SORTILEGES
RAVEL

them inappropriate and too specific, not Sendak's skill as a draftsman.

As Tyler Fallas suggests in his essay about Sendak's later Bell Atlantic *Wild Things Are Happening* campaign, the malleability of the Wild Things—their ability to be both disturbing and comforting, strange and familiar, explains their enduring popularity. They can be all *things* to all people, and yet each one is rendered with sufficient detail and clarity that they retain their individuality, what Sendak might call their truth. Their universality is not a matter of making them bland or indistinct, but instead drawing them as if they fully exist somewhere. In 1967 Sendak followed up *Where the Wild Things Are* with *Higglety Pigglety Pop!*, the story of the dog Jennie's existential quest to find "something" she does not have. She finds it, but the reader is left to imagine what it is. As Sendak told me in 2003, his most famous books have titles that point to undisclosed locations; we follow their heroes to a place far away, but we never exactly find out where it is, or how exactly we should behave once we get there.

"There can't be anything different than Mahler, and what I'm working on. And yet there are, in Mahler, moments when the pain becomes almost too intense to bear, and he goes bananas. He starts chirping like a bird. Something is happy."

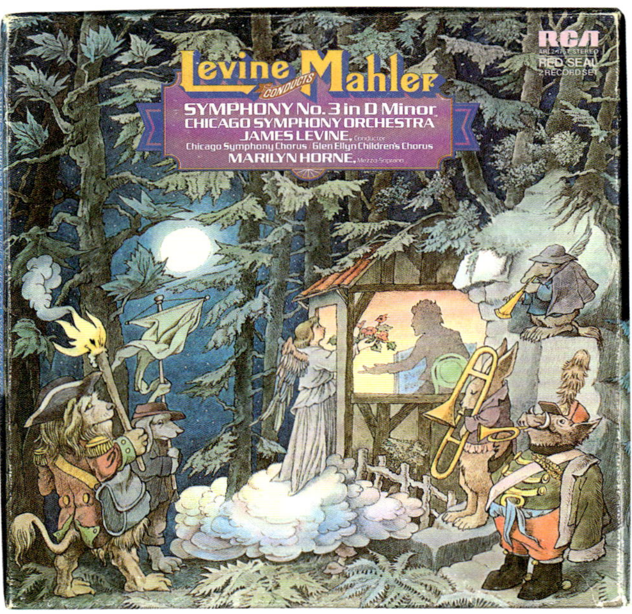

James Levine, *Levine Conducts Mahler, Symphony No. 3 in D Minor*, Box Album Cover

The openness of Sendak's narratives is essential to their radicality. It is not just that he sometimes includes disturbing content—after all, monsters and death are a common place of children's literature from the Brothers Grimm to J.K. Rowling. It is Sendak's refusal to tell children what to do that makes his work so different from typical books targeted at children, and in particular, picture books. Even when *The Nutshell Library's Pierre* includes the line: "The moral of Pierre is care!", Sendak does not ask that his hero do anything particularly good; rather he is commanded to simply feel and be passionate about something. Indifference is the sin, not bad behavior. More than anything else, Sendak rejects the cherished notion that childhood is a lost paradise, or that children live in blissful ignorance. Another Henry James story Sendak loved was *What Masie Knew*, in which the parents are completely unaware that their little girl knows all about their scandalous secrets and hypocrisy. In a conversation with Art Spiegelman, immortalized in a comic strip the two artists drew together in 1994, Sendak remembers that when he was a child he "knew terrible things . . . but I mustn't let adults know I *knew* . . . it would scare them." Once again these "things" are left for the reader to imagine.

In emphasizing the openness of Sendak's work, and his emulation of past styles and artists, I don't mean that he didn't at times take on contemporary themes and politics or that his work is anachronistically stuck in the past. Even as he immersed himself in the nineteenth century, listening to Mozart, Schubert, and Mahler, or reading Melville and Keats, Sendak was an avid television watcher, and he read *The New York Times* cover to cover every morning. When he became excited or outraged by what he saw in the news, particularly the suffering of children, it made its way into his books. Certainly, Max's rebellious nature and Mickey's nakedness are a response

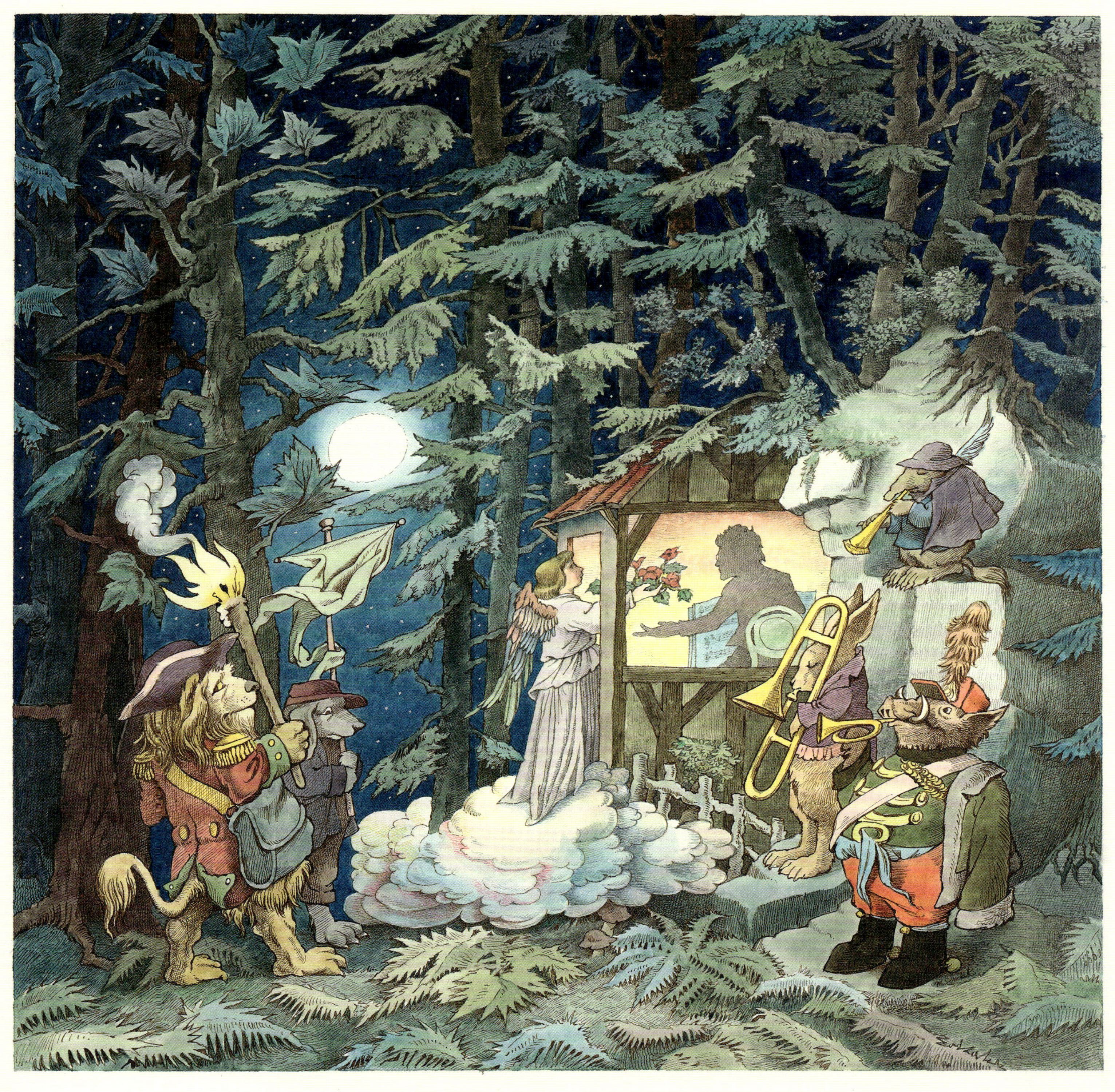

Maurice Sendak, *Mahler's Symphony No. 3*, 1976, watercolor on paper, 14½ × 14½ in.

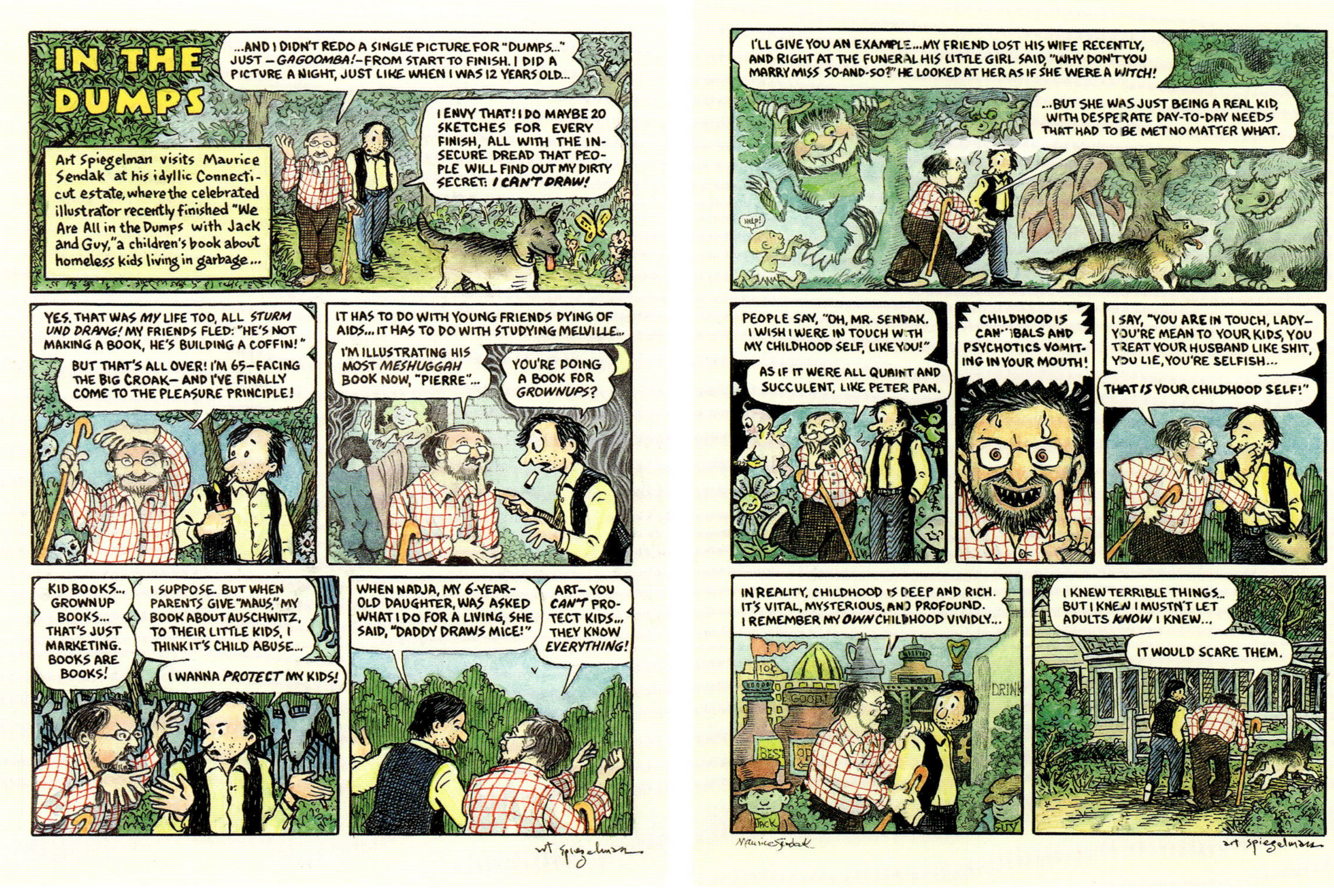

Maurice Sendak and Art Spiegelman, *In the Dumps*, 1993, watercolor on paper and digital reproduction (left side original), 9 × 12½ in.

to the counterculture of the 1960s, while the images of poverty at the foot of the Trump Tower of *In the Dumps* were protests against the crisis of homelessness and child starvation of the 1980s and 90s that continues to this day.

If Sendak's children are innocent, it is not because they are angels who are guilt free—Max, Pierre, and Ida are capable of cruelty and great selfishness—but because they are not yet responsible for the sin of their parents. The grownups make all the real choices, and no matter how they try, children cannot be shielded from the knowledge that people do all kinds of terrible things and death is everywhere. It is only in fantasy that children have control over their lives and thus tame their fears and inner demons that they unfortunately carry into adulthood. In this sense the child is the stand-in for the artist, who, through imagination, creates a world where like Max, he is King of the Wild Things.

It may seem like a paradox that Sendak, who is so celebrated for his ability to delve into the most primal emotions of children, was so unchildlike in his structured work habits and in the meticulous way he constructed his art, but the whole logic of his practice was to create the illusion of autonomy and the sensation that we not only can control our fears and desires, but that they can be our salvation too. It was in the studio, and on the drawing table that Sendak

opposite: Maurice Sendak, Cover of *The New Yorker*, September 27, 1993

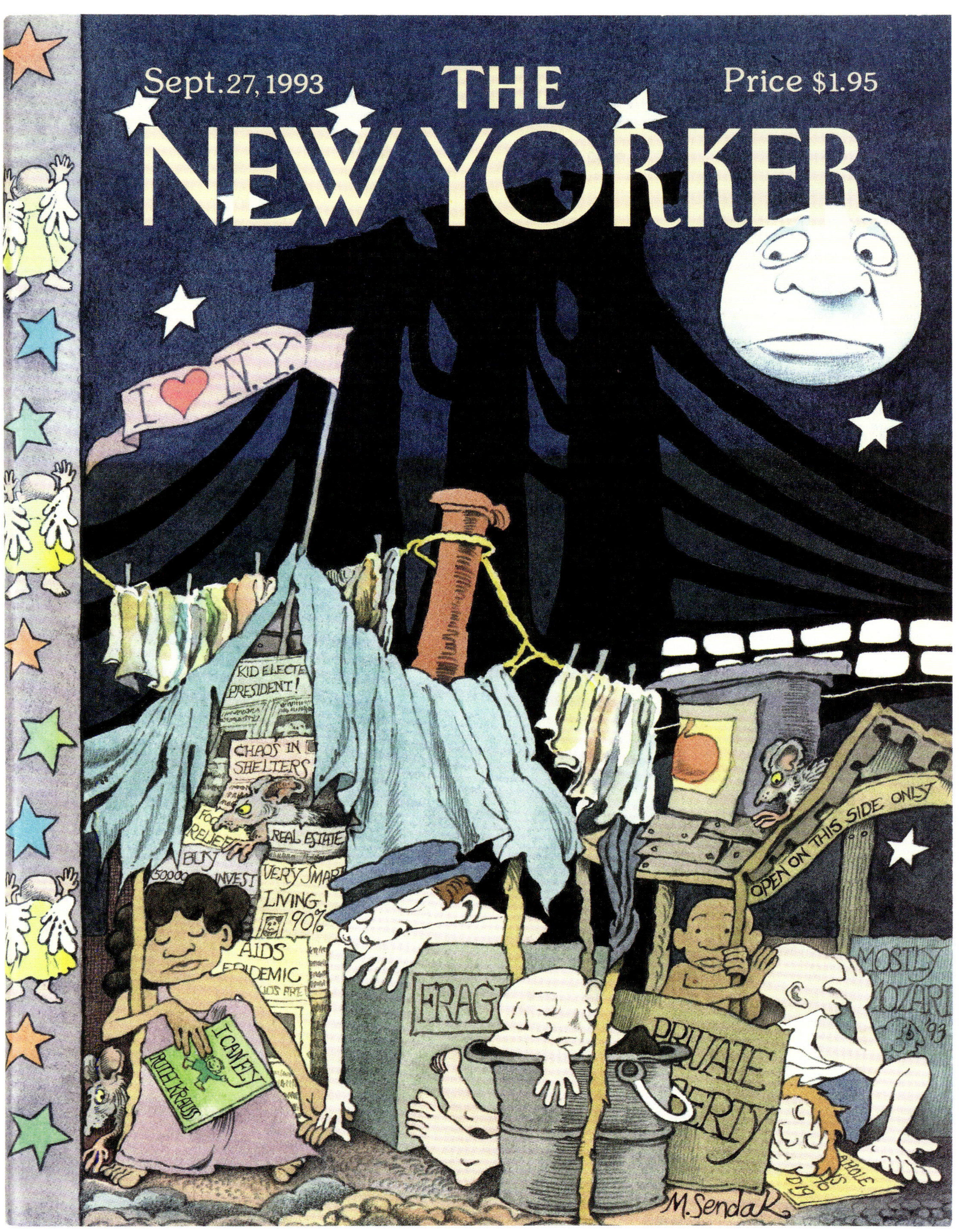

Sept. 27, 1993
THE NEW YORKER
Price $1.95
I ♥ N.Y.
KID ELECTE
PRESIDENT!
CHAOS IN
SHELTERS
REAL ESTATE
BUY
INVEST
VERY SMART
LIVING!
90%
AIDS
EPIDEMIC
OPEN ON THIS SIDE ONLY
FRAG
MOSTLY
MOZART
'93
M. Sendak

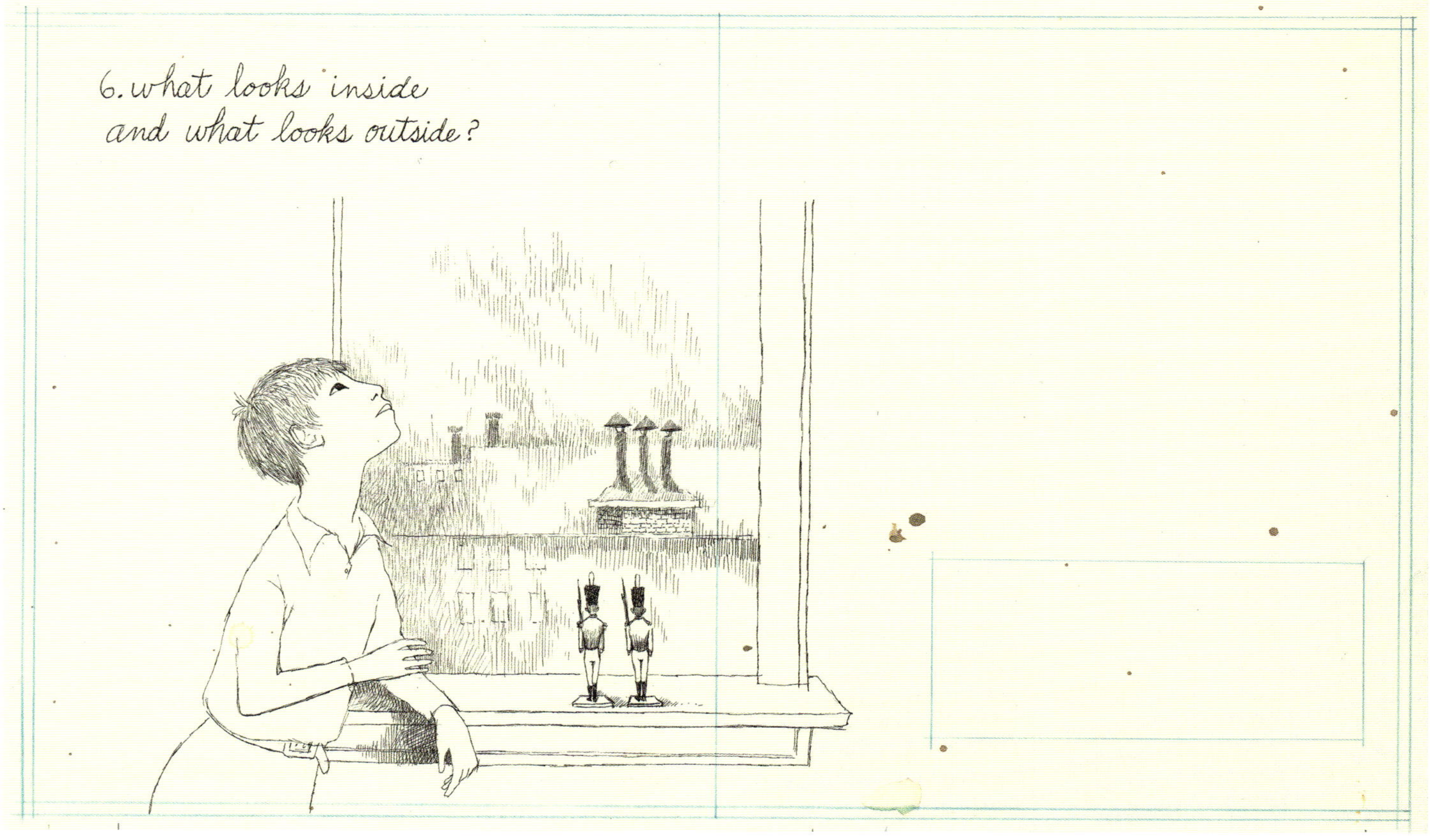

6. what looks inside and what looks outside?

Maurice Sendak, *Kenny's Window*, 1956, ink on paper, 10¾ × 17¼ in.

could take the raw material of his fantasies and convert them into images that for all their disturbing content have generosity and wholeness of form. Crow, in his beautiful essay, suggests the way Sendak's grid-like cross hatching in *Where the Wild Things Are* serves to not only animate the figures and shapes, but also to order them.

In his ink illustrations for the fairy tales of the Grimm Brothers or of Isaac Bashevis Singer, Sendak purposely flattens the space, so that the face of the stepmother or of the devil is pushed toward the picture plane, but simultaneously the rectangle of the border rhymes with the strong vertical and horizontal lines of the composition, to lock everything down. The almost claustrophobic quality of Sendak's proscenium-like spaces— derived from scrutiny of print artists like Dürer—heightens and controls the disturbing content. Often, we feel we are looking at the action on a narrow stage, or better yet, through a window. Sendak liked to tell people that he had been a sickly child, who had to stay indoors where his grandmother would entertain him by pulling a window shade up and down, pretending the view was a magic screen.[19] Fittingly, Sendak's first self-authored children's book, *Kenny's Window*, tells the story of a boy who mostly experiences the world from the contained safety of his room, looking out.

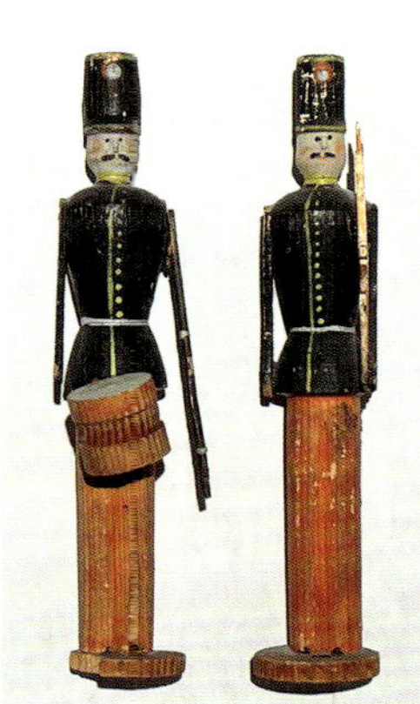

Toy Soldiers, FAO Schwarz, c. 1950

"*Kenny's Window* was a story of a little boy who has contradictory attitudes toward life, and toward his toys and toward his parents."

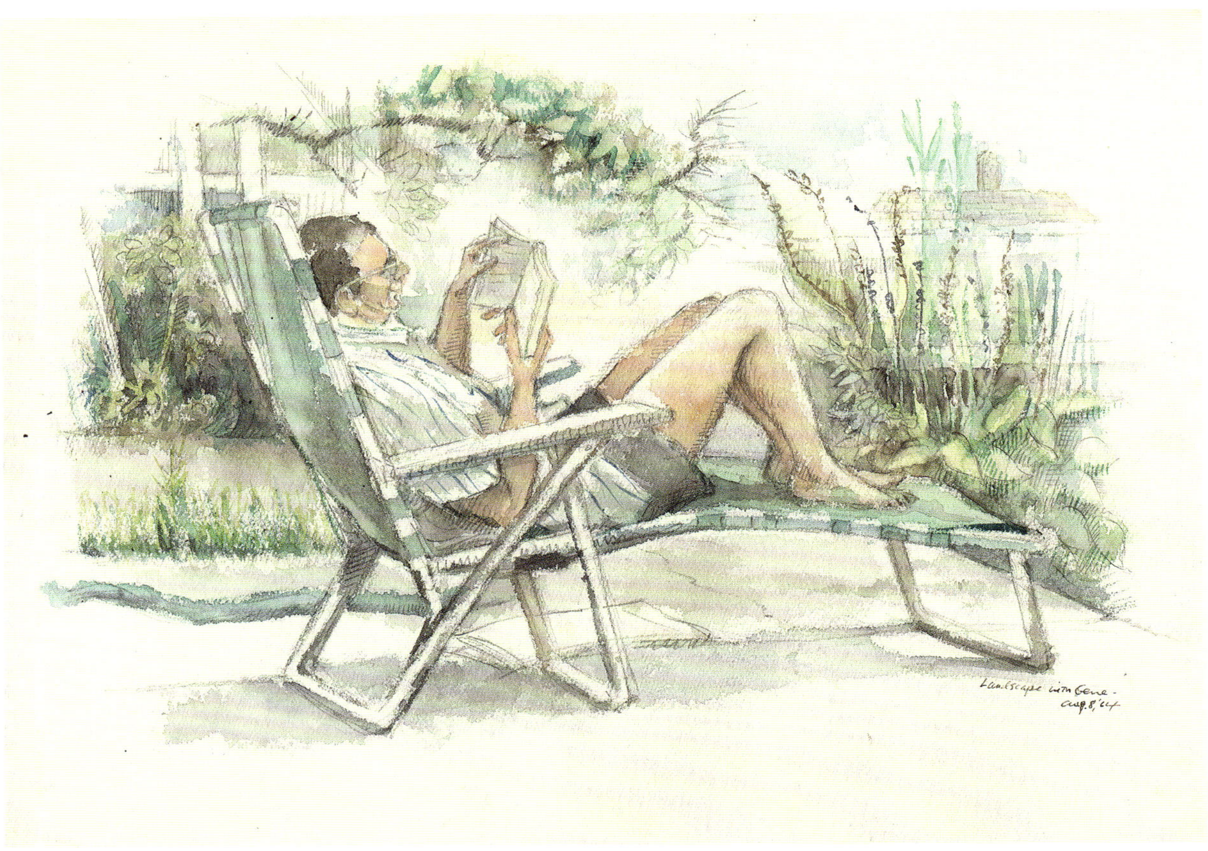

Maurice Sendak, *Landscape with Gene*, 1964, watercolor and pencil on paper, 10 × 14 in.

I hesitated before mentioning Sendak's childhood memory of illness, because I feel too much of the writing on his art dwells on such stories. Sendak's companion, Eugene Glynn, in his writing about psychoanalysis and art, frequently cautioned about the tendency to reduce the work of art to stories of childhood suffering leading to neurosis.[20] One of the dangers of dwelling on trauma in Sendak's biography and art is that it deflects from the sheer joy of creation and his extraordinary sense of humor. Sendak may sometimes depict a world of potentially anxious challenges, where death lurks behind every corner, and yet his heroes are usually cheerful and confident. He may have obsessed over the Lindbergh kidnapping, and the horror of the holocaust, but he also loved to play with his Mickey Mouse toys, and his god was Mozart, whose music contains both joy and melancholy in equal measure. The memories of his collaborators and friends, like Twyla Tharp and John Dugdale, are included in this book, to give a sense of the enormous vitalism of the man.

When Lynn Caponera and I conduct interviews, we always ask people for their funniest Sendak story, because in our experience there was no one who was funnier or fuller of what Spike Jonze called "mischief" than Sendak. Whatever his personal demons—his unhappy childhood or his frequent bouts of depression—his finest work right up to the last was often about what the director Carroll Ballard called, "the foibles of human nature" and "just how absurd we can be." After all, the book he was working on at his death was the Nikolay Gogol-inspired story of a man in search of his lost nose.

And so, when someone who is close to me suffers a great loss, I send them to one of Sendak's saddest *and* funniest books, *Higglety Pigglety Pop!* which he wrote when his dog Jennie was dying. In the beginning of the story Jennie leaves her loving owner in quest of the meaning of life. After several Kafkaesque misadventures trying to get an obstinate baby to eat, and herself avoid getting eaten by a lion, she becomes "the leading lady" in The World Theatre. In other words, she becomes an artist who entertains the world. Personal grief is crafted by Sendak into a book of charm and beauty. Making art healed himself and in the process consoles us all. It ends with a letter from Jennie to her owner, letting him know she is doing alright, but now I hear in it my friend Maurice's voice: "I can't tell you how to get to the Castle Yonder because I don't know where it is. But if you ever come this way, look for me."

Notes

1. Jonathan Cott, *There's a Mystery There: The Primal Vision of Maurice Sendak* (New York: Doubleday, 2017), 1.
2. Charles Baudelaire, *The Painter of Modern Life and Other Essays*, trans. Jonathan Mayne (New York: De Capo Press, 1986), 8.
3. This interview is published in Carin Kuoni and Amanda Parmer, eds. *An Index to Art & Politics: 25 Years of Vera List Center Fellowships* (New York: Vera List Center for Art and Politics, The New School, 2018).
4. Morton Schindel, producer, "Maurice Sendak" (Weston Woods, 1965).
5. Maurice Sendak, "Introduction," Oliver Knussen and Maurice Sendak, *Higglety Pigglety Pop! Opera*, original manuscript copied by Oliver Knussen from Maurice Sendak's handwriting and dated April 9, 1984, pg. 1. In the collection of The Maurice Sendak Foundation.
6. Virginia Haviland, "Questions to an Artist Who Is Also an Author: A Conversation between Maurice Sendak and Virginia Haviland," *Quarterly Journal of the Library of Congress* 28, no. 4 (October, 1971). Reprinted in Maurice Sendak and Peter C. Kunze, *Conversations with Maurice Sendak*, Literary conversations series (Jackson: University Press of Mississippi, 2016), 32–3. Kindle Edition.
7. Stephen Heller, *Innovators of American Illustration* (New York: Van Nostrand Reinhold, 1986), selections reprinted in *Conversations with Maurice Sendak*, 95.
8. Haviland, 33.
9. Sendak began to mention Mantegna's painting in public events almost immediately after he saw it hanging at the Metropolitan Museum of Art in 1988 and he discussed this painting with me in the public interview I conducted with him at the Vera List Center for Art and Politics on October 30, 2003, excerpted in this book.
10. Cott, *There's a Mystery There: The Primal Vision of Maurice Sendak*, 92.
11. Antony Griffiths and Frances Carey, *German Printmaking in the Age of Goethe* (London: British Museum Press, 1994), 119.
12. Robert Rosenblum, *The Romantic Child: from Runge to Sendak*, twentieth Walter Neurath memorial lecture (New York, N.Y.: Thames and Hudson, 1989), 29.
13. Interview with Bill Jersey and Terry Strauss for the television program *First Edition*, PBS, 1994, excerpted in this book.
14. Sendak claimed he couldn't draw horses well and told the story about his Jewish relatives being the inspiration for the Wild Things in Selma Lanes, *The Art of Maurice Sendak* (New York: Harry N. Abrams), 1980, 88.
15. See Patrick Rodgers, "Selected Sendak: Interviews by the Rosenbach," in *Conversations with Maurice Sendak*, 183. Interestingly, Sendak himself says the translation of vilde chayes is "wild thing," but literally it is "wild animal." In this interview he also talks about his relatives being escapees from Nazism.
16. A recent example of the discussion of *Where the Wild Things Are* is the exhibition *Vilde Chayes/Wild Things: Childhood Through the Eyes of Maurice Sendak*, curated by Clara Nguyen and Avinoam Patt, Richard H. Schimmellfeng Gallery, UConn Library, 2021. For a discussion of issues of both Jewish and gay identity in Sendak's work see Golan Moskowitz, *Wild Visionary: Maurice Sendak in Queer Jewish Context* (Redwood City, CA: Stanford University Press, 2020).
17. *L'Enfant et les Sortilèges*'s influence on *Where the Wild Things Are* became obvious when Sendak designed a production of the opera for Glyndebourne in 1987. While Tony Kushner briefly discusses it in his *The Art of Maurice Sendak, 1980 to the Present* (New York: Harry N. Abrams, 2003), 158–9, and John Cech refers to it in passing in his *Angels and Wild Things* (University Park, PA: Pennsylvania University State Press, 1995), it is rarely considered in terms of troubling the biographical impetus of most of the approaches to *Where the Wild Things Are*.
18. This story seems to have its origins in Edith Wharton's 1934 memoir, *A Background Glance* (Moorside Press, 2013) accessed online at https://books.google.com/books?id=w2pTCAAAQBAJ&pg=PT117&source=gbs_toc_r&cad=4#v=onepage&q&f=false on 29 November 2021.
19. See Weinberg interview with Sendak in this book.
20. See Eugene D. Glynn, *Desperate Necessity, Essays on Art and Psychoanalysis* (New York: Periscope Publishing: 2008).

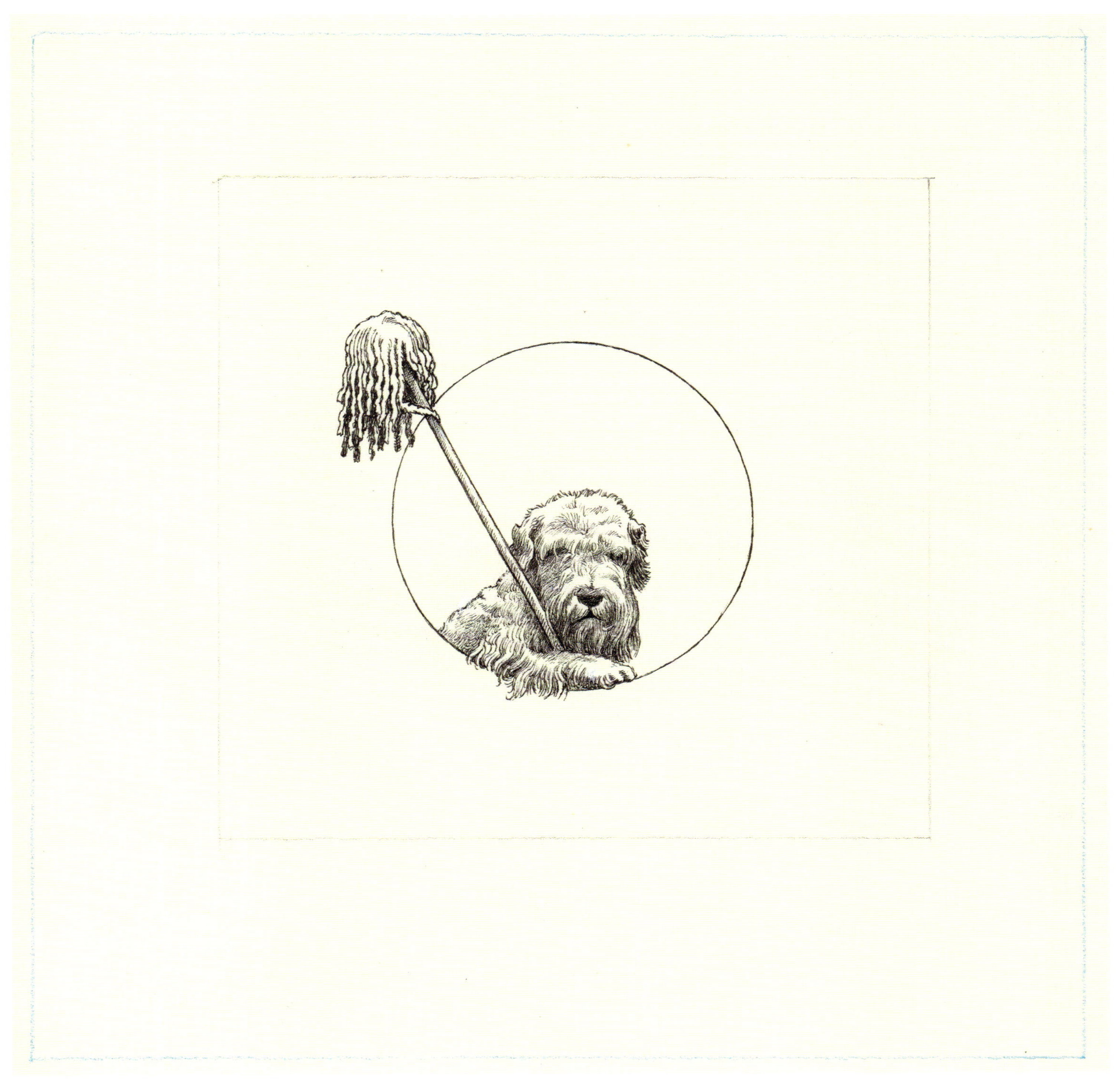

Maurice Sendak, *Higglety Pigglety Pop! Or There Must Be More to Life*, 1967, ink on paper, 11½ × 9 in.

Fantasy Sketches

"Music, which accompanied the creation of these pages, is the catalyst that brought them to life . . . Music helped unravel my imaginary scenes; it pressed the button, turned the key, kept my pen moving across the paper. My homework consisted of letting whatever came into my mind come out on the paper, and my only conscious intention was to complete a whole 'story' on one page, to compose the whole sheet, beginning and ending, if possible, with the music itself."

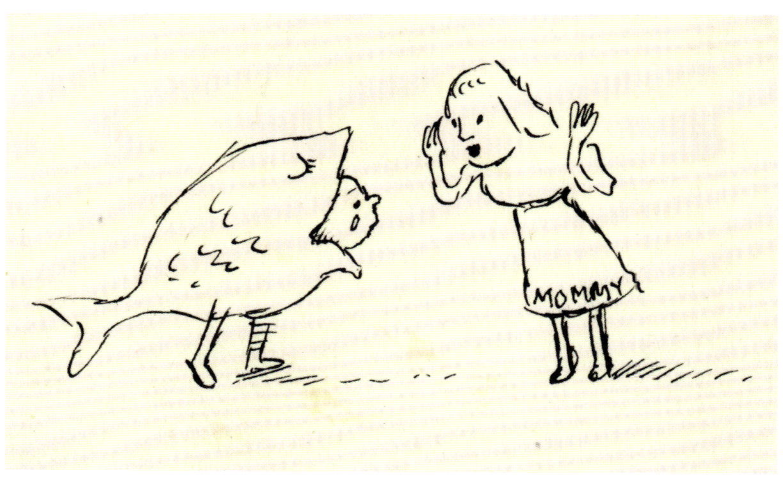

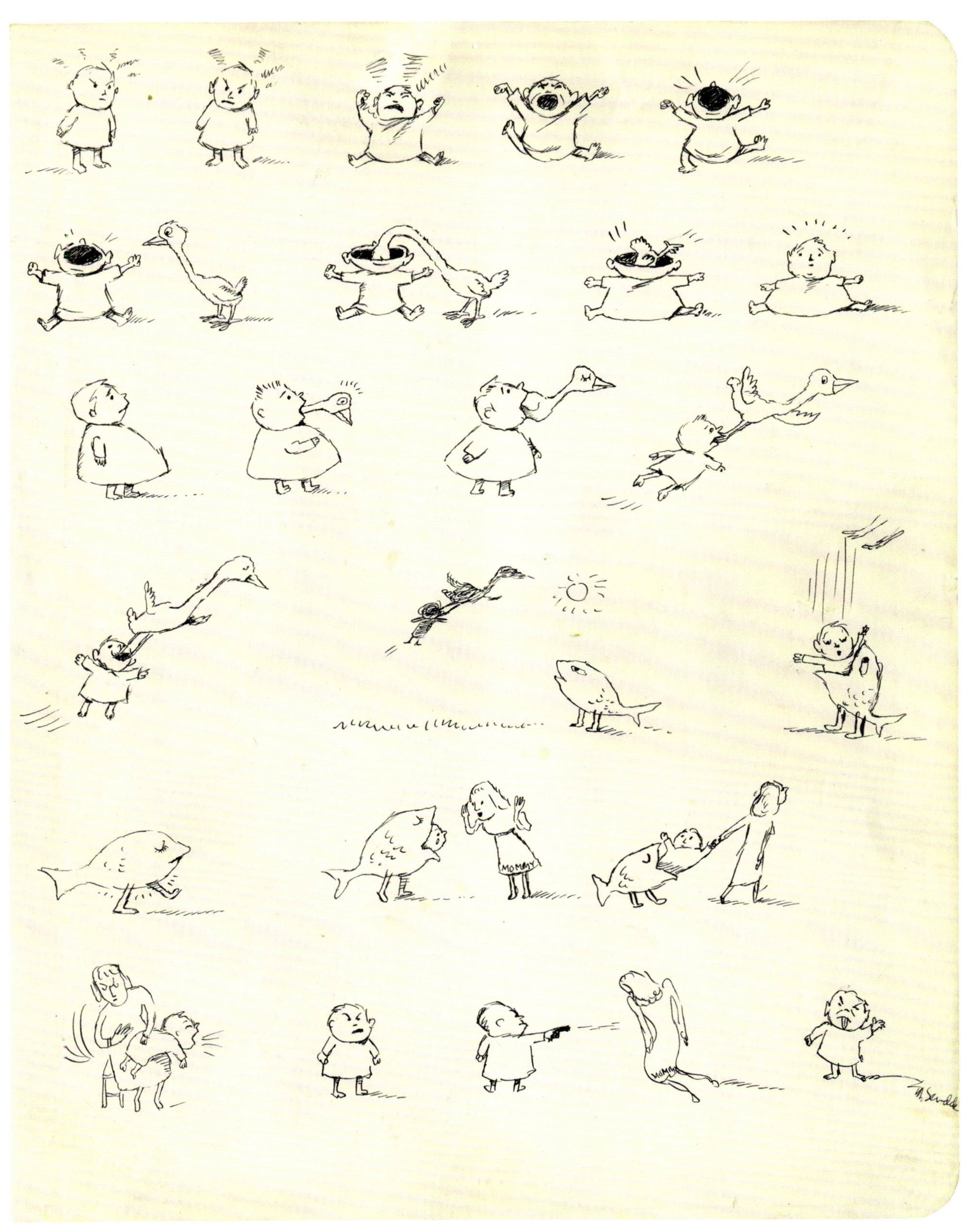

Maurice Sendak, Fantasy Sketch: *Fish Boy*, c. 1950, ink on paper, 10 × 7½ in.

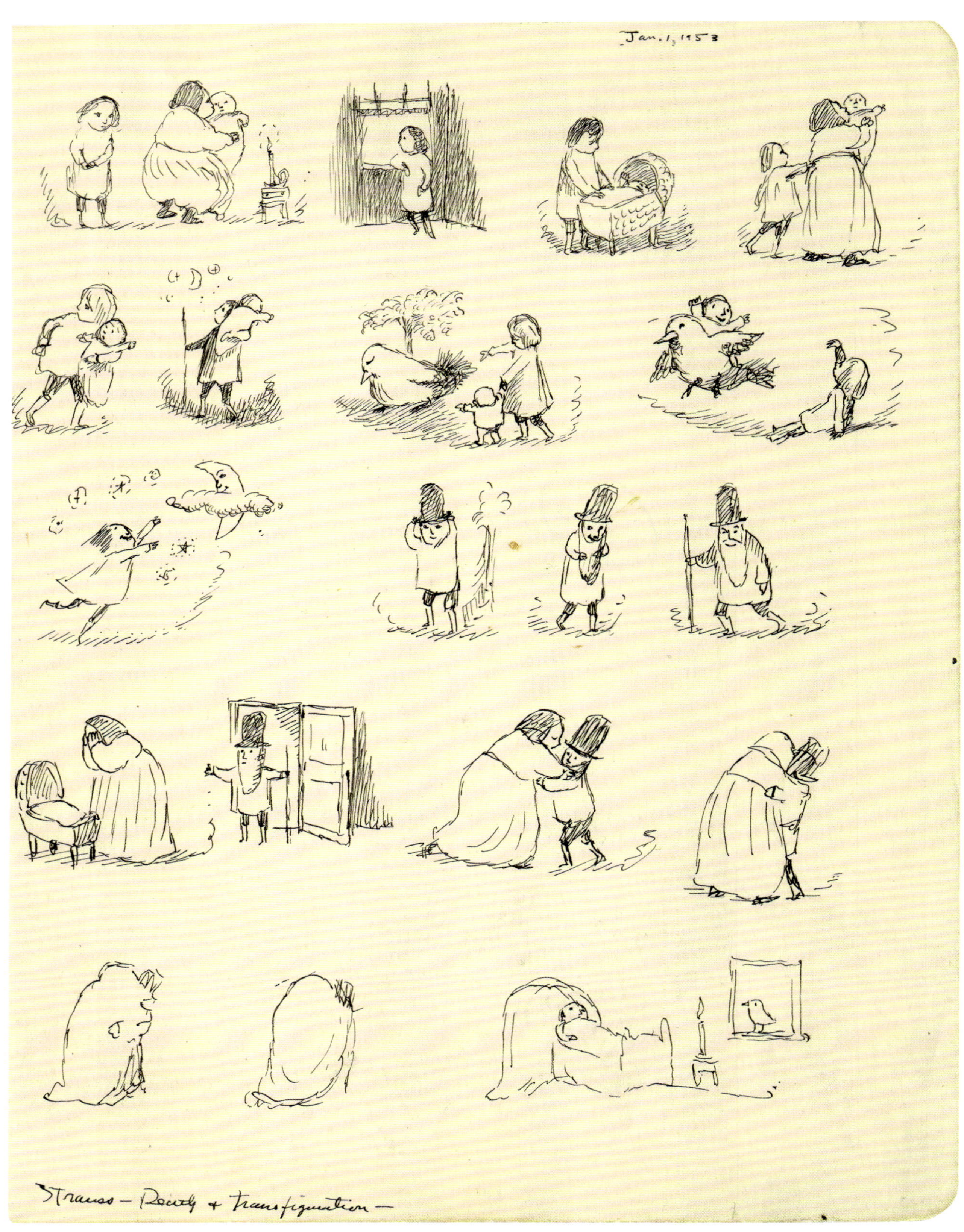

Maurice Sendak, Fantasy Sketch: *Strauss—Death and Transfiguration*, 1953, ink on paper, 10 × 7½ in.

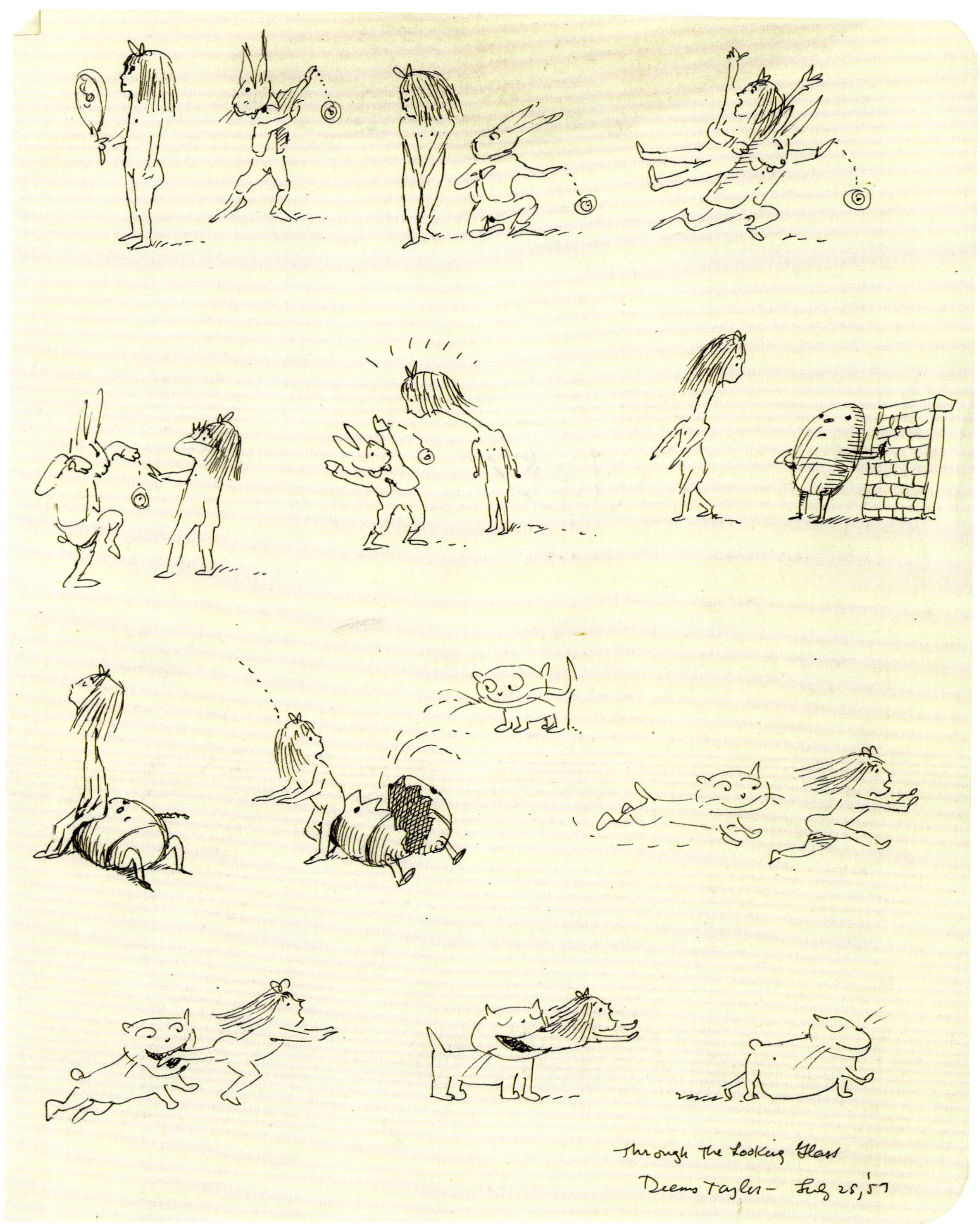

Maurice Sendak, Fantasy Sketch: *Through the Looking Glass—Deems Taylor*, 1957, ink on paper, 10 × 7⅝ in.

A Hole Is to Dig

"Ruth was way ahead of women's lib. She wouldn't let me get away with any myths about what little boys did and what little girls did. We did six books together and that was my education in bookmaking, book layout and typography."

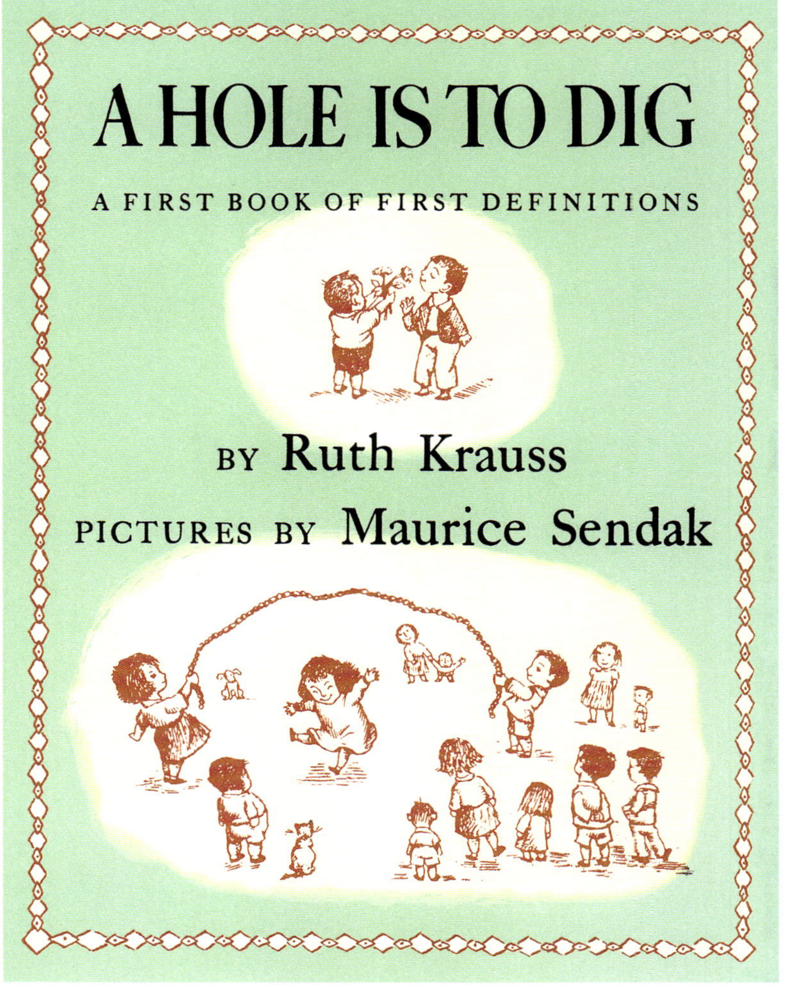

Ruth Krauss, Pictures by Maurice Sendak, *A Hole Is to Dig* (New York, Harper & Brothers: 1952)

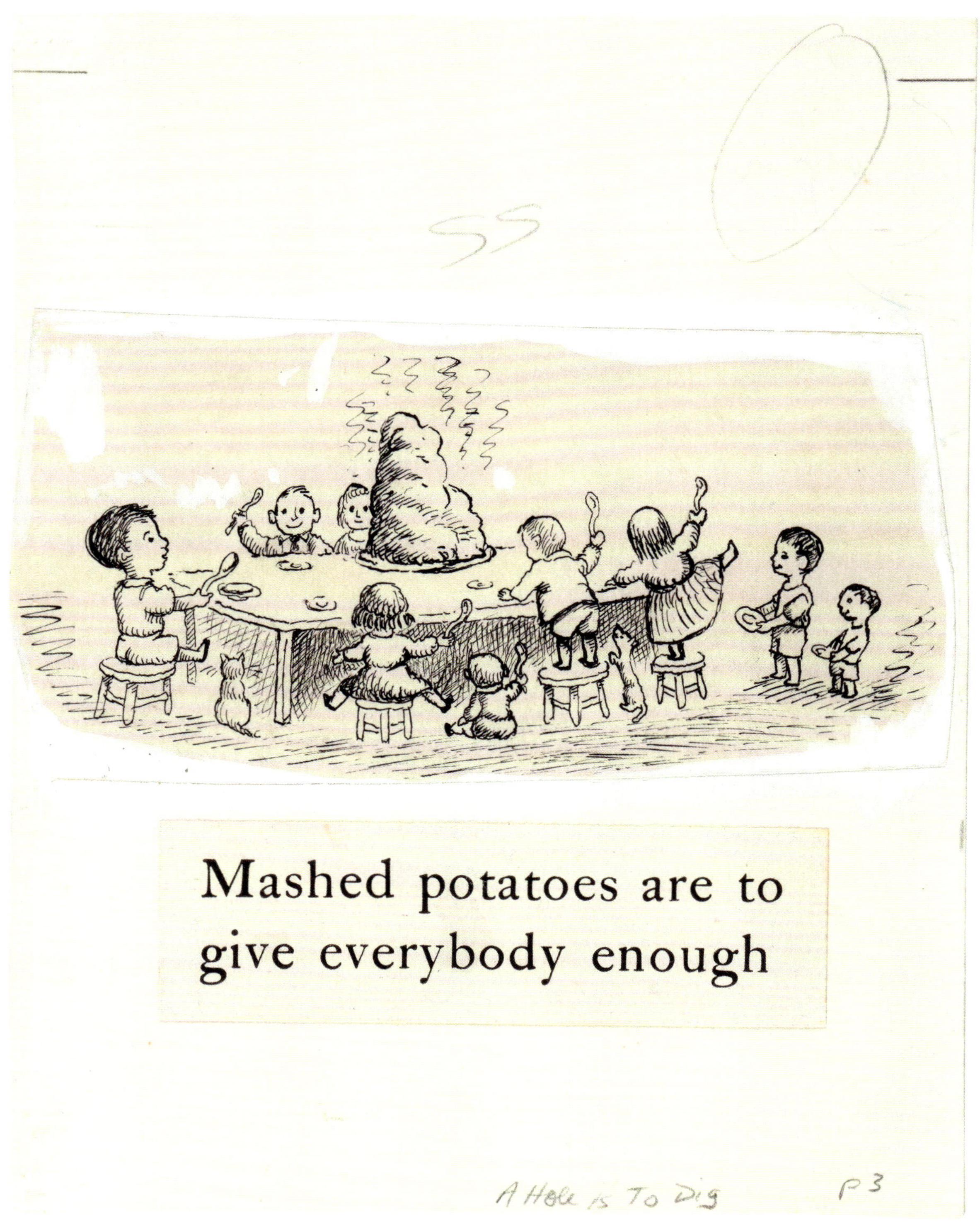

Maurice Sendak, illustration for *A Hole Is to Dig*, 1952, ink on paper with paste-up lettering, 6¾ × 5½ in.

A face is so you can make faces

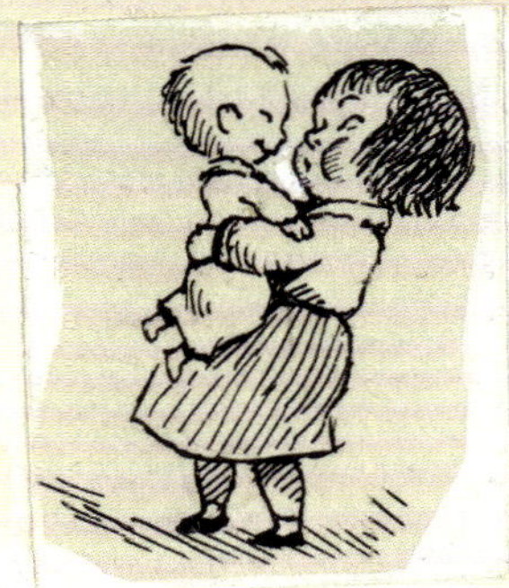

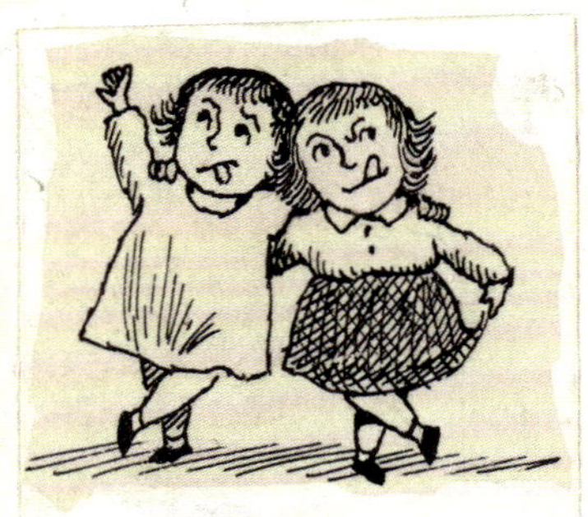

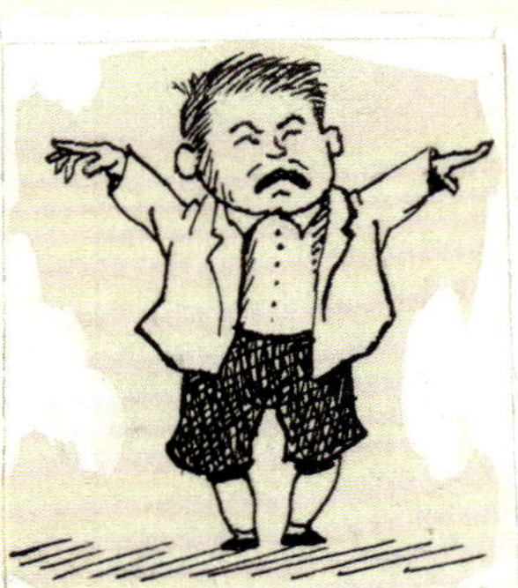

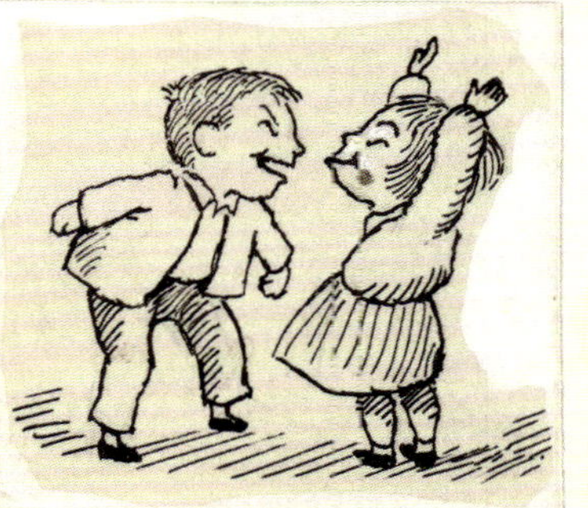

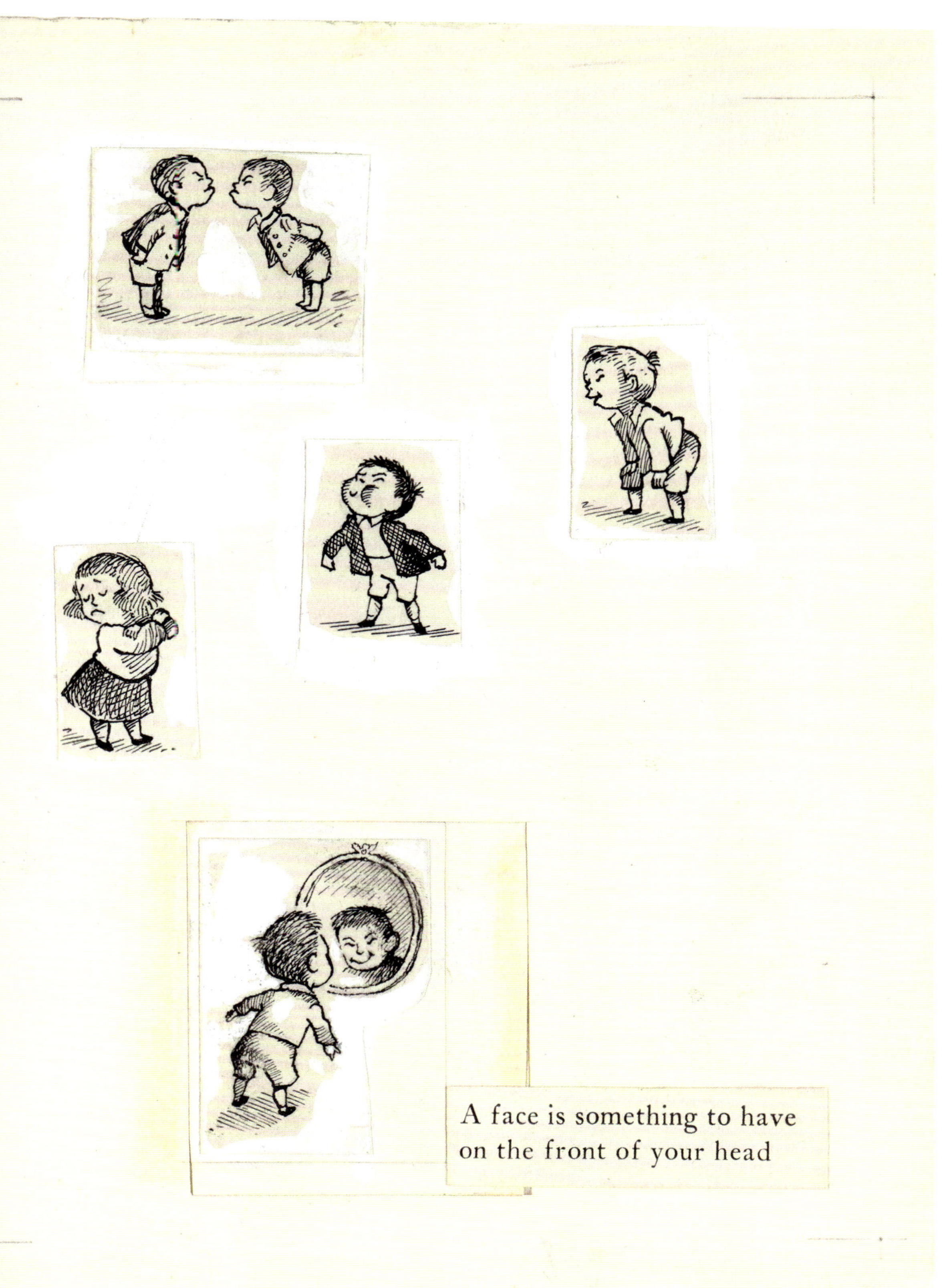

Maurice Sendak, illustration for *A Hole Is to Dig*, 1952, ink on paper with paste-up lettering, 6¾ × 10 in.

Right as Rain

Quests and Transformative Garments in the Major Books of Maurice Sendak

THOMAS CROW

Amid the prosperous times of 1950s America, graphic art and illustration emerged into their own era of abundant talent and innovation. Young practitioners arrived in New York from a remarkable gamut of backgrounds and professional formations. Edward Gorey's Harvard experience in literature and amateur theatricals yielded in 1953 the fully realized *Unstrung Harp*, announcing the monochrome manner and gothic sensibility that would sustain a storied career. Jules Feiffer had spent a decade after leaving his Bronx high school assisting the *noir*-comic master Will Eisner, then emerging out from under the heavily inked panels of the *Spirit* with the lightly fluent calligraphic line with which he would dissect the anxious self-consciousness of aspirational urbanites. A similarly loose, improvised feel found its way into John and Faith Hubley's designs for their animated shorts, where the pair found fresh psychological authenticity in the improvised dialogue and untrained voices of their own children. Tomi Ungerer emigrated to the city from the French region of Alsace, bringing a spare but tensile ink line that would lend itself to expressing the political and sexual upheavals on the horizon.

For all the incomparable qualities that would distinguish Maurice Sendak's work as an illustrator, this array of talent formed a professional milieu that affirmed a valid artistic path to one side of gallery fine art. Most of these artists had been born within a few years of his birthdate of 1928, with some becoming friends and supportive colleagues. While the capsule characterizations above indicate how widely their range of work extended beyond Sendak's early, firm choice of children's books, there ran through virtually all of their output, even that directed to adults, a privileged place for the child as exemplary presence and guarantee of authenticity. Veteran William Steig, future creator of Shrek, populated his *New Yorker* covers with gamboling, slightly feral tykes. The worldliest among these artists turned their hands to illustration for children. Even the unique books that Andy Warhol created for friends followed a child's rubric of alphabets and whimsically anthropomorphic animals, flowers, and shoes. He even assumed something of a juvenile, toy-like persona within the magazine and advertising world, regularly typecast as Raggedy Andy for his unassuming carelessness in dress and winsome personal manner.

This cohort of artists nonetheless displayed mastery over line fully on a par with exemplars such as Paul Klee or Georg Grosz, but the reigning criteria for high art in the museums and 57th-Street galleries—abstraction, wall-dominating scale—excluded them from similar aspiration. Their luster offers a lesson in how historical phases of art succeed one another, in that putatively outmoded formations are rarely, if ever, exhausted; rather they migrate to more hospitable, less policed ground. Children's literature offered one such refuge, while the accompanying diminution of status found a figure in the analogically reduced persona of the child.

There were compensating advantages to staking out this ground, however, as these artists could also call on the deeply ingrained cultural associations of childhood with truthful, unaffected vision. That foundation allowed the Hubleys brilliantly to adapt avant-garde idioms from the cubists and expressionists to their animated lyricism. The exquisite sophistication of Warhol's fashion illustrations and the taste of those who commissioned them were only enhanced via his disarming affinity to the cult of the child. It thus followed that his distinctive manner of drawing and dye washes would not change between what appeared on a page in the *New York Times* and his handmade cute-cat codices.

Consistency of a signature style, handy for commissioning editors needing a certain look, typifies this group of postwar graphic artists. Warhol began with one that usefully resembled the manner of the blacklisted leftist Ben Shahn; but the career of the younger artist also demonstrates the vulnerability to external changes that this seeming professional necessity brought in its wake. By the close of the 1950s, both magazine art directors and advertisers were curtailing their longstanding reliance on illustration in favor of newly artful applications of photography, a shift that spurred artists dependent on freelance commissions toward other pursuits. Alongside his weekly strip in the *Village Voice*, Feiffer emerged as a novelist and playwright of some consequence, one of his unproduced scripts eventually becoming the screenplay for the Mike Nichols film *Carnal Knowledge*. Warhol went so far as to abandon commercial illustration in favor of the fine-art career that Pop had opened to his skill set.

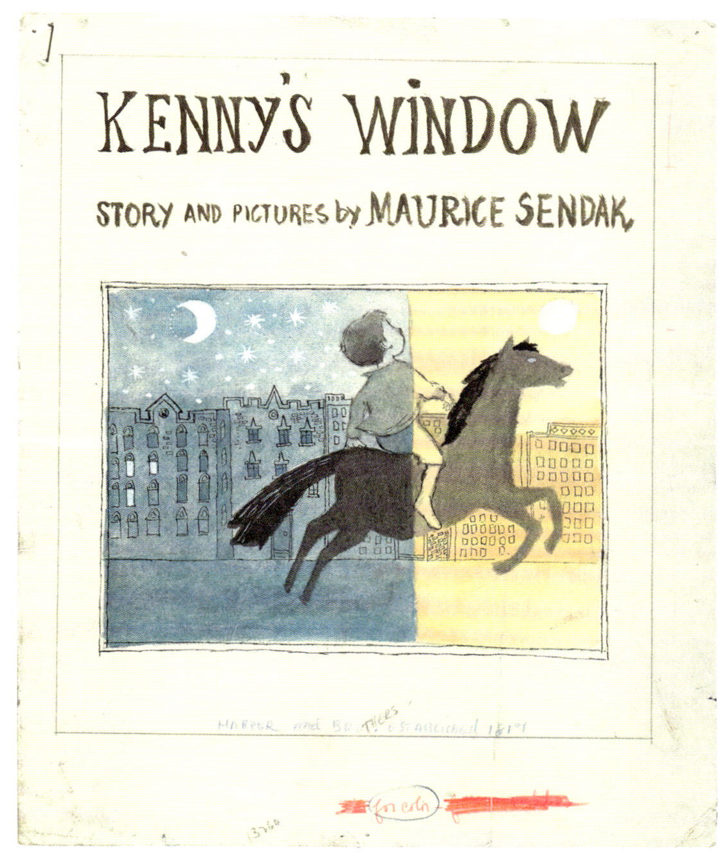

Maurice Sendak, Study for the Cover of *Kenny's Window*, 1956, ink and watercolor on paper, 11 × 9 in.

And the steady market for illustrated children's literature became ever more attractive.

Sendak had of course been there all along. Over the period of his self-driven formation, he had ranged across various distinct manners cognate to the ones his peers would make their exclusive signatures, but never fixed on any of them. The well-known page from the 1956 *Kenny's Window*, where the boy kneels upright at the foot of his curvilinear Victorian bed frame, relies on a density of ink and inflection of silhouette that recalls the distinctive manner of Gorey, its darker implications surely touched by Sendak's own memories of sickly isolation in childhood. The rollicking angularity of *Alligators All Around*, part of the miniaturized 1962 *Nutshell*

following pages: Maurice Sendak, *Kenny's Window*, 1956, ink on paper, 10¾ × 17¼ in.

7. do you always want
what you think you
want?

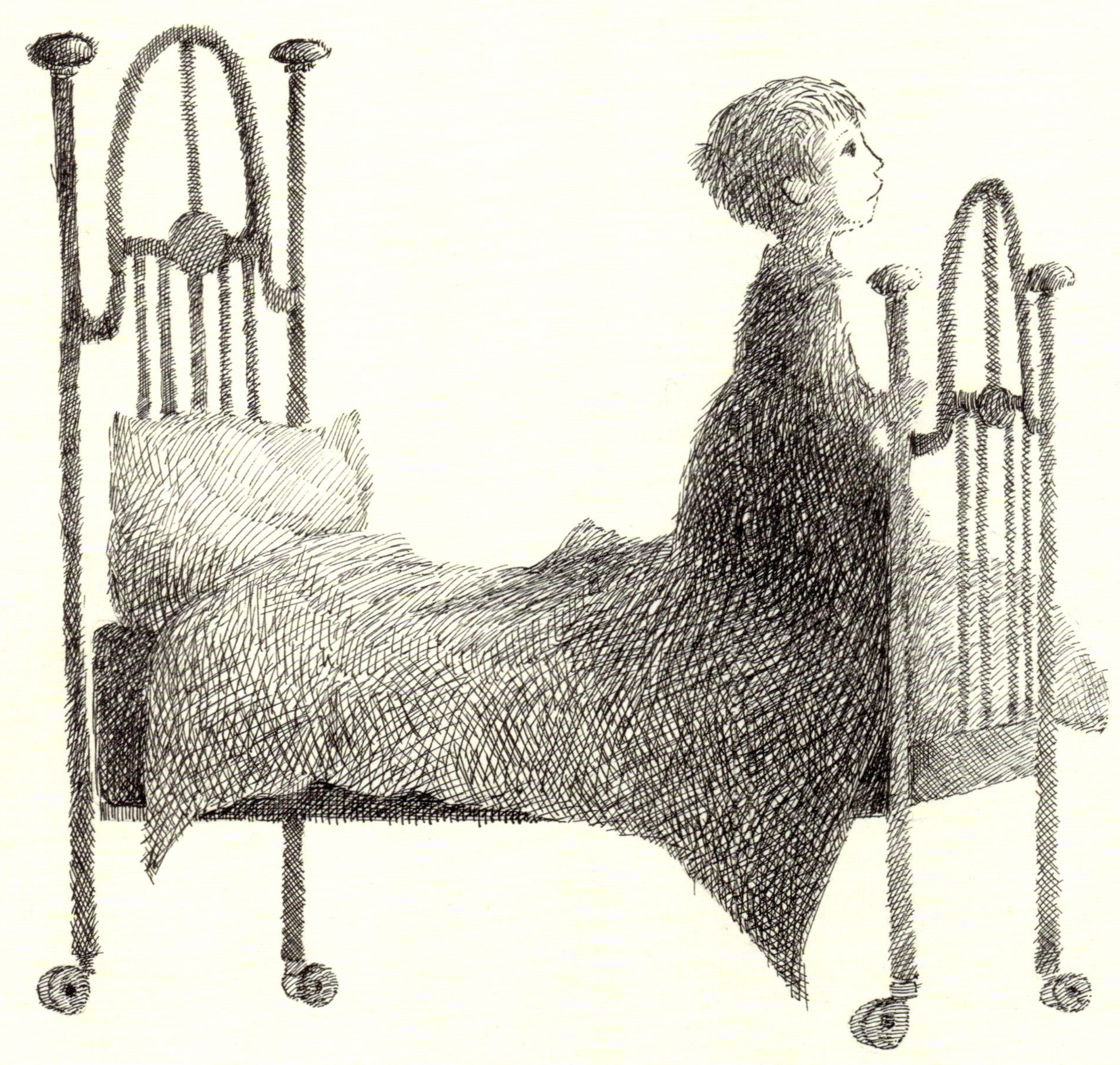

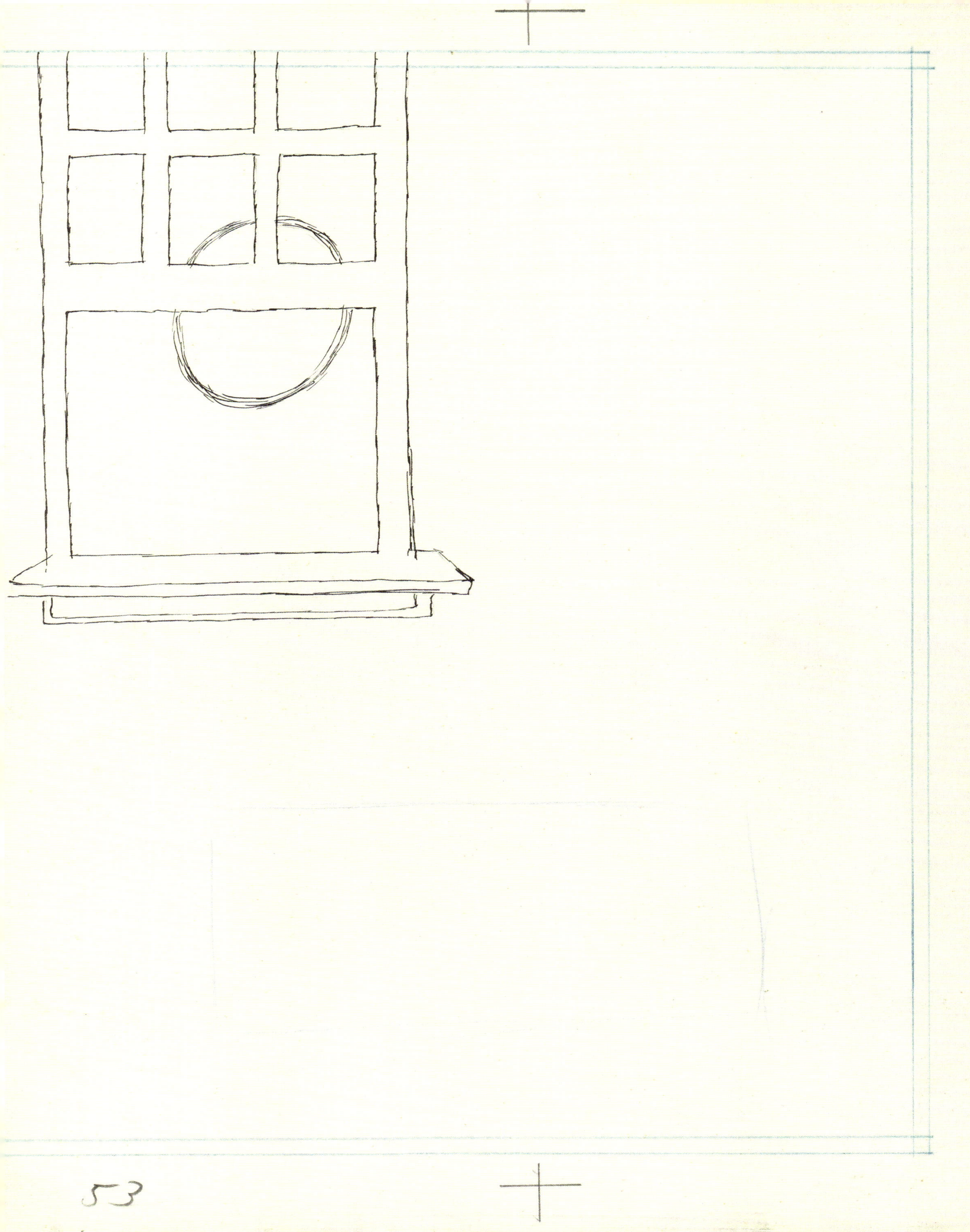
53

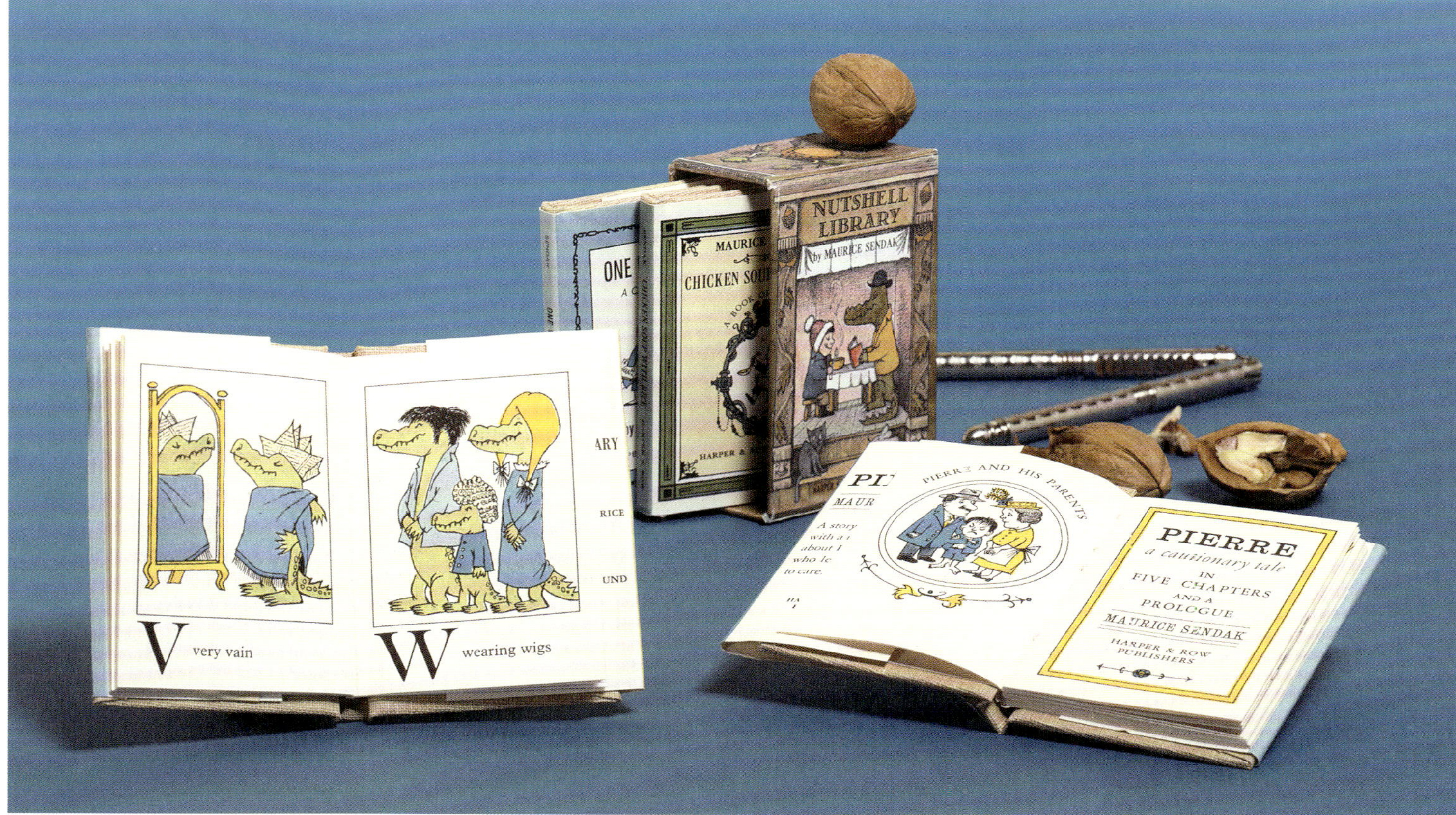

Maurice Sendak, *Nutshell Library* (New York: Harper & Row: 1962)

Library, carries echoes of both Ungerer and Warhol, while the melting watercolor illustrations for *Mr. Rabbit and the Lovely Present* of the same year, nearly forgoing defined contours altogether, swerves in the direction of the Hubleys.

Over the course of Sendak's early personal odyssey, one nonetheless came to recognize a work as being by him even if it didn't necessarily resemble the previous one. But that nearly paradoxical achievement depended on his finding some foundation that felt securely his own, against which every departure might be measured. Opening the way toward a firmer personal foundation were his illustrations from around 1960 for Else Holmelund Minarik's primer series *Little Bear*, where he turned away from the contemporary gamut of styles toward one that evoked a bygone era of Victoriana.

There are the inner borders with Sendak's own delicate floral filigree, and there is the characters' nineteenth-century dress; but most of all, there is the crosshatching pen technique for generating gradations of tone from light to dark using only overlaid thin lines. Such building up of tonal modulation to suggest shading and volume was the stock in trade of the engraver using a sharp burin to incise the wood or steel printing plate, the roughness of the cut holding the ink for a run through the press after the smooth surface had been wiped clean (cutting lines into a wax covering allowed an acid bath to etch the surface with less effort). Even as advances in lithography made engraving and etching obsolete in mass reproduction, its special texture retained an enduring appeal in hand-drawn illustration. Sendak achieved his special fineness and fragility of line by using what was practically the simplest instrument available, the steel crow-quill nib, itself a nineteenth-century survival, which required dipping into the ink bottle at frequent intervals and wore out rapidly. Edward Gorey, whose consistently archaizing manner in pen and ink offered a certain parallel,

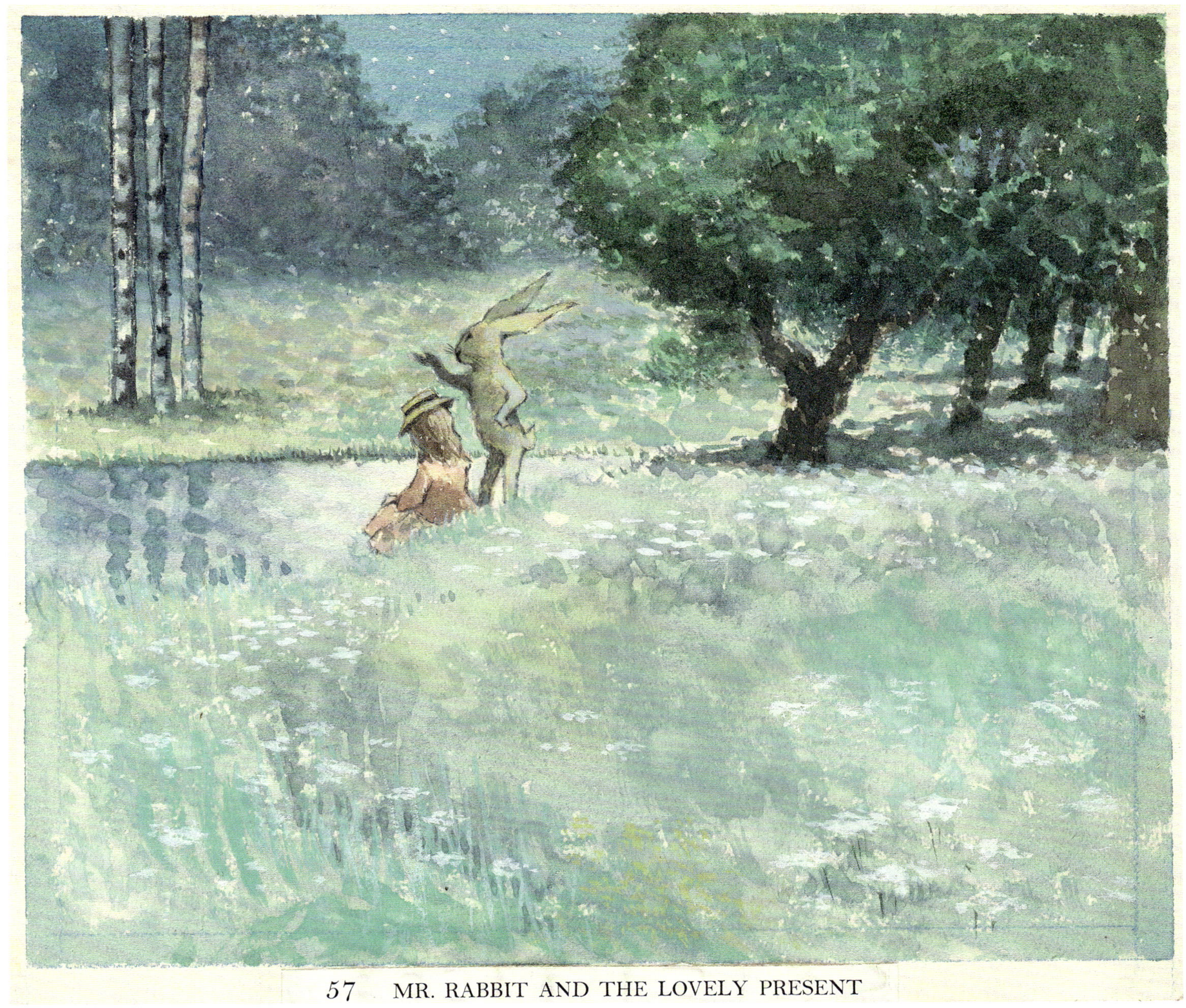

Maurice Sendak, *Mr. Rabbit and the Lovely Present*, 1962, watercolor on paper, 7¾ × 9⅜ in.

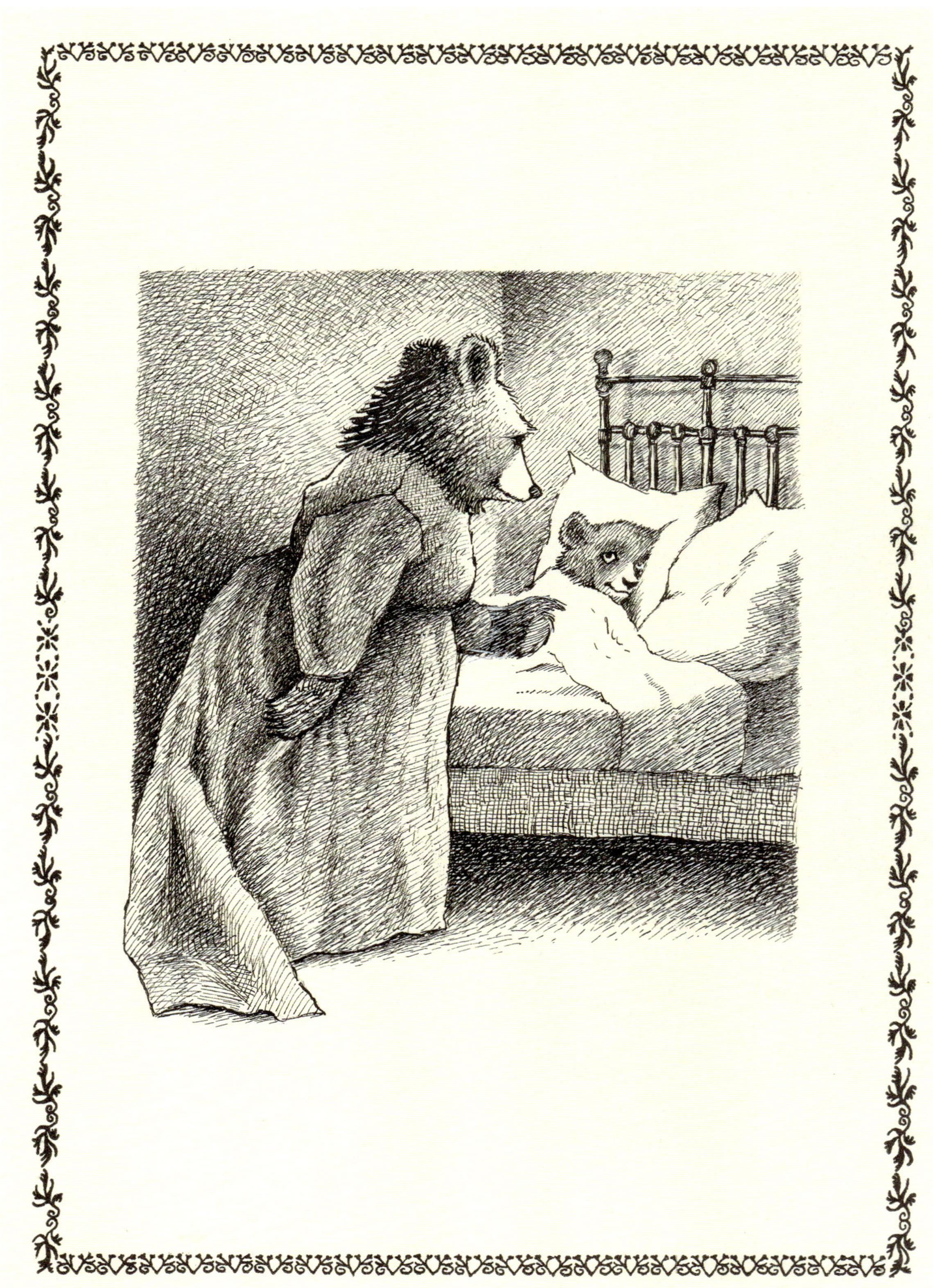

Maurice Sendak, *Little Bear*, 1957, ink on paper, 10¾ × 8¼ in.

nonetheless attested that Sendak drew "much more finely" than he did.[1]

By the time that Sendak came to fashion his watershed *Where the Wild Things Are* in the early 1960s, that crosshatched texture, now divested of period connotations, had become something of a character unto itself—starting with the Matisse-like floral pattern of the endpapers, which would have been blandly out of character with the book had they lacked their scratchily textured overlay. He generated that effect by straightforward means: horizontal and vertical passes of the fine pen point at nearly equal intervals. But that pattern arises from dozens of conjoined patches, each one only as large as a single load of ink in the nib would generate, which Sendak emphasized by taking no trouble to align each passage with the ones next to it—thus engendering a secondary wandering pattern along the seams, like looking through a patched window screen in what amounts to the book's ingratiating overture.

For an artist on Sendak's level, it would be implausible to imagine him putting so much time and application into a technique without making it an instrument of thought. The first two illustrated pages of what remains Sendak's most famous work further emphasize the black ink crosshatching, its density suited to these tightly configured panels, confined as they are to centered rectilinear formats floating inside large white margins. In the first, the child protagonist Max, already wearing his curious wolf suit/all-in-one pajamas, engages in maximum mayhem. He makes an indoor tent by hanging a blanket over a chain of tied-together bed linens, which recall the clichéd means of a prisoner's escape—or, more ominously, prison suicide as mimicked by the suspended stuffed bear—all reinforcing the book's opening statement of compression and confinement. Max wields a hammer like a battle-axe half his height to pound an anchoring nail into the wall, and little that follows in the land of the Wild Things quite equals the violent agitation and turmoil that Sendak intimates in his claustrophobic opening vignette.

The following, slightly larger scene appears even more thoroughly governed by the crosshatched grid (save only for the opening at the left through which the alarmed pet dog escapes). But the implication of captivity, against which Max raises his fearsome hammer, here gives way to orderly domestic decorum suddenly invaded by the bestialized boy, a pinwheeling, be-clawed changeling whose borrowed animal energy overwhelms the actual fleeing animal, the two of them colored and modeled alike. Every component of Max's figure forms an angle to the verticals and horizontals that dominate the whole, most dramatically expressed in the relationship of the costume's tail to the wall behind it. The disproportionate size and contrastingly dark color of the appendage attaches it less to the foreground figure and more to the crosshatched field, where it functions like a zone of turbulence collapsing the regularity of the grid into something dynamic and disturbing, capped at the tip by a cresting wave out of Hokusai. Within a balancing rectangle on the upper left of the wall is the unmissable anticipation of the fantasy adventure to follow, as well as a conflation of creator with protagonist: the drawing inscribed "by Max" of a saw-toothed, bug-eyed beast, rhino horn on its snout. Whether its prominence represents parental pride or palliative remains unanswered, as does the question of whether "*by* Max" signifies a self-portrait "*of* Max."

Turning the page to the next, again slightly larger panel reveals Max sent to his room without his evening meal (the moon through the window establishing the time). Though this turn of events has been deemed a path-breaking acknowledgment of anger in a child, Max appears distinctly subdued compared to the ferocious acting-out evident on the opening page. His room is now a calm, foursquare enclosure, contained by radiating perspective lines where the sidewalls meet the ceiling and floor. So far, so straightforward; but Sendak handles these spatial cues in a way that positions the implied eye level of the viewer well above the child's head, thus reinforcing his temporary subordination, from which he will rise on the strength of his imaginative resources rather than any physical prowess. Over the next four pages, while the crescent moon maintains its position, the illustrations keep growing larger and larger in line with the recovery of Max's spirits, until the art fills the entire surface of the right-hand page and his room has vanished, adult perspective nullified,

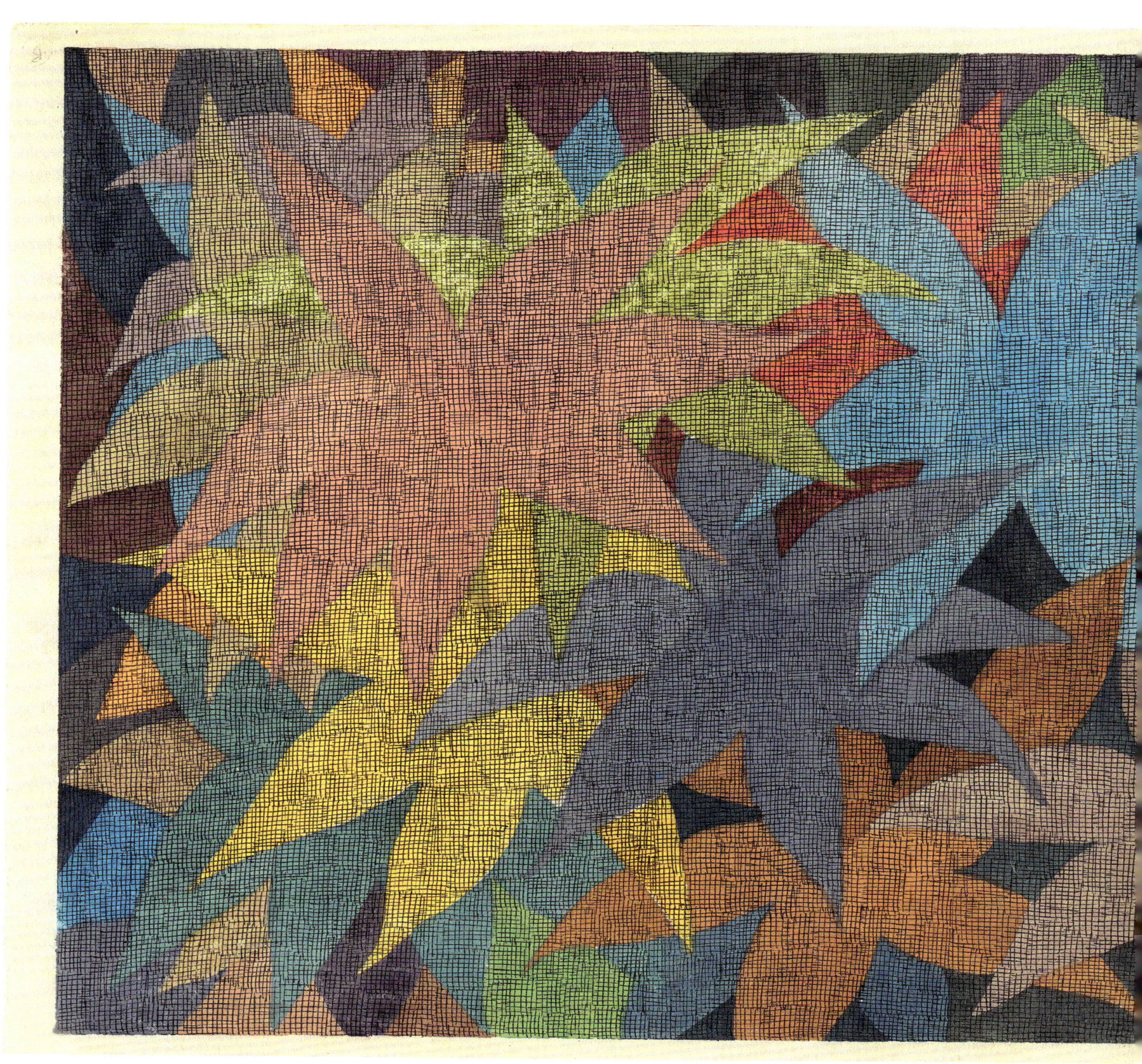

Maurice Sendak, *Where the Wild Things Are*, Endpaper, 1963, ink and watercolor on paper, 10 × 22 in.

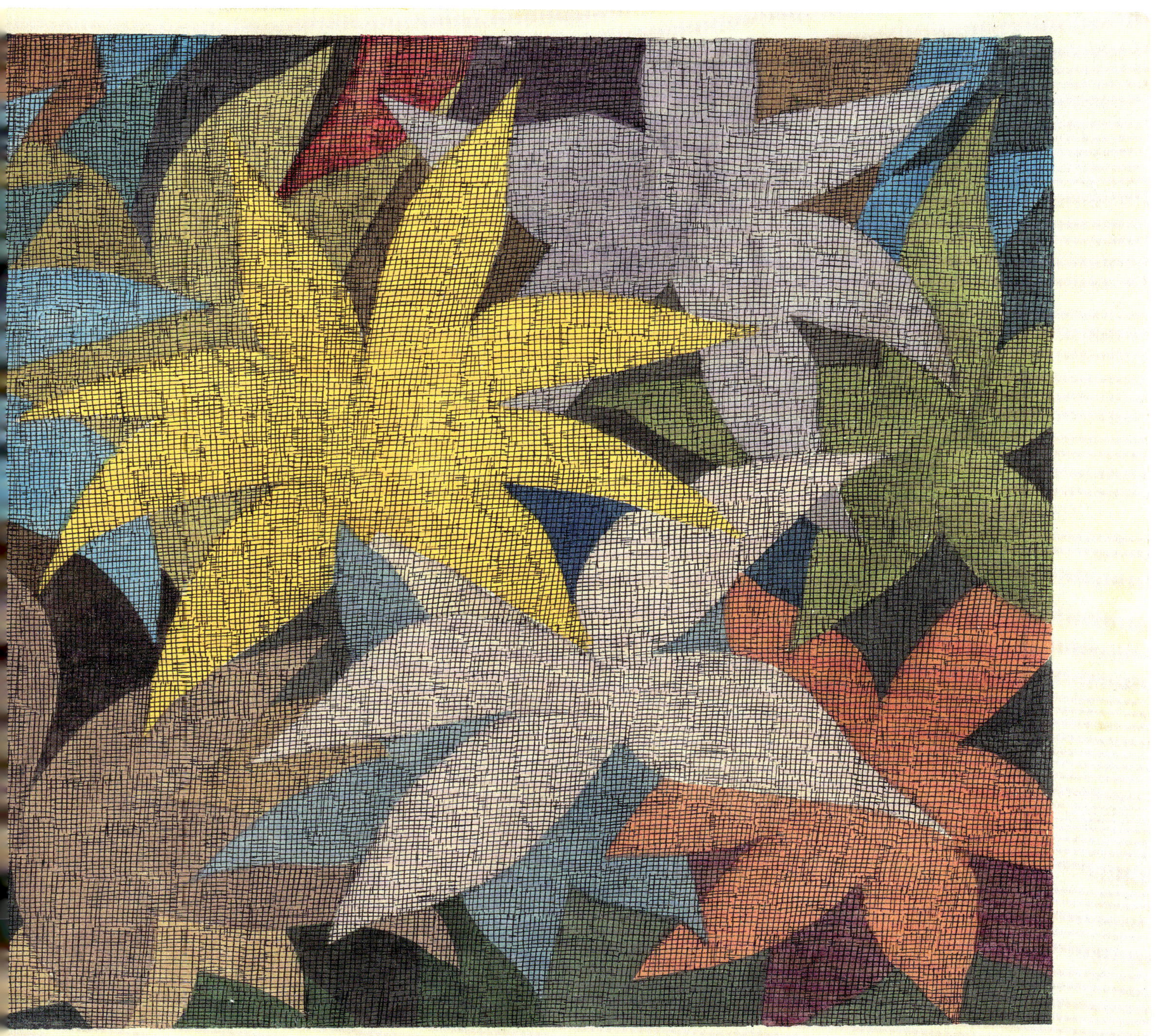

overwhelmed by the primeval forest he has mentally conjured into being. Human face hidden, he limbers up his claws like a fledgling predator in training.

When his personal boat arrives, the illustration for the first time breaches the gutter to occupy a portion of the facing page; by the time he reaches the shore of the Wild Things, the frieze-like composition has reached the far edge, with text migrating from its old position at the left to span the open band across the bottom of both facing pages. Three further openings and the art expands to fill the entirety of the double-page spread, coinciding with the creatures' stomping celebration of the moon, the "rumpus" ordered by Max, now crowned their king. As his idyll fades and he makes his way home, the size of the illustrations begins its retreat, finishing with the art safely contained once again on the right-hand page, the closing, comforting text about the waiting supper appearing on the left.

Compared to the "wild" goings-on within the boundaries of the art, abstract considerations of page layout might seem something of a dry side-issue. But the systematic character of Sendak's progressions offers insight on another level that concerns his small protagonist's psychological trajectory. The step-by-step growth and diminution of the illustrated panels is not in the end symmetrical; it stops at the right-hand full-bleed page and does not recapitulate in reverse the progression of inset illustrations seen in the first five openings. The final scene matches in scale the wall-to-wall transformation of Max's room into the moonlit subtropical forest. Such an invitation to equate the two illustrations entails recognition that the boy's successful journey through his own rebellious impulses has suspended, at least for this moment, the conflict between the world he wants and the world he already possesses.

Max's quest, the strength he manifests, and harmony he achieves, all belong in their sequence to ancient conventions of allegory. Like the traditional resources of figurative graphic art, these survivals likewise eluded obsolescence by migrating to more propitious climes, among them children's literature. A prominent case in point is C.S. Lewis, whose immensely popular *Chronicles of Narnia* wrap their tales of daring children's adventures around a Christological allegory involving the regal lion Aslan (both Lewis and Sendak shared a passion for the fantasy writer George MacDonald). Lewis was moreover a formidable scholar of medieval allegories in both Christian and secular form. His remarks on Chrétien de Troyes, the twelfth-century codifier of allegorical romance, shed light on Sendak as his distant descendent. Chrétien, Lewis observes:

> [C]an hardly turn to the inner world without, at the same time, turning to allegory . . . It is as if the insensible could not knock at the doors of the poetic consciousness without transforming itself into the likeness of the sensible; as if men could not easily grasp the reality of moods and emotions without turning them into shadowy *persons*.[2]

The predominant themes in this bygone body of poetry were drawn from tales of the Arthurian court, quests undertaken to prove the virtue of the knight; but, as Lewis observes, such tales figured the interior conflicts of the protagonist within a culture that yet lacked an introspective vocabulary for such an undertaking. Like a great many narratives directed at children, the *Narnia* stories among them, *Where the Wild Things Are* is likewise a quest, if one that does without an elaborate, medievalizing script. Max calms himself by externalizing the conflicted parts of himself, the ones that had sent him into a destructive frenzy and sparked his defiant riposte to his mother: "I'LL EAT YOU UP!" It is standard practice in the writing of allegory for the unresolved components and experiences within the hero to distribute themselves over an array of external antagonists who stand in his way. In the words of another great authority on the genre, the late Angus Fletcher: "The allegorical hero is not so much a real person as he is a generator of other secondary personalities, which are partial aspects of himself."[3] When Max faces down the Wild Things and becomes their king, he is becoming the master of the refractory parts of his inner self rather than their victim.

Despite the alarms about scaring children that greeted the book's first publication, Sendak is gentle with Max's inner demons, rendering them friendly enough to have set the stage for Jim Henson's Muppets and Disney/Pixar's *Monsters, Inc.*, that is, for a virtual industry devoted to shaggy, shambling, big-eyed beasts as companions to children. Parade mummers, not frightening fiends out of Bosch, populate the boy's psychic landscape, drawing a line between what Sendak knew from the interminable process of psychoanalysis to be an adult's intractably internalized enemies and the helpful emotional projections that land Max safely home in next to no time at all. The boy's playful exorcism thus comes wrapped within a zone of safety, worn like a second skin in the improbably all-covering wolf suit, one he never need shed (in a gesture of reconciliation, Max lowers the hood of the costume in the final scene).

—

Sendak's practice of crafting different styles for different occasions takes on added significance in light of his penchant for wrapping his child-protagonists in such enclosing costumes. When a core theme remains so consistent, there arises the need to introduce variation on another plane. He intimated the terms of this running preoccupation in a remark on the mother's garments in his illustrations for Else Holmelund Minarik's *Little Bear* primers:

> I dressed her in Victorian costume, because those voluminous skirts, the voluminous sleeves, and her voluminous figure all made for the strong and comforting tenderness I wanted her to exude. And when Little Bear sat in her lap, I had her envelop him. The folds of her skirt surrounded him. There couldn't be a safer place in all the world . . . [4]

Max's ferally formfitting pajamas, presumably his mother's gift, envelop him just as completely and in the end just as protectively, armoring him for his trial and test.

The next book in what Sendak came to regard as his core trilogy of self-authored works, *In the Night Kitchen* of 1970, entailed clothing both creator and protagonist in protective guises. Having achieved a sense of ownership over the visual style of *Wild Things*, he predictably threw it over for the new book, emulating, in undisguised homage, the signature strip cartoons fashioned in the early twentieth century by the masterful Winsor McCay. The character of Little Nemo, McCay's prime creation, anticipated Sendak's wayward boys, falling asleep at the beginning of every full-page layout to dream himself into a continuing adventure in the fantastic realm of Slumberland, then to find himself back in his room at the bottom right corner after falling out of bed. Such is the trajectory of Sendak's child-protagonist Mickey. His more compact book format offered little opportunity for the epic sweep of a *Little Nemo* episode, which covered whole broadsheet pages. McCay took splendid advantage of the already phantasmagoric architecture of Manhattan's Wall Street and Flatiron districts in order to generate elastically vertiginous settings, miracles of foreshortening, which seem to suspend gravity as the characters rise and tumble over their ornamental facades, cornices, and rooflines. In an inspired re-interpretation of his predecessor's architectural fantasies, Sendak deployed analogously fluent outlines in a paradoxical miniaturization of New York—one congruent with a child's fascinated perspective—by enlarging to skyscraper proportions the branded, Depression-era containers found in virtually every American domestic kitchen,

Reaching back to the more distant past represented by McCay brought with it an overlay of the artist's own childhood, a time when he fixated on Mickey Mouse, namesake of his diminutive hero. Despite decidedly conflicted childhood memories, Sendak intended the design of the book to conjure the best of them, the exhilaration of Coney Island rather than claustrophobic confinement under the feet of his unstable mother: "McCay's mature style," he writes, "reflects the carnival poster's demand for vivid, clear shapes and showy motifs. The grandiose façades, the freaks, clown, fancily tricked-out dancers and comic-mirror distortions become the raw material from which he fashioned Nemo's world."[5] The wild rides of the fairground, the exhilaration of gravity defying swoops and swings, lend Mickey his untethered movements, as sounds in the night jolt

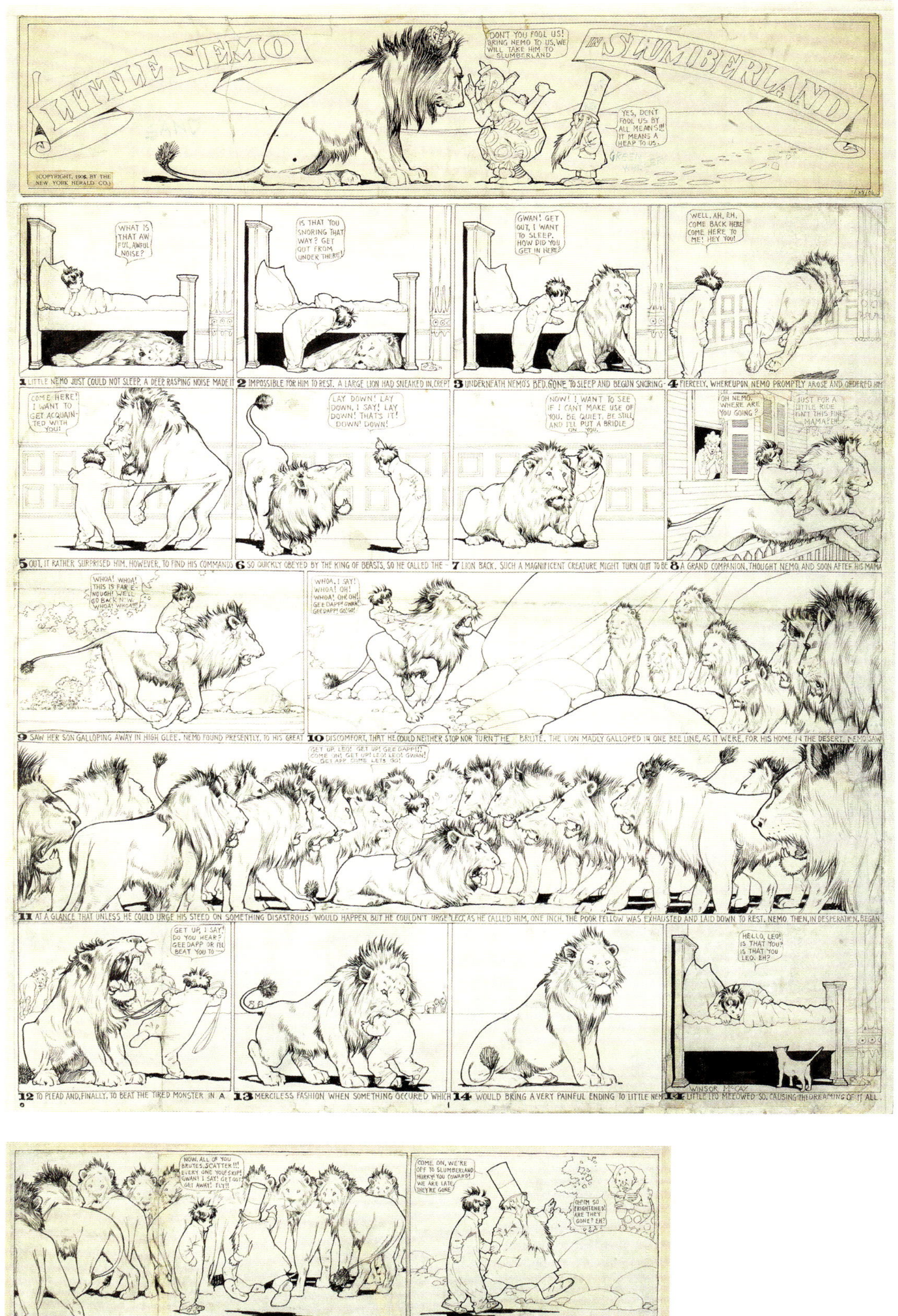

Winsor McCay, *Little Nemo in Slumberland*, ink on paper, Original line drawing including unused section where the Lion swallows Nemo, 1906, 34 × 22 in.

“McCay and I serve the same master, our child selves. We both draw not on the literal memory of childhood but on the emotional memory of its stress and urgency. And neither of us forgot our childhood dreams.”

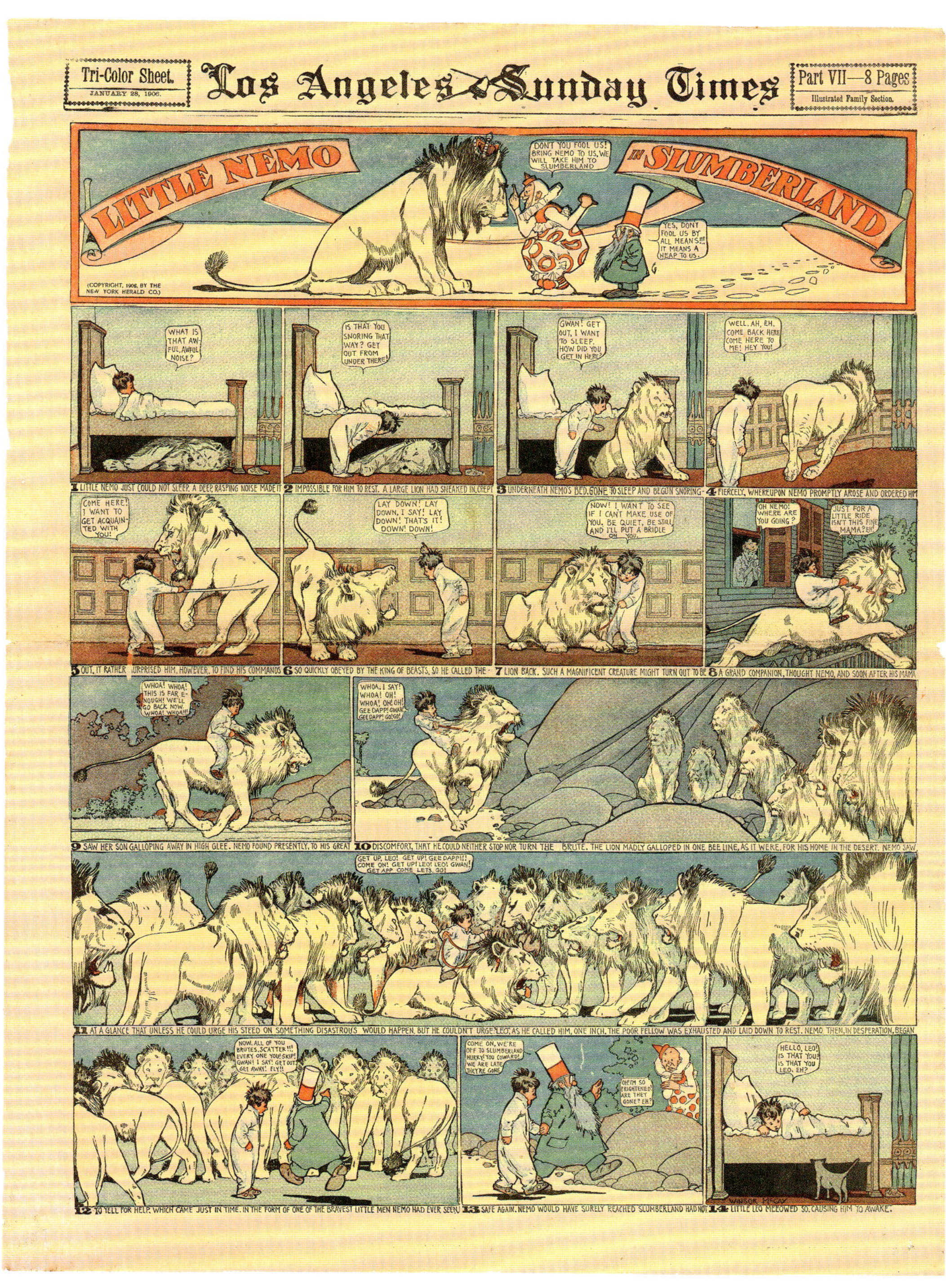

Winsor McCay, *Little Nemo in Slumberland*, *Los Angeles Sunday Times*, 28 January 1906, 22 × 16 in.

following pages: Maurice Sendak, *In the Night Kitchen*, 1970, watercolor on paper, with mylar overlay of black outline, 13½ × 19¾ in.

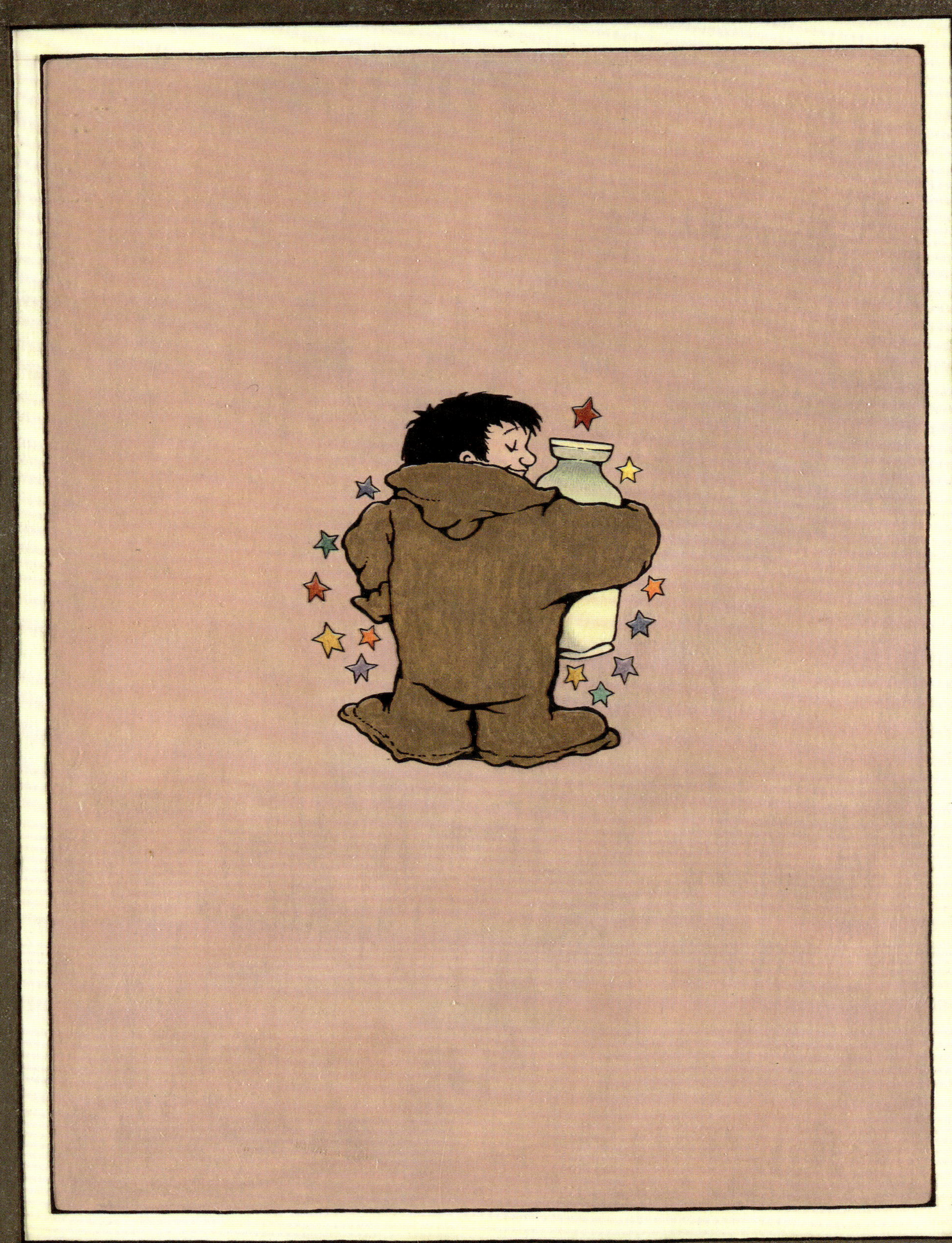

IN THE NIGHT KITCHEN

MAURICE SENDAK

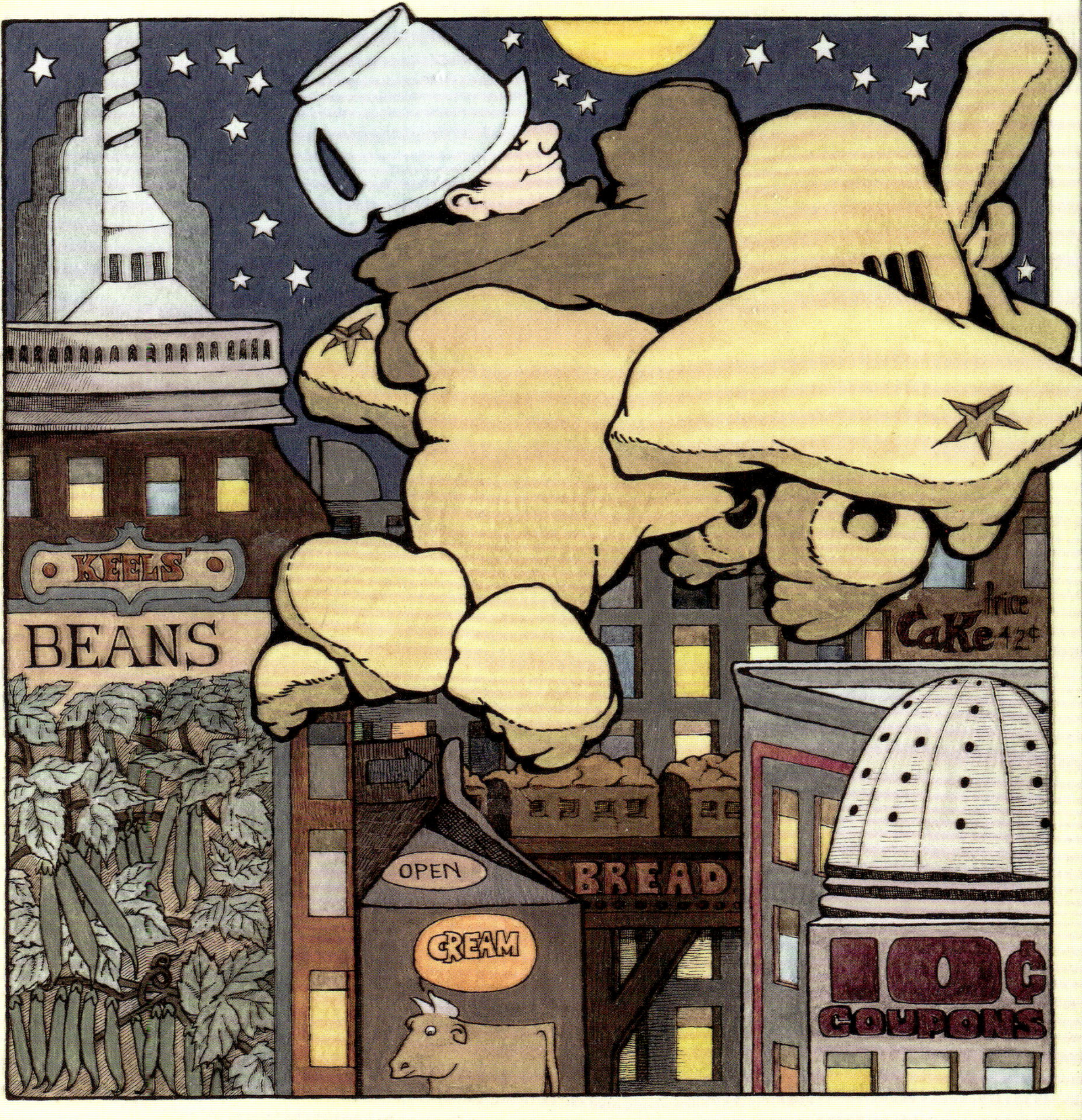

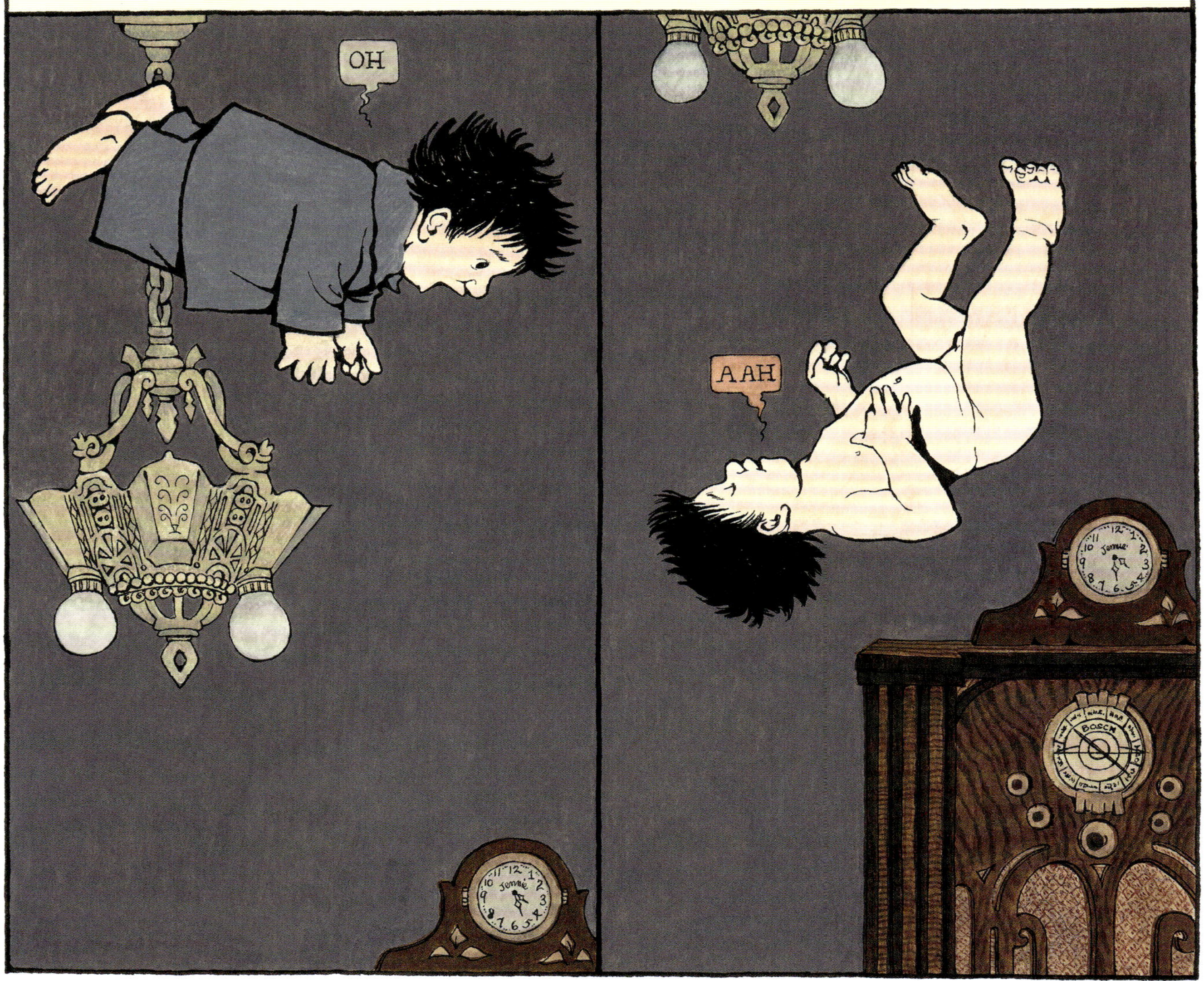

Maurice Sendak, *In the Night Kitchen*, watercolor and ink on paper as printed in color in Maurice Sendak, *In the Night Kitchen* (New York: Harper & Row, 1970)

him from the Nemo-like bed and he lets out a shout conveyed by a speech balloon that fills an entire frame. Then, like other misbehaving children from earlier tales, he suddenly finds himself falling head over heels into a strange and disorienting world.

Mickey falls out of his nightclothes on the way, allowing Sendak the frank nakedness that struck a blow for realism consistent with his prior highlighting of Max's anger. But the boy is no sooner revealed than covered up again as he lands in the dough being mixed by the monstrous bakers, appearing for a moment on the verge of submerging altogether, only a waving hand visible, then disappearing to be baked into the "delicious Mickey-Cake." That nightmare (which Sendak frankly called "terrifying")[6] ends when the boy bursts from the pan fully covered, the dough transformed into an enveloping all-in-one costume, brown like an animal pelt, complete with integral booties, mittens, and hood. So armored, he lands in a previously unseen heap of dough, from which he fashions a ramshackle airplane and escapes over the heads of the "howling" cannibalistic bakers.

Naturally he triumphs, his aerial stunts securing the needed milk from a monumental bottle for the now benignly toqued trio, he steps forth naked again as conquering hero, only to find himself back in his pajamas tucked into bed. *Night Kitchen* thus adds the rhythm of exposure to the quasi-bestial envelopment of the boy established in *Wild Things*, which reinforces its more fantastical transformations. As Sendak later told interviewer Jonathan Cott:

> Obviously I have one theme . . . It's not that I have such original ideas, just that I'm good at doing variations on the same idea over and over again . . . That's all we need as artists—one power-driven fantasy or obsession, then to be clever enough to do variations, like a series of variations by Mozart.[7]

He refused Cott's request that he divulge the "one theme," saying he found it impossible to put into words. But the transformative, hybrid human-animal cloak provides the animating device in both books. *Night Kitchen* extends this magic from Mickey's costume to the small, single-prop plane, a prosthetic extension for the body doubly enveloped inside it. And it requires only basic knowledge of Disney history to see in the pliable craft a direct allusion to the inaugural appearance in an animated film of the boy's namesake Mickey Mouse, *Plane Crazy*, which happened to be in 1928, the year of Sendak's birth. In the inspired designs by animator Ub Iwerks, the rascally early incarnation of the character concocts two airplanes from the junk (and one turkey's tail) found around a farmyard. All sorts of mayhem and near-disasters ensue before the final crash into blackout oblivion (nothing gentle about the humor in early animation).

It is made plain at the start of the film that the inspiration for the mouse's antic flight experiment came directly from Charles Lindbergh, who had successfully flown the Atlantic only the year before. Twice the character is shown gazing at a tabloid

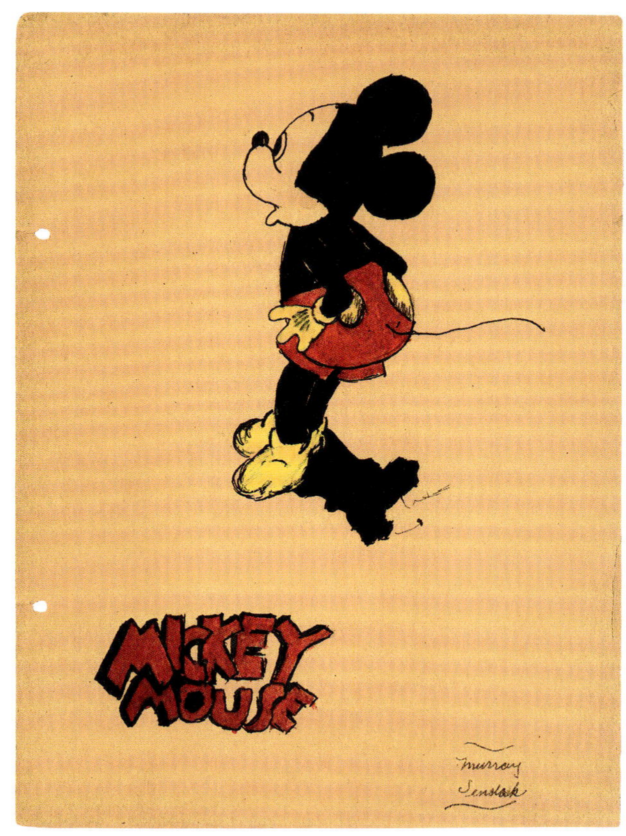

Maurice Sendak, *Mickey Mouse*, 1934, watercolor on paper, 11½ × 8 in.

cover portrait labeled "LINDY," rendered in a naturalistic, non-cartoon manner, and the mouse for a moment acquires human hair so he can tousle it in the Lindbergh style. That topical allusion can only have reinforced the already strong set of meanings that *Plane Crazy* would have had for Sendak, which take their most overt form in *Night Kitchen* but would go deeper in the next major project, the culmination of his core trilogy of sole-authored picture books in *Outside Over There* (1981).

—

In his remarks to interviewers, Sendak is fond of finding significance in convergences between letters and names. That he, Maurice, came to life in the same year that his beloved original Mickey began to move on screen surely kept *Plane Crazy* regularly

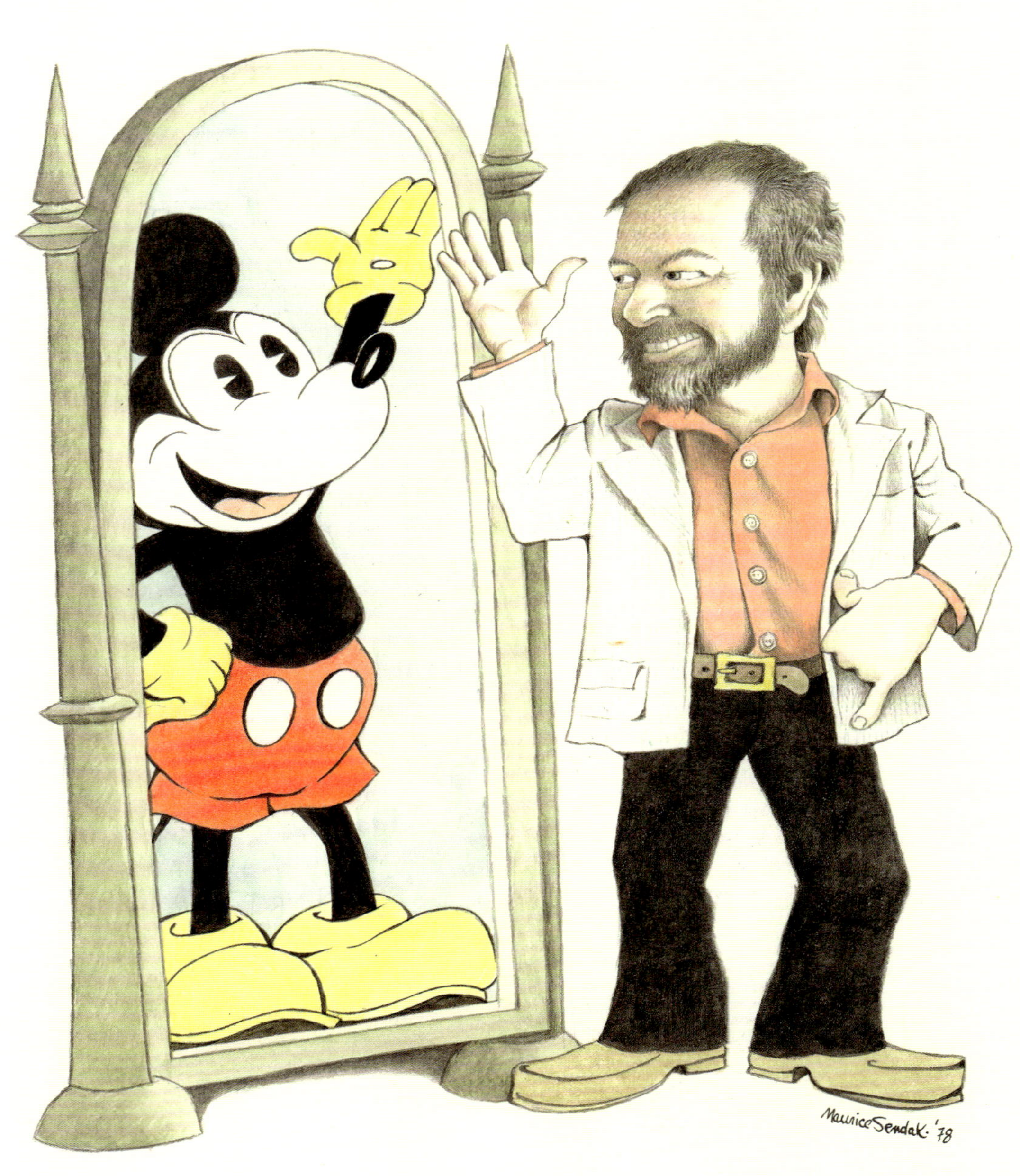

Maurice Sendak, *Me and Mickey*, 1978, watercolor on paper, 6 × 4½ in.

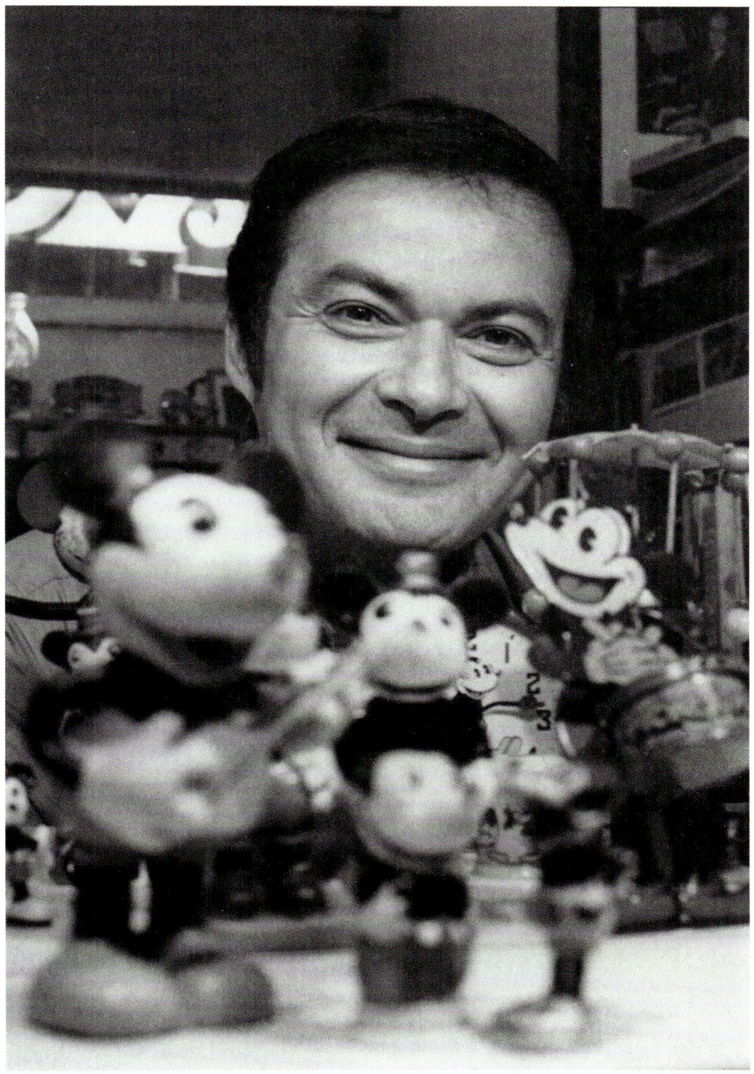

Maurice Sendak in his New York City 9th Street Studio, 1970

"[Mickey Mouse] was our buddy. My brother and sister and I chewed his gum, brushed our teeth with his toothbrush, played with him in a seemingly endless variety of games . . . Best of all, our street pal was also a movie star. In the darkened theater, the sudden flash of his brilliant, wild, joyful face—radiating great golden beams—filled me with an intoxicating, unalloyed pleasure."

in his thoughts. The common initial M likewise signaled the revered McCay, one of the inventors of cartoon animation (*Gertie the Dinosaur* in 1914) alongside his resplendent strip cartoons. But the abiding bearer of that initial in the Sendak imaginative universe was Mozart, the creative exemplar that surpassed all others. In the mid-1970s, a few years after the contested success of *In the Night Kitchen*, he began feeling his way toward a new picture-book narrative that would make concrete his adoration of the composer, though his initial inspiration made this no more explicit than setting his story in early nineteenth-century northern Europe. Despite choosing a maritime backdrop some distance from Vienna and a decade or two after Mozart's death, it must have seemed proximate enough, while enabling visual homages to the German Romantic painters Philipp Otto Runge and Caspar David Friedrich. The multiple analogues to Mozart animating the project were similarly indirect, among the most important of them being the core narrative of the quest, implicit in the two major precedents explored above, but at this juncture brought more decisively to the fore. Sendak's mastery of allegory as a genre would have derived in part from his devotion to opera, to the high artifice of its story lines, and no work manifested such qualities more completely than did Mozart's *Magic Flute*, the masterpiece that looms largest in his recorded remarks on Mozart and indeed music in general.

At the heart of the *Magic Flute*, moreover, is a knightly quest, undertaken by Tamino as a test of virtue in the mold of late-medieval Romances in the style of Chrétien de Troyes. The hero must rescue his promised princess Pamina from captivity and sets out, so he thinks, with blessing of his requisite Lady, her duplicitous mother, the Queen of the Night. In Sendak's enthusiasm for the opera, however, his admiration tends to settle on Pamina at the expense of her chivalric protector (who indeed frequently fails to inspire confidence, requiring rescue at the start of the first act by the three female attendants to the Queen). From suicidal despair Pamina rises, in his words, to "absolute assurance." As he reflects further, "She's looked at something that's cost her life . . . But from having looked and

"... in Mozart, there is the most quintessential perfect balance. There is suffering and everything you expect a grown man would have experienced in life, and, yet, in a way no other creature has done it. They are the pluses and minuses in my personal algebra."

---

come back she's turned into the great woman she is at the end of the opera."[8] Sendak's own heroic female in *Outside Over There* is of course a child, the nine-year-old Ida, not the victim of kidnapping but herself the rescuer when three monkishly garbed goblins, faces hidden in hooded shadow, steal her infant sister away by climbing a ladder to the nursery window.

With her sea captain father away on a voyage, Ida's mother has lapsed into torpor—she is shown seated beneath an arbor in near catatonia, indifferent to the little sister's cries as she struggles in Ida's arms. No malevolent plotter like the Queen of the Night, the mother nonetheless leaves her older daughter entirely to her own devices in pursuing the goblins as far as their underground lair. Across the character spectrum, women re-enact Sendak's Pamina-focused optic on Mozart: "It's a female world," he acknowledged, "and to tell you the truth," he added disarmingly, "I don't know what that means or why it's so, but I just know that it's right as rain."[9]

The old-fashioned phrase "right as rain," with its folksy connotations of safety and security, does double duty here, as it calls pointed attention to the book's resplendent reinvention of the enveloping, protective, and transformative garment central to the entire sequence of Sendak's major picture books. As the characters, in keeping with the decorous bourgeois milieu, are already clothed from their necks to their ankles, Sendak finds his needed covering garment in the exceptionally voluminous yellow rain cloak belonging to the immobilized mother, which Ida commandeers to aid in her quest.

By its size and color, the cloak might well be a seaman's slicker, as the succession of disparate sea views, each uncannily corresponding to Ida's emotional state, pass across the window behind her like a series of scenes in a film. At the peak of her anger, a raging storm swamps the port and sinks a ship, while a lesser squall lashes the seascape when she settles her mind and dons the cloak, swimming inside its cascade of elaborate folds, only her face and hands visible. It provides pockets so large that her hunting horn (a further power object) can fit inside one. But this apparently cumbersome raiment confers the power of flight, as Ida discovers when she mistakenly tumbles backward though the window, so losing sight of the goblin party carrying off her sister to be betrothed in a sinister wedding.

Though this paraphrase might already seem a long one, it does scant justice to the complexity of inner relationships that Sendak built into and across each of the book's illustrations (the outsized sunflowers out of Runge, for example, that crowd into the nursery from the garden side like an accusing Greek chorus). The composite character of *Outside Over There* follows from the disparate points of entry that led him into Ida's quest narrative, of which the *Magic Flute* was only one. The enveloping garment possesses its own genealogy within the artist's personal repertoire, assuming in this third iteration its greatest measure of autonomy. Sendak treats its eight appearances as opportunities for virtuoso cadenzas of elaborate drapery in implicit homage to the masters of the exercise, preeminently Leonardo da Vinci. The self-involved convolutions of the cloak, marked out by yellow watercolor, set its successive appearances apart from their surroundings like self-contained appliqué—perhaps most dramatically in the two-page spread where Ida magically hears the voice of her father sing from way off at sea "If Ida backwards in the rain / would only turn around again / and catch those goblins with a tune / she'd spoil their kidnap honeymoon!" Below the girl's suspended figure in a vignette of flight recalling Michelangelo or Titian, Sendak has arrayed every element of the story's time, place, and chain of events within a compartmentalized composition fitted together like fine marquetry, the layered intricacy of an opera scenario in a single tableau.

Just as Sendak has been entirely forthcoming about the homage to Mozart he sought to build into *Outside Over There*, so he has been equally candid about other strands of reference and points of entry into the story. Though he at first held back any comment on the Lindbergh kidnapping, not wanting to tie the book's initial reception to such a dark folk memory, he became more than forthcoming on the topic as the years went on. Four years old during the agonizing weeks before the body of toddler Charles Lindbergh Jr. was found, Sendak, by his own testimony, carried for the remainder of his life the fear and anxiety implanted by the clamor of press and radio reports on the crime, search, manhunt, and trial that followed. He has recounted making a kind of pilgrimage to the small town of Hopewell, New Jersey, where the crime occurred, circling the house for a look at the upstairs nursery window where the ladder had been propped and the child stolen away.

That excursion into adulthood makes sense as a way to render an inchoate bundle of threatening fantasies into a concretely manageable set of memories. *Outside Over There* likewise played its therapeutic part in Sendak's rehearsing the details of the crime: the ladder; the open window; and the guard dog (modeled after his own German Shepherd) that fails to protect or even raise an alarm. As the allegorist confronts the refractory components of the self by reimagining them as external apparitions, so the demonic goblins understand Ida's ambivalence toward the sister she has been left to tend by default; thus they leave behind a changeling baby, a surrogate made of ice that makes manifest that disavowed coldness inside of her. When turning the page from the operatic dreamscape where Ida hears her father's distant song, the first-time reader shares Ida's surprise in discovering the kidnapping demons to be outsized babies themselves, naked under their sinister cloaks.

As always in Sendak's thinking, there is a practical grasp of children's emotions as these persist in his own. In this case, it is sibling rivalry, in which his was the part of the burdensome younger sibling. As he characterizes the fraught relationship with his older sister Natalie:

> I remember her demonic rages. I remember her losing me at the New York World's Fair of 1939 . . . my parents were working very hard and

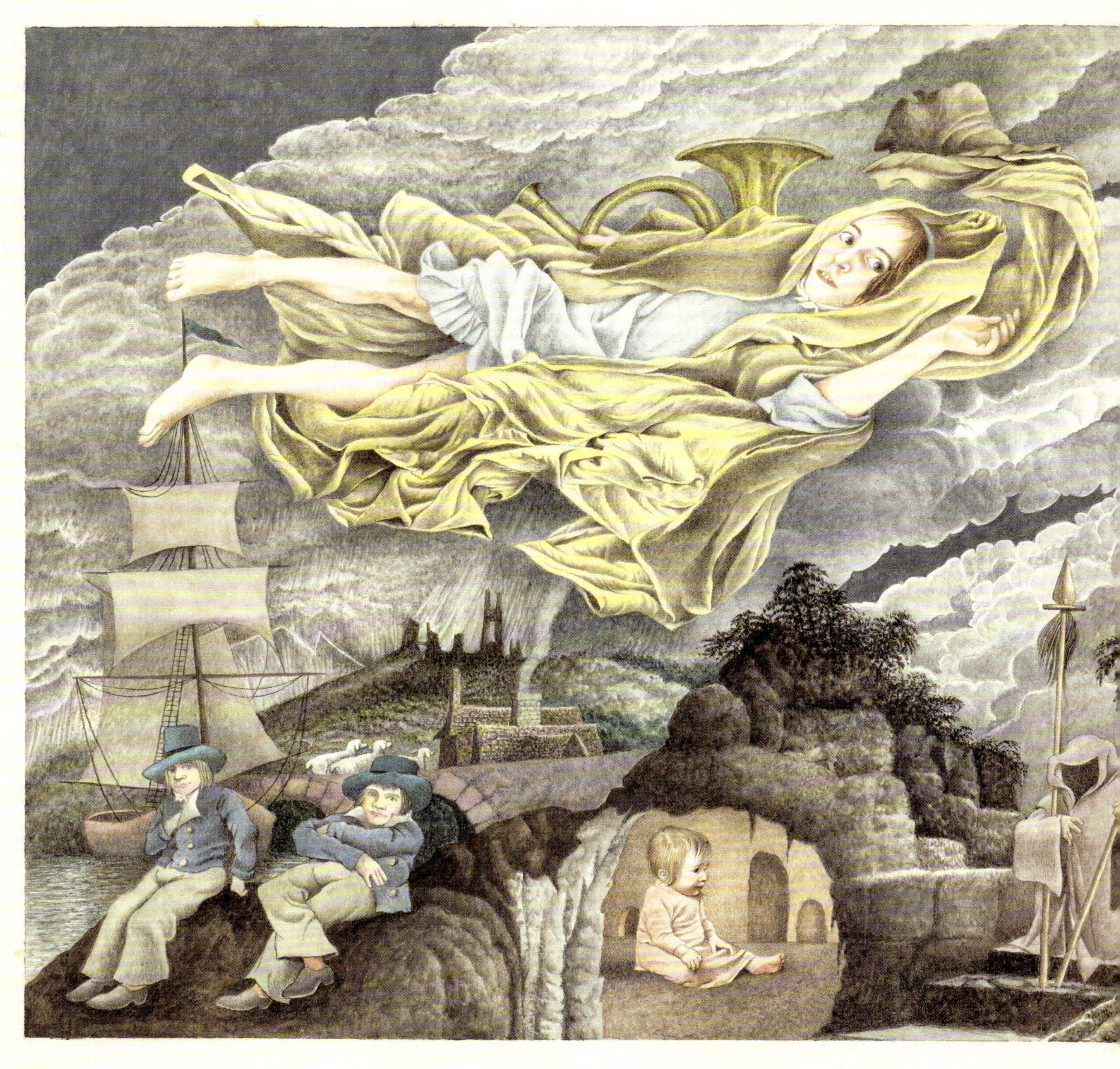

Maurice Sendak, *Outside Over There*, 1978, watercolor on paper, 16 × 19⅞ in.

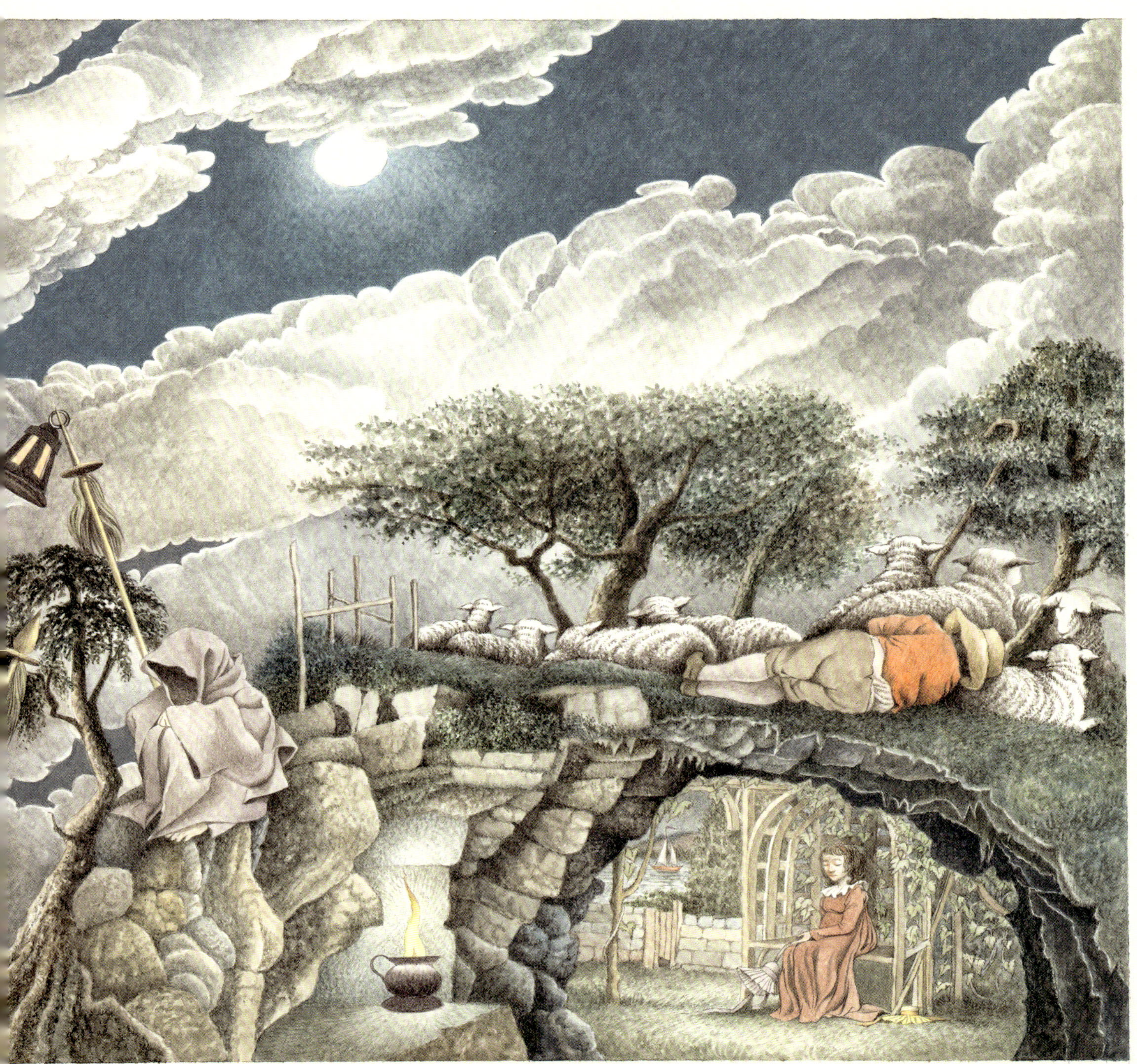

"*Outside Over There* was the most painful experience of my creative life. It brought on a catastrophe. It was so hard it caused me to have a breakdown . . . At that point in my still-young life, I felt I had to solve this book; I had to plummet as far down deep into myself as I could: excavation work."

> didn't have enough time, and so I was dumped on her. And that is the situation in *Outside Over There*: a baby is taken care of by an older child . . . who both loves and hates the newcomer.[10]

Under the premises that govern the story, how could Ida not blame the helpless younger sister for alienating her mother as much as had the absence of her husband and helpmate? How could Ida avoid resenting being required to manage this endlessly needy sibling, who appears to be nearly as large as she is? Naturally Ida nonetheless succeeds in neutralizing, if not extirpating, the bad babies who have escaped from her own tangle of emotions. Exercising preternatural skill in coaxing "a captivating tune" out of her natural horn, the goblins cannot resist dancing themselves to the point of such frenzy that they dissolve into the underground stream. Here it is easy to spot a rare explicit lift from *The Magic Flute*: Ida deploys her horn just as does Papageno his enchanted bells when the comic bird-catcher neutralizes the minions of the demonic Monostatos, thereby rescuing Pamina by forcing them to dance against their will. That same feat accomplished, Ida's horn tucked away behind her gown, the affecting reunion between the two sisters can occur, the interplay of their hand gestures a lyrically musical passage on its own.

While Sendak was immersed in his homage to Mozart, Ingmar Bergman's 1975 film of the *Magic Flute* saw its American premiere, offering a rare view into the stage settings and practices familiar to its composer. The Drottningholm Palace Theater, just outside Stockholm, was and remains one of the last European theaters to survive as it had been in Mozart's lifetime. When the structure proved too fragile to withstand the rigors of filming, Bergman had an exact replica of its interior constructed in the studio, which included the period painted wings and drops, all conveyed with subtle richness by the cinematography of Sven Nykvist. The opening combat with the dragon makes full use of the fantastically craggy mountains, illuminated by lightning flashes, reproduced from the theater's stock scenery.

Sendak employed a cognate scenic repertoire on the left side of his opening two-page spread. The stage-setting title card, "When Papa was away at sea," hovers in front of the towering landscape, all geological uplift of eccentric rock formations, a vigilant castle clinging to the slope (the hooded goblins bide their time below with ladder and boat). To its right, riding the calm waters, a ship borrowed from the early romantic painting of Friedrich raises sail, attended by the three female principals in the story there to see off Papa's voyage, the mother's full skirt and scarf billowing in the fresh breeze. Like Ida, she looks away, face hidden by the flaring cone of her bonnet; only the baby in Ida's arms turns to confront the viewer's regard. All of these details do their work, the Mother's long wafting scarf in particular guides one's eye to the next opening, which transports the reader to the domestic outdoor setting where the three are meant to await his return.

At the outset of the painting process, Sendak employed a subtle stippling technique in watercolor linked to examples by William Blake. Contemporary with the Drottningholm scenery, that style helped generate the suggested patina of age, along with the softly articulated Rococo vegetation in the park-like setting of the house and garden. A seeming world away from the dramatic harbor, a small sailboat floats in a pond just where the stately merchant vessel had appeared in the previous opening. Indeed, there is something there of Sendak's own rural Connecticut retreat in the profusion of trees and the characteristically New England dry stone wall—adding a personal dimension, consistent with his Lindbergh preoccupations, to its coming violation by the unheeded goblins. And it is to this same setting that Ida returns with her sister extracted from the dank gothic cavern, but not before traversing hilly terrain seeded with stock devices from European pastoral (and Mozart playing harpsichord in his garden hut), then skirting one last threat in a corner of dark woodland out of the Brothers Grimm, spectral white moths hovering before tree branches that resemble grasping arms. The mother, spirits revived by a letter from her husband, extends her arms in greeting on their arrival home. The father's message—in keeping with his earlier song from afar—makes plain that he knows what Ida has accomplished. Like Pamina, her trial overcome, she will replace her mother as guardian of the hallowed place.

The one element that fails to make the return journey is the yellow rain cloak, the power talisman borrowed from the parent but no longer required. And this abandonment appears likewise to be Sendak's farewell to the enabling device that had served him so well across the trio of major, self-authored picture books. Given how active he remained for another three decades, the fact that he has repeatedly referred to them as his trilogy must be predicated on some significant closure achieved at the conclusion of *Outside Over There*. And in light of Sendak's penchant for trusting in providential confluences, the resolution of the book well might be further ascribed to intervention by a higher power. He had come to an impasse in 1978, stalled at page 12 (the single panel where Ida first dons the rain cloak and stands in the center like a pyramid), when out of the blue came a call from an opera producer to design a new production of *The Magic Flute* for the Houston Grand Opera. The immediate effect of what became a celebrated commission, the onset of a second career in opera, was to lift his depression and spur the completion of Ida's story. "Yes," he affirmed to Cott,

> *Outside Over There* is my attempt to make concrete my love of Mozart . . . It's my imagining of Mozart's life. I sometimes think of it as an opera in pictures, and that's why after I'd designed the sets and costumes for *The Magic Flute*, I cried during the performance.[11]

Not to put too much weight on the construction of that last sentence, its implication at least is that his 1980 triumph in the opera house was the confirmation of his own opera, not the one he had embellished but the one he had scripted and orchestrated himself, with Mozart less a posthumous partner than a tutelary deity. Having met that test, a certain phase in his self-realization as an artist could thus be brought to a conclusion.

Notes

1. Gorey made this remark on The Dick Cavett Show (November 30, 1977), https://www.youtube.com/watch?v=cng3K8FGj28&list=PL5ZxYsLy1tzGBy6dFBLWE6YsBuk4Yzi3E&index=5
2. C.S. Lewis, *The Allegory of Love: A Study in Medieval Tradition* (Oxford: Oxford University Press, 1936), 30.
3. Angus Fletcher, *Allegory: The Theory of a Symbolic Mode* (Princeton: Princeton University Press, 1970), 35.
4. Maurice Sendak, quoted in Selma G. Lanes, *The Art of Maurice Sendak* (New York: Abrams, 1980), 55.
5. Maurice Sendak, *Caldecott and Co.: Notes on Books and Pictures* (New York: Farrar, Strauss and Giroux, 1988), 79–80.
6. Sendak, quoted in Jonathan Cott, *There's a Mystery There: The Primal Vision of Maurice Sendak* (New York: Doubleday, 2017), 118.
7. Ibid., 74–5.
8. Ibid., 101.
9. Ibid., 99.
10. Sendak, *Caldecott and Co.*, 209.
11. Sendak, quoted in Tony Kushner, *The Art of Maurice Sendak, 1980 to the Present* (New York: Abrams, 2003), 79.

The Sign on Rosie's Door *and* Really Rosie

"These early, unprecise, wavery sketches are filled with a happy vitality that was nowhere else in my life at the time. They add up to the first rough delineation of the child all my future characters would be modeled on. I loved Rosie. She knew how to get through a day."

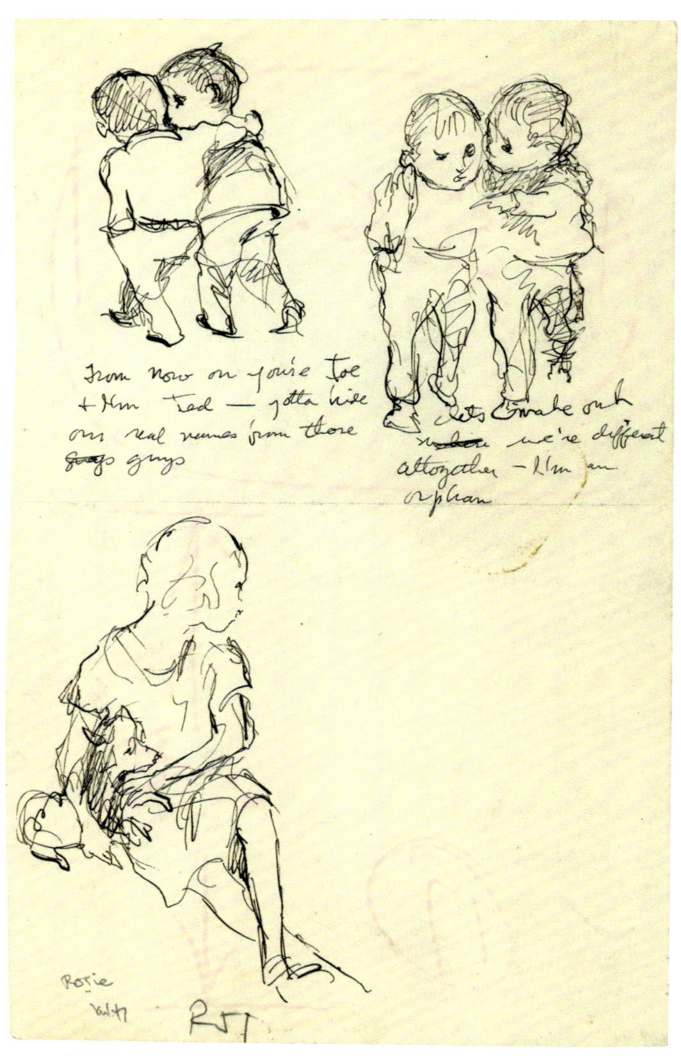

Maurice Sendak, *Sketches of Rosie and Other Children*, 1947, ink on paper, 8¼ × 5¼ in.

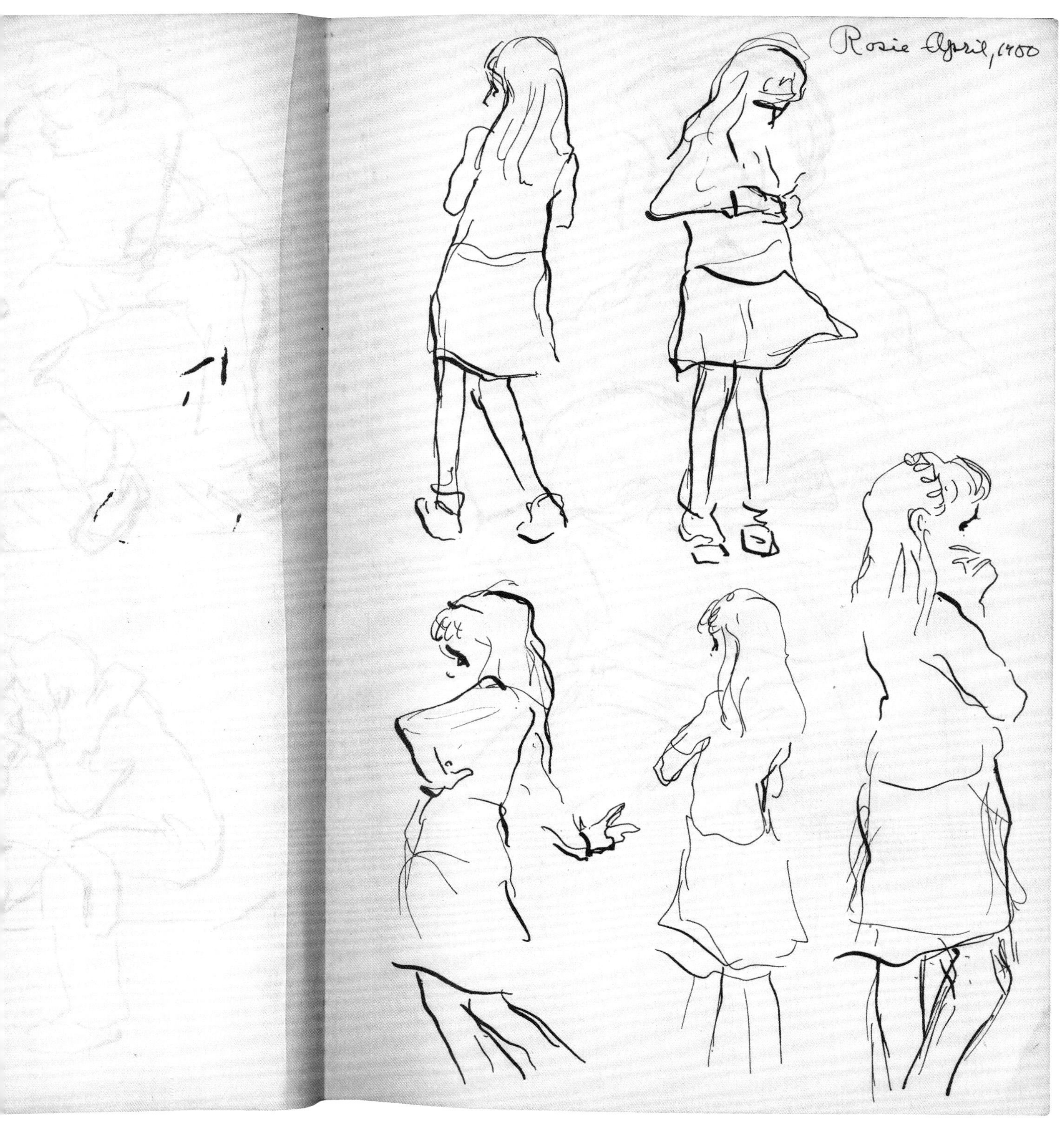

Maurice Sendak, *Rosie Sketchbook*, 1950, ink on paper, 8⅘ × 11 in.

following pages: Maurice Sendak, Title Page, *The Sign on Rosie's Door*, 1960, ink on paper and paste-up lettering, 12 × 15¼ in.

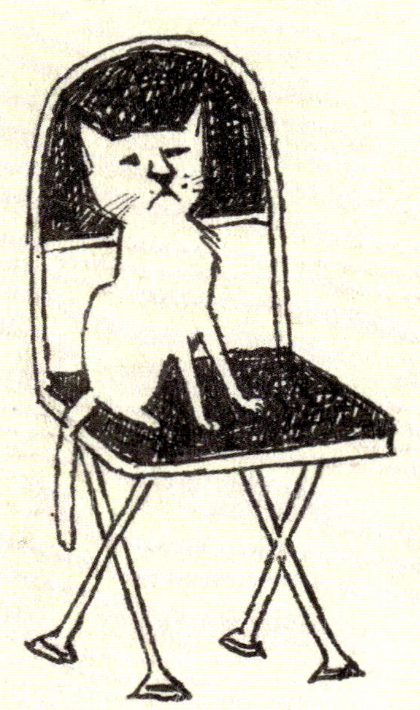

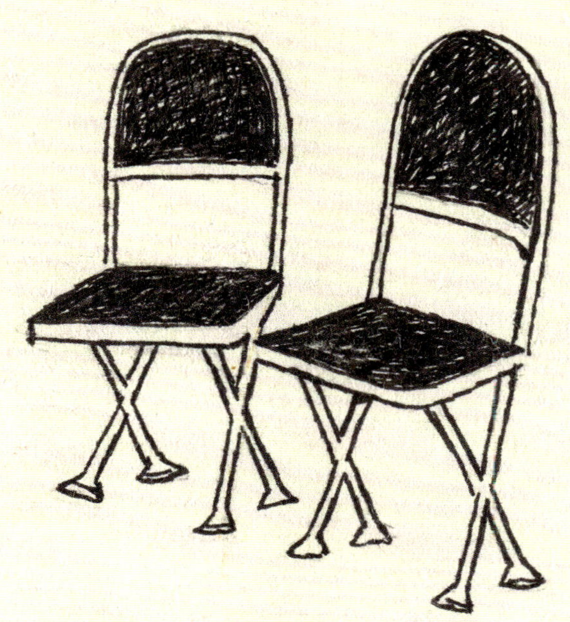

The SIGN on

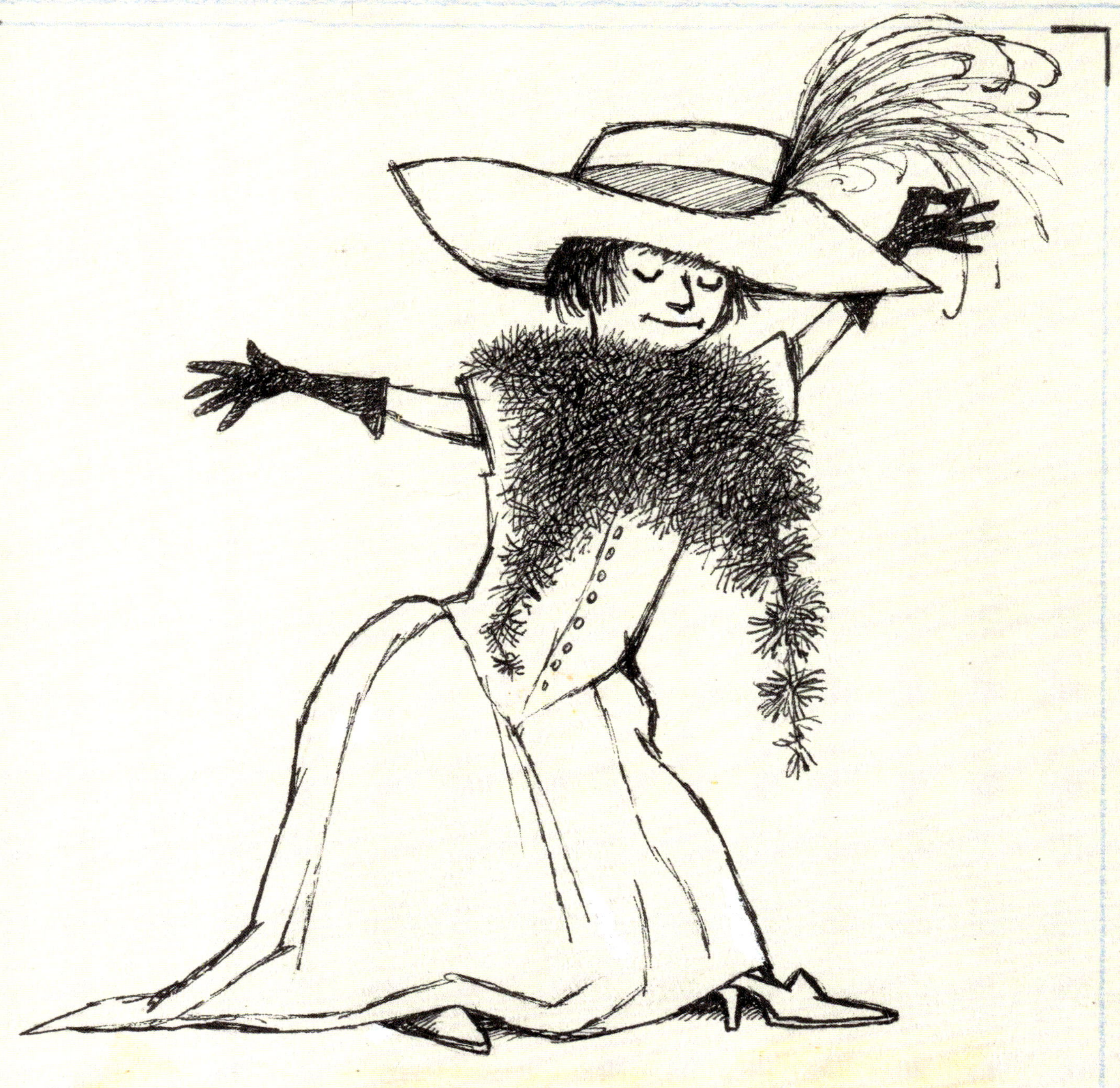

ROSIE'S DOOR

Story and pictures by MAURICE SENDAK

HARPER & BROTHERS *Publishers* NEW YORK

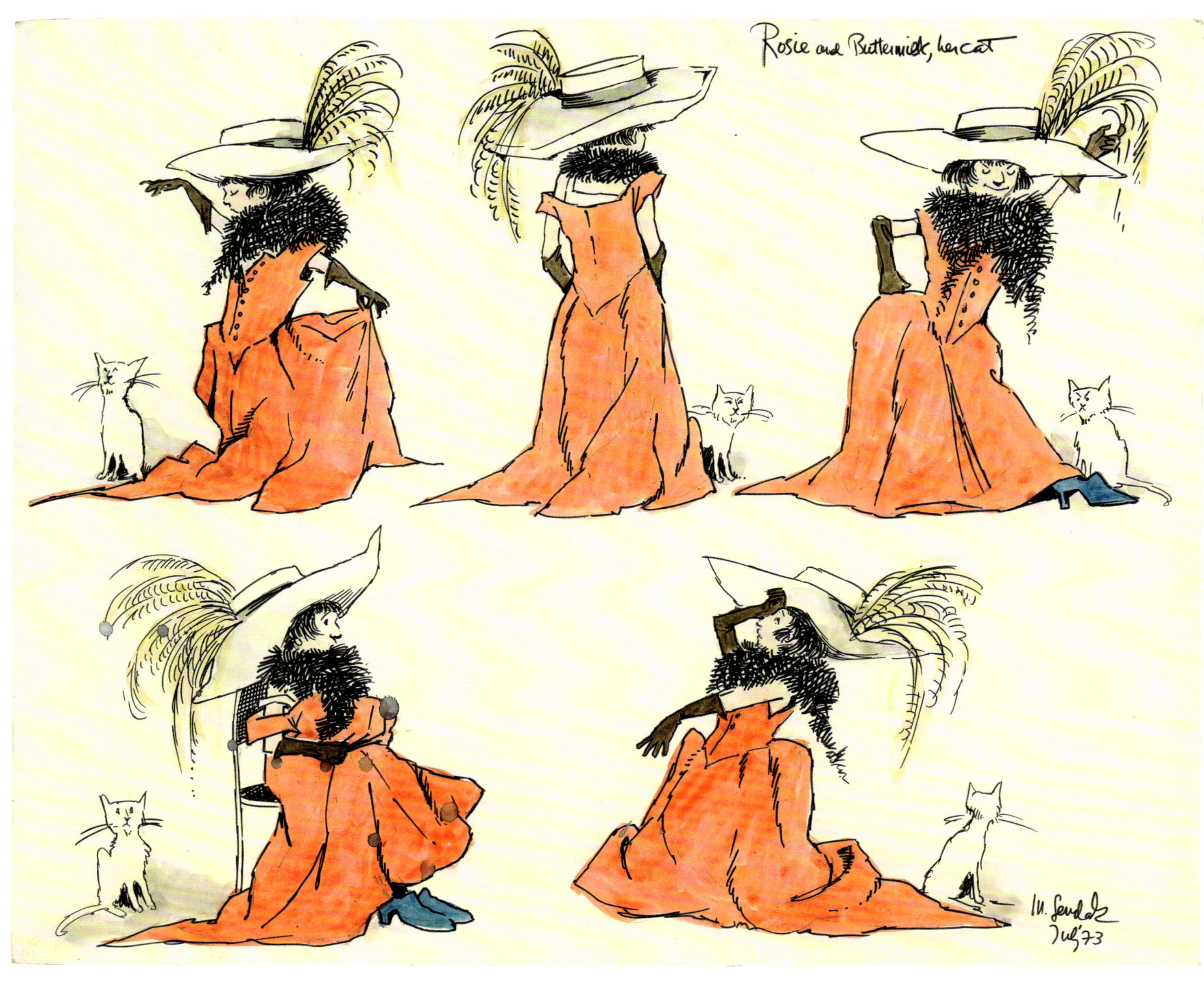

Maurice Sendak, *Rosie and Buttermilk, her Cat*, character studies for *Really Rosie* animation, 1973, watercolor and ink on paper, 13¾ × 15⅝ in.

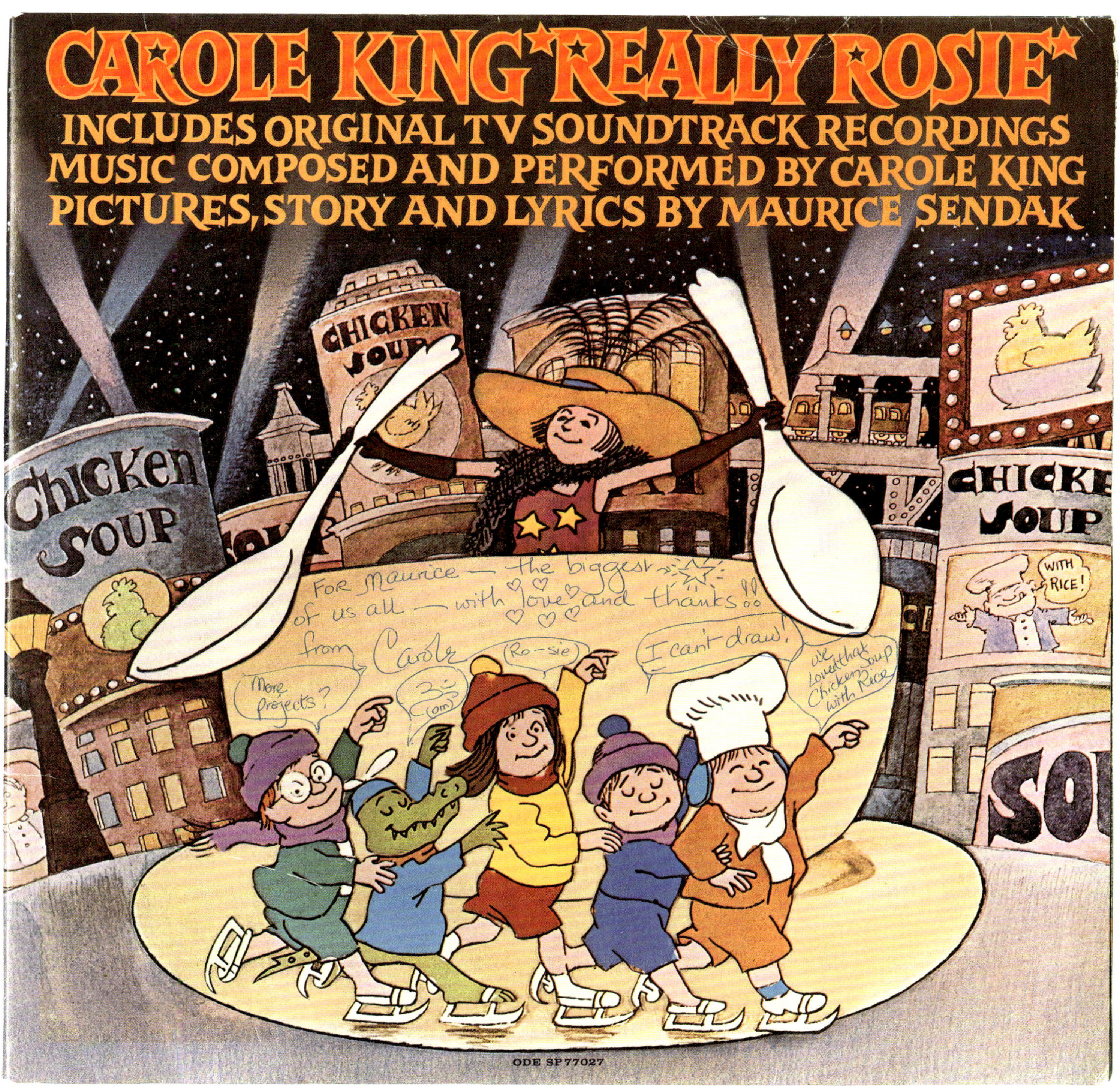

Carole King and Maurice Sendak, *Really Rosie*, album cover, 1975 inscribed by Carole King to Maurice Sendak

The Nutshell Library

"Pierre, perhaps, is the most typical of all my published children—he could be Rosie playing Pierre!—and it was only a short step from Pierre to Max of *Where the Wild Things Are*."

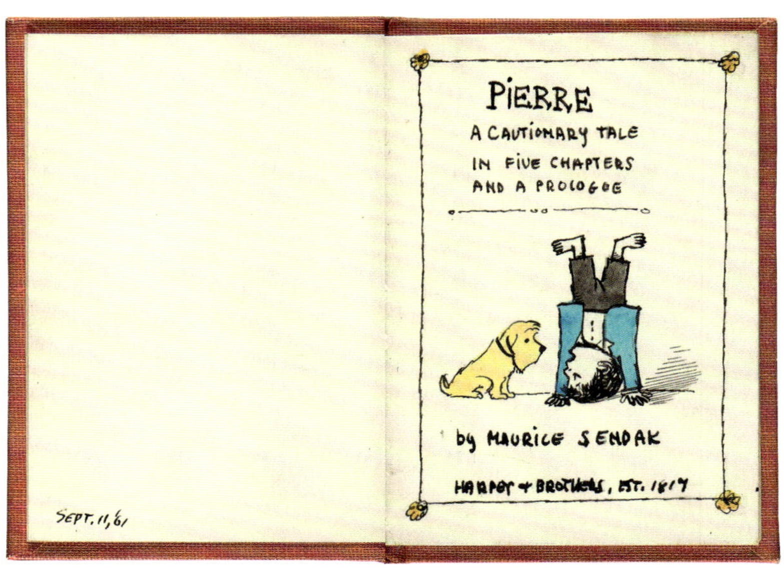

Maurice Sendak, Dummy for *Pierre* from *Nutshell Library*, 1961, ink on paper, 4¼ × 7 in.

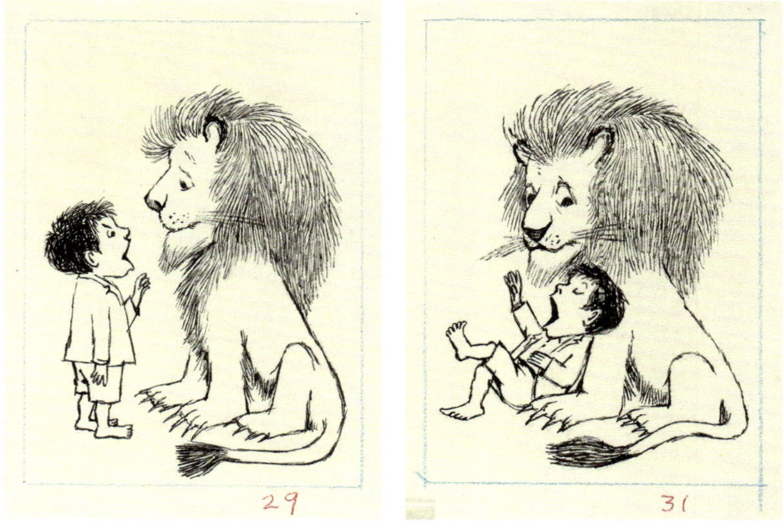

Maurice Sendak, *Pierre*, 1961–2, ink on paper, each 4¼ × 3½ in.

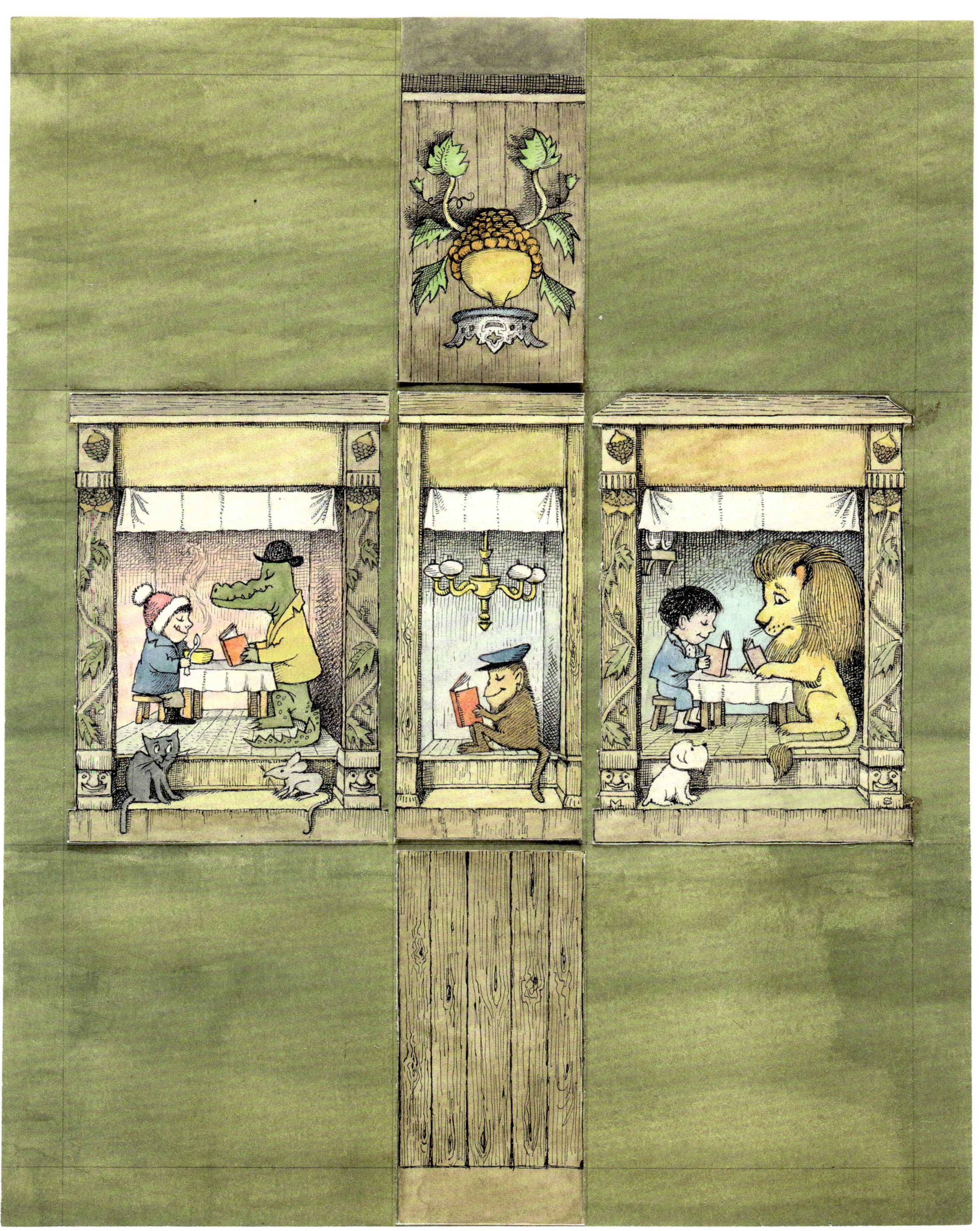

Maurice Sendak, Cover mockup for *Nutshell Library*, 1962, ink and watercolor, 10⅜ × 8⅛ in.

Where the Wild Things Are

"With *Where the Wild Things Are* I feel that I am at the end of a long apprenticeship. By that I mean all my previous work now seems to have been an elaborate preparation for it."

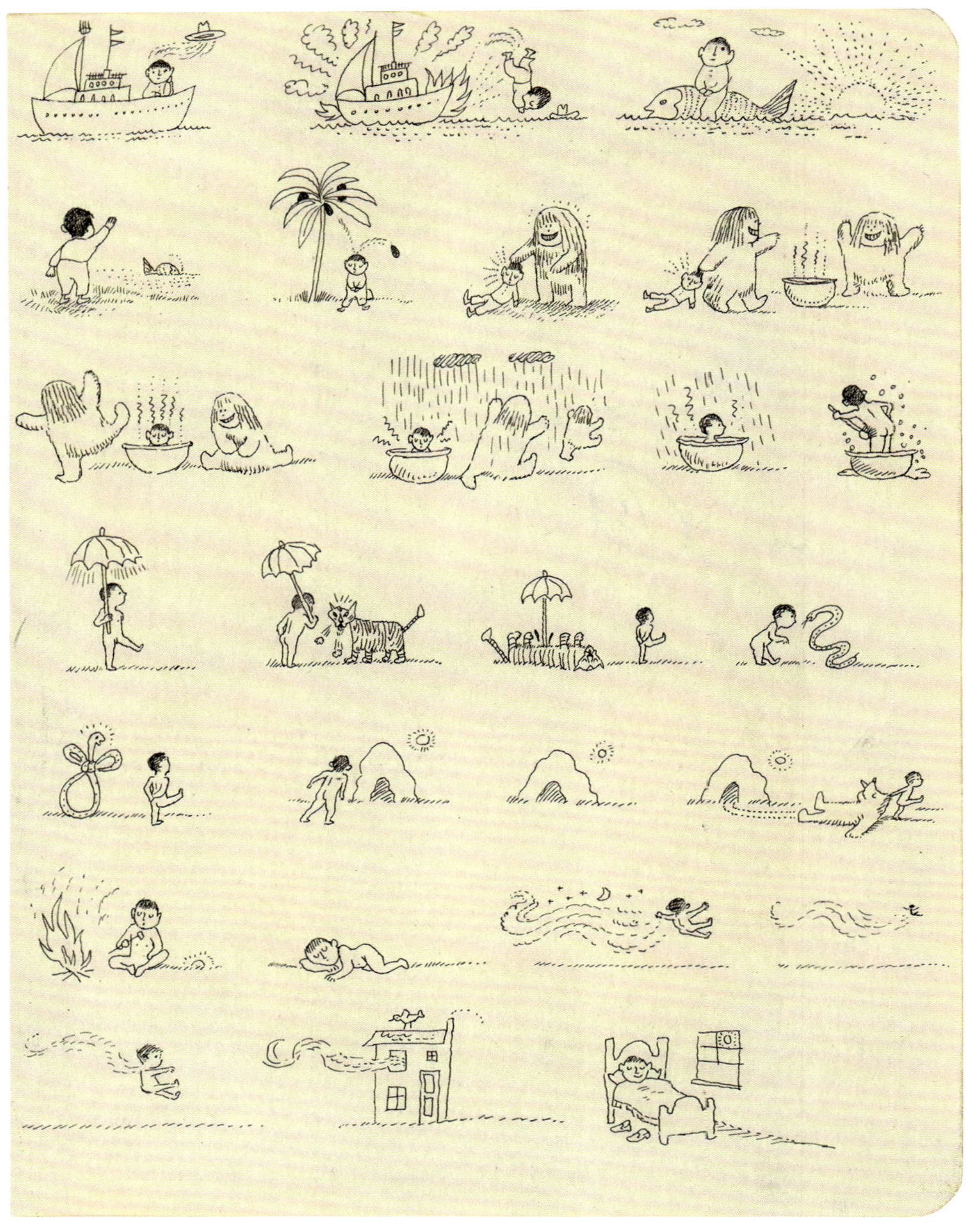

Maurice Sendak, *Fantasy Sketch* (*Boy in Ship*), c. 1953, ink on paper, 10 × 7⅝ in.

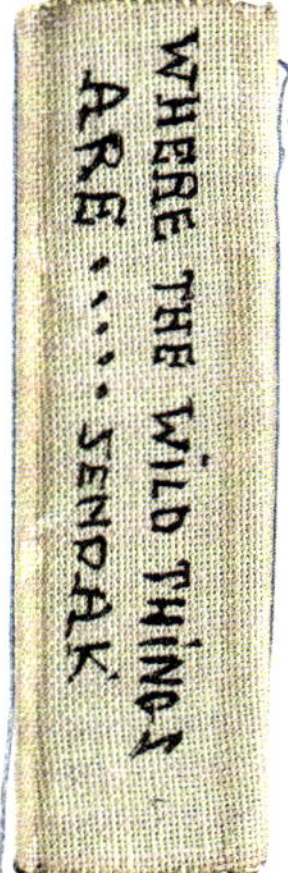

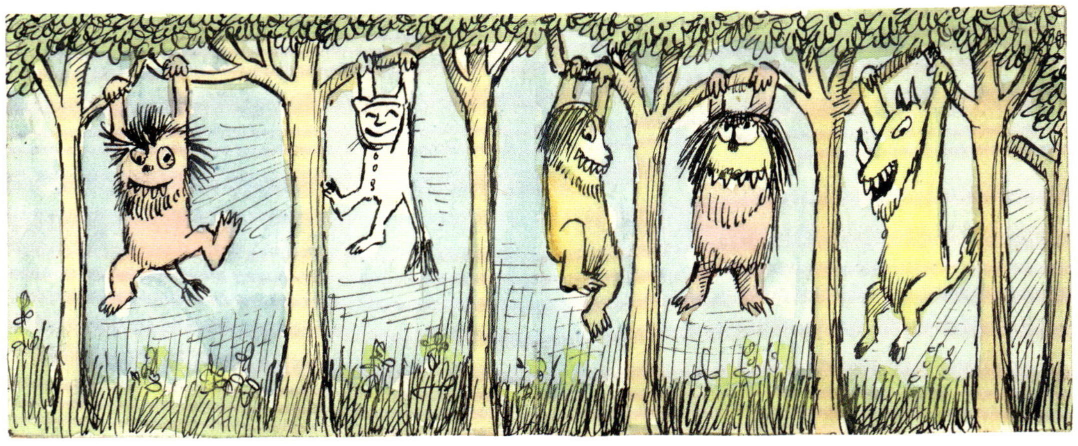

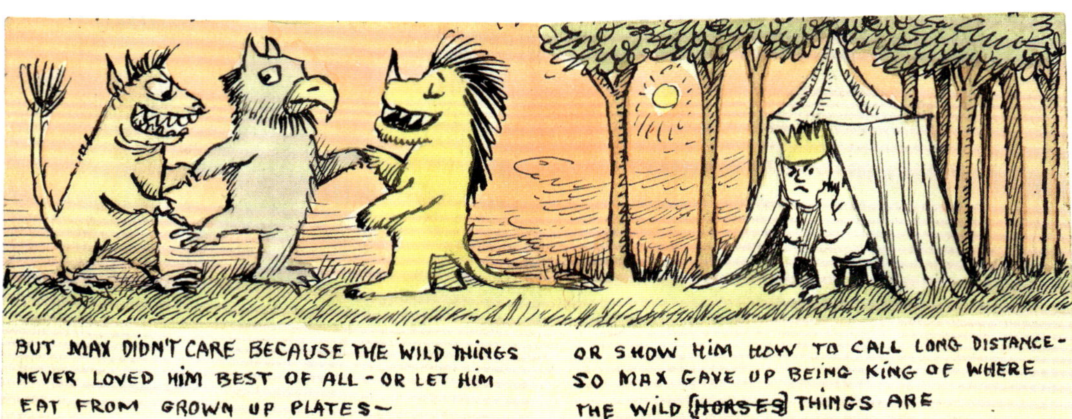

Maurice Sendak, *Where the Wild Things Are*, Dummy, 1963, watercolor and ink on paper, $2\frac{3}{8} \times 6$ in.

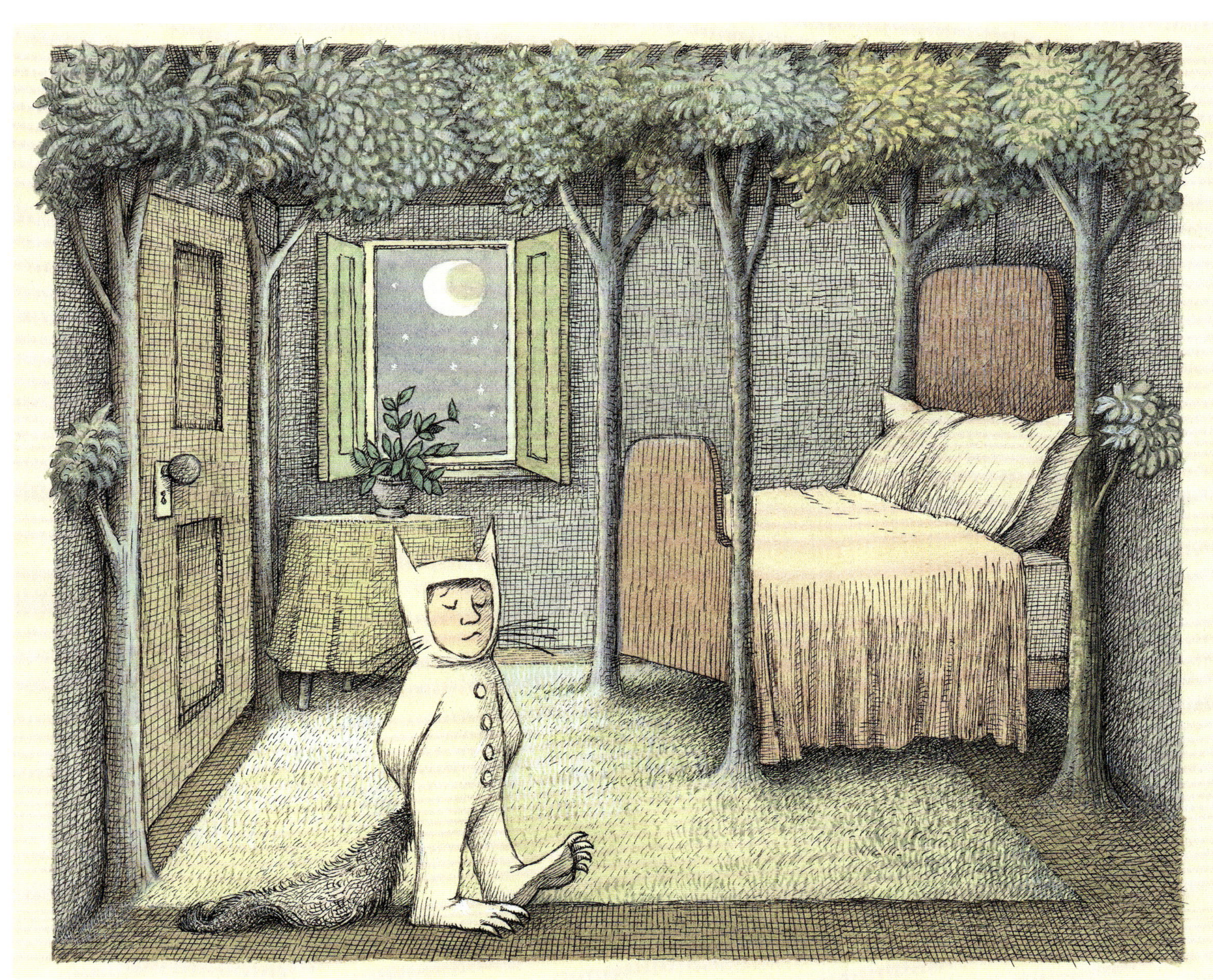

Maurice Sendak, *Where the Wild Things Are*, 1963, watercolor on board, 10 × 10¼ in.

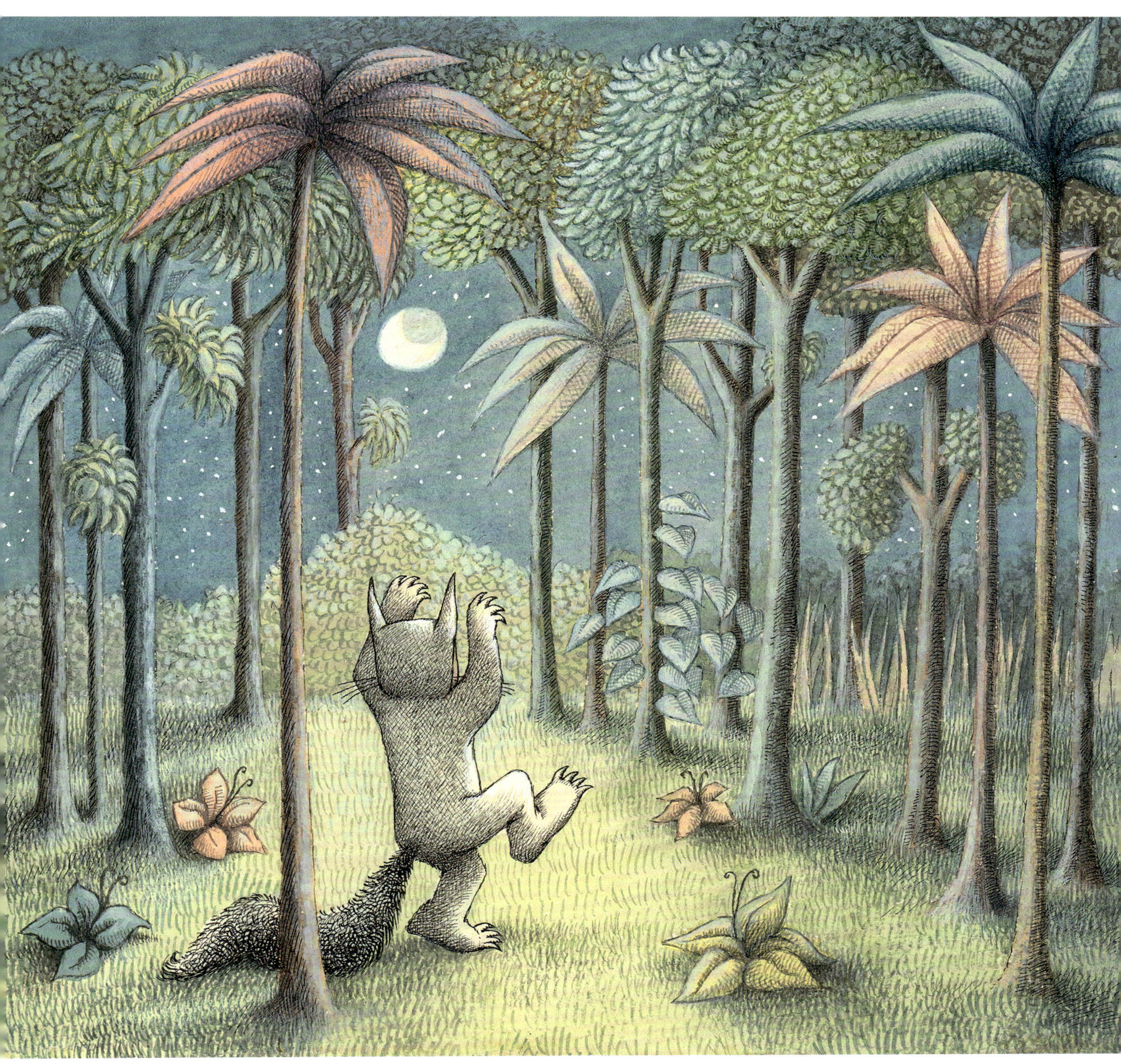

Maurice Sendak, *Where the Wild Things Are*, 1963, watercolor on board, 9¾ × 11 in.

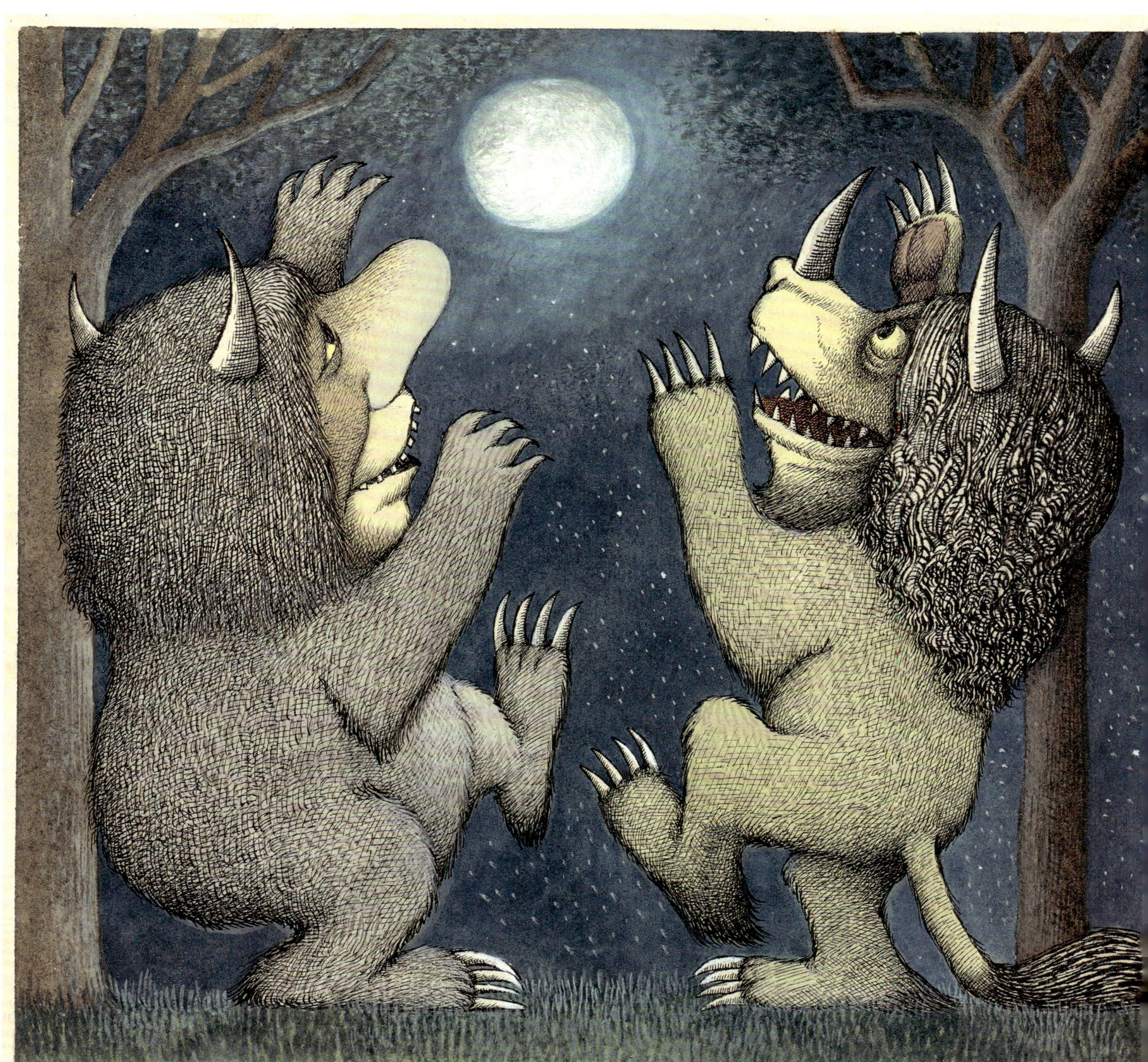

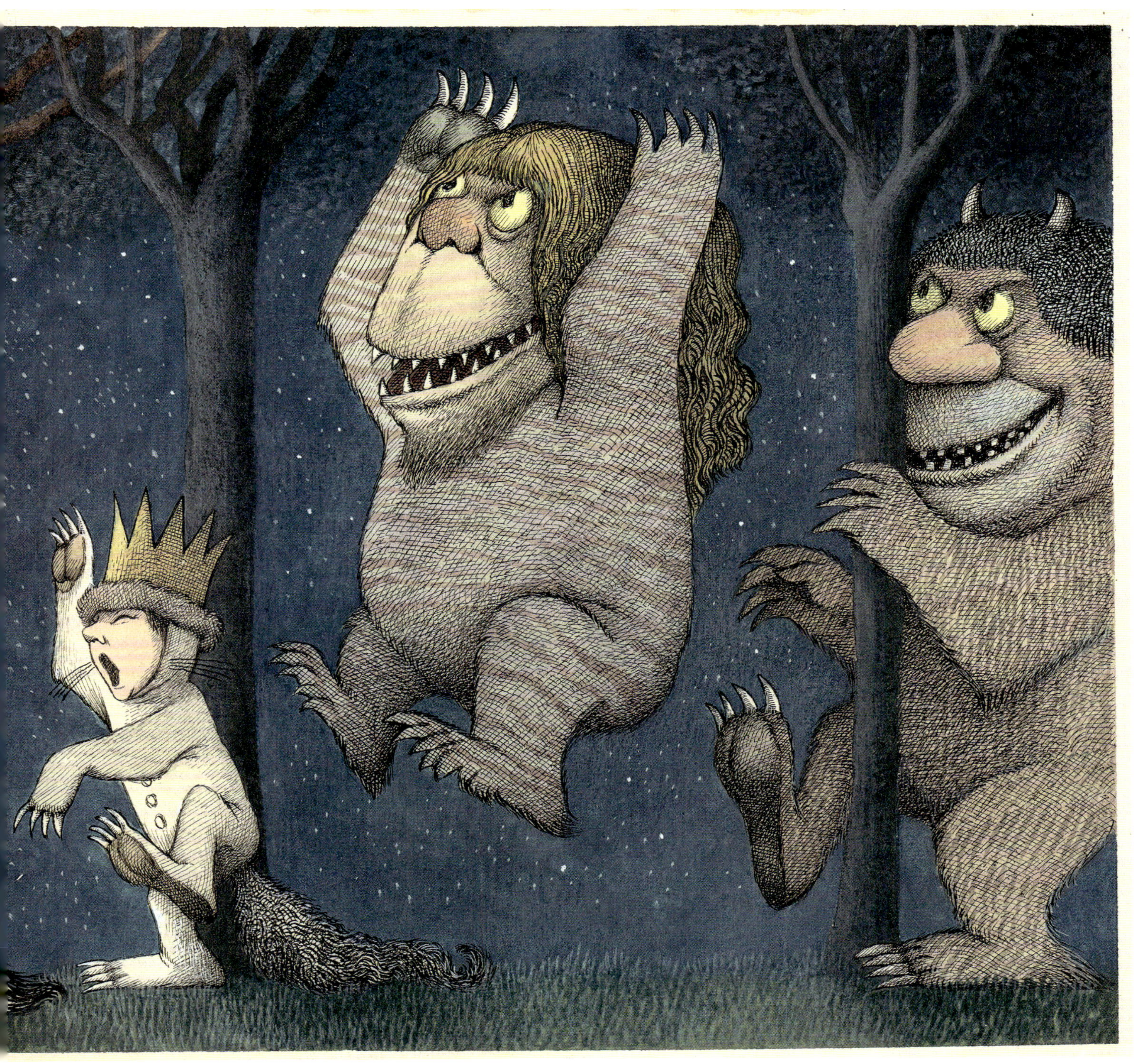

Maurice Sendak, *Where the Wild Things Are*, 1963, watercolor on board, 10 × 22 in.

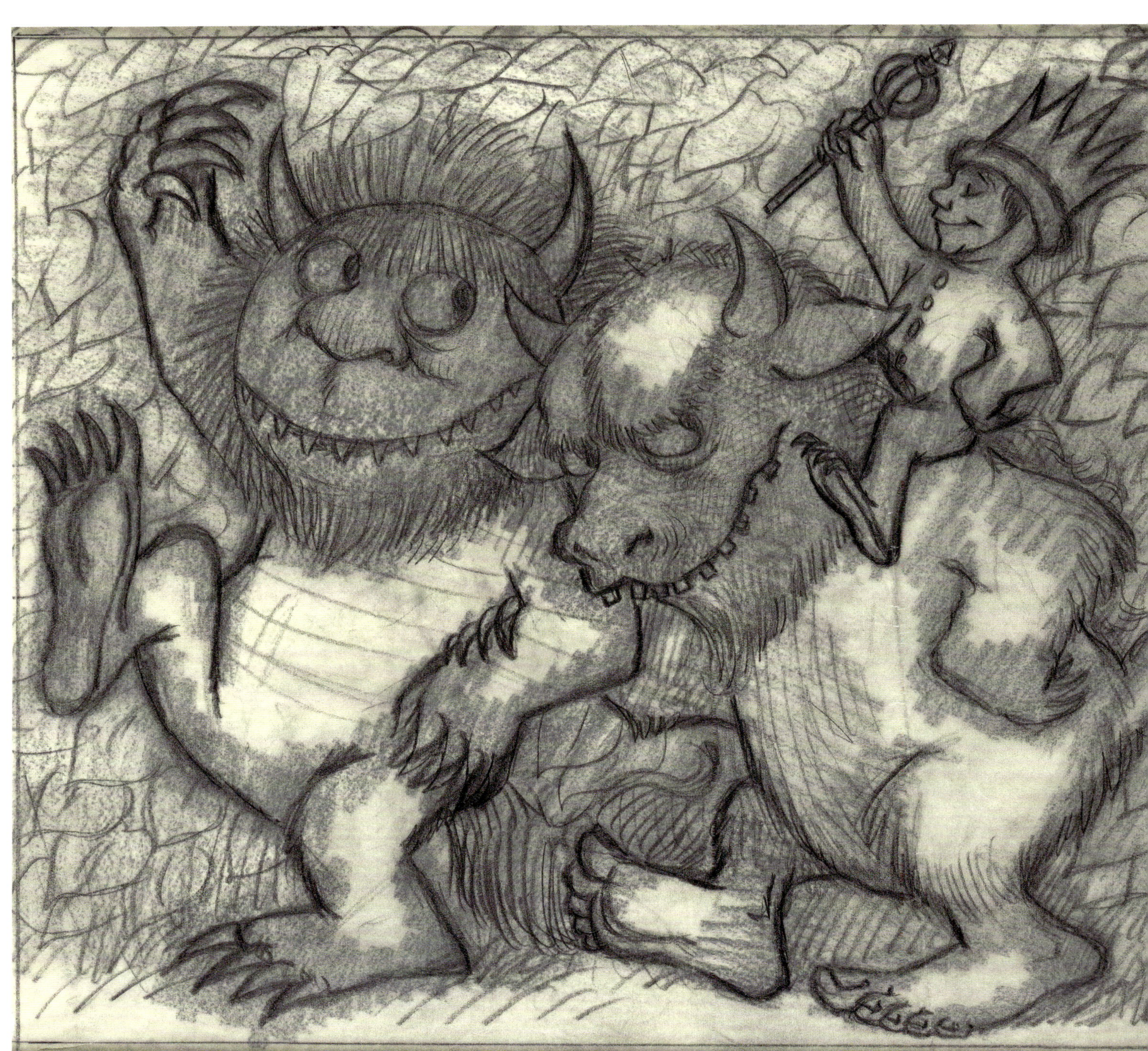

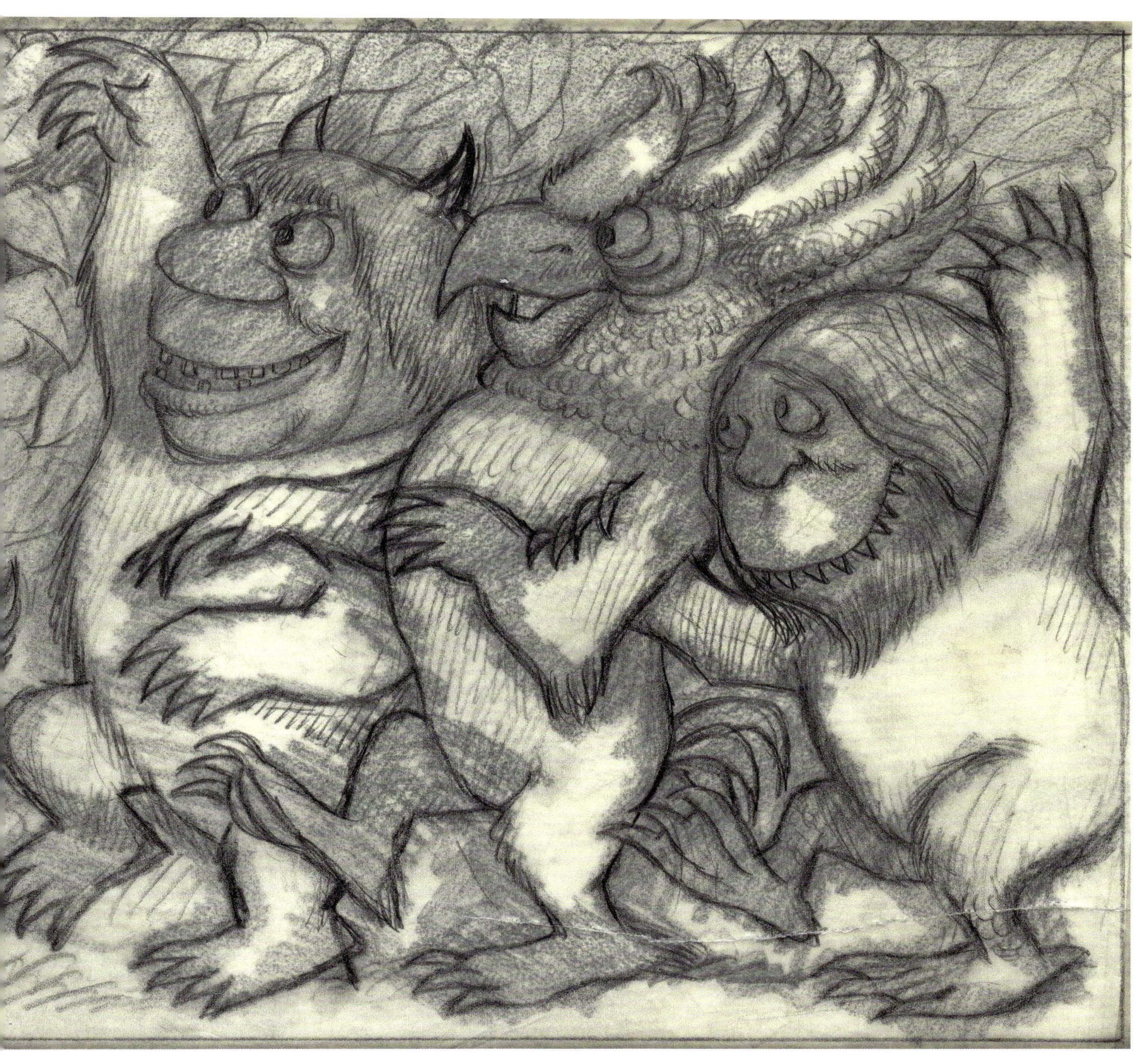

Maurice Sendak, Study for *Where the Wild Things Are*, 1963, pencil on tracing paper heavily outlined to transfer the drawing to the watercolor spread on the following pages, 11¼ × 21 in.

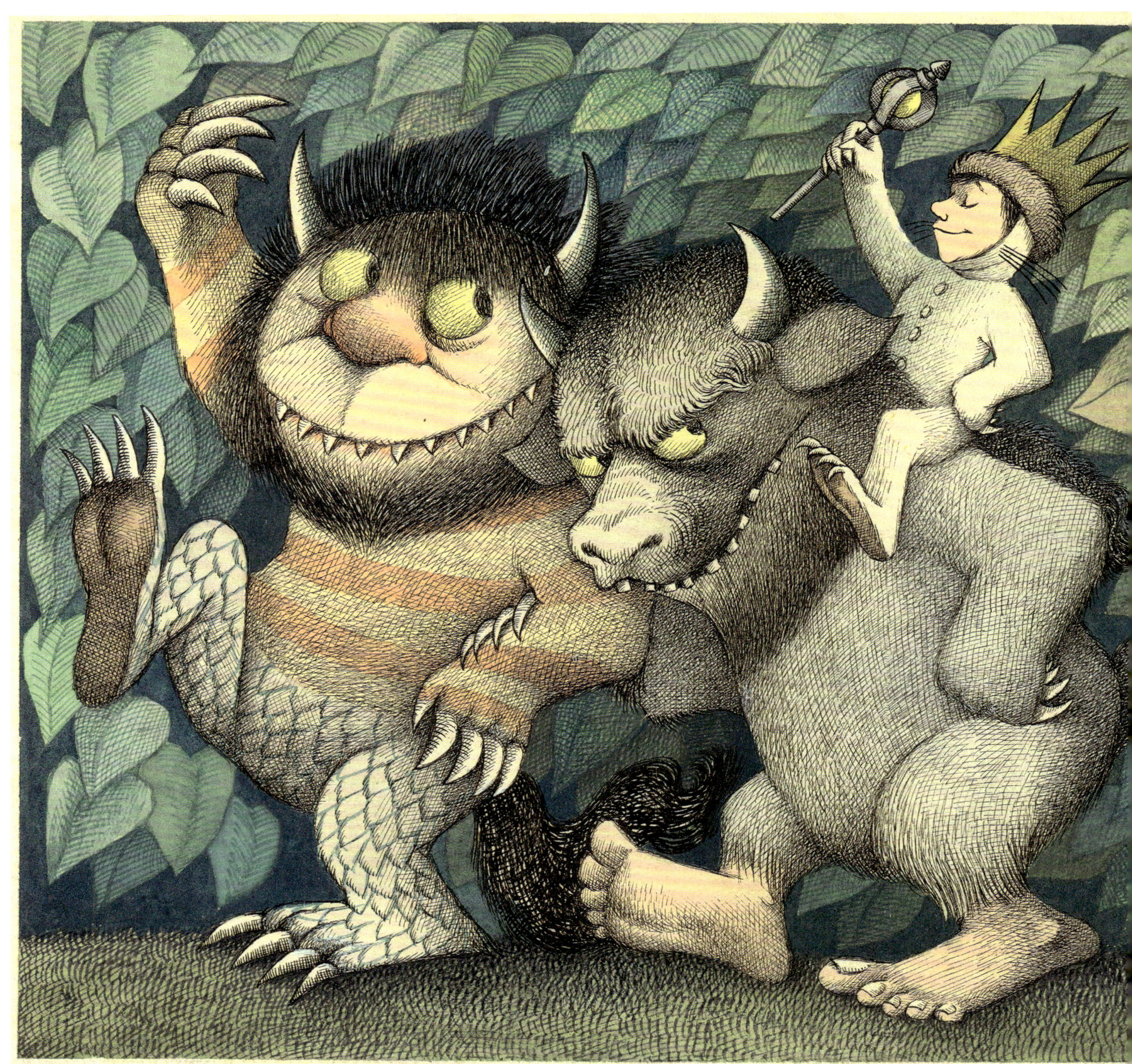

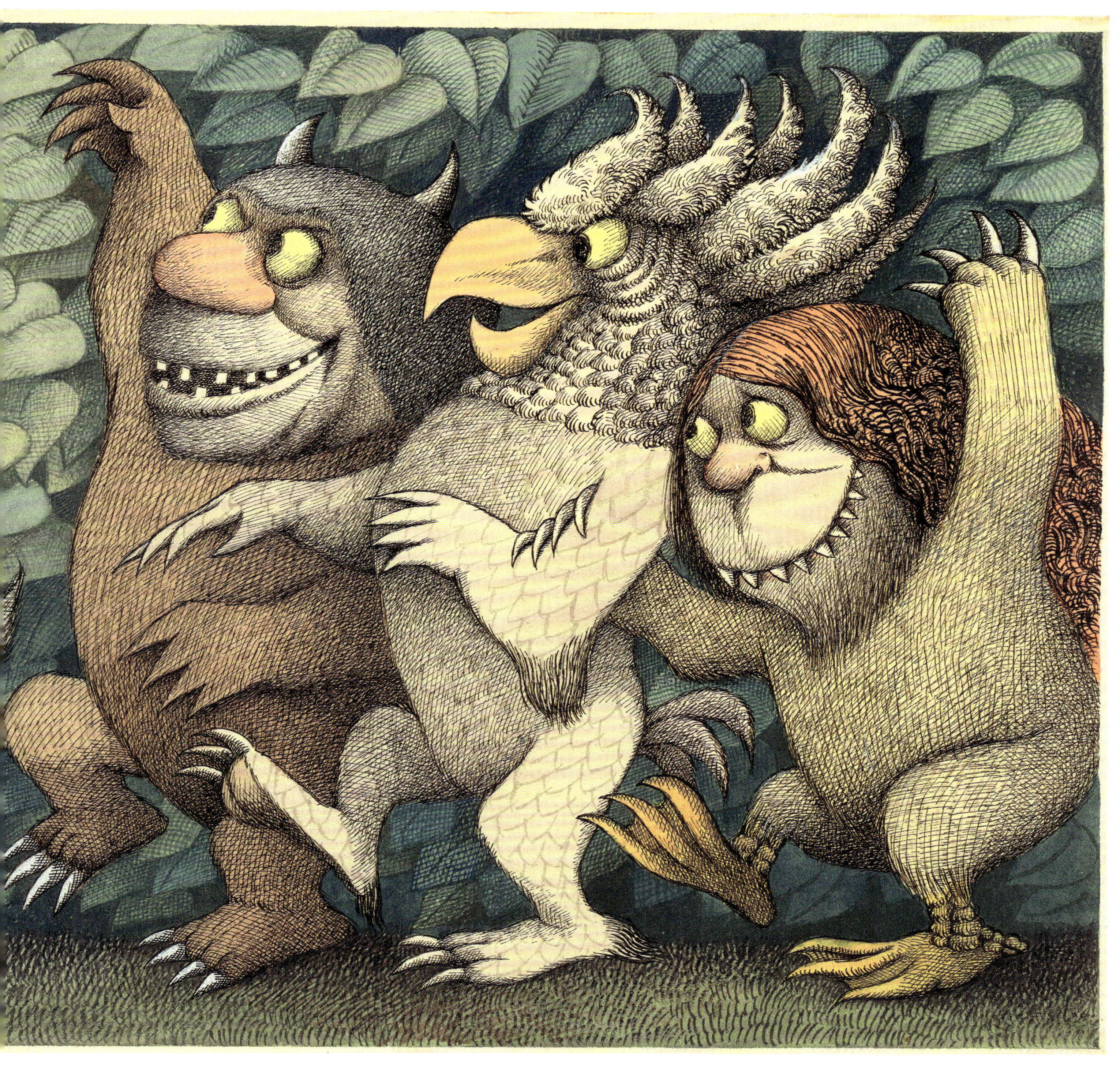

Maurice Sendak, *Where the Wild Things Are*, 1963, watercolor on paper, 9¾ × 22 in.

"Through fantasy, Max, the hero of my book, discharges his anger against his mother, and returns to the real world sleepy, hungry, and at peace with himself."

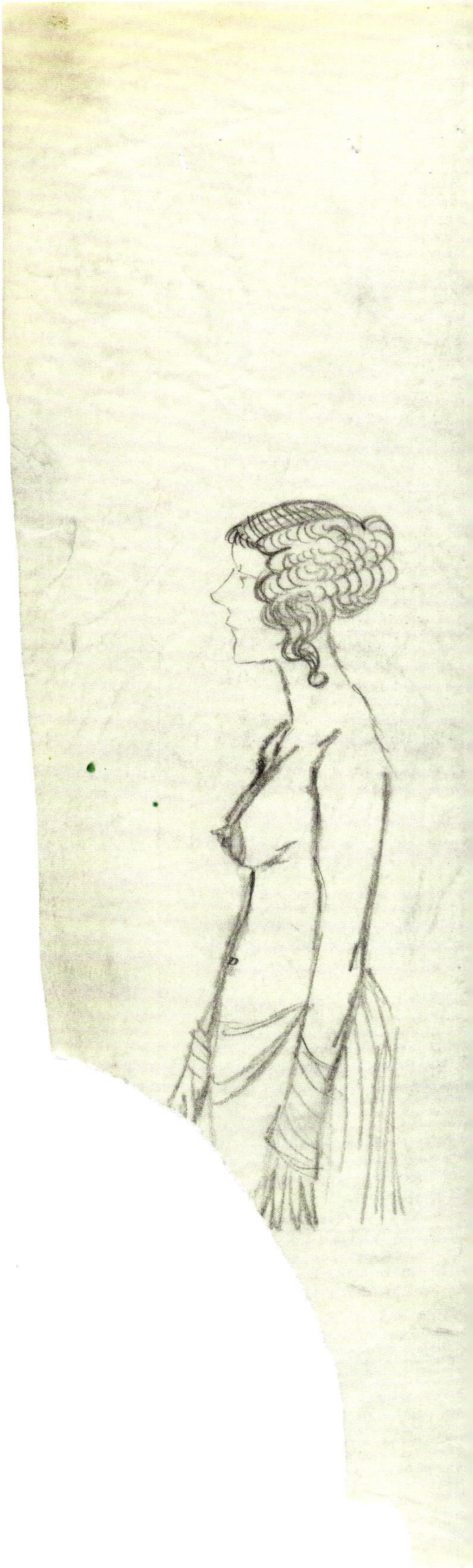

Maurice Sendak, Study for *Where the Wild Things Are*, 1963, pencil on tracing paper, 13¾ × 16½ in.

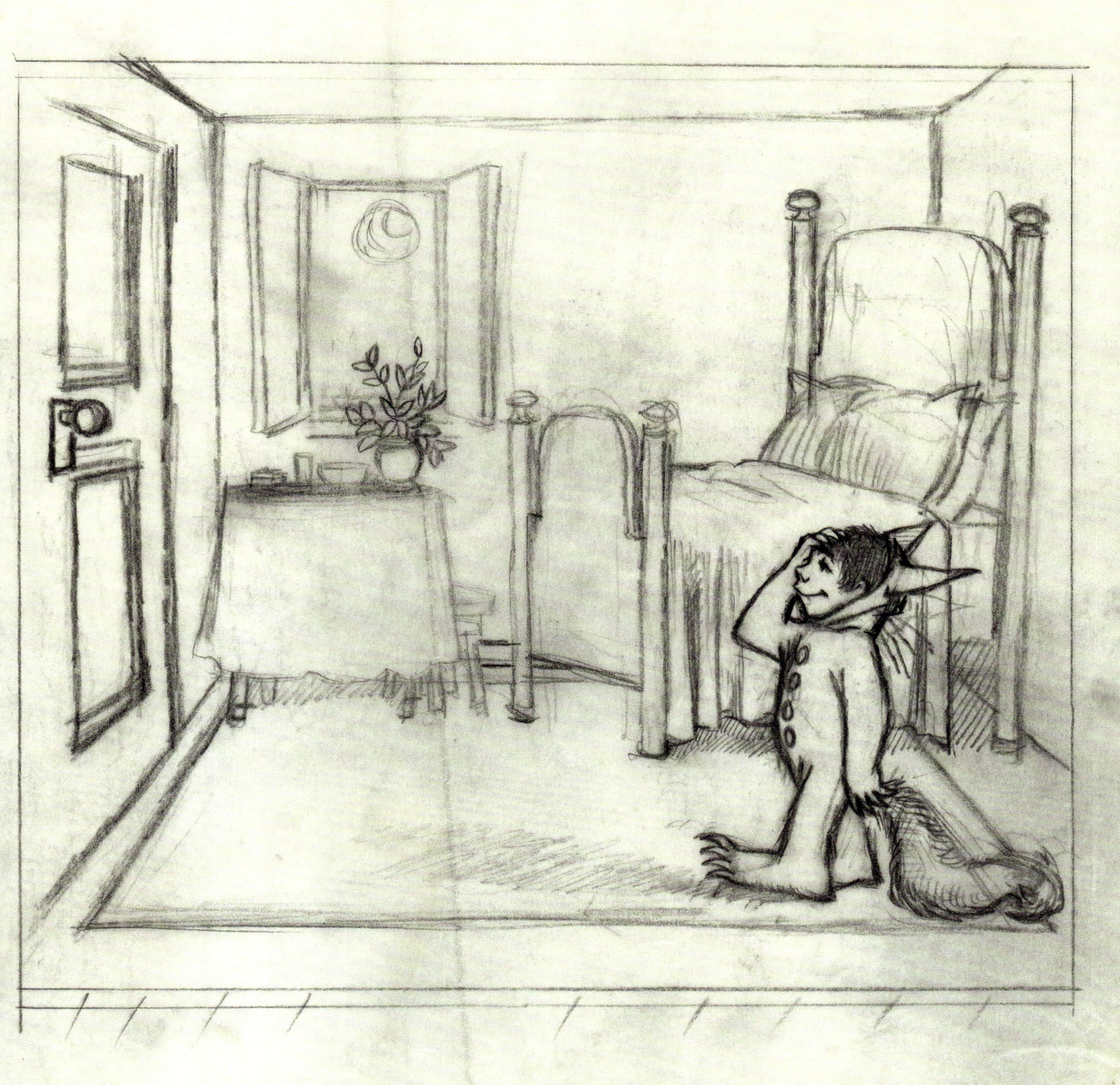

"Swing into Action"

Maurice Sendak and the Worlds of Puppetry

JOHN BELL

Maurice Sendak was not a puppeteer, but he understood the nature of puppetry's never-ending fascination with objects, images, movement, music, and text, and how the creation of those combinations with a collaborative team of artists can make a puppet show work.

Sendak primarily created images for the page, but he was not limited by that concentration: he kept other elements in mind. He famously absorbed music while drawing—creating his many "fantasy" sketches while listening to works of Mozart and other composers—and was fascinated by the possibilities of image and movement. In his 1964 essay "The Shape of Music" he elaborates upon the importance of music to his drawing, but his writing suggests an even wider combination of preoccupations. He begins the essay with an immediate concern for image and movement:

> *Vivify*, *quicken*, and *vitalize*—of these three synonyms, *quicken*, I think, best suggests the genuine spirit of animation, the breathing of life, the swing into action, that I consider an essential quality in pictures for children's books.[1]

That "breathing of life," that "swing into action" is the animating spirit of puppet and object performance as well, and even though Sendak was not a puppeteer, his work continually brushed up against the material world in performance, in convivial ways. Walt Disney's expressive combinations of image and movement in *Fantasia* (1940) enthralled Sendak as a child, inspiring his life-long admiration of Disney animation and his growing collection of Mickey Mouse miniatures and paraphernalia. In high school he got a job building window displays (another job

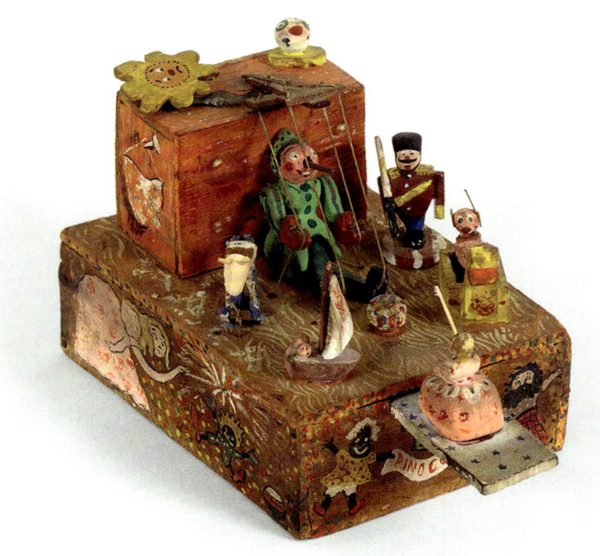

Maurice and Jack Sendak, *Pinocchio*, 1948, mechanical toy, 3½ wide × 6¾ deep, base height 1⅝ in.

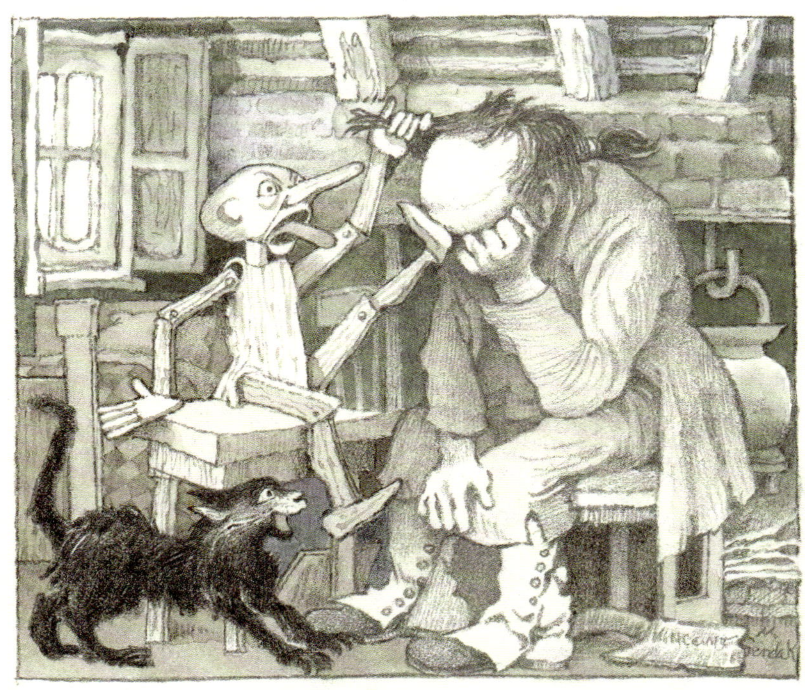

Maurice Sendak, *Pinocchio*, 2004, ink on paper, 7¾ × 8⅛ in.

often taken by puppeteers), including life-size figures of Snow White and the Seven Dwarfs he made "out of chicken wire overlaid with papier-mâché."[2] In 1948, he and his brother Jack collaborated on simple but evocative automata based on children's stories. Jack, Sendak later said, "did all the carving, the figuring out of how it worked, and I did all the painting."[3] The brothers' attempt to sell their creations to the FAO Schwartz toy store did not work out but did lead to Maurice designing window displays there.

Sendak's professional work as a children's book illustrator began in 1950. Around this time, his deep interest in graphic design led him to focus on nineteenth-century English and German illustrators, who worked in a dynamic, early modernist era

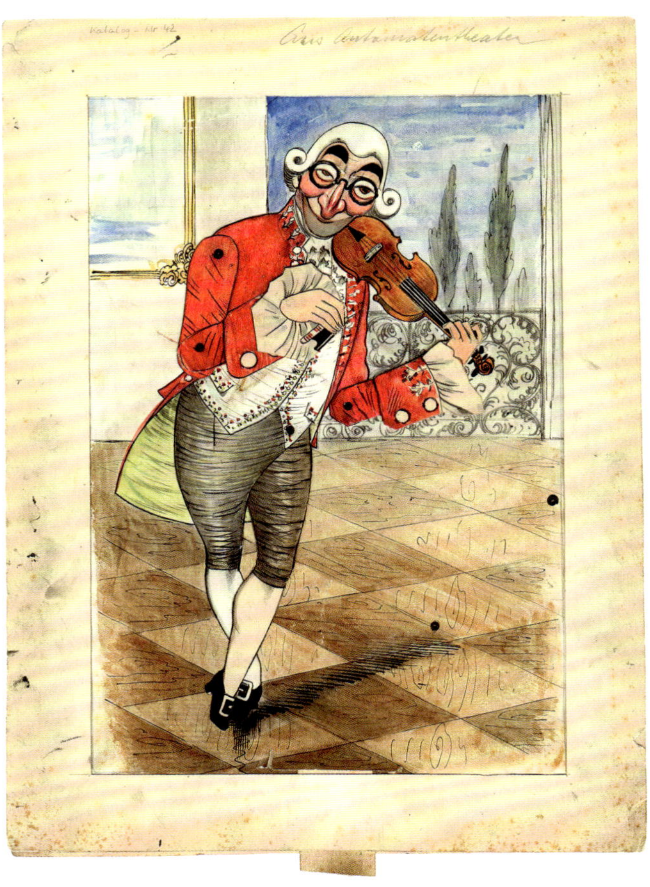

Lothar Meggendorfer, *The Dancing Master*, original painting for his *Lustiges Automaten-Theater*, 1890, watercolor, ink and pencil, $13\frac{1}{2} \times 10\frac{1}{8}$ in.

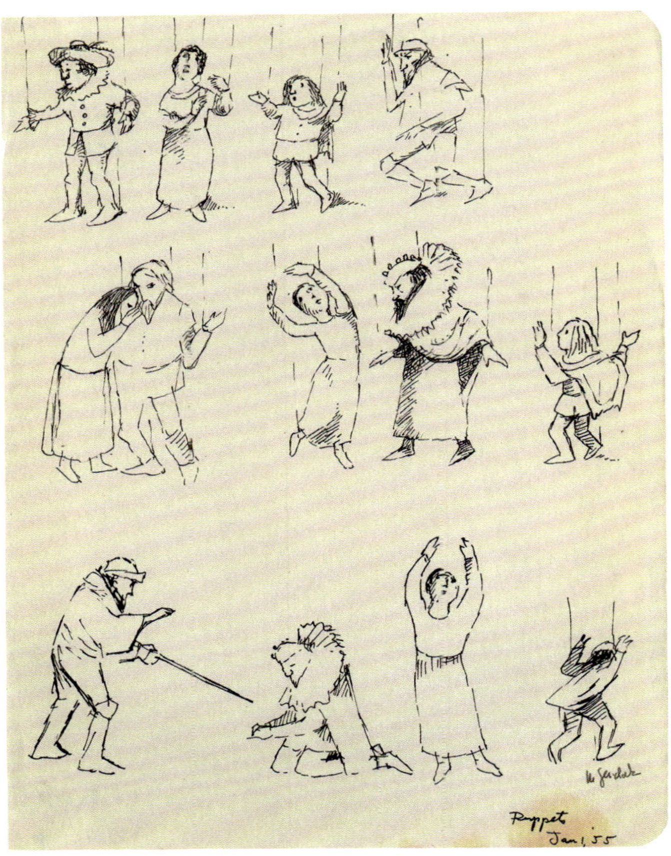

Maurice Sendak, *Fantasy Sketch: Puppets*, 1955, ink on paper, $10 \times 7\frac{5}{8}$ in.

where art, technology, and the possibilities of image and movement were developed in an array of new techniques, including moving panoramas, toy theater, magic lanterns, shadow theater, stroboscopes, kinescopes, and other innovative media. Sendak's interest in the transformation illustrations of German graphic designer Lothar Meggendorfer is part of this fascination, and another moment where Sendak appreciated the combination of visual art and movement. Similar to nineteenth-century toy theaters, the animated figures of Meggendorfer and others combined the mass-production technology of the printing press with the possibilities of two-dimensional movement. Paper toy theater figures performed on miniature proscenium stages, while Meggendorfer's paper creations remained on the page; but with the simple pull of a tab, the designs could move like their similarly two-dimensional toy theater relatives. For Sendak, Meggendorfer's "fantastical" work was "a dream come true," because the German artist was able to use the form's simple technologies to "[turn] the mechanical toy book into a work of art."[4]

In 1963 Sendak's life and work changed forever with the publication of *Where the Wild Things Are*. At first it shocked, but then inexorably broadened the world of children's literature to include complicated and often difficult emotions and experiences. The hero Max's wolf costume, the sea monster he meets on his voyage, and of course the Wild Things are all glorious invitations to imagine extravagant non-human beings, and they naturally inspired puppeteers to put those characters in motion on puppet stages.

An American puppeteer in Italy, Amy Luckenbach, was the first to take up this challenge, creating

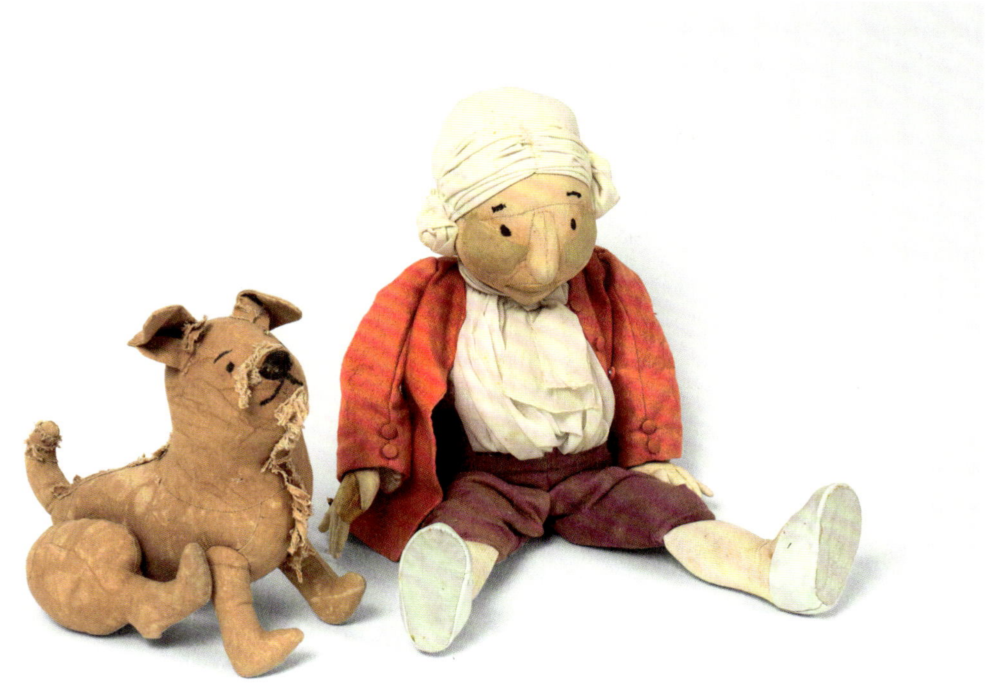

Amy Luckenbach, *Mozart and Bimberl, his Dog*, 2001 (Mozart is 20 in. high, the dog is 10 in. high)

a rich and dynamic hand-puppet version of the show in 1974, which she performed in Florence and nearby towns with her company Burattini a Spasso (the Meandering Puppets). Luckenbach wrote Sendak to let him know about the production, but he never responded. The success of her *Wild Things* production inspired Luckenbach to design, build, and perform other puppet shows, and her reputation began to grow in puppetry circles worldwide. In 1988 at the Bologna Children's Book Fair, she finally met Sendak, telling him she had written to him years ago about her *Wild Things* production. "I hope I answered," Sendak responded. Luckenbach said no, he hadn't, but that she wanted to propose a new idea: a puppet production of Sendak's *In the Night Kitchen*, with music by Philip Glass. Surprised, Sendak replied that Glass himself had only recently proposed writing an opera based on the same story, and the serendipity of this meeting of minds began a long friendship between the artist and the puppeteer.

Luckenbach and Sendak's next collaboration was not *In the Night Kitchen*, but instead a realization, through puppetry, of Sendak's "stream-of-consciousness" *Fantasy Sketches*, for which Luckenbach built Bunraku-style puppets operated by black-clad puppeteers.[5] The production, premiered at the 2001 Festival of Arts and Ideas in New Haven, included new sketches about the life of Sendak's favorite composer, Mozart, whose music was played on instruments including a glass harmonica. After seeing the performance, Sendak wrote an appreciation of his relationship with Luckenbach, pointing out that they both "enjoy conundrums, mysteries and fantasies," and that he had in her "the perfect friend, playmate and collaborator."[6]

Composer Oliver Knussen's opera version of *Where the Wild Things Are* was first produced in 1984 by the National Opera of Belgium and remounted in London in 2001. Sendak sent Luckenbach a DVD of the London production, which prompted her to

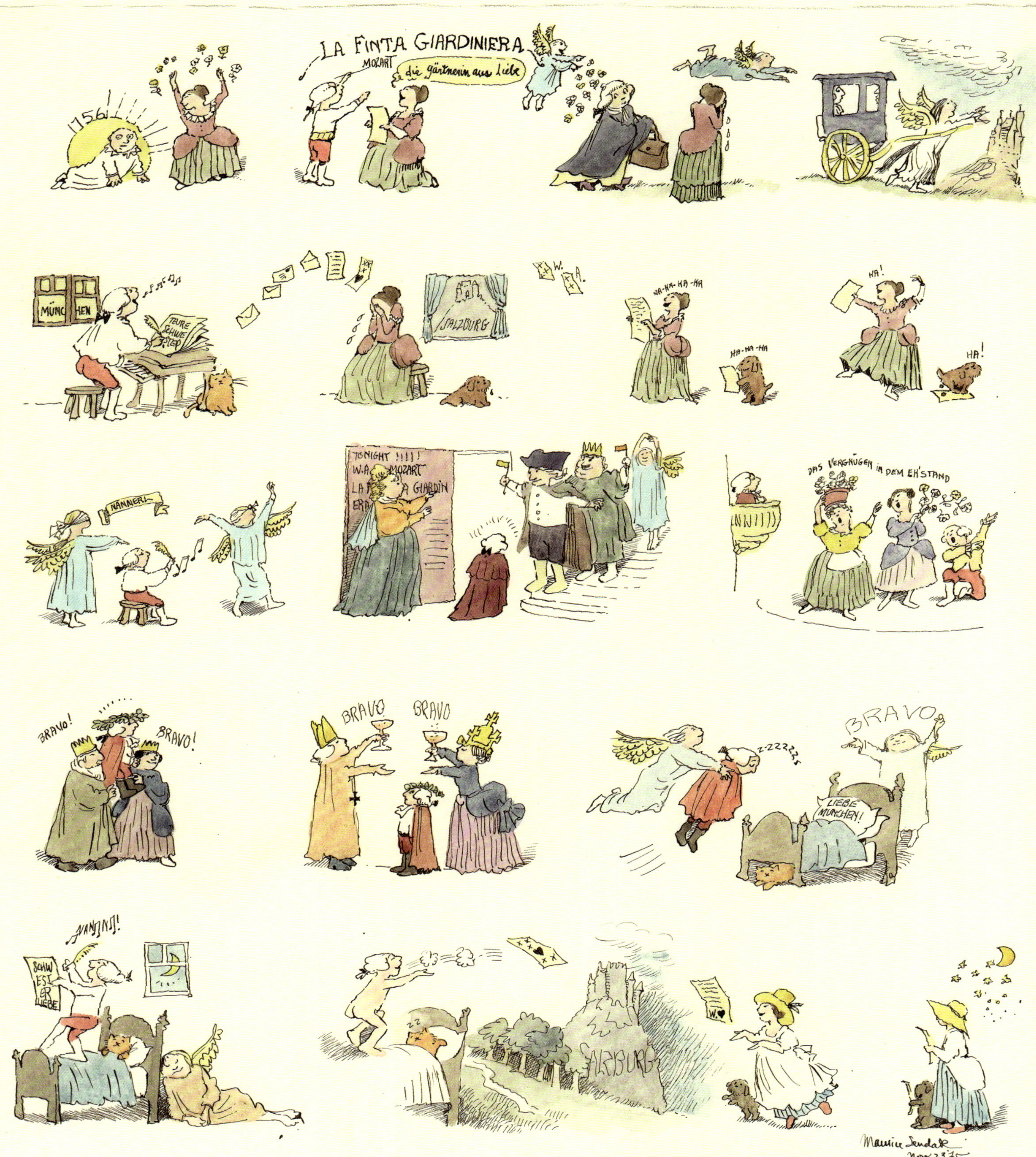

1756
LA FINTA GIARDINIERA
MOZART
die gärtnerin aus Liebe
MÜNCHEN
TEURE SCHWESTER
SALZBURG
W.
A.
HA-HA-HA-HA
HA-HA-HA
HA!
HA!
NÄNNERL
TONIGHT !!!!
W.A. MOZART
LA FINTA GIARDINIERA
DAS VERGNÜGEN IN DEM EH'STAND
BRAVO!
BRAVO!
BRAVO
BRAVO
Z-ZZZZZS
BRAVO
LIEBE MÜNCHEN!
NANNERL!
SCHWESTER LIEBE
SALZBURG
W.♥
Maurice Sendak
Nov. 23, 75

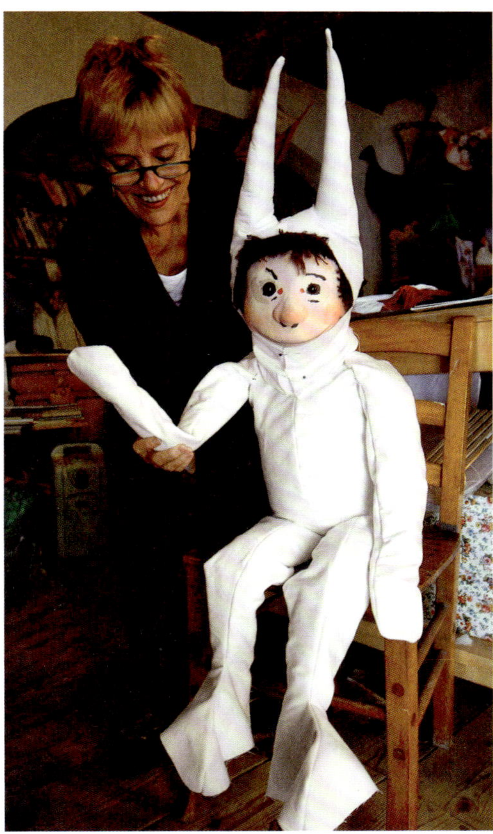

Amy Luckenbach with her unfinished puppet *Max* from her 2005 Production of *Where the Wild Things Are*

comment on the awkwardness of the over-life-size monsters. Luckenbach proposed to produce the opera instead with a child-sized puppet as Max, and masked and costumed adults as the monsters, who would be able to gesture and move more gracefully. Thrilled by her proposal, Sendak approved, and Luckenbach directed the opera in 2004 in Florence's Teatro Communale. She still pursued her plans to produce *In the Night Kitchen* with Sendak and Glass in the following years, but died in 2009, before the project could be realized. In a letter of condolence to her husband, Sendak wrote that he was heartbroken, and that he had "trusted her creatively, totally."[7]

As a result of Sendak's increasingly prominent profile following the publication of *Where the Wild Things Are*, and his creation of more personal expressions such as *Outside Over There* (1981), there occurred what playwright Tony Kushner called a "sea change" in Sendak's work, and the development of a second career as a set, costume, and puppet designer for opera, ballet, theater, and film.[8] His collaborations with director Frank Corsaro, beginning with the 1980 Houston Opera production of Mozart's *Magic Flute*, developed his reputation as a notable designer of classic works for the stage. Sendak's interests in graphic design, animation, and object performance were a natural match for the stage, although as Kushner has pointed out, Sendak had a conservative approach to stage design, embracing "strictly wing-and-drop-style scenography" reminiscent of the seventeenth and eighteenth centuries, rather than the postmodern approaches of Robert Wilson and other stage designers.[9] This conservative vision of the proscenium stage was also wholly in line with similarly traditionalist theater forms; not only opera and ballet, but also European puppetry and toy theater, which also thrived within the confines and accoutrements of the proscenium frame and the clearly stated theatrical artifice of such stages.

The *Where the Wild Things Are* monsters demanded theatrical realization through masks and puppetry, not only in the various productions of Knussen's opera, Luckenbach's puppet versions, and in countless amateur productions in schools across the U.S., but also in a giant inflatable puppet for Macy's Thanksgiving Day Parade (1998), and in the puppets Jim Henson's Creature Shop built for Spike Jonze's 2009 *Wild Things* feature film. Sendak must have become intrigued with the possibilities of puppet performance as far back as the late sixties, when he and Jim Henson served on the Children's Television Workshop advisory board during the development of *Sesame Street*.[10] The age-old demands of theater spectacle so routinely a part of classic European ballet and opera also found a willing partner in Maurice Sendak.

opposite: Maurice Sendak, Mozart's *La Finta Giardiniera*, Fantasy Sketch, 1975, ink on paper with watercolor added c. 2000, 13⅜ × 11 in.

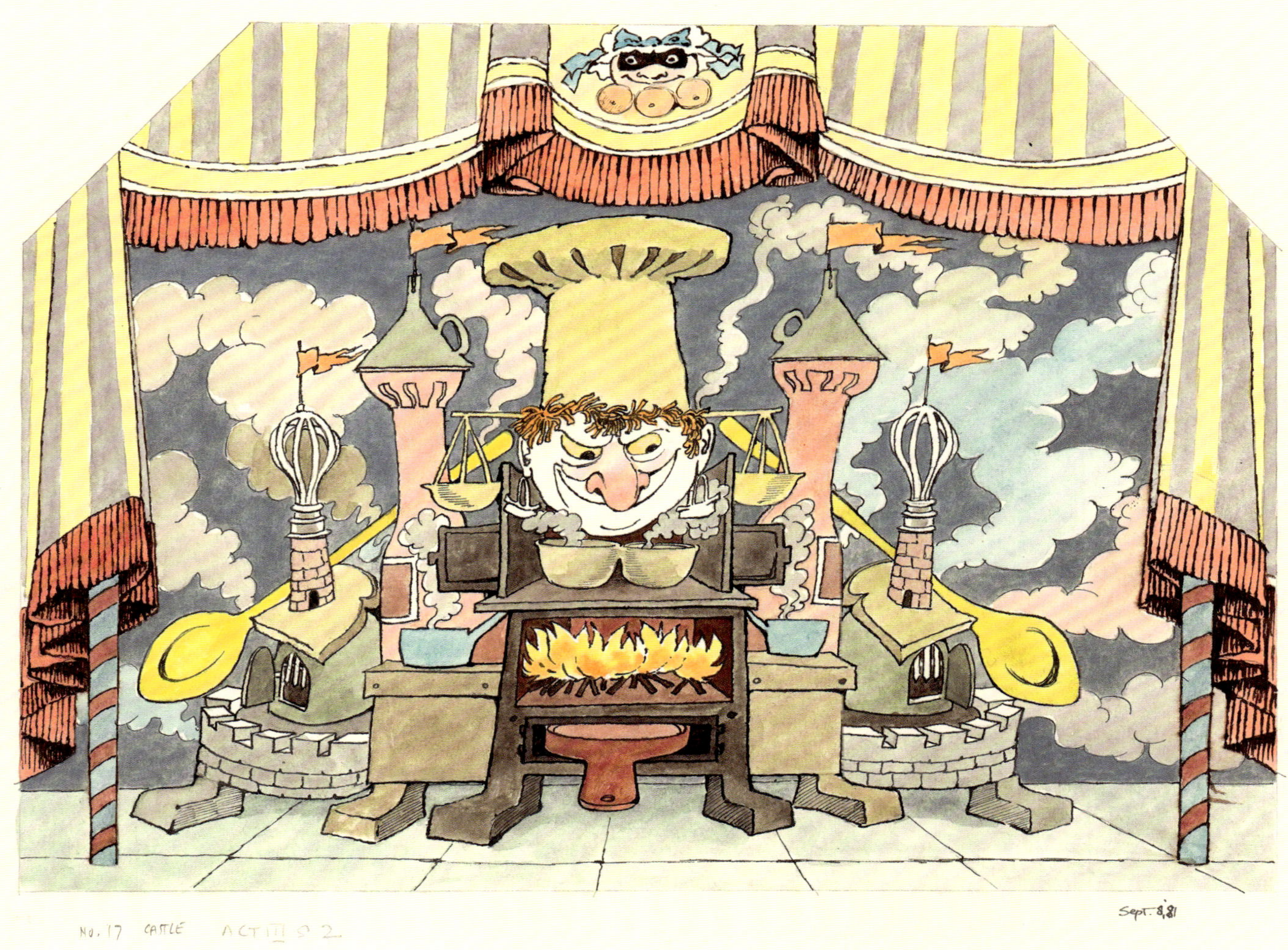

Maurice Sendak, *The Love for Three Oranges: Scene Design for the Castle, Act 3, Scene 2*, 1981, gouache and graphite pencil, 13 11/16 × 18 15/16 in., The Morgan Library & Museum

Sendak's love of image, object, and movement found powerful matches in the *commedia dell'arte*-influenced Prokofiev opera *Love for Three Oranges*, for which Sendak could reference Giovanni Battista Tiepolo's seventeenth-century sketches of masked *commedia* characters. The joyous theater-within-a-theater conceit of the opera inspired Sendak to design not only beautifully classic *commedia* masks; but also an oversize inflatable puppet of the witch Fata Morgana; two giant, moveable, flat cut-out Punchinello figures on either side of the proscenium stage (reminiscent of the Meggendorfer "Dancing Master"); three oversized animal masks for the Act 2 divertissement; and a hobby-horse-style gondola that the King (disguised in a Punch mask) could wear with shoulder straps.[11]

Sendak was equally inspired in his puppet and mask designs for the 1983 Pacific Northwest Ballet production of Tchaikovsky's *The Nutcracker*. Like so many of the E.T.A. Hoffman stories that fueled Romantic-era and nineteenth-century ballets and operas, it is full of fantastic characters begging to be portrayed with masks and puppets. In addition to over-life-size masks for the Nutcracker, Princess Pirlipat, the seven-headed Mouse King, and his army, Sendak designed a similarly scaled mask for the magician Drosselmeier, and his version of a traditional "bighead" puppet for a vaguely Asian

Tiger Boy dancer. He was even able to reprise his idea for giant flat cut-out proscenium puppets with a 35-foot-tall version of Drosselmeier, whose legs could bend and dance (again, Meggendorfer on a giant scale).

Even more puppet fun was to be found in the 1982 Kansas City Opera production of Mozart's incomplete *opera buffa*, *The Goose of Cairo*. Sendak had to design a giant "mechanical" Goose in which the romantic hero could hide as he was smuggled into a castle to save his love.

In his puppet and theater designs, Sendak seems to have found a welcome alternative to the solo processes of drawing in his studio. Collaborative art-making may have begun with the automata he and his brother Jack made in 1948, but he seems also to have cherished his work collaborations with Amy Luckenbach, Frank Corsaro, Arthur Yorinks, Tony Kushner, the various builders of his puppet, set, and costume designs, and other professionals who could direct, choreograph, write, and compose in partnership with him. Puppetry, in particular, was deeply connected to his visual designs, to which it added "the breathing of life, the swing into action" that brought them from the page into active existence, where they could be augmented with new languages of gesture, dance, and music, which Sendak so admired.

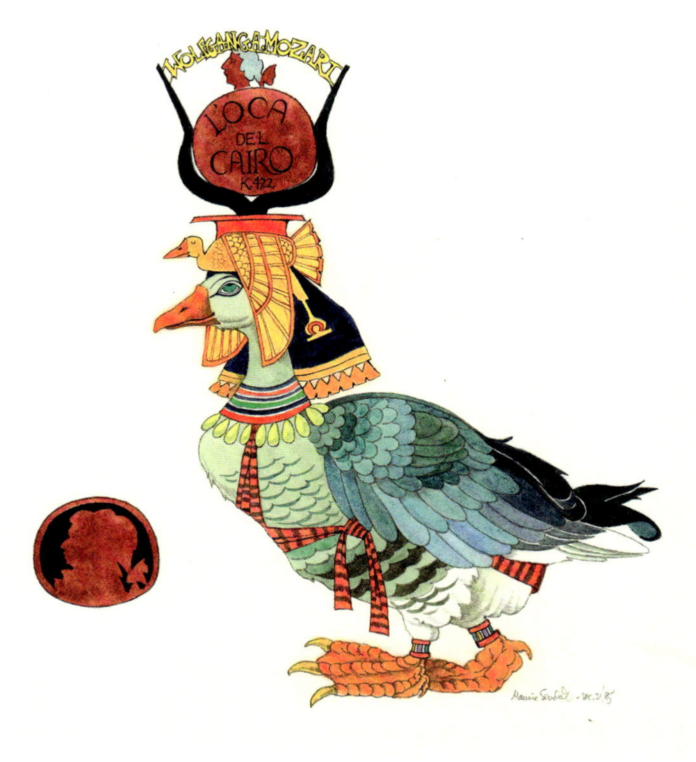

Maurice Sendak, Design for the Goose, *The Goose From Cairo*, 1985, watercolor and ink on paper, 11¼ × 9¾ in.

Notes

During the run of the exhibition *Wild Things Are Happening* at The University of Connecticut's Benton Museum in 2022, John Bell and Emily Wicks curated an exhibition at the University's Ballard Institute and Museum of Puppetry devoted to Maurice Sendak's connections to puppetry and performance objects.

1. Maurice Sendak, "The Shape of Music," *Caldecott and Company: Notes on Books & Pictures* (New York: Farrar, Straus and Giroux, 1988), 3.
2. Selma G. Lanes, *The Art of Maurice Sendak* (New York: Harry N. Abrams, 1984), 29. Notable puppeteers who also created window displays include Tony Sarg, Remo Bufano, and Paul McPharlin.
3. *Tell Them Anything You Want: A Portrait of Maurice Sendak*, a film by Lance Bangs and Spike Jonze (HBO Documentary Films, 2009). 7:58 to 8:07.
4. Maurice Sendak, "Lothar Meggendorfer," *Caldecott and Company: Notes on Books & Pictures* (New York: Farrar, Straus and Giroux, 1988), 52.
5. Sendak, "The Shape of Music," 4.
6. Maurice Sendak, quoted in Swietlan Nicholas Kraczyna, *Amy Luckenbach: Love and Life of Puppets and Dolls / Amore e Vita di Burattini e Bambole* (Florence: Labyrinth Press, 2012), 143.
7. Maurice Sendak, quoted in Kraczyna, *Amy Luckenbach*, 225.
8. Tony Kushner, *The Art of Maurice Sendak: 1980 to the Present* (New York: Harry N. Abrams, 2003), 14.
9. Kushner, 92.
10. "4/18/1980—Meet with Jon Stone and Maurice Sendak—talk about idea. Go to Boston—see Brian." Jim Henson's Red Book. Accessed 31 October 2021, https://www.henson.com/jimsredbook/2011/04/4191980/. *Where the Wild Things Are* and *Outside Over There* also inspired aspects of Henson's film *Labyrinth*. See "Maurice Sendak." Muppet Wiki. Accessed 31 October 2021, https://muppet.fandom.com/wiki/Maurice_Sendak.
11. See Rachel Federman, *Drawing the Curtain: Maurice Sendak's Designs for Opera and Ballet* (New York: Morgan Library & Museum, 2019), 19, 102–17.

Where the Wild Things Aren't

The Bell Atlantic Advertising Campaign

TYLER FALLAS

In 2012, while brandishing a copy of *Where the Wild Things Are*, Stephen Colbert asked, "Why not do a sequel?" to which Maurice Sendak replied, "because it is the most boring thing imaginable."[1]

True to his word there was never a sequel, though *Where the Wild Things Are*, *In the Night Kitchen*, and *Outside Over There* together form a self-proclaimed trilogy. The *Wild Things* characters, however, appear constantly in later posters and toys, those yellow eyes signaling something familiar and fantastical. In particular, Moishe, as Sendak affectionately called the monster who most resembled him, crops up regularly. Sendak reveals his characters' lasting impression by saying, "when I meet young people, or older people . . . it's almost as though they go back into a non-verbal condition, to the time when I first met them, and they were picking up signals in the book that are pre-language signals."[2] These pre-language signals embedded in *The Wild Things* live off the page, and if there were anything called "Where the Wild Things Are II" it would be in the continuing life of the characters. The Wild Things' success in later advertisement campaigns for American Express and Sony, and in opera, stage, and film adaptions is proof enough that nobody wanted the rumpus to end.

In 1996 Bell Atlantic was one of the largest telecommunication companies in the world, operating predominantly overseas and in the mid-Atlantic states (it is the antecedent of Verizon). Market deregulation provided an opportunity for Bell Atlantic to expand, but its size and legacy as one of the heirs to the mega monopoly, Bell Telephone, made it unattractive to a new generation of entrepreneurs from the world of cyberspace. Bell Atlantic wanted to emerge from the pack, while quelling a rising fear of behemoth companies that could march in and dominate the market, offering impersonal customer services. As one company executive put it: "this campaign will remind our customers—and reassure them, too—that we are there for them

opposite: Maurice Sendak, *New York is Book Country*, 1979, poster, 24 × 19 in.

NEW YORK IS BOOK COUNTRY

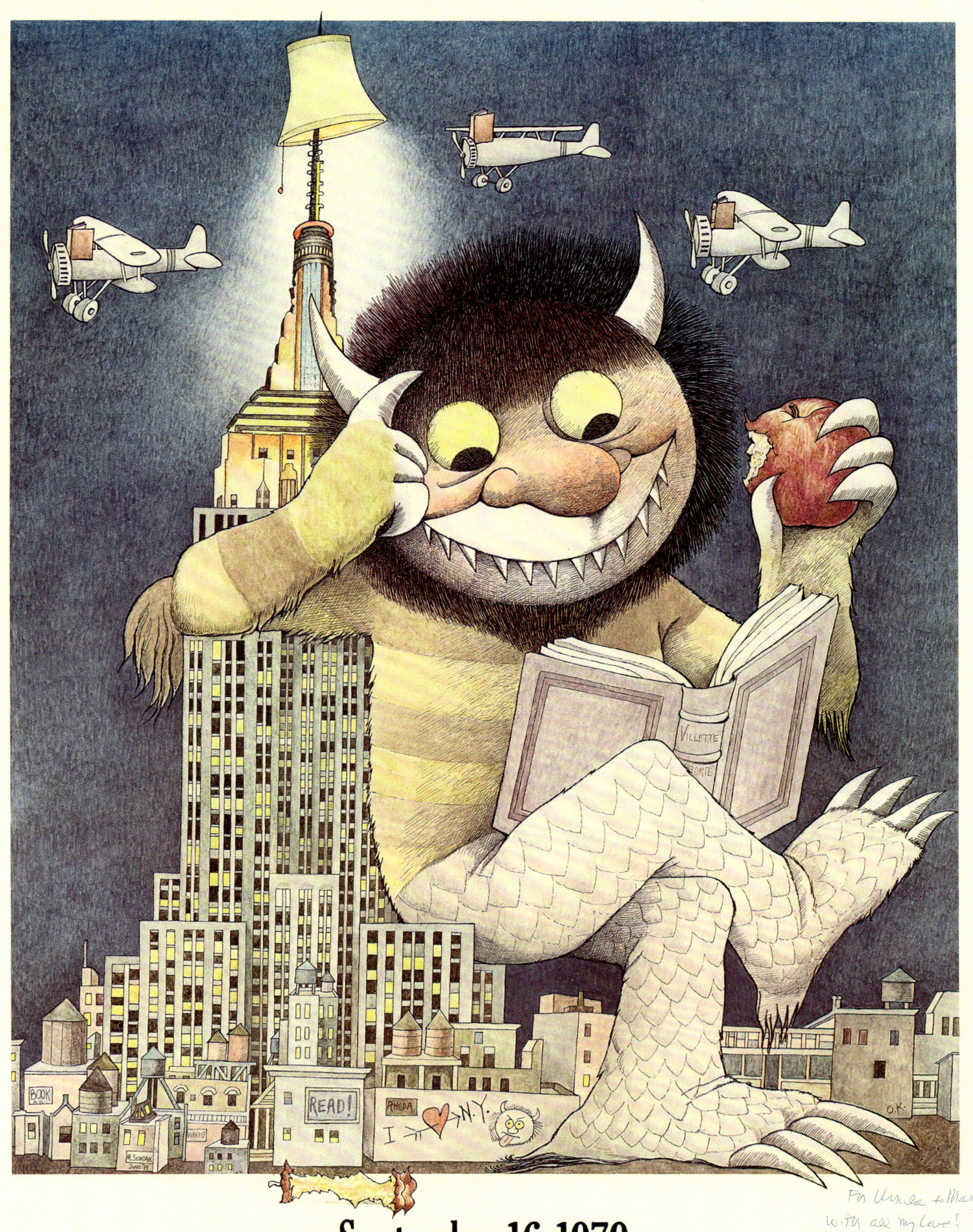

September 16, 1979

For Ursula + Mary –
with all my love!
Maurice Sendak
Sept. 79

Illustration by MAURICE SENDAK · All net proceeds benefit Children's Services, New York Public Library · Design by Barbara G. Hennessy · Production by Eileen G. Schwartz · Printing and production courtesy of Viking Penguin, Inc.
Distribution courtesy of Harper & Row, Publishers, Inc. ·

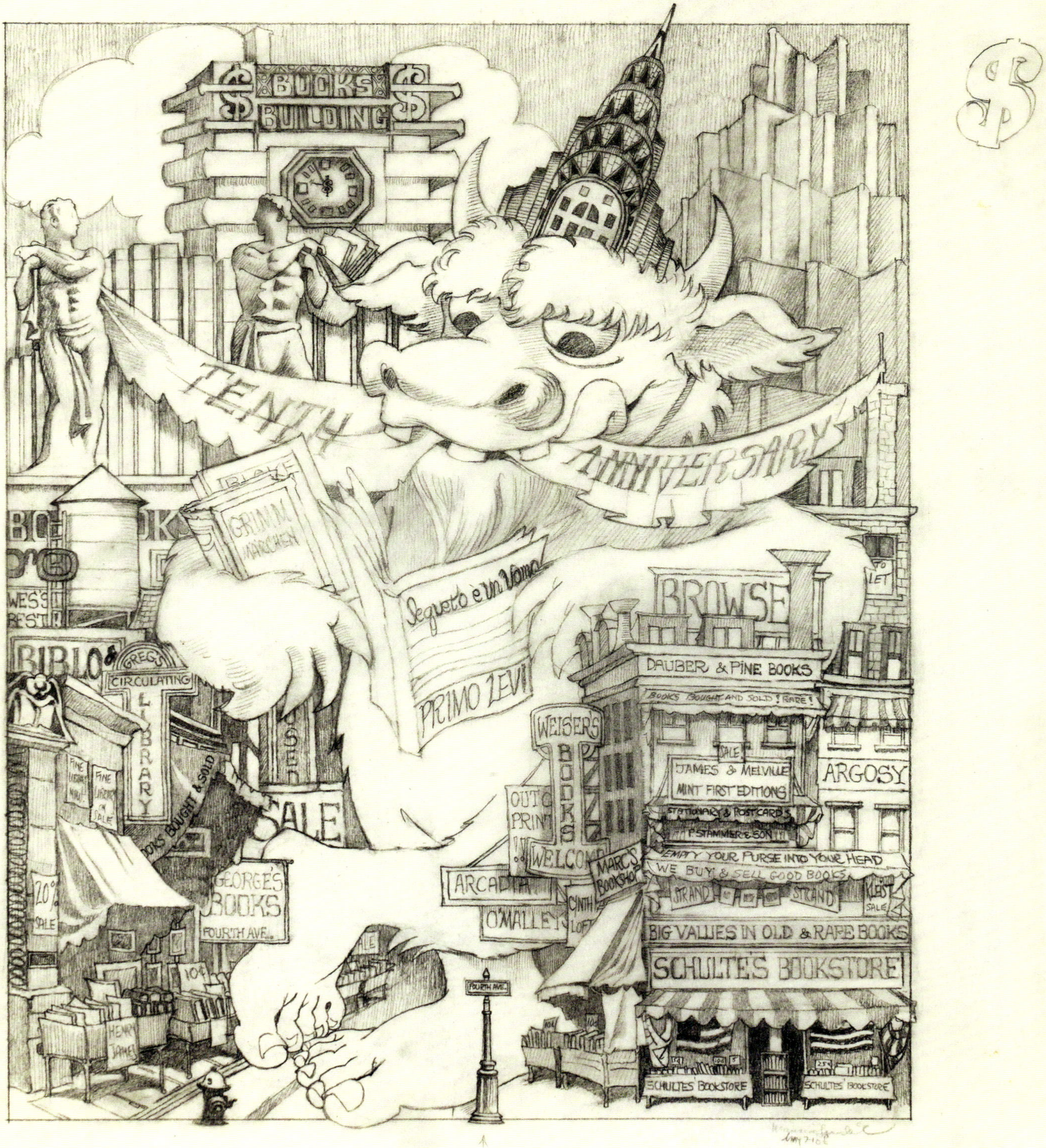

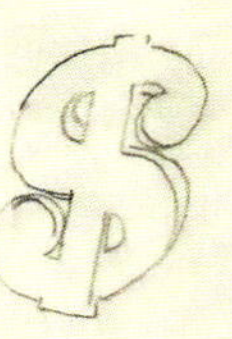

BUCKS BUILDING
TENTH ANNIVERSARY
GRIMM MÄRCHEN
PRIMO LEVI
BIBLO &
GREG'S CIRCULATING LIBRARY
BROWSE
TO LET
DAUBER & PINE BOOKS
BOOKS BOUGHT AND SOLD! RARE!
SALE
JAMES & MELVILLE MINT FIRST EDITIONS
ARGOSY
WEISER'S BOOKS
WELCOME
MARC'S BOOKSHOP
ARCADIA
O'MALLEY
GEORGE'S BOOKS FOURTH AVE.
EMPTY YOUR PURSE INTO YOUR HEAD
WE BUY & SELL GOOD BOOKS
STRAND
STRAND
BIG VALUES IN OLD & RARE BOOKS
SCHULTE'S BOOKSTORE
FOURTH AVE.
SCHULTES' BOOKSTORE
SCHULTES' BOOKSTORE
HENRY JAMES
10¢
20% SALE

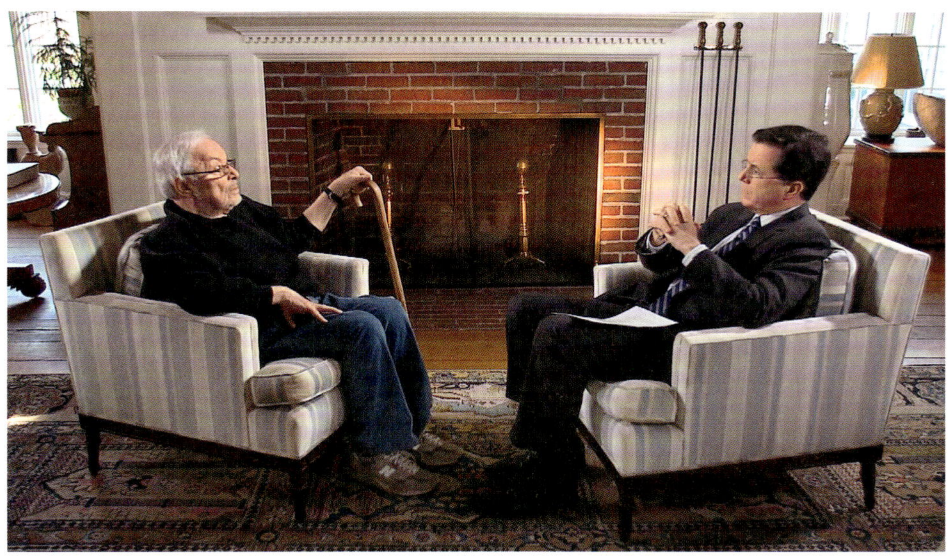

Maurice Sendak and Stephen Colbert, 2012 © copyright Comedy Central

through this figurative jungle of communication choices."[3] Jim Ritterhoff and Tony Kobylinski, creative directors at the advertising firm, The Lord Group, suggested Bell Atlantic clip their terrible claws to become synonymous with Maurice Sendak's gentle giants. After approaching the artist, they pitched putting *Wild Things* into a series of Bell Atlantic advertisements. What emerged was the "Wild Things Are Happening" campaign: a series of posters, billboards, and animated commercials.

A sense of what Sendak and The Lord Group accomplished is revealed by watching a commercial by competitor, Comm South Telephone (1998).[4] It's an assault: a pantomimic narrator yelling numbers and pitching deals, while lurid dollar signs bounce on and off screen. In contrast, "Wild Things Are Happening" avoids such desperate frenetic energy. Instead of bombastic technical jargon you hear waves lap, monkeys whoop, a Wild Thing murmur. A child sails frothing seas towards a tropical island, where he is greeted by Moishe, and led by the hand through a lush jungle, passing gleaming fruits, and employing a snake to traverse a ravine. Finally, James Earl Jones announces, "Wild Things Are Happening" and the Bell Atlantic logo reveals itself in the trail of that boy swinging by a vine. This ad evokes a comforting nostalgia and the thrill that we have suddenly been allowed to revisit, even if only fleetingly, the island of the Wild Things.

Though he did not write the scenes, Sendak had control over all the images, and personally drew the storyboard for each cartoon before they were sent to Jonathan Hodgson and finished at his studio in London. Throughout the animation process Sendak sent pencil sketches and alterations to Hodgson, replacing vines with snakes or a girl's drum for a horn, and Hodgson would incorporate those changes into the final animation. In one note Sendak drew a grinning Wild Thing head with the advice that Hodgson should "think Harpo Marx!!!." This hand-drawn animation style was Sendak's favorite. He preferred the likes of Disney's *Pinocchio*, and in his own 1975 *Really Rosie* cartoon, laboriously drew each frame, cell by cell. Likewise, Sendak did the pictures for all the print ads and billboards, and finally realized one of his fantasies when Bell Atlantic commissioned a Wild Things balloon for the Macy's Thanksgiving Day parade. The campaign was a critical success, winning an Effie

opposite: Maurice Sendak, *New York is Book Country*, 1988, pencil on tracing paper, 24 × 19 in.

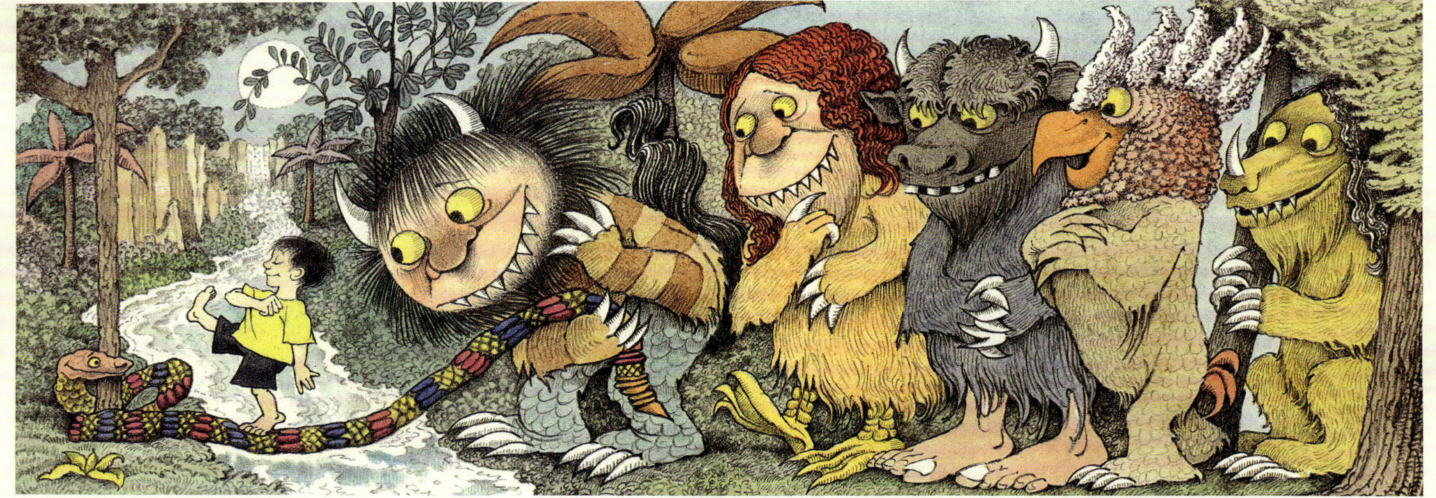

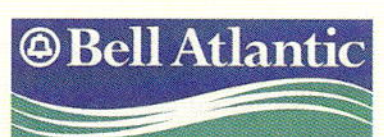

Maurice Sendak, *Wild Things are Happening*, Bell Atlantic, 1997, poster, 24 × 36 in.

award for creative commercials, and Sendak won a Clio award for his innovate pictures in advertisement.

It's not as though a phone company ad targets children. However, the children of the sixties, who were so devoted to the monsters of *Where the Wild Things Are*, had become the adults of the nineties, dazzled by the Bell Atlantic Campaign. But can that campaign realized by Sendak's own hand, beautiful though it was, be called "Where the Wild Things Are II?" Though the ads may seem an addition to the well-loved world, inhabited by familiar characters, they could not possibly constitute a "Where the Wild Things Are II," because Sendak did not write the stories. Indeed, it isn't really plausible to call any of the myriad adaptations and reuses of *Wild Things* sequels.

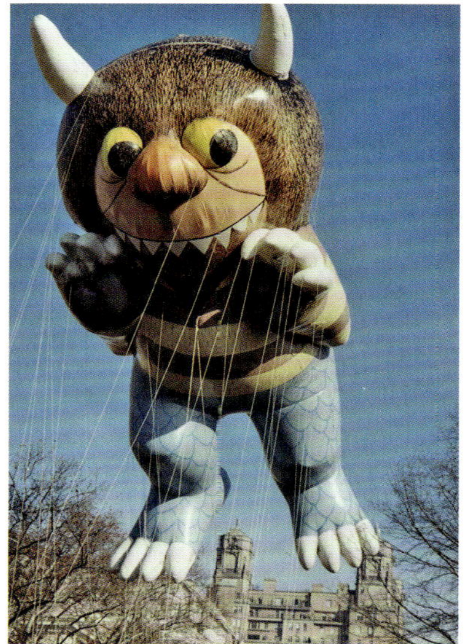

Maurice Sendak, *Where the Wild Things Are*, Macy's Thanksgiving Day Parade Float, 2002

opposite: Maurice Sendak, *Wild Things Are Happening*, Bell Atlantic, 1998, poster, 36 × 21 in.

Wild things are happening.

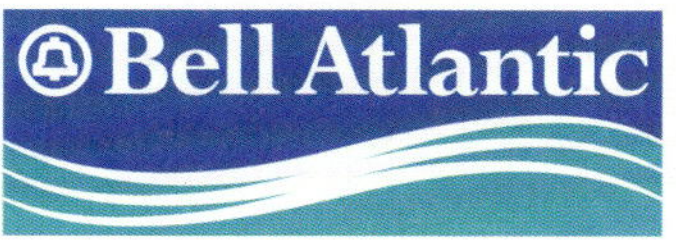

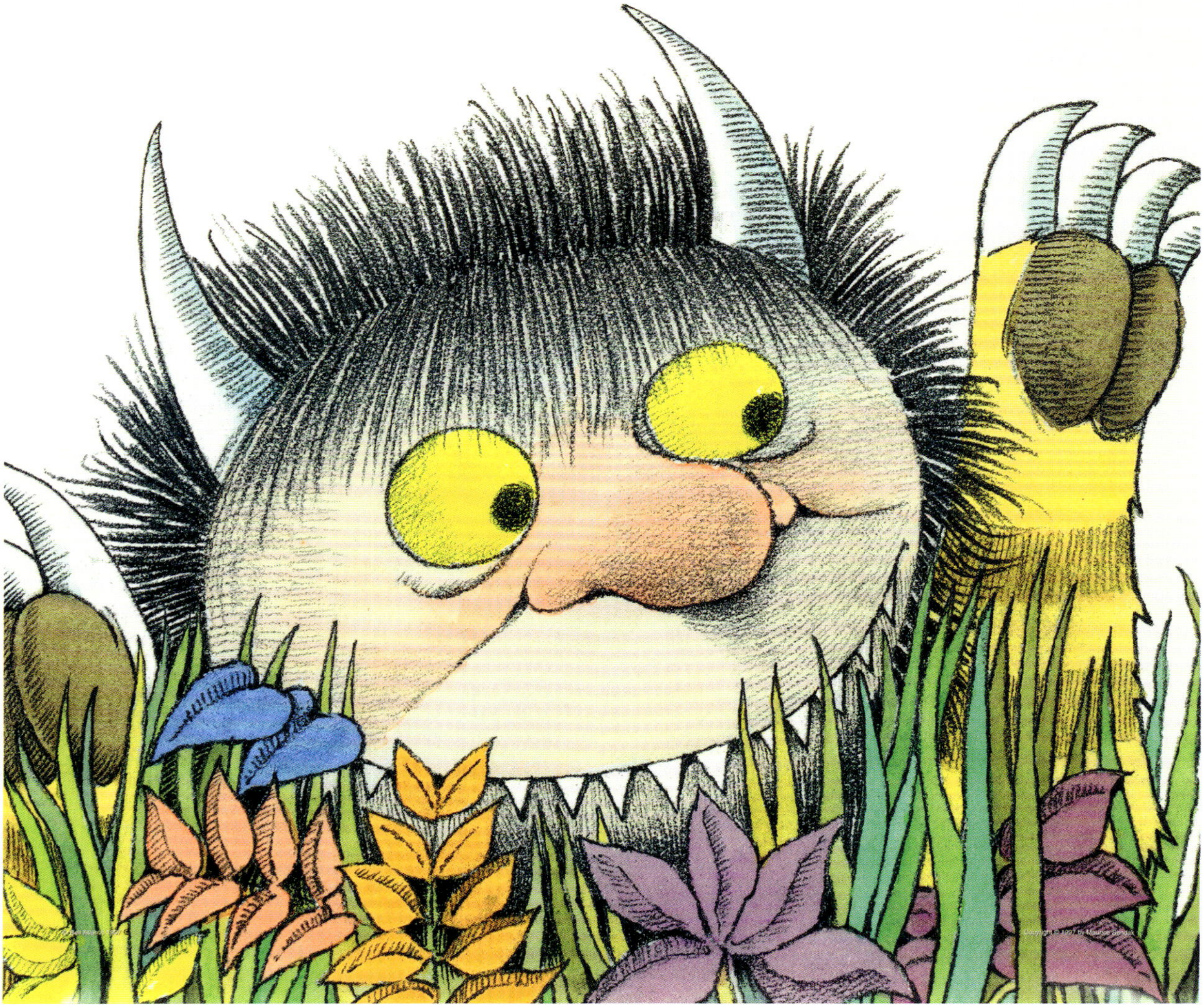

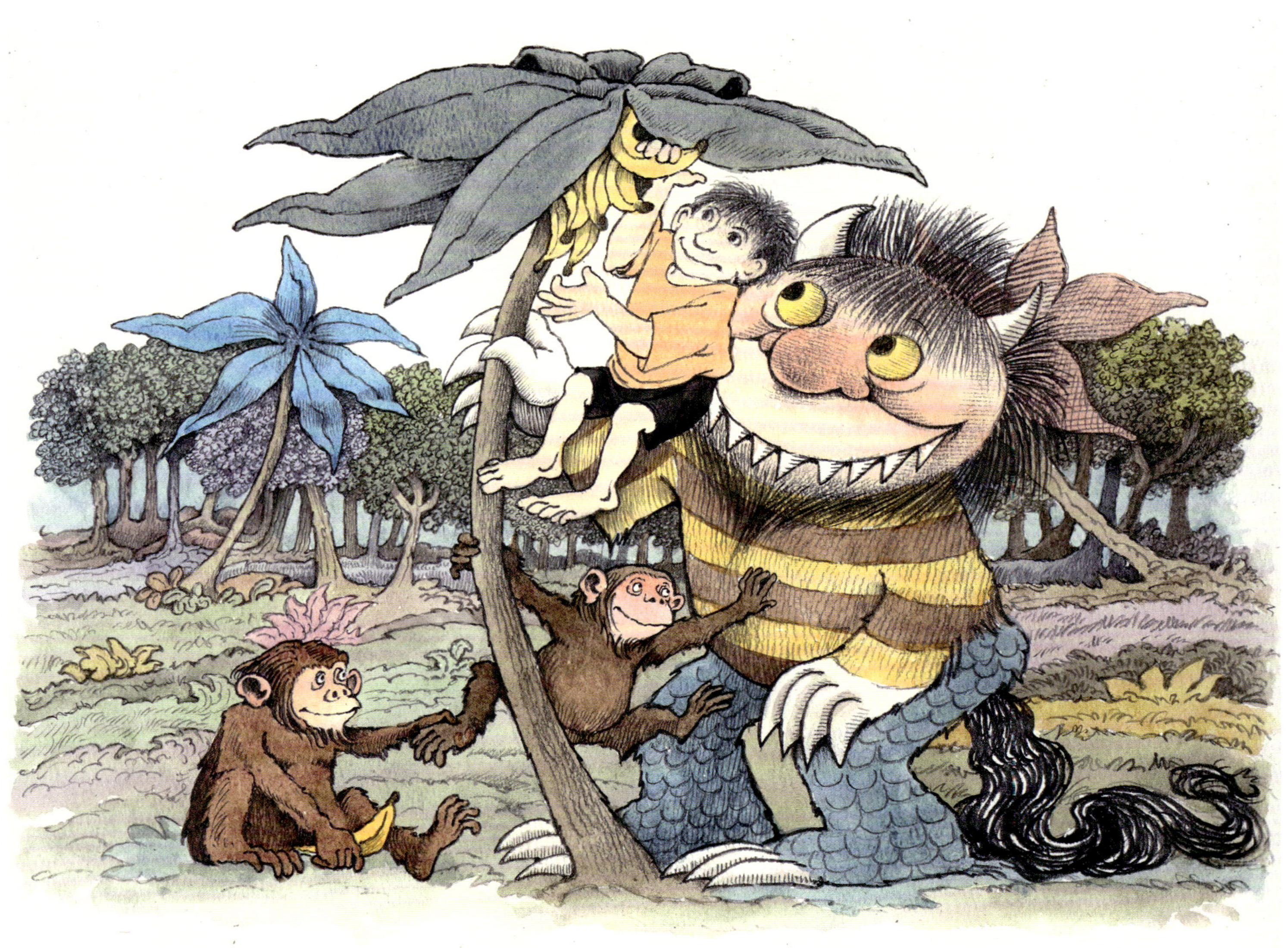

Maurice Sendak, Study for *Wild Things are Happening* Animated Commercial, Bell Atlantic, 1997, watercolor and ink on paper, 7¼ × 10 in., private collection

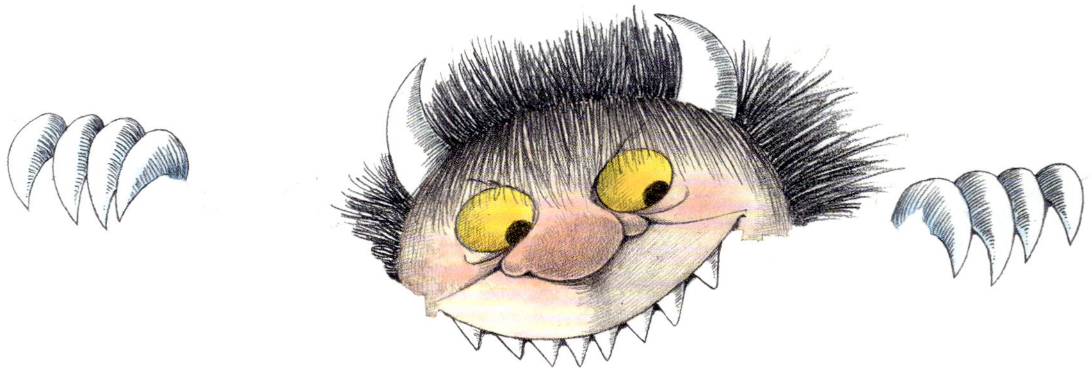

Maurice Sendak, *Wild Things are Happening*, 1997, ink and watercolor on paper, 5⅞ × 16¹⁵⁄₁₆ in., private collection

From the outset, Sendak's Bell Atlantic animations departed stylistically from the book. The color pallet for the animations was expanded: new reds and yellows appeared in a butterfly's wings, pinks and purples in a boomerang tossed into a Wild Thing's mouth. Alligators, monkeys, snakes, and even a UFO appeared in the cartoons, where they never could have in the original. And Max was nowhere to be seen. While Sendak's books were not made specifically for children, a Bell Atlantic phone advertisement was most certainly made for an adult audience by a mature artist. Despite the tropical-island setting, it is no vacation resort. Sendak's rigorous work ethic is exemplified by the factory line of children making masks. And the boy chomping on an apple, who uses the serpent's body to stride across the ravine before landing safely on the other side, is an allusion to Adam and Eve's fall from grace.

Most telling of all is that in the "Wild Things Are Happening" commercials, the Wild Things never need taming. They simply lead children by the hand, without any threat or protest; though they may roar, they are never terrifying. Instead, the Wild Things serve a function. They are bent into a promotional narrative to establish a connection between the frightening yet benevolent beasts and an intimidating mega corporation. From the start, the advertisements were an interpretation of what the Wild Things are, what they represent, and what they mean to generations of fans. Yet the very fact that Sendak didn't consider them an extension of Max's story allowed him to experiment with new possibilities and a new palette. What would more children of different genders and ethnicities do on the island? What else happens there? It's like a lucid dream in which Sendak can color a familiar landscape in the shades of some thirty years of experience, all without ever actually setting foot where the Wild Things are.

Notes

1. Stephen Colbert, Interview with Maurice Sendak, *The Colbert Report*, 24 January 2012.
2. Thomson, Sedge, Interview with Maurice Sendak. City Arts and Lectures Radio Program, 7 December 1987.
3. "New Bell Atlantic Taps Maurice Sendak", *Verizon News Archives*, 10 August 1997. https://www.verizon.com/about/news/press-releases/new-bell-atlantic-taps-maurice-sendaks accessed on 11 November 2021.
4. Comm South Telephone (1998), YouTube, uploaded by PastMeetsPresent, 6 July 2017, www.YouTube.com/watch?v=uEmwfi1Jt2g.

How to Make a Picture Book

Maurice Sendak's *Hector Protector and As I Went Over the Water*

CLARA NGUYEN

The creation of children's books is a laborious, detail-oriented, and demanding endeavor. Maurice Sendak knew this fact well, utilizing the medium to develop complex worlds in which his characters played out their stories. Drawing on text as the point of inspiration, Sendak extended the meaning of the written word by purposefully interpreting the brief stories in unexpected ways. Rather than illustrating the narrative verbatim, he construed events in nuanced ways by exploring characterization and developing new storylines that are not explicit in the text.

This playful interpretation is readily seen in Sendak's books featuring Mother Goose rhymes, such as the 1965 *Hector Protector and As I Went Over the Water*. In it, Sendak treats the two rhymes as separate visual narratives. The first is brief and vague: "Hector Protector was dressed all in green; Hector Protector was sent to the Queen. The Queen did not like him; No more did the King; So Hector Protector was sent back again." Armed with the text and ideas, Maurice Sendak often began his projects by creating tiny hand-made paper books, dummies in which he would sketch out the major narrative, or he would create a storyboard, with a pane to represent each page. In the case of *Hector Protector and As I Went Over the Water*, he created both and in several variations.

In an early storyboard version, Sendak illustrated Hector Protector, not as the boy of the published book, but as a vain and unkind man who visits the Queen to win her affection. Unsurprisingly, the Queen "did not like him." Aiming for Hector, she unintentionally hits the King on the head with a frying pan and Hector is sent spinning through the air by a kick from a horse. The last image in the sequence shows Hector Protector sporting a bandaged head and foot and tearfully looking at his reflection in a mirror.

In the final dummy book and storyboard version, Hector Protector has become a young boy who rebels against being dressed in green, and who is reluctant to be sent to the Queen with a cake. He meets a lion and a snake on his journey and surprises the Queen sitting on the throne. The story ends with Hector

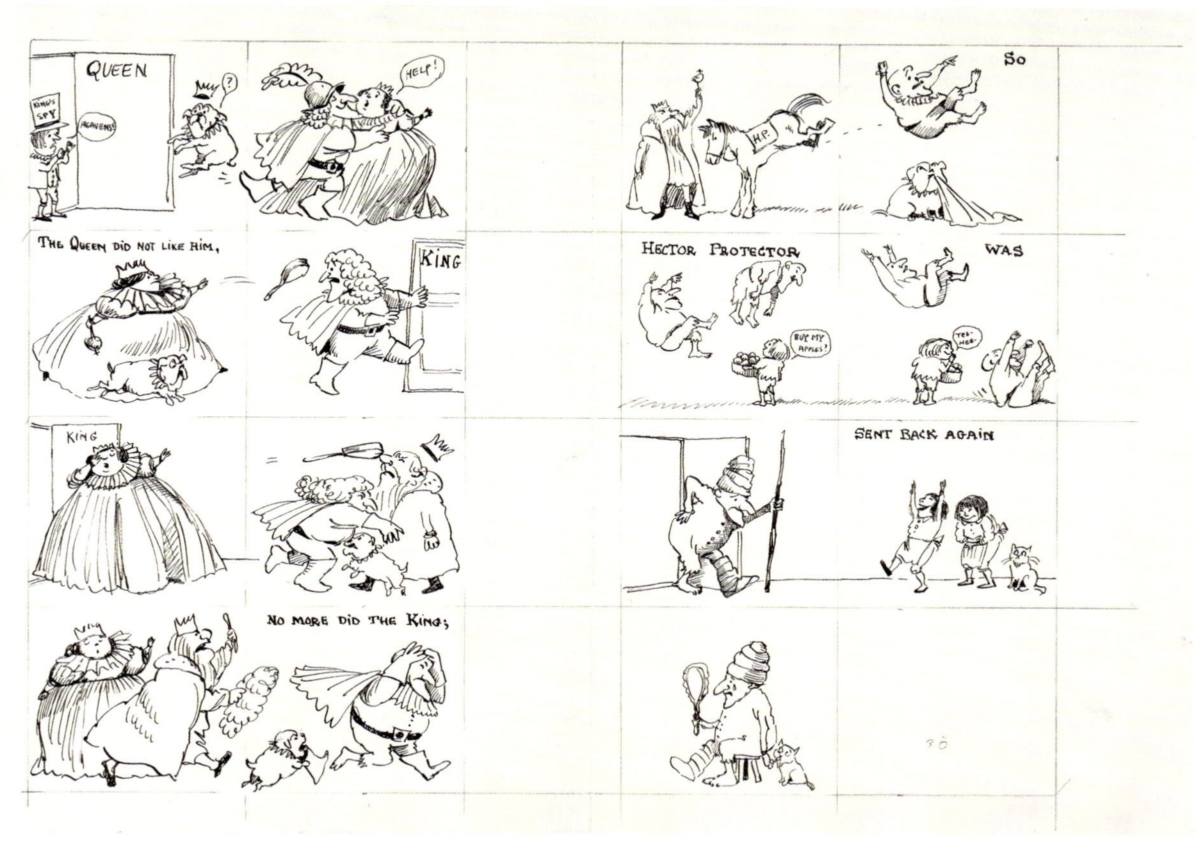

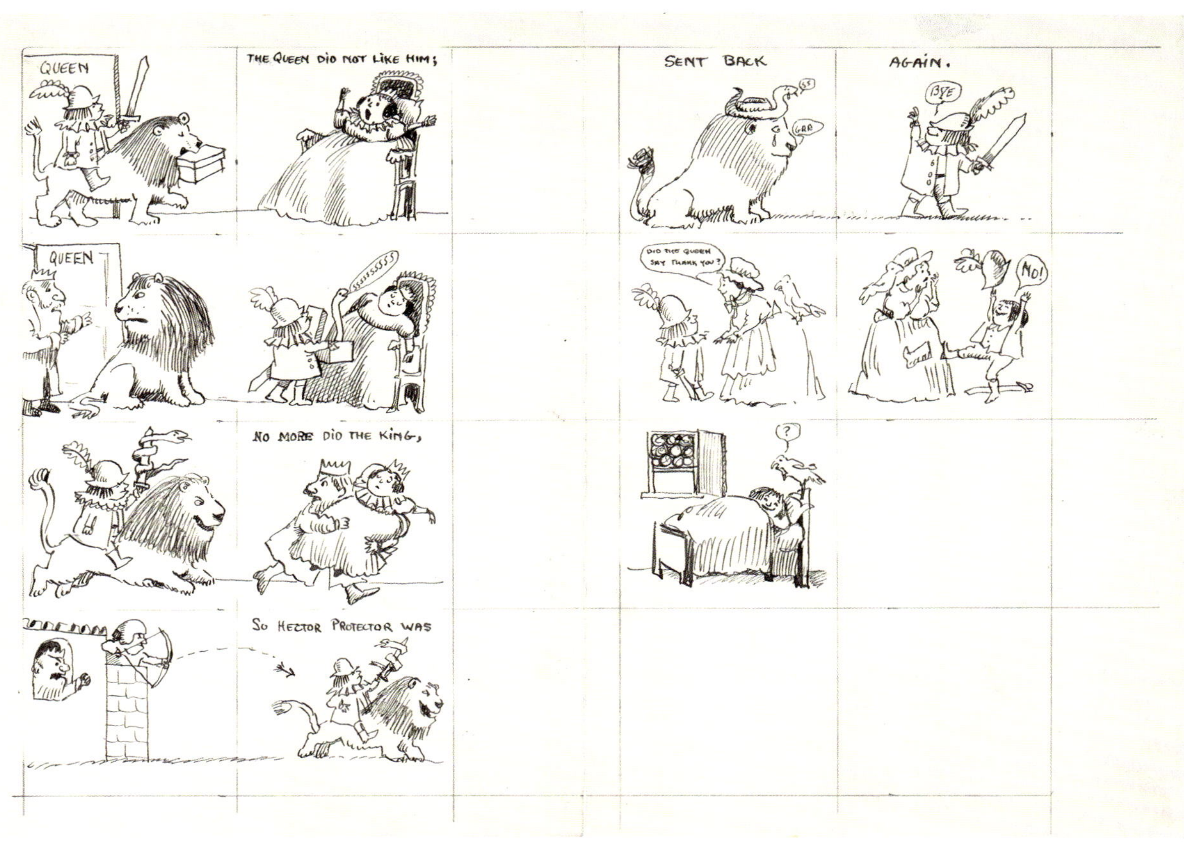

Maurice Sendak, *Hector Protector*, Storyboards, 1965, ink on paper, 8⅞ × 12⅜ in.

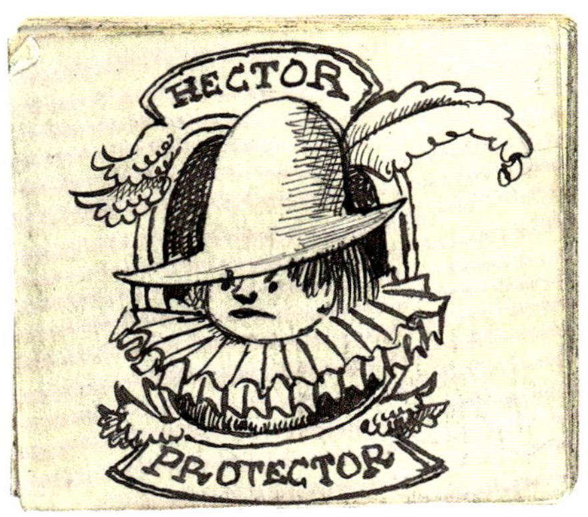

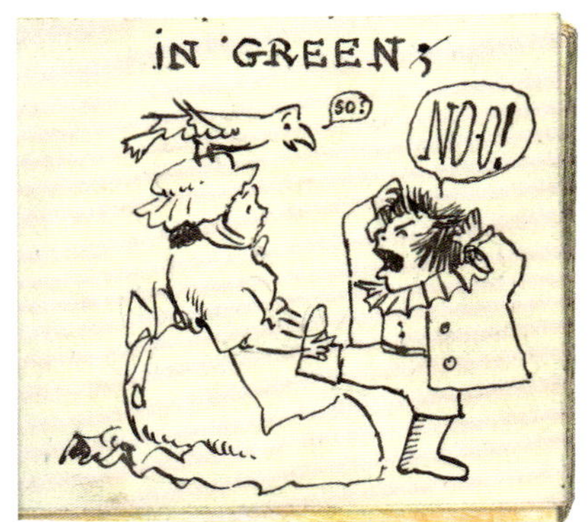

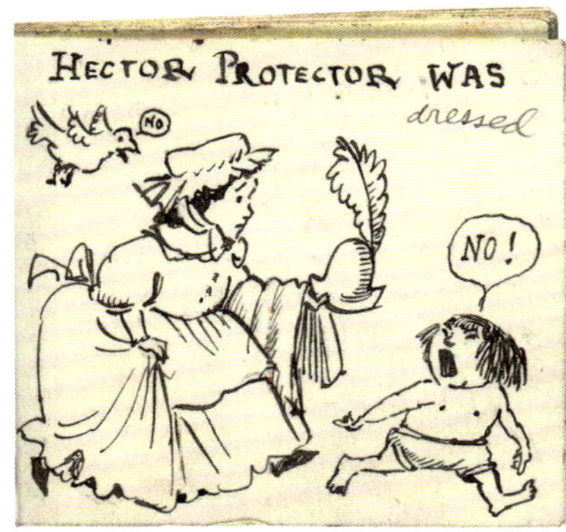

Maurice Sendak, *Hector Protector*, final Dummy book, 1965, watercolor and ink, 2 × 2¼ in.

Protector being sent home to his bed, where he gleefully laughs at the antics of the day. Sendak derived the visual narrative of the finished book from this dummy but in the process of getting there he had explored the merits of two radically different versions from the same rhyme, with each story featuring a unique protagonist on a distinctive journey.

For publication, Sendak illustrated *Hector Protector and As I Went Over the Water* using a method of preseparation. This time-consuming manual technique involved creating two different layers for printing. Sendak employed the process as the result of his dissatisfaction with the initial printing of his 1963 book, *Where the Wild Things Are*. The fine black ink cross-hatching and intense color that are so vivid in the original watercolor paintings appeared muddy in the first edition due to the limitations of mass-market printing at that time. (Fortunately, with all the advancements in color reproduction, the current edition closely captures the original artwork). Hence for *Hector Protector*, Sendak made a black-ink layer outlining shapes and details, and a watercolor layer for the various tones. Consequently, the printed book has greater clarity and brilliance of color. This method underlines how carefully Sendak considered the printing process and how, for him, the printed book was the work of art, not the paintings and drawings on which it was based. He went to great lengths to provide the best images for reproduction and whenever possible he carefully monitored the actual printing of his books as they came off the press. Arguably, this process of separating the black lines from the color influenced Sendak's art. In this instance, by emphasizing the black line Sendak recalls the look and feel of comic strips. He employed the same technique again for *In the Night Kitchen* (1970). It begins with Mickey awaking and ends with him drifting off to sleep—two scenes that clearly duplicate the comic strip format of *Little Nemo* in a direct homage to American cartoonist Winsor McCay.

Sendak had utilized preseperation previously as a means of bringing color to his books while keeping them affordable.[1] For *Little Bear* and *Very Far Away*,

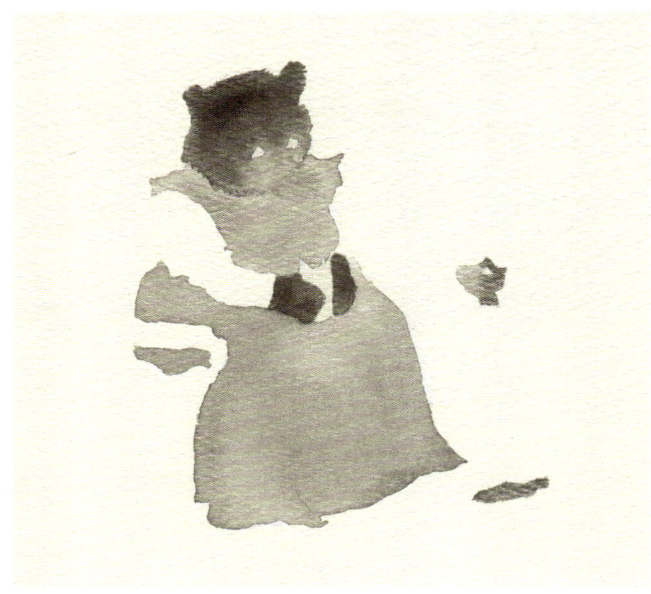

Maurice Sendak, *Little Bear* color separation (detail), 1957, ink on paper, 11⅛ × 8¼ in.

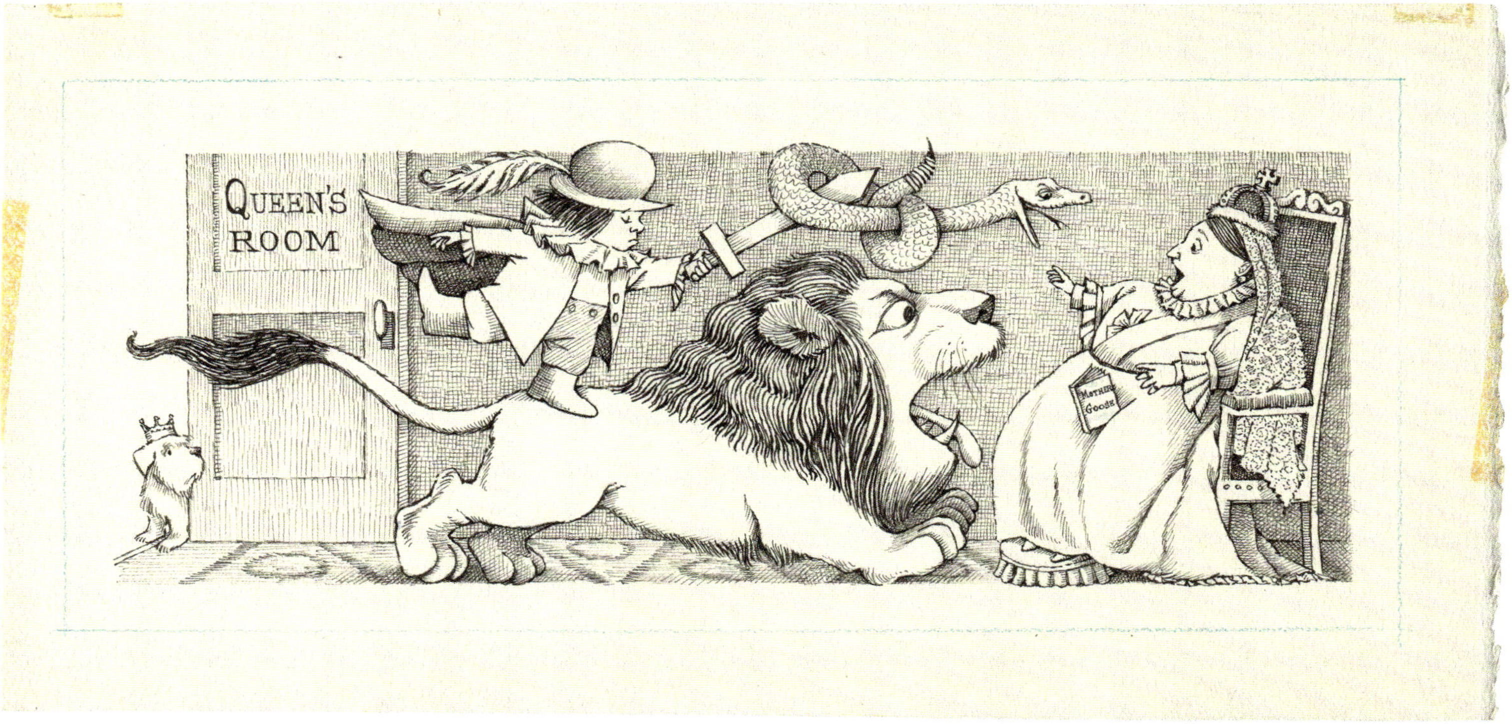

Maurice Sendak, *Hector Protector*, 1965, ink on paper, 7½ × 18¾ in.

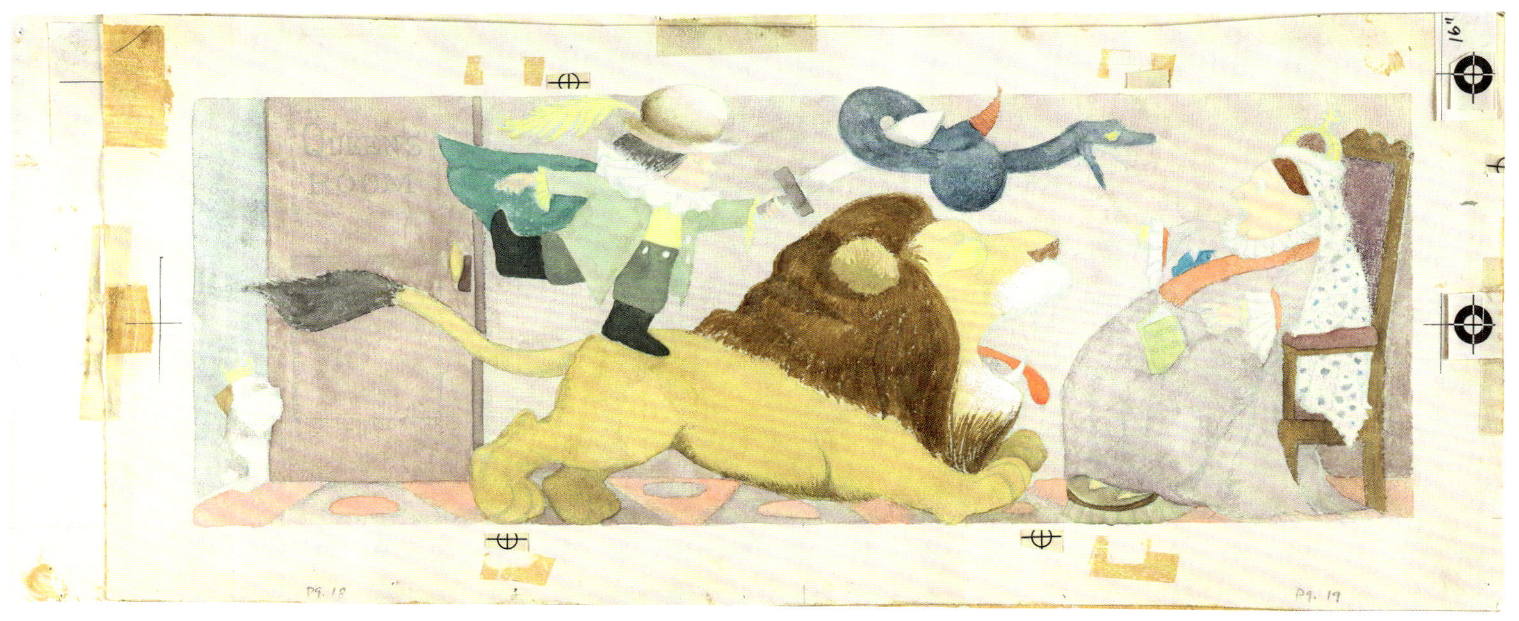

Maurice Sendak, *Hector Protector* color separation, 1965, watercolor and ink, 7½ × 18¾ in.

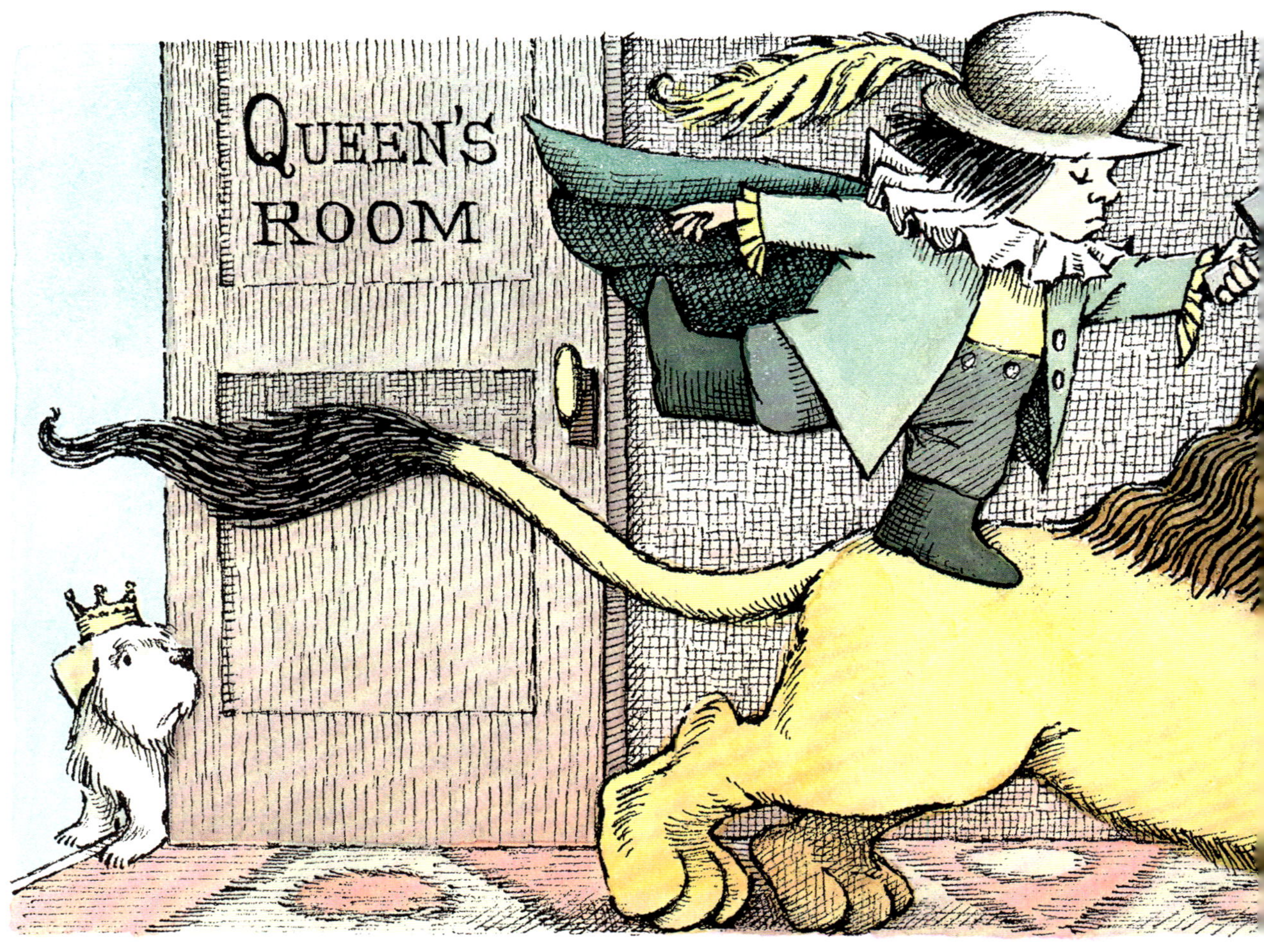

both of which were published in 1957, he created individual layers for each color. The process required that all the overlays were prepared in black and then printed in the different colors, such as the tan of *Very Far Away*, or the blue, yellow, and brown of *Little Bear*. This technique is particularly difficult as it demands that the artist must visualize the color scheme of the final ensemble but make each layer in shades of grey. By the time of the publication of *Outside Over There* in 1981, and all Sendak's later books, advances in color printing had made the earlier techniques unnecessary. Sendak cared deeply about making the final book look as good as possible, given the limitations of mass-market printing. To him, the quality of the reproduction outweighed the need to capture an exact color match to the original artwork.[2]

In 1965, just as he was creating *Hector Protector*, Maurice Sendak penned an essay on Mother Goose. He writes,

> If full measure of the rhymes isn't taken in the pictures, then the artist has failed Mother Goose. And her revenge is swift, for no other writing I know of so swiftly exposes the illustrator's strengths and inadequacies. So it is with trepidation that the artist must confront this formidable muse.[3]

From Hector Protector, he went on to illustrate *Higglety Pigglety Pop! Or There Must Be More To Life* (1967) and *We Are All in the Dumps with Jack and Guy* (1993). In these books, once again Mother

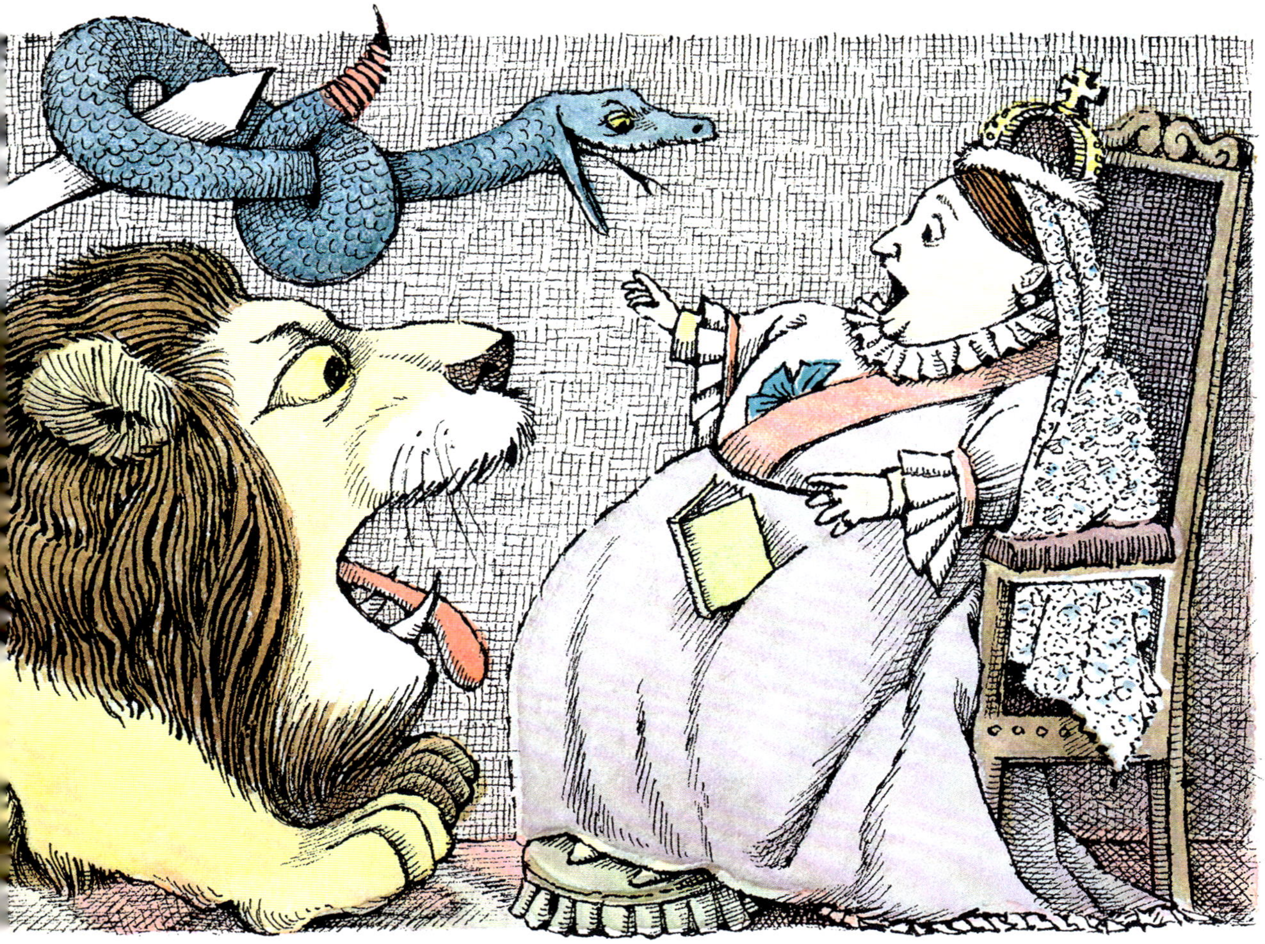

Maurice Sendak, *Hector Protector and As I Went Over the Water* (New York: Harper & Row, 1965)

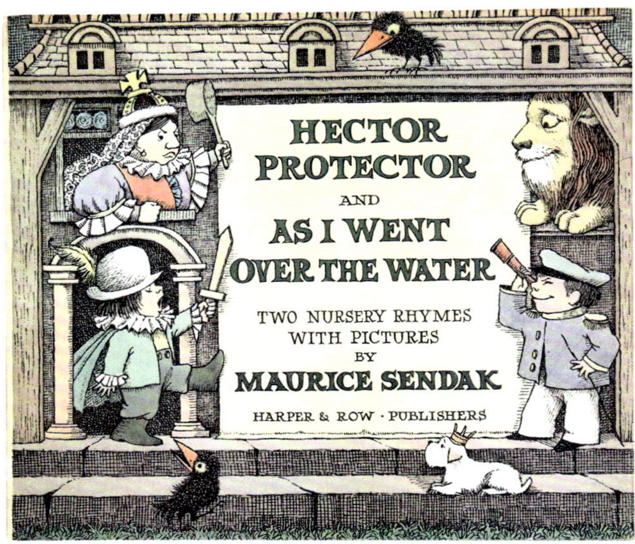

Maurice Sendak, *Hector Protector and As I Went Over the Water* (New York: Harper & Row, 1965)

Goose rhymes provide the backbone of the stories, but his treatment of the narratives is significantly more serious, reflecting on personal fulfillment and social issues such as poverty and hunger.[4] And Mother Goose rhymes also crept into his teaching practice. Due to their ambiguity and open interpretation, he liked to assign them as an illustration exercise for his students.[5] In each one of his projects Sendak's imaginative interpretation turns anticipated narratives upside down. By imbuing the imagery with liveliness and musicality, he captivates the viewer with his own particular brand of humor, while at the same time enriching the tales with profound significance.

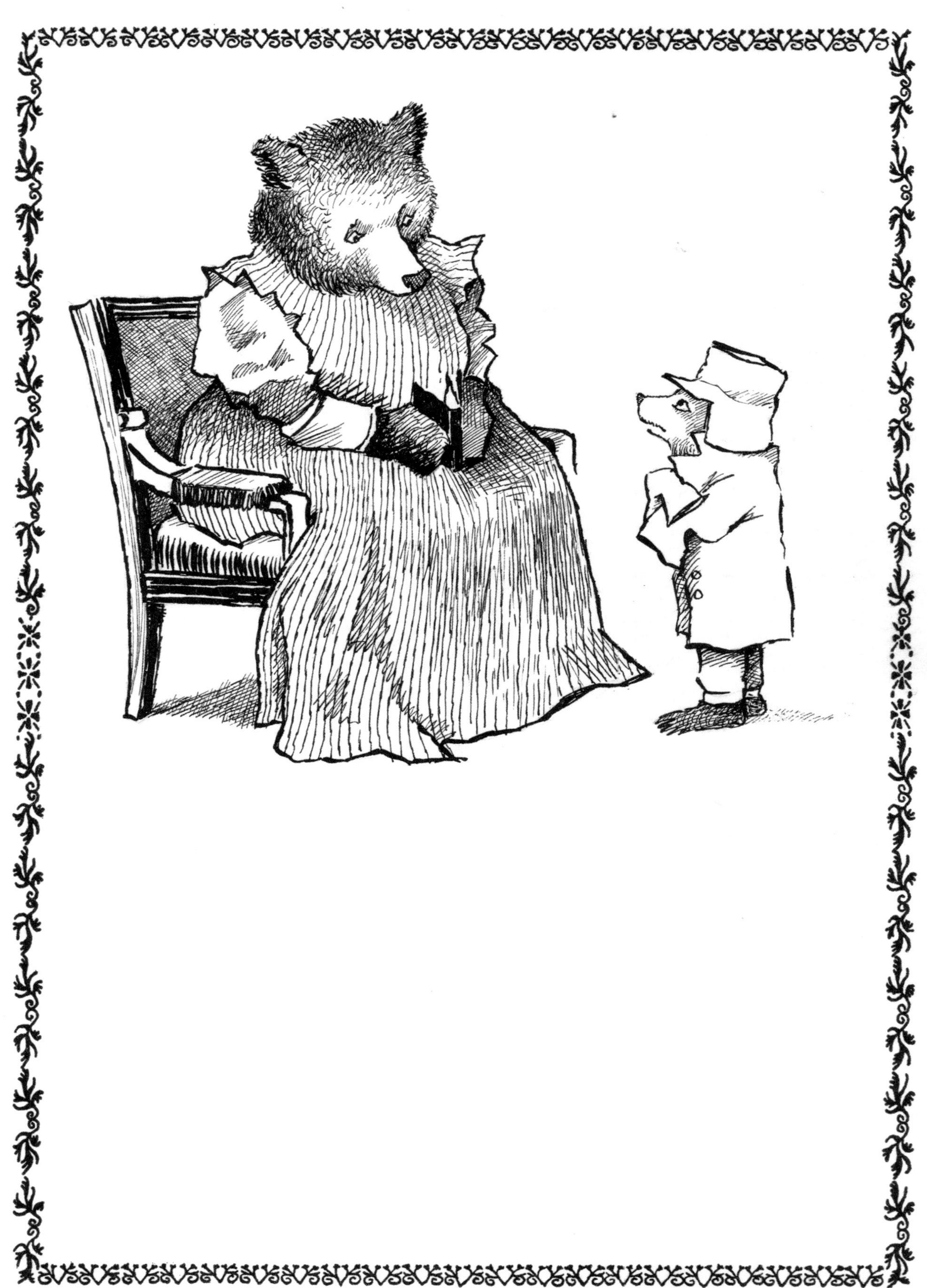

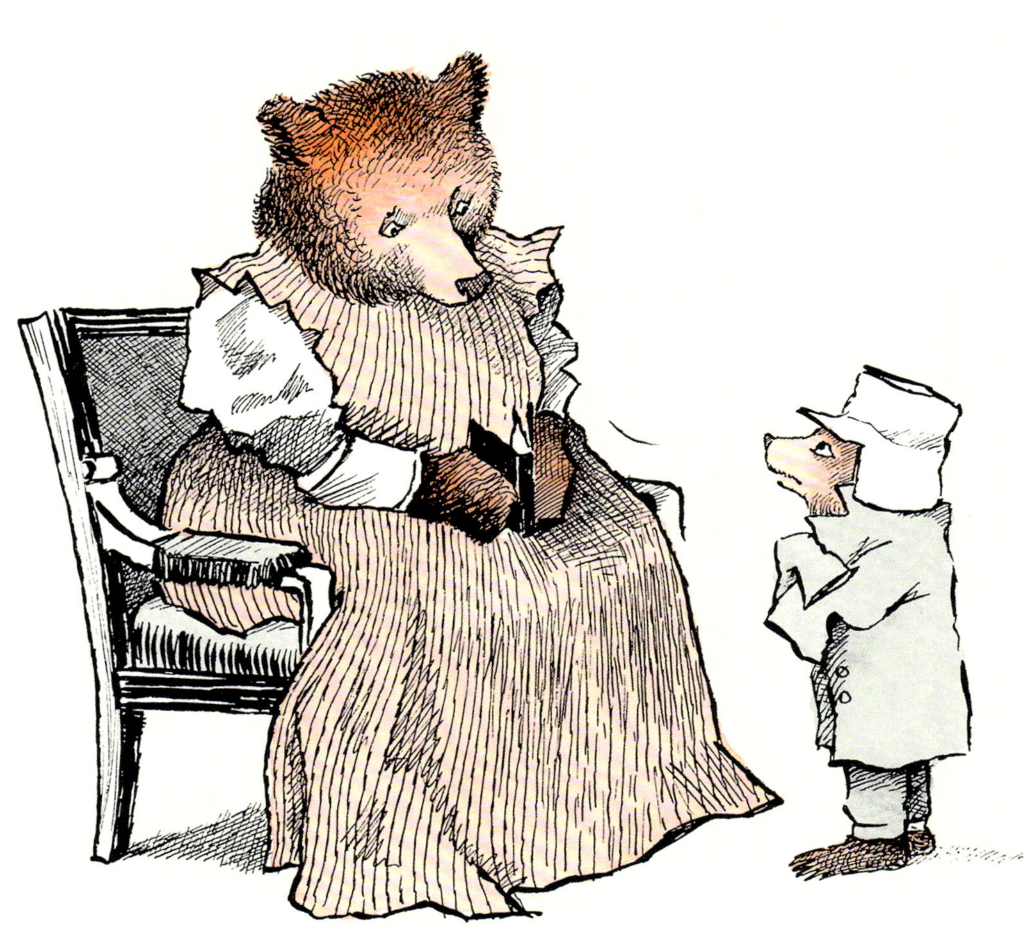

Maurice Sendak, *Little Bear*, ink on paper and watercolor wash, as printed in color in Else Holmelund Minarik *Little Bear*, pictures by Maurice Sendak (New York: Harper & Row, 1957)

Notes

1. Uri Schulevitz, *Writing with Pictures: How to Write and Illustrate Children's Books* (New York: Watson-Guptill Publications, 1985), 216–18.
2. Lynn Caponera (Executive Director of The Maurice Sendak Foundation) in discussion with author, December 2021.
3. Maurice Sendak, "Mother Goose," *Book Week, The Sunday Herald Tribune*, 31 October 1965, reprinted in Maurice Sendak, *Caldecott & Co.* (New York: Michael di Capua Books, Farrar, Straus and Giroux, 1988), 14.
4. Clara Nguyen. "Imagining Mother Goose: Exploring Maurice Sendak's Visual Interpretation of Nursery Rhymes" (Feb. 2021–Jan. 2022). https://lib.uconn.edu/sendakcollection/exhibitions/2/ (accessed December 9, 2021).
5. Jonathan Weinberg (Curator and Director of Research of The Maurice Sendak Foundation) in discussion with author, December 2021.

opposite: Maurice Sendak, *Little Bear*, 1957, ink on paper, 11 × 8½ in.

"If any name deserves to be permanently joined with that of Mother Goose, it is Randolph Caldecott. His picture books should be among the first volumes given to every child."

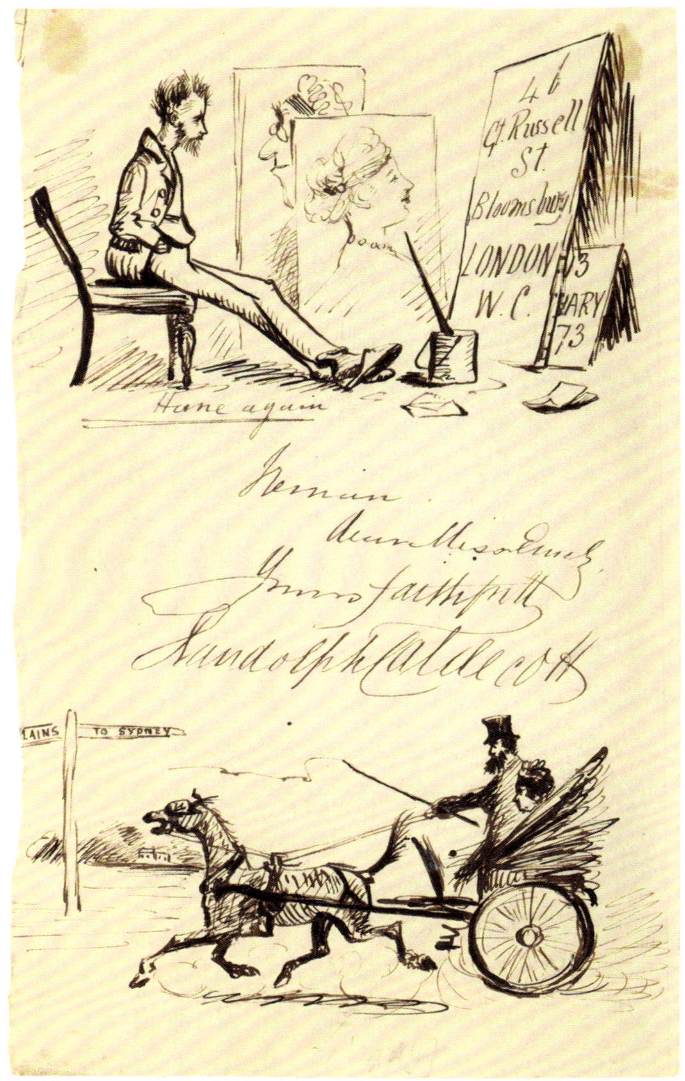

Randolph Caldecott, *Letter to a Friend*, 1873, ink on paper

opposite: Maurice Sendak, *The Horn Book Magazine* (poster version of the cover design for the magazine, depicting Randolph Caldecott sketching, with a Sendak Wild Thing, and some of Caldecott's own beloved characters), 1985, offset lithograph, 24⅛ × 16⅓ in.

The Horn Book

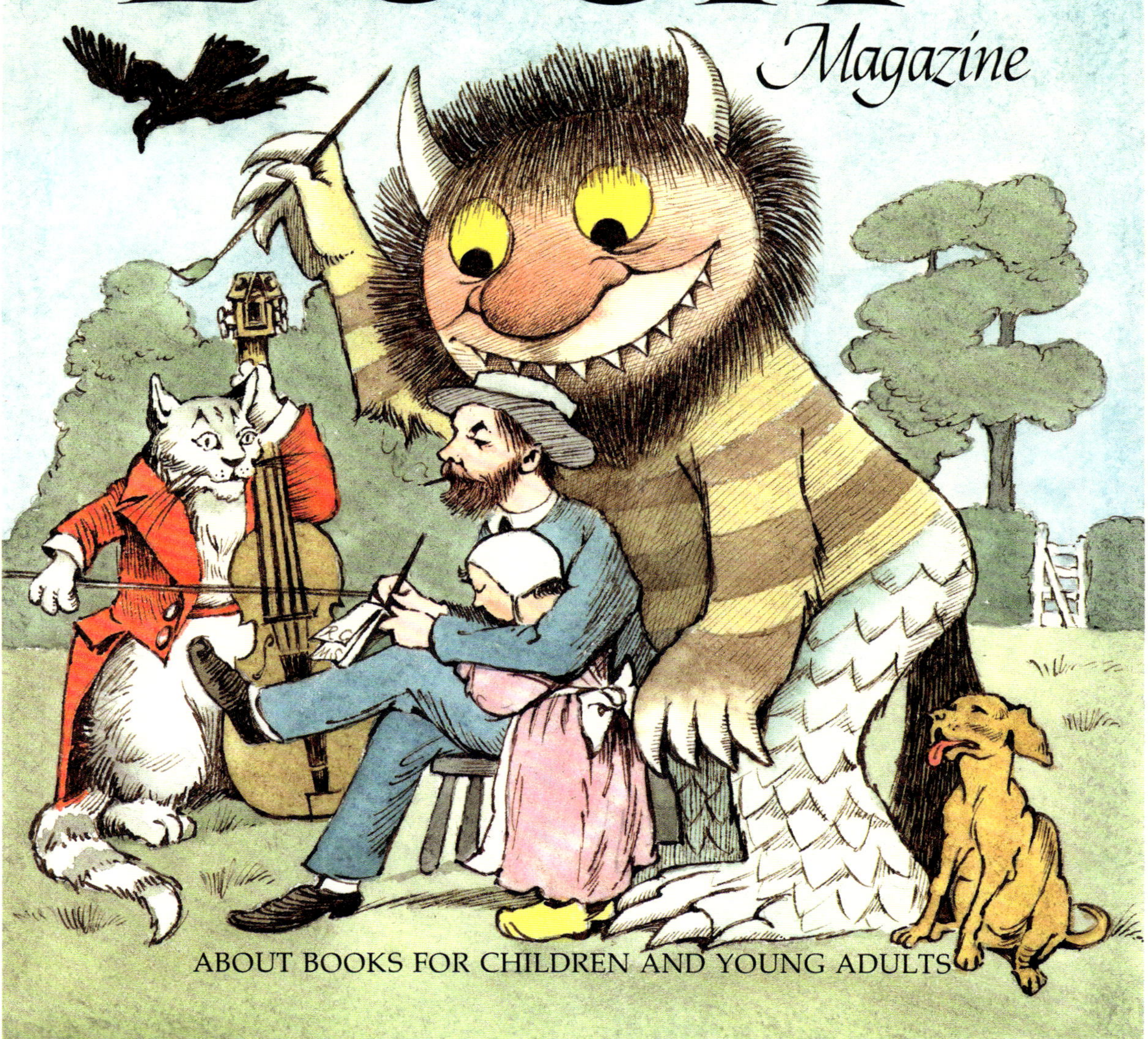

Higglety, Pigglety, Pop!
or There Must Be More to Life

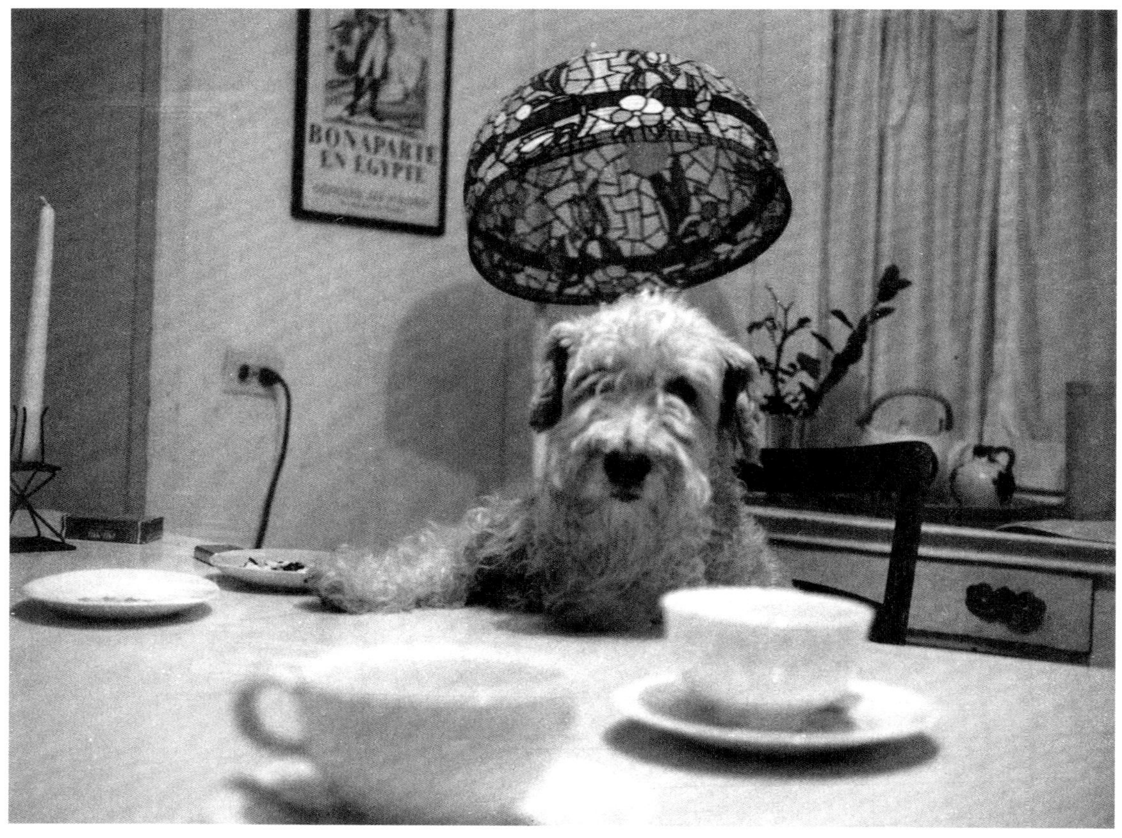

Maurice Sendak, source photograph for *Higglety, Pigglety, Pop!*, 16 August 1966

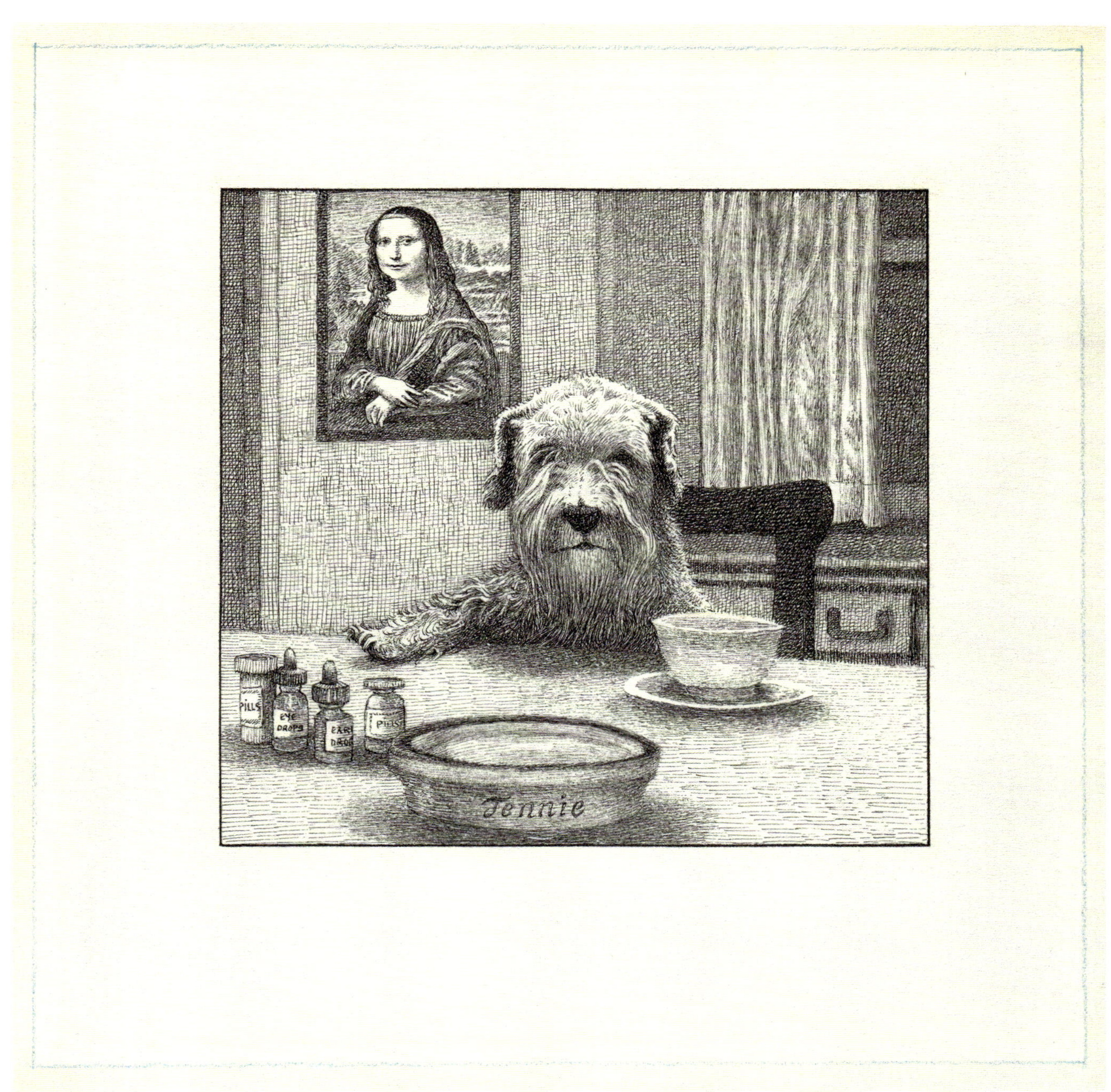

Maurice Sendak, *Jennie, Higglety, Pigglety, Pop!*, 1967, ink on paper, 11½ × 9 in.

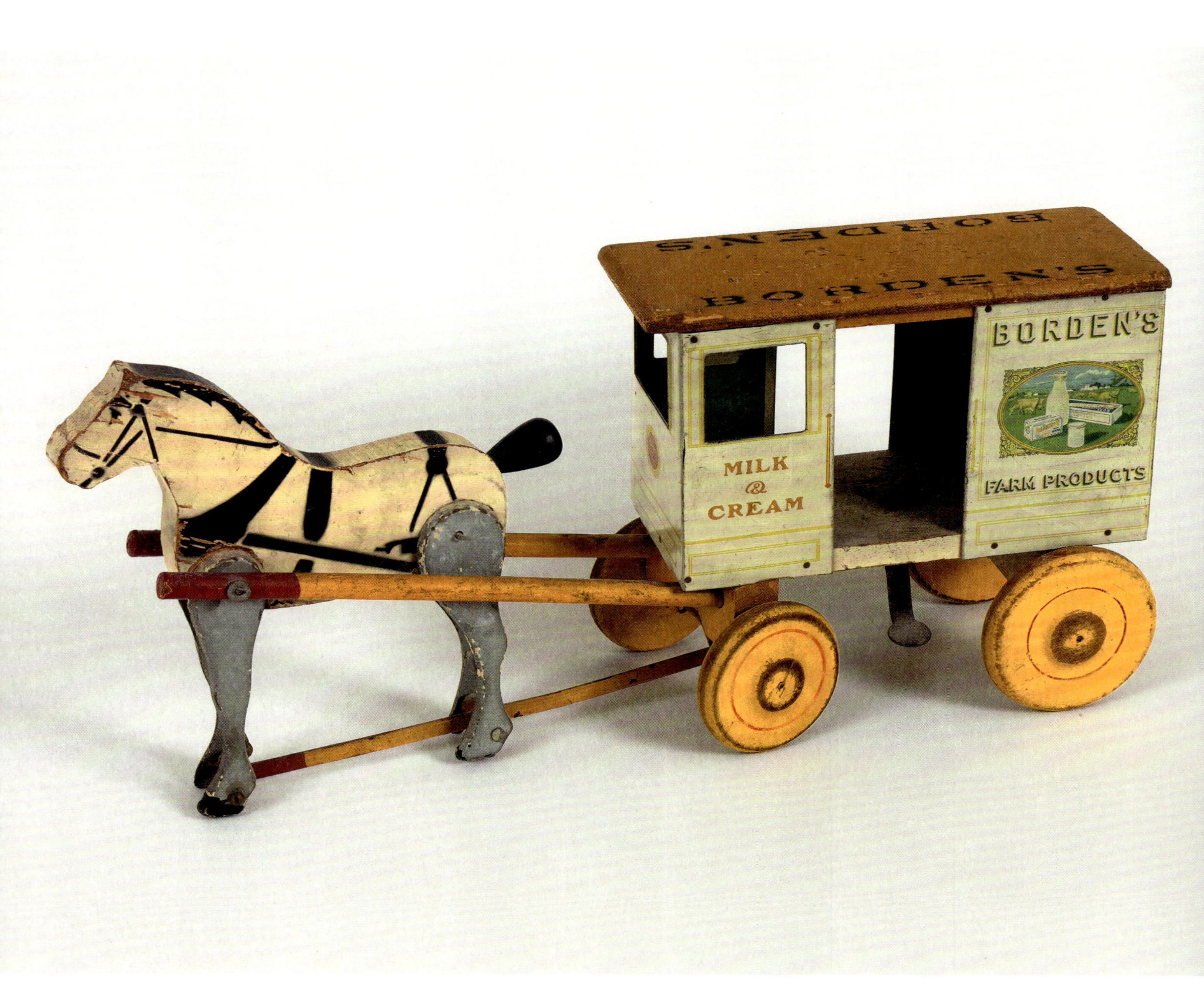

Borden's Milk Truck Toy, c. 1930, 8¼ h × 19½ l × 3½ in.

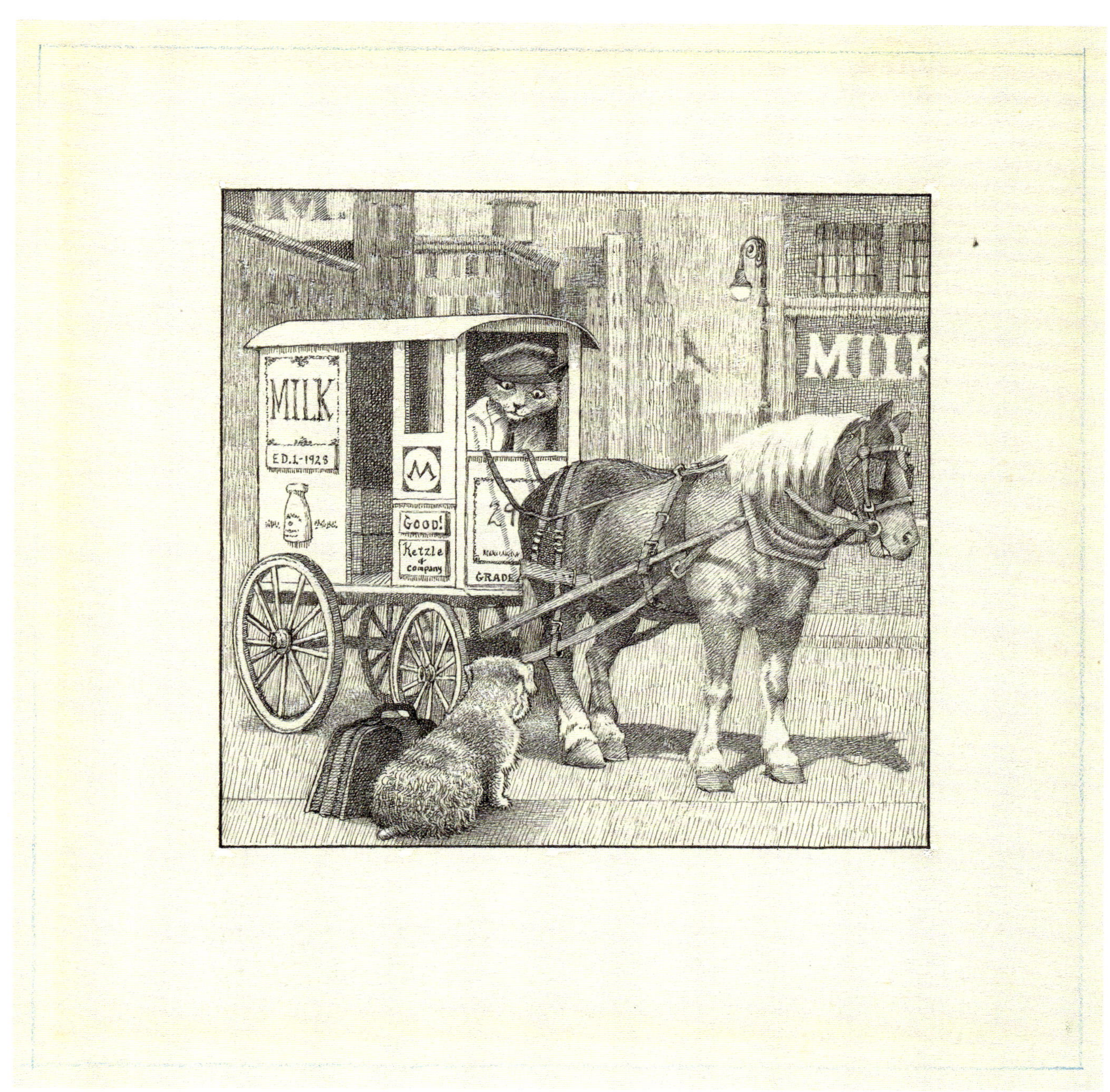

Maurice Sendak, *Higglety Pigglety Pop! or There Must Be More to Life*, 1967, ink on paper, 11½ × 9 in.

"I wrote it when Jennie was getting old, and I was afraid she was going to die. Somehow it was easier to work up an anxiety about the dog's dying than about my mother, because that was just too much to go for. Then, when the book was finished, I went to England and had my coronary."

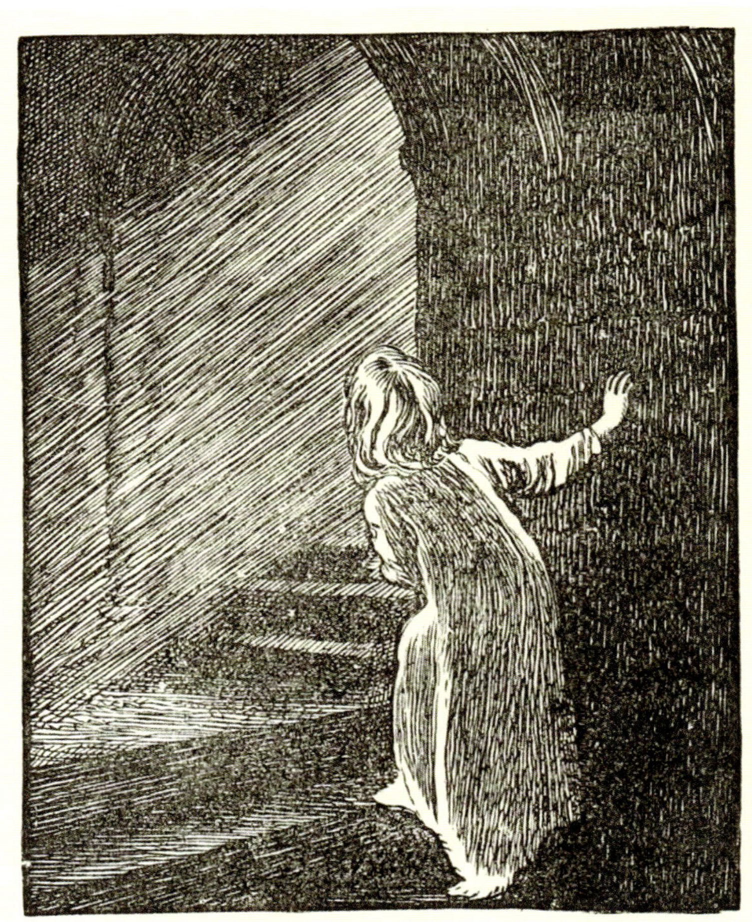

Arthur Hughes, illustration for George MacDonald, *The Princess and the Goblin* (London: Strahan & Co., 1872), p. 112

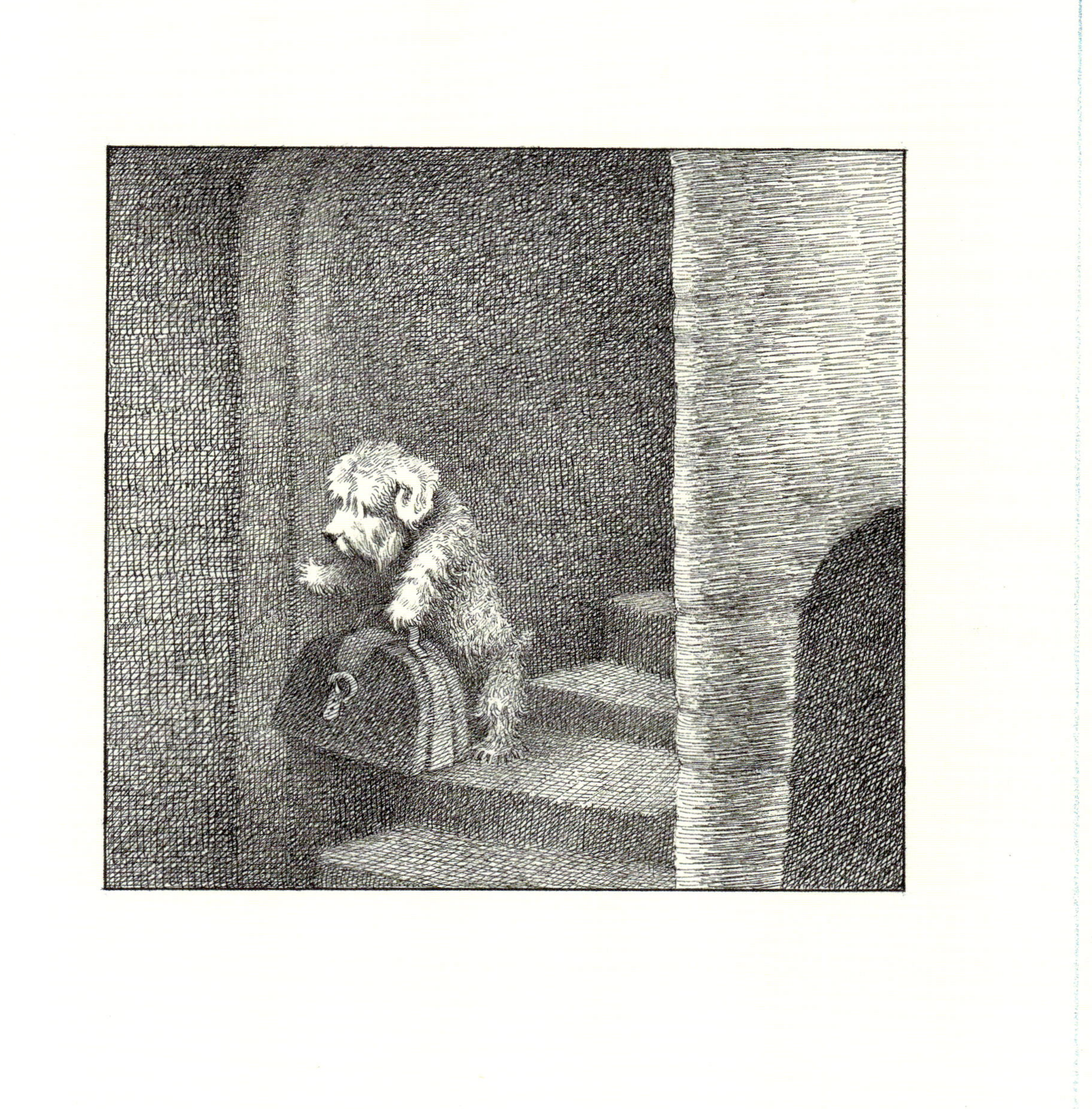

Maurice Sendak, *Higglety Pigglety Pop!*, 1967, ink on paper, 11½ × 9 in.

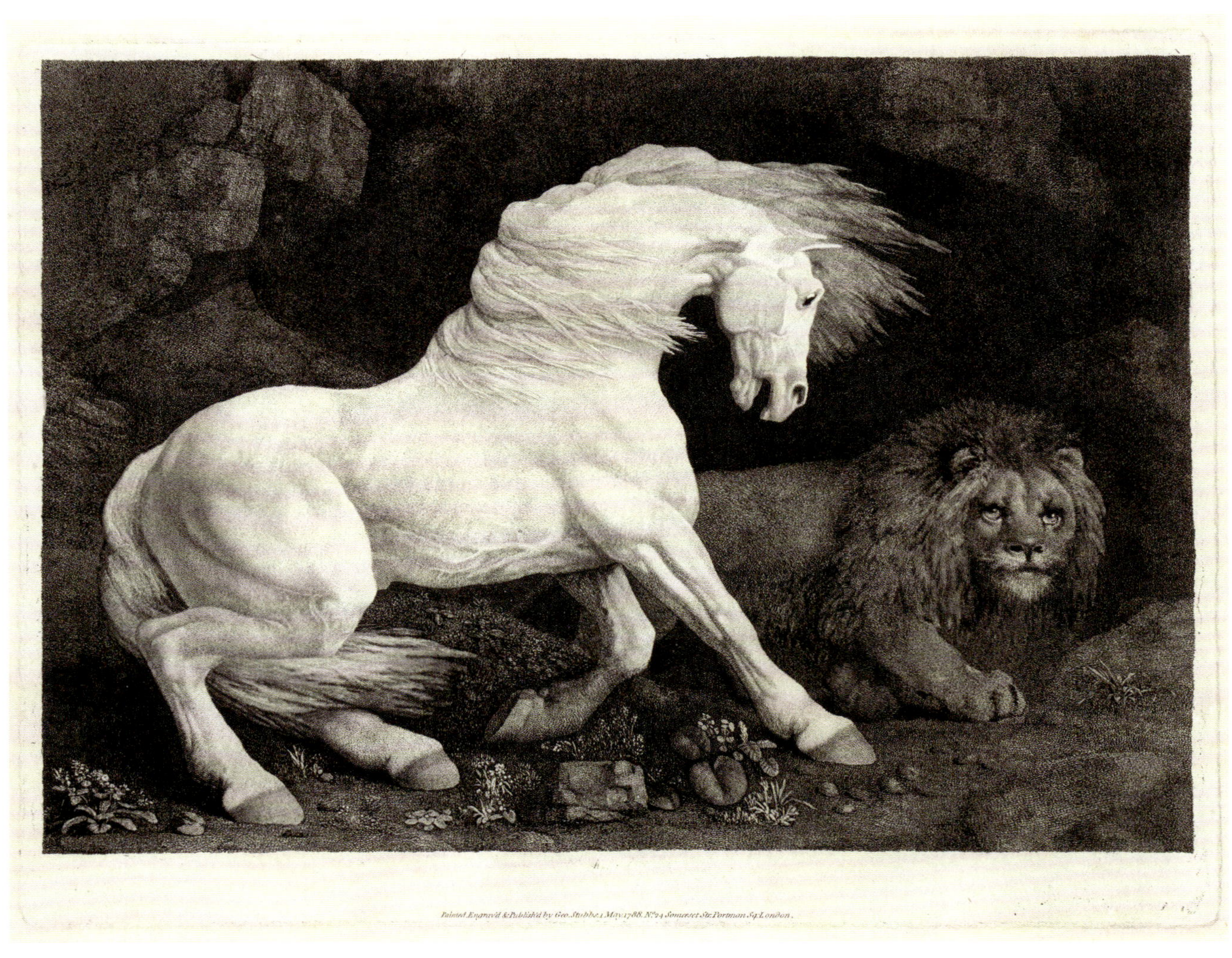

George Stubbs, *A Horse Frightened by a Lion*, 1788, mixed method engraving, 9¾ × 13 in.

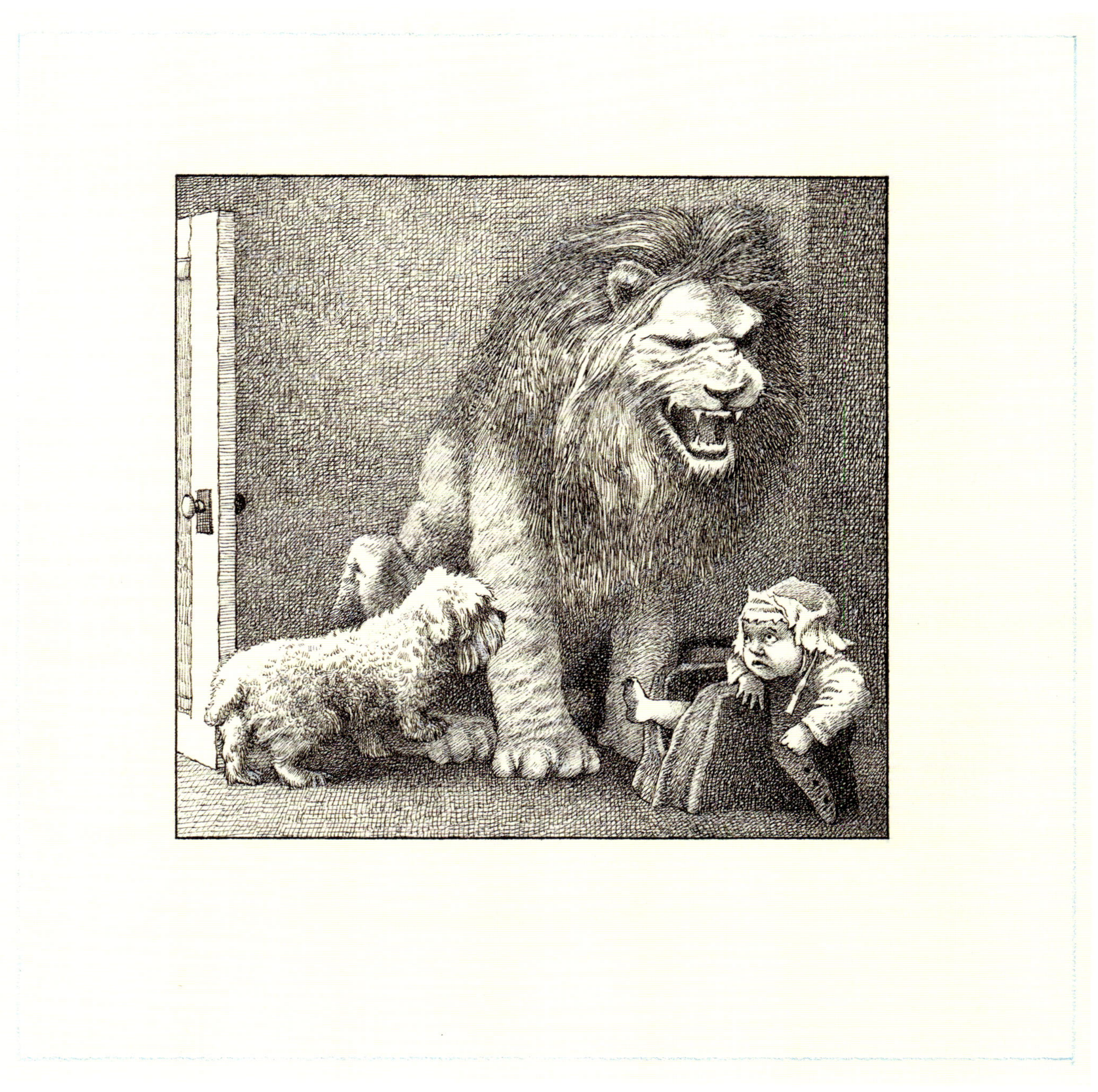

Maurice Sendak, *Higglety Pigglety Pop!*, 1967, ink on paper, 11½ × 9 in.

HIGGLETY-PIGGLETY POP!

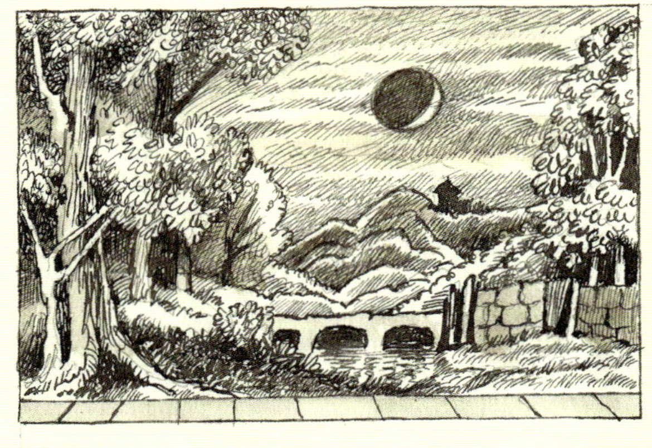

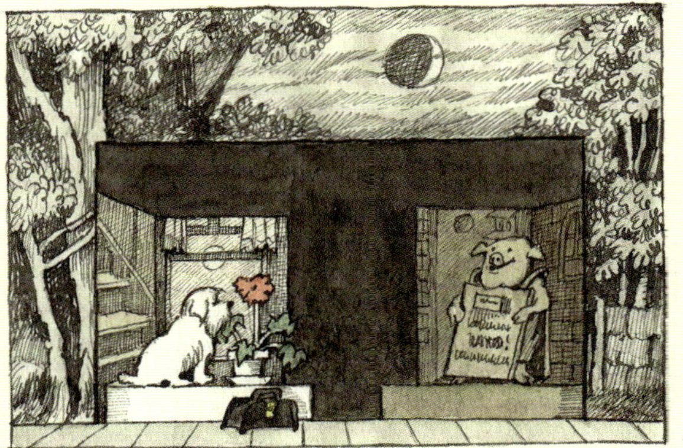

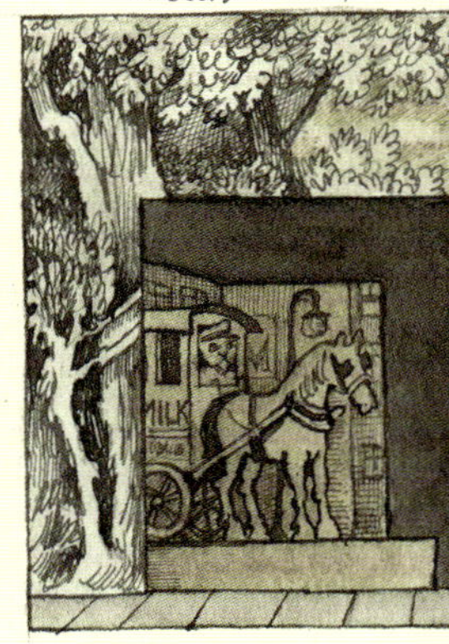

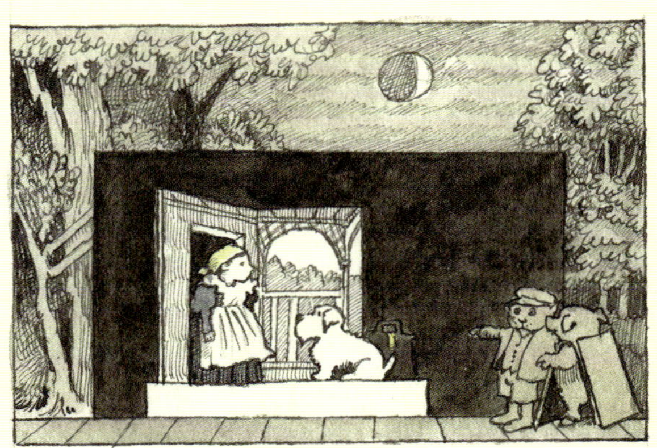

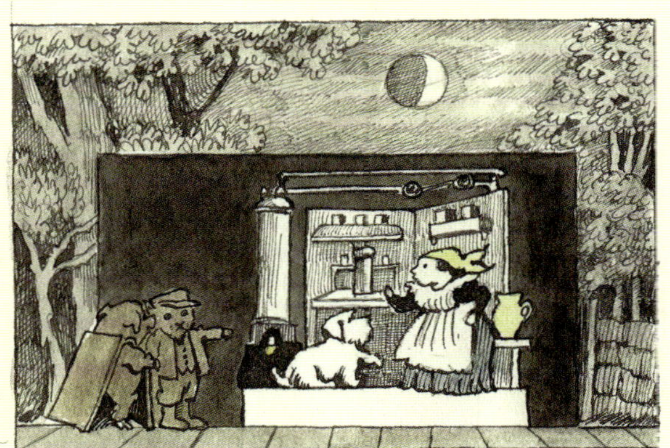

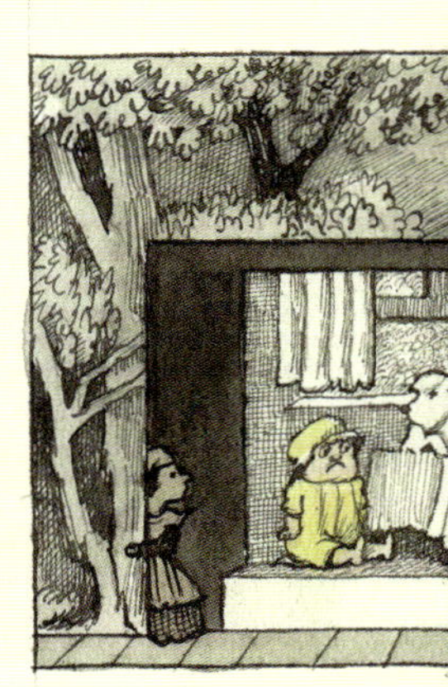

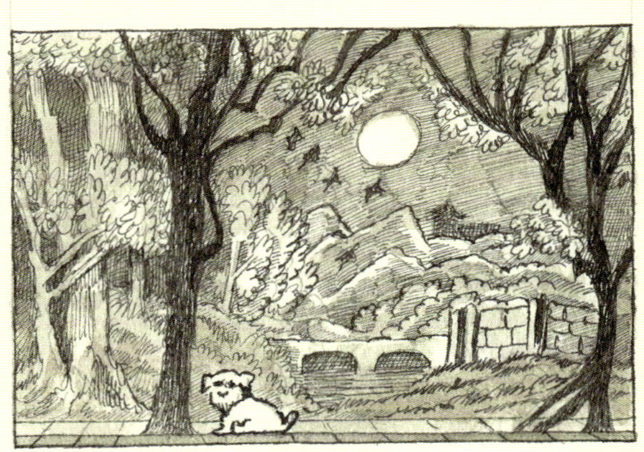

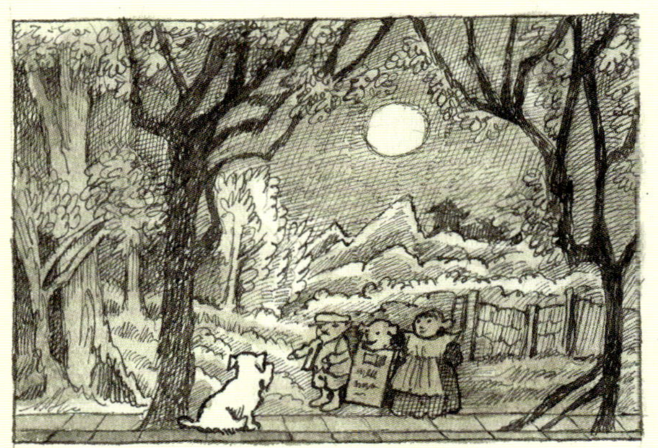

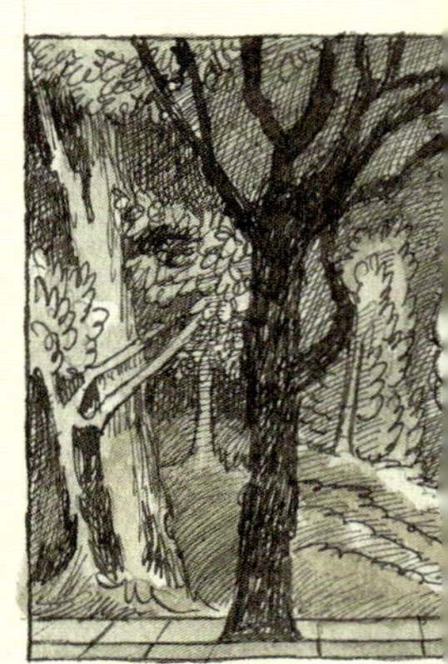

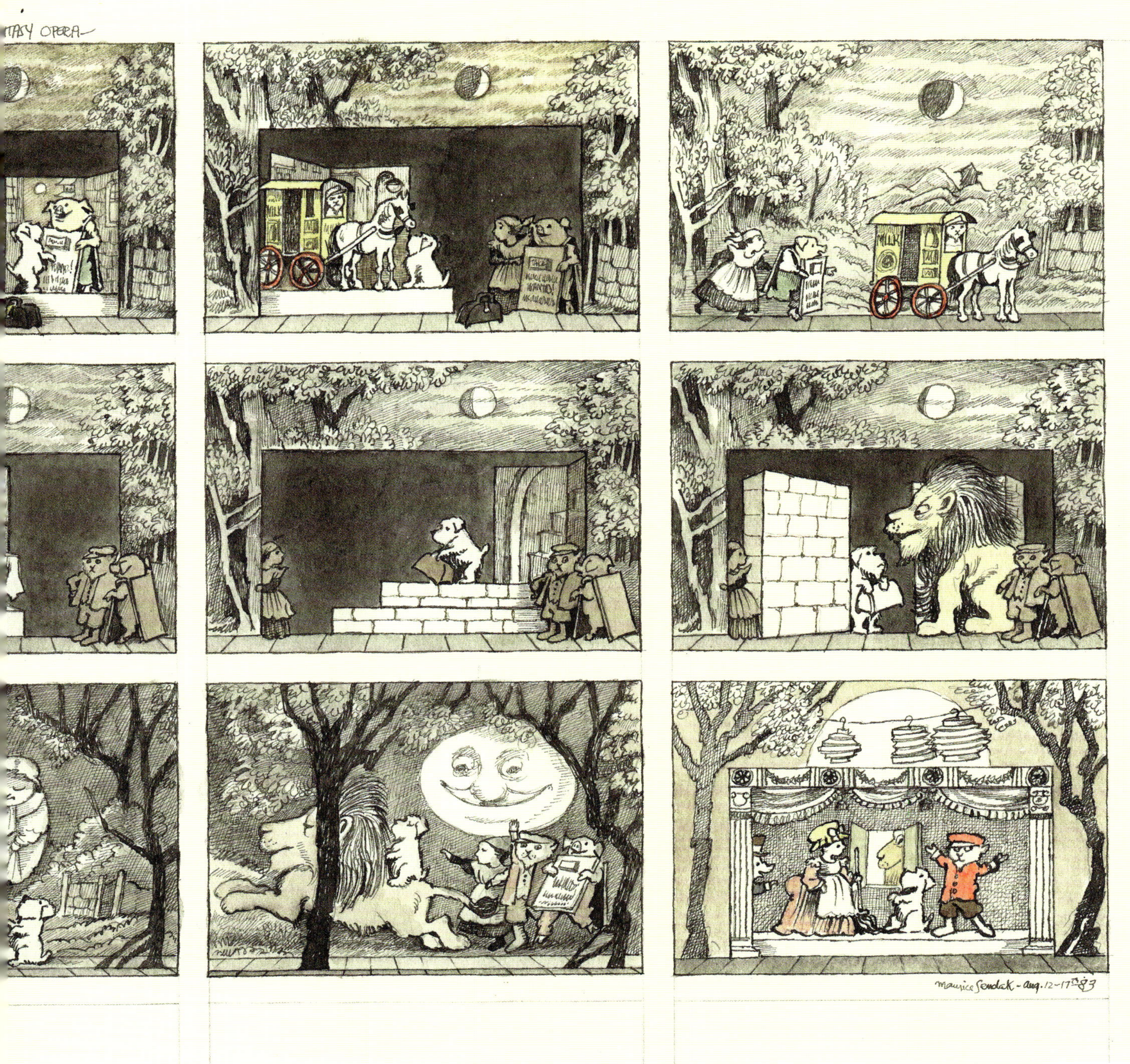

Maurice Sendak, Storyboard for *Higglety Pigglety* Opera, 8¼ × 19½ in.

Michael di Capua

Michael di Capua is one of the most admired and influential children's book editors in our time. Di Capua was the official editor and art director for almost all Sendak's books after *Outside Over There*, and he served as a sounding board and the unofficial editor for virtually every book that Sendak did after 1962, including *Where the Wild Things Are*, *In the Night Kitchen*, and *Outside Over There*.[1]

MICHAEL DI CAPUA The first time I met Maurice we discovered that so many things that mattered to each of us were identical: Mahler, Mozart, Verdi, Kleist. It was like running into your doppelganger.

I was working at Macmillan, and I stumbled on *Schoolmaster Whackwell's Wonderful Sons*. And the jacket just caught my eye. I was really struck by the art. And then I started spending time at the 8th Street Bookstore, Scribner's, the children's room at the Public Library, looking up Sendak books.

The more I saw, the more impressed I was . . . and especially with the fact that virtually each book had a disparate style, but no matter how much he modified his style or invented a new style to go with the text, you could always tell it was Sendak.

And so I wrote him a letter by hand. "I've seen these books of yours and you seem to be very interested in German Romanticism. So I was thinking that maybe it would be good if you illustrated Grimm." The phone rang in my cubicle. And it was Maurice Sendak and he said, "I'd love to illustrate Grimm. Let's have lunch."

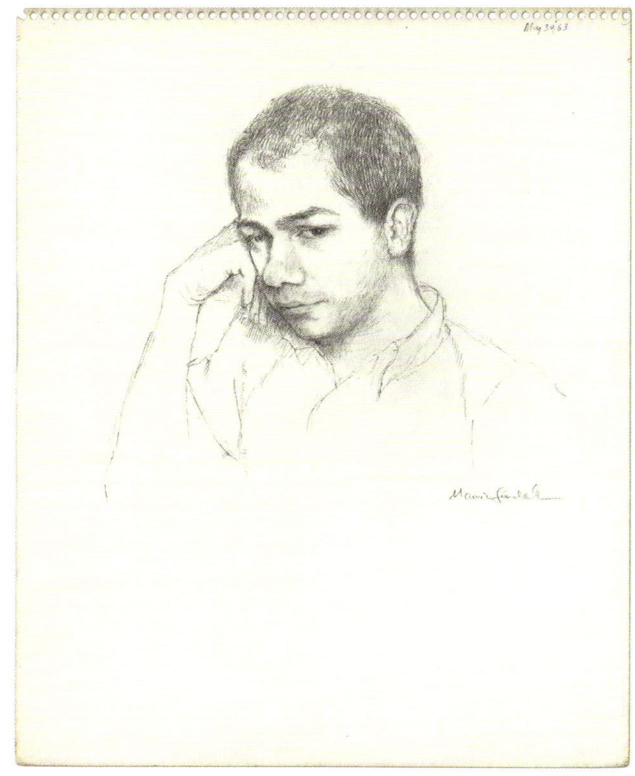

Maurice Sendak, *Michael di Capua*, 1963, pencil on paper, collection of Michael di Capua

We developed a custom, we would spend most of Saturdays touring second-hand bookstores all over the city, print stores. We would just spend every Saturday together.

He respected me. Let's say the first time he asked me something about this layout or whatever, whatever I said, his reaction could have been "Jesus

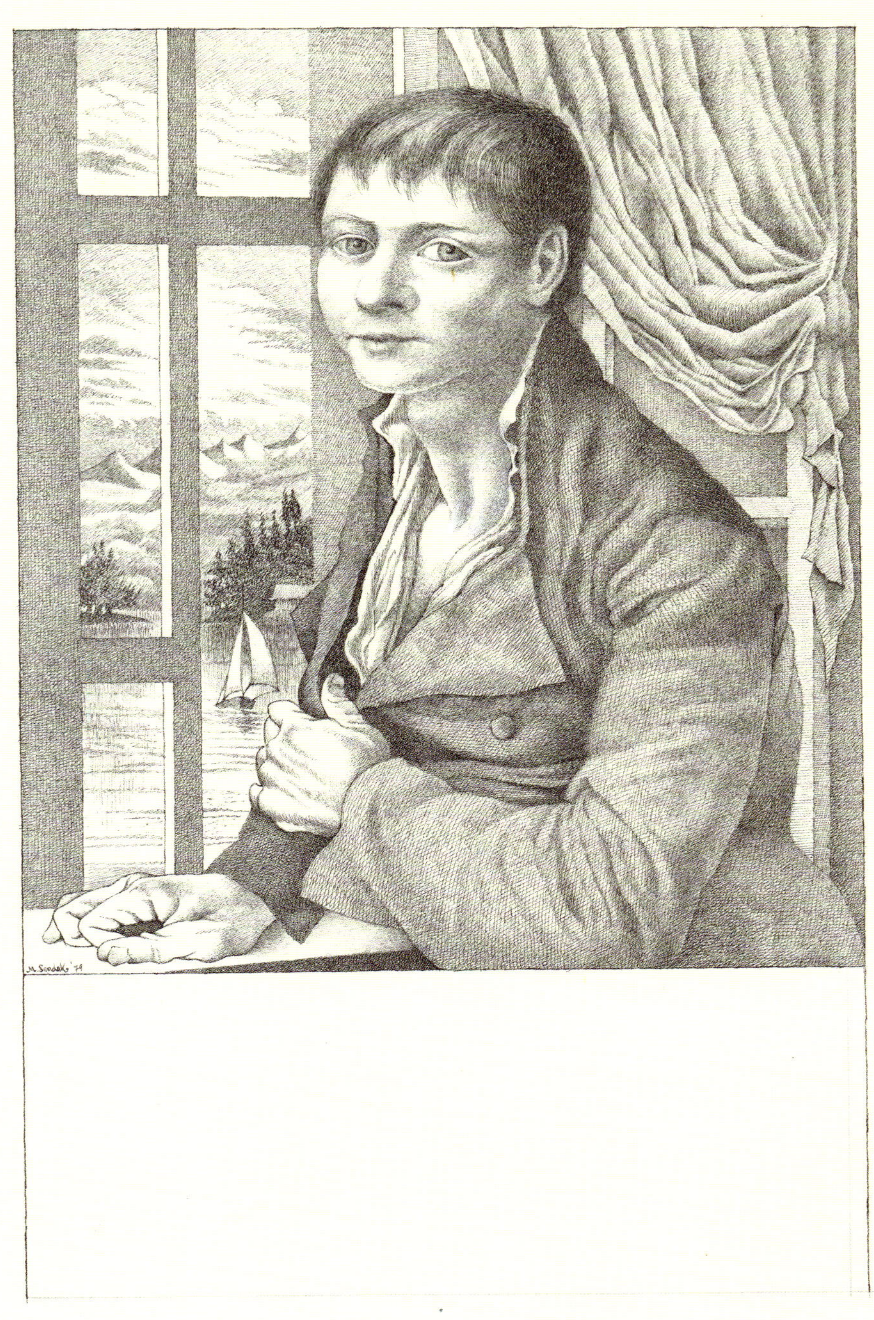

Maurice Sendak, *Heinrich von Kleist*, pen and ink, 12¼ × 9 in.

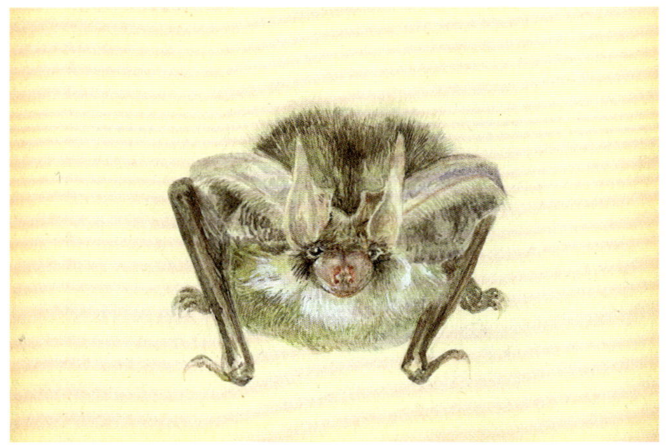

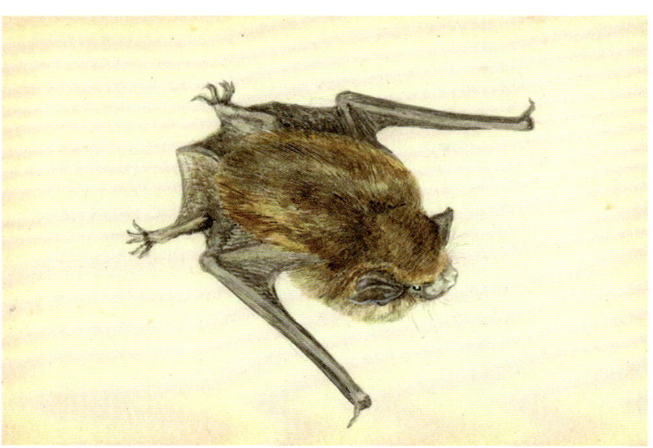

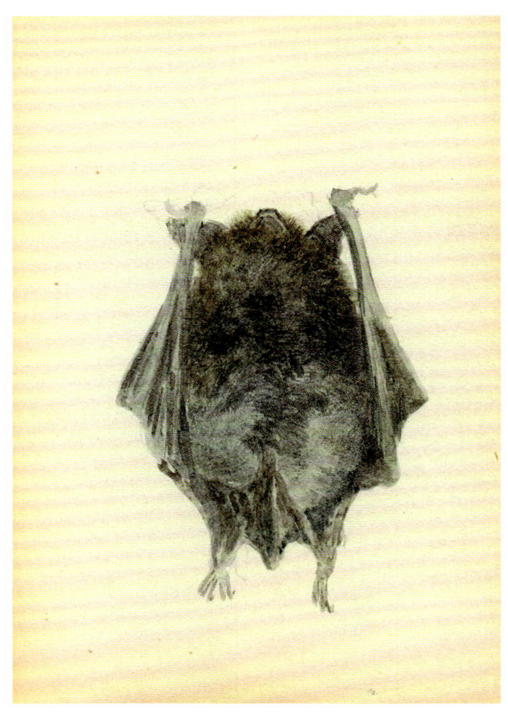

Beatrix Potter, *Three Bats*, n.d., watercolor, 4½ × 3½ in. approx.

Christ, that was ridiculously stupid." But apparently he liked what he heard. And that just grew and grew. The very first thing we worked on together was *Wild Things*. The second thing was *The Bat-Poet*.

Night Kitchen was published in '70. The way *Night Kitchen* was written is that Maurice and I would take a long walk at night. And he would tell me the text that he had so far, and I would edit it verbally while we were taking long walks. I think the way I functioned was as a sounding board. One word would strike me as not right. Or too much. And I would comment on that.

JW Was there a discussion of what the book meant?

MdC No. The only thing he talked about was that he was devoted to Winsor McCay, and movie atmosphere and movie culture of the time. Maurice never said one word about what anything meant. The closest he would come to that is in talking about *Outside Over There*; that it was all inspired by his relationship with Natalie and the Lindbergh baby.[2]

LC It seems like you did much more than what a typical editor does.

MdC All right, one thing that is different about me from most other quote "editors" is that I'm *bisexual.* I work on verbal, and I work on visual. And I'm credited on all my books as not only the editor but the art director—both. I don't know of anybody else who does both.

LC Was there anxiety about Mickey falling out of his clothes in *Night Kitchen*?

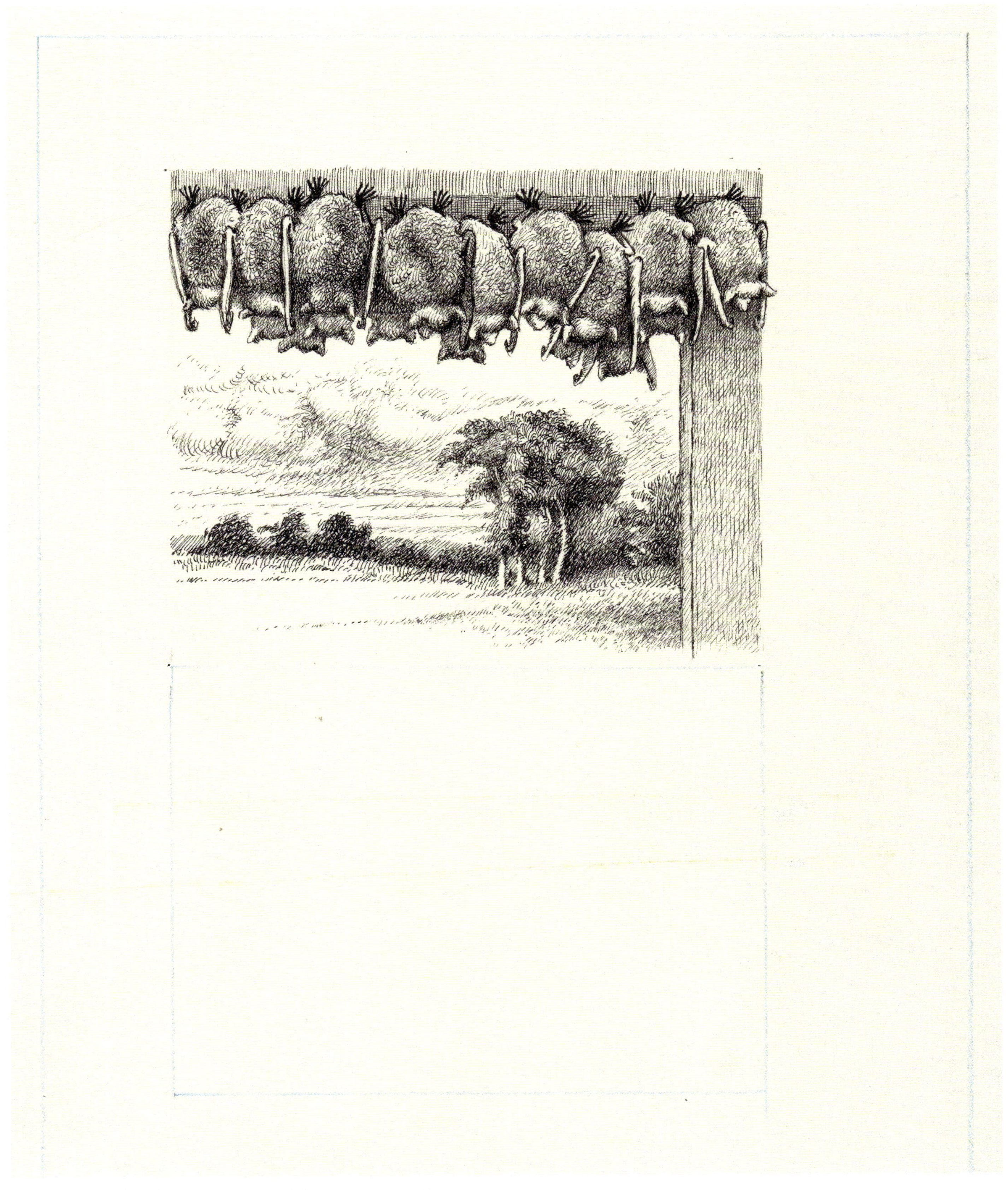

Maurice Sendak, *The Bat-Poet*, 1964, ink on paper, 9 × 8 in.

MdC No, we never gave it a second thought . . . You might recall that the frontispiece of *The Light Princess* is a close-up of the Light Princess as an infant floating in the air. And her legs are spread apart, and you get a nice close view of her vagina. And that was in 1968. No one ever said "Oh you can't do that." I don't remember any reviewer ever commenting on it.

JW What are some other books you gave input on in the 1960s?

MdC *Higglety Pigglety Pop!*, which was published in 1967, and where the writing was paramount. And paramount in the sense that there was so much more of it compared to *Wild Things* or *Night Kitchen* or *Outside Over There*. And Maurice would give me a hardcopy manuscript which he must have typed up himself. And I would make handwritten notes and write on the manuscript, circling things or crossing out things or adding words or whatever. And I did that very, very extensively. *Wild Things*, and *Night Kitchen*, and even *Outside Over There*, in terms of quantity, were minimum, because the texts were minimum. Let me put it this way: Maurice didn't do anything unless I looked it over. And that includes when he would be asked to write a blurb for somebody.

LC Do you have a favorite book you worked on with Maurice?

MdC I'm interested in the fact that I thought of *We Are All in the Dumps with Jack and Guy*. I could have thought of *Brundibar*, I could have thought of *Bumble-Ardy*, but I thought of *Dumps* because, with both *Brundibar* and *Bumble-Ardy* a great portion of

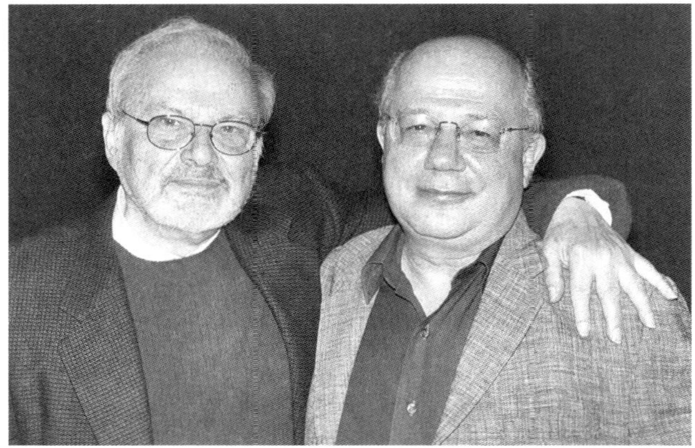

Maurice Sendak and Michael di Capua, 2003

the work was a struggle for Maurice. It was difficult. It was hard work. Whereas *Dumps*, to me, compared to those books, was just shot out of a cannon.

He knew from day one what he was going to do. Once the dummy was done—the reworking of the 1965 dummy—he just sat down, and the pictures just fell out of his hand. There was no struggle. No hard work. It was so clear to him what he wanted to do. What this book was meant to show. What this book was meant to say. And the fact that the book is so incredibly complex, that the story it tells, from first page to last, is so complicated, and on top of that making what would appear to be two totally disparate halves into a seamless whole. Both *Brundibar* and *Bumble-Ardy* were extremely difficult and challenging for him. *Dumps* was pure joy for him.

Notes

1. Michael di Capua interviewed by Lynn Caponera and Jonathan Weinberg, July 9, 2017, East Hampton, New York.

2. Natalie was beloved older Sendak's sister. He dedicated *Dear Mili* to her. Sendak was obsessed with the 1932 kidnapping and murder of Charles Lindbergh's baby.

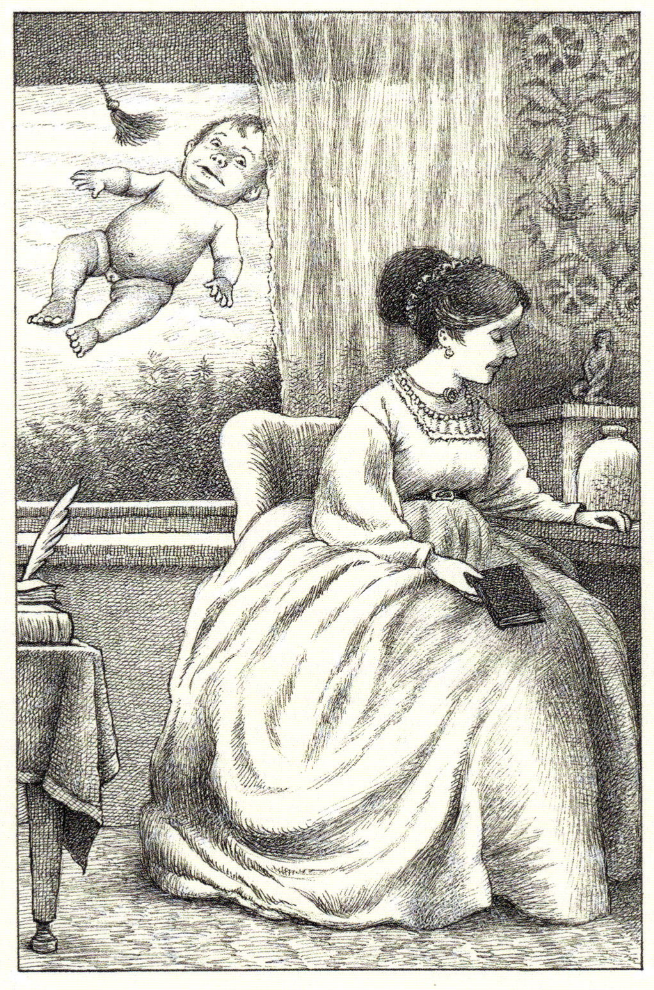

Maurice Sendak, *The Light Princess*, pen and ink on paper, 5 1/16 × 3 3/16 in.

In the Night Kitchen

"Apparently, a little boy without his pajamas on was more terrifying to some people than any monster I ever invented."

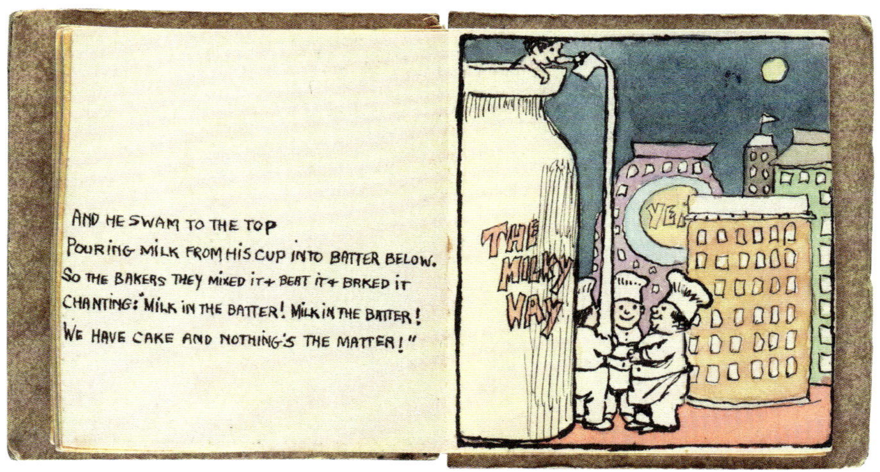

Maurice Sendak, Dummy for *In the Night Kitchen*, 1969, watercolor and ink on paper, 2⅜ × 4¾ in.

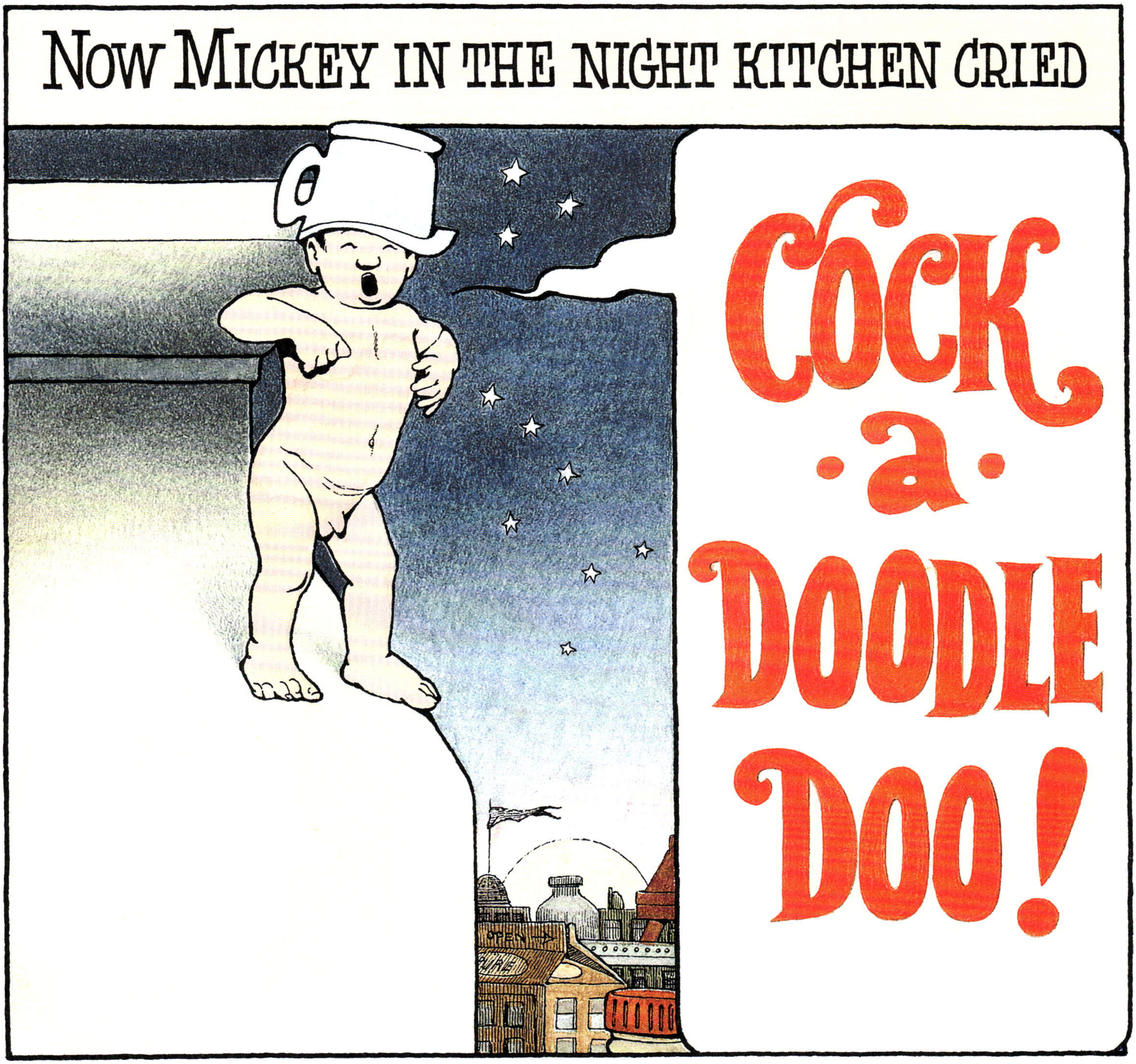

Maurice Sendak, *In the Night Kitchen*, watercolor and ink on paper as printed in color in Maurice Sendak, *In the Night Kitchen* (New York: Harper & Row, 1970)

"When I was a child, there was an advertisement which I remember too clearly. It was for the Sunshine Bakers. And the advertisement read 'We Bake While You Sleep!' It seemed to me the most sadistic thing in the world, because all I wanted to do was stay up and watch."

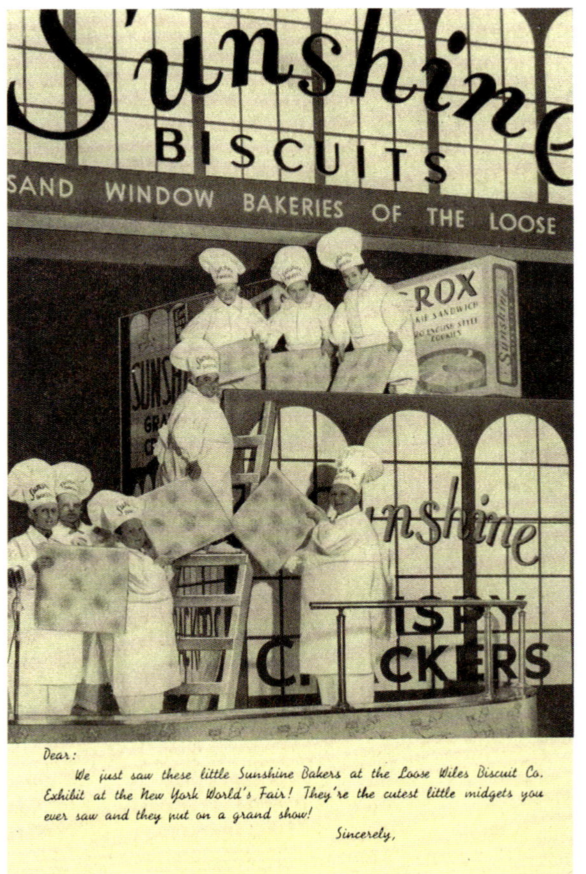

Sunshine Biscuits Exhibit, 1939 World's Fair, postcard, $3\frac{1}{2} \times 5$ in.

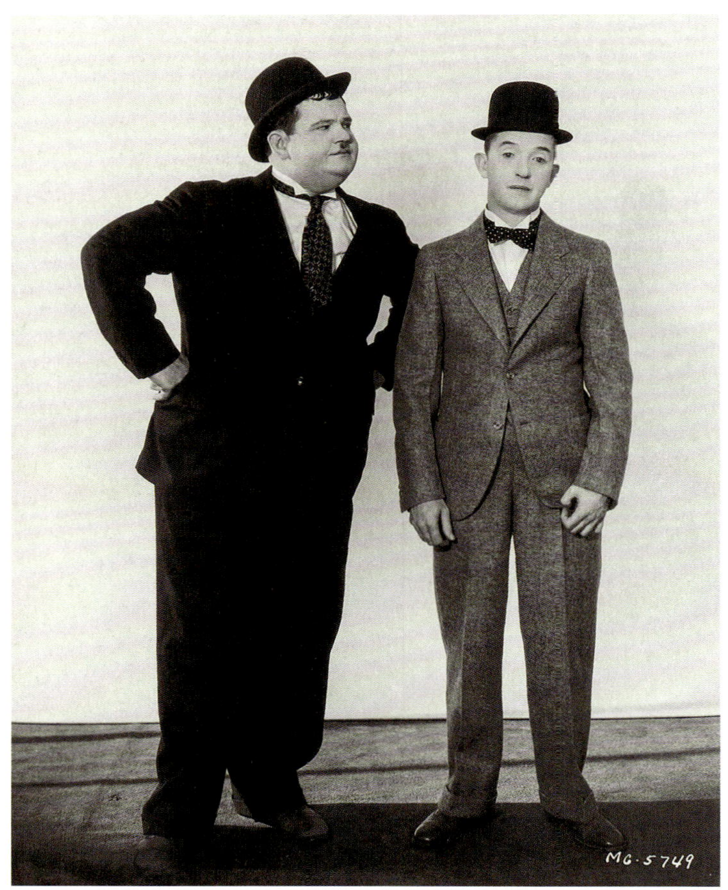

Laurel and Hardy Publicity Shot, c. 1930s

opposite and following pages: Maurice Sendak, *In the Night Kitchen*, watercolor and ink on paper as printed in color in Maurice Sendak, *In the Night Kitchen* (New York: Harper & Row, 1970)

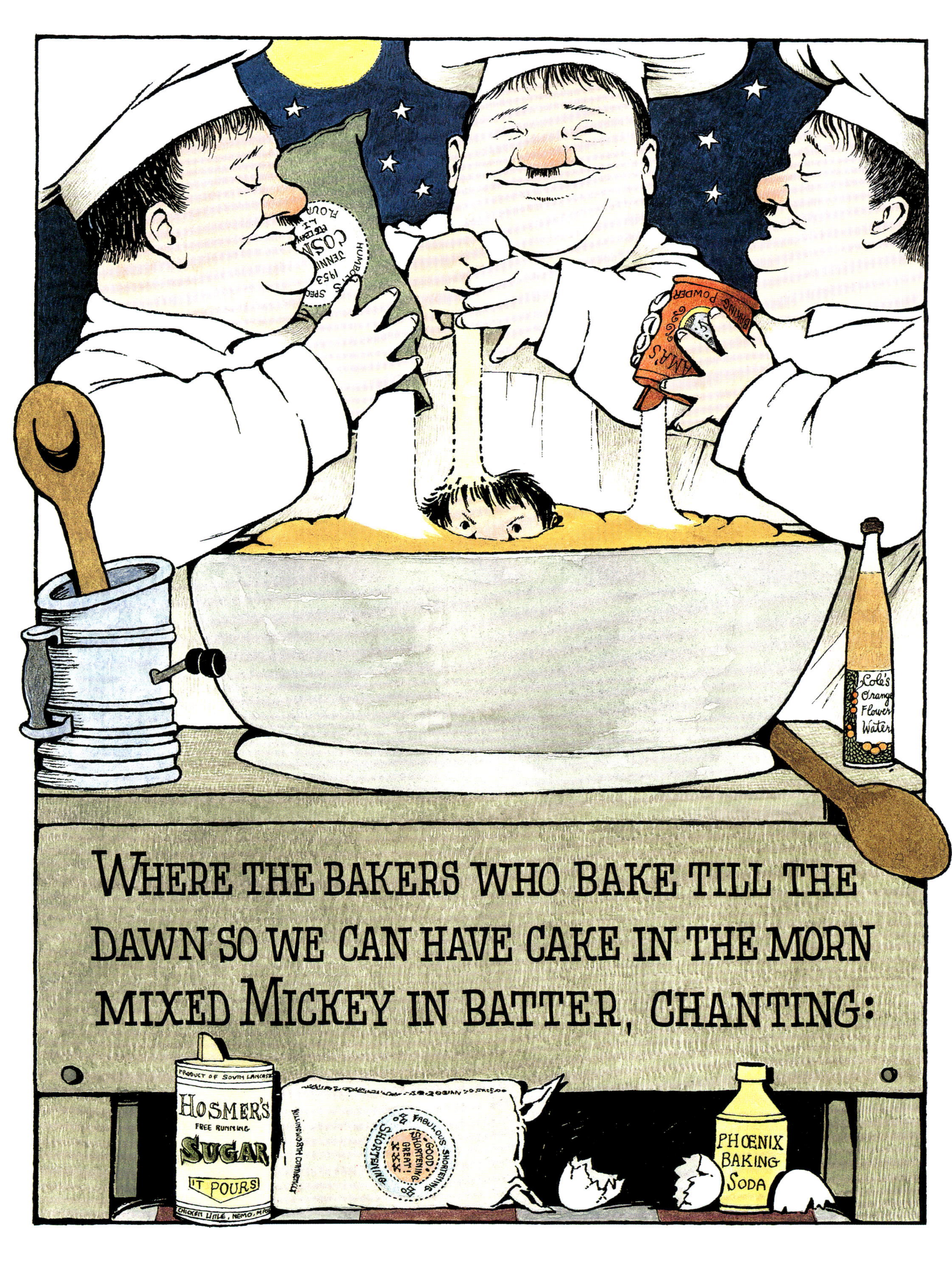

WHERE THE BAKERS WHO BAKE TILL THE DAWN SO WE CAN HAVE CAKE IN THE MORN MIXED MICKEY IN BATTER, CHANTING:
BAKING POWDER
Cole's Orange Flower Water
PRODUCT OF SOUTH LANCASTER
HOSMER'S
FREE RUNNING
SUGAR
IT POURS
CHICKEN LITTLE, NEMO, MASS.
FABULOUS SHORTENING
GOOD SHORTENING GREAT! XXX
PHOENIX BAKING SODA

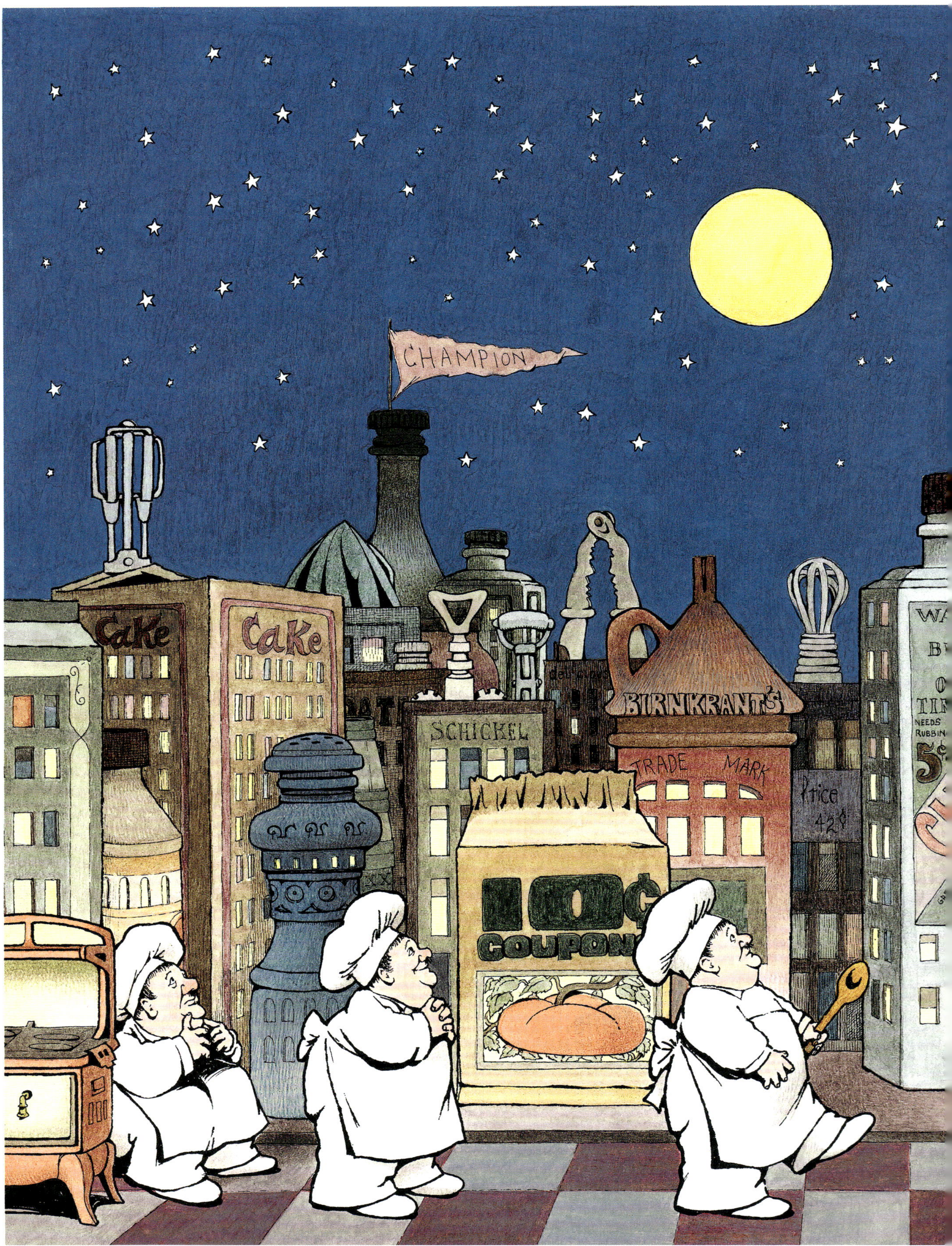
CHAMPION
Cake
Cake
SCHICKEL
BIRNKRANT'S
TRADE MARK
Price 42¢
10¢
COUPON

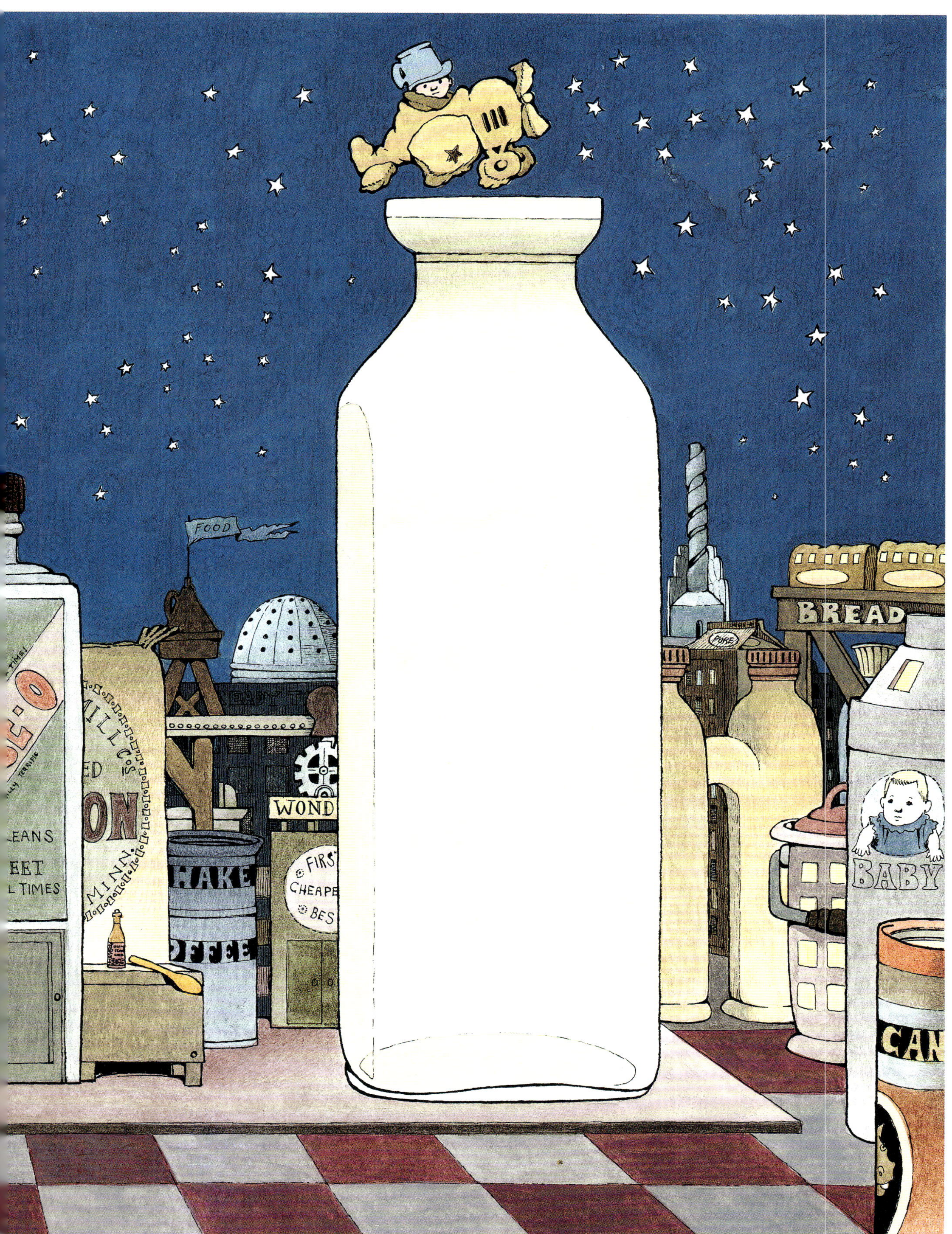

FOOD
BREAD
PURE
WOND
FIRST
CHEAPE
BES
HAKE
OFFEE
BABY
CAN
LEANS
EET
L TIMES
MINN.

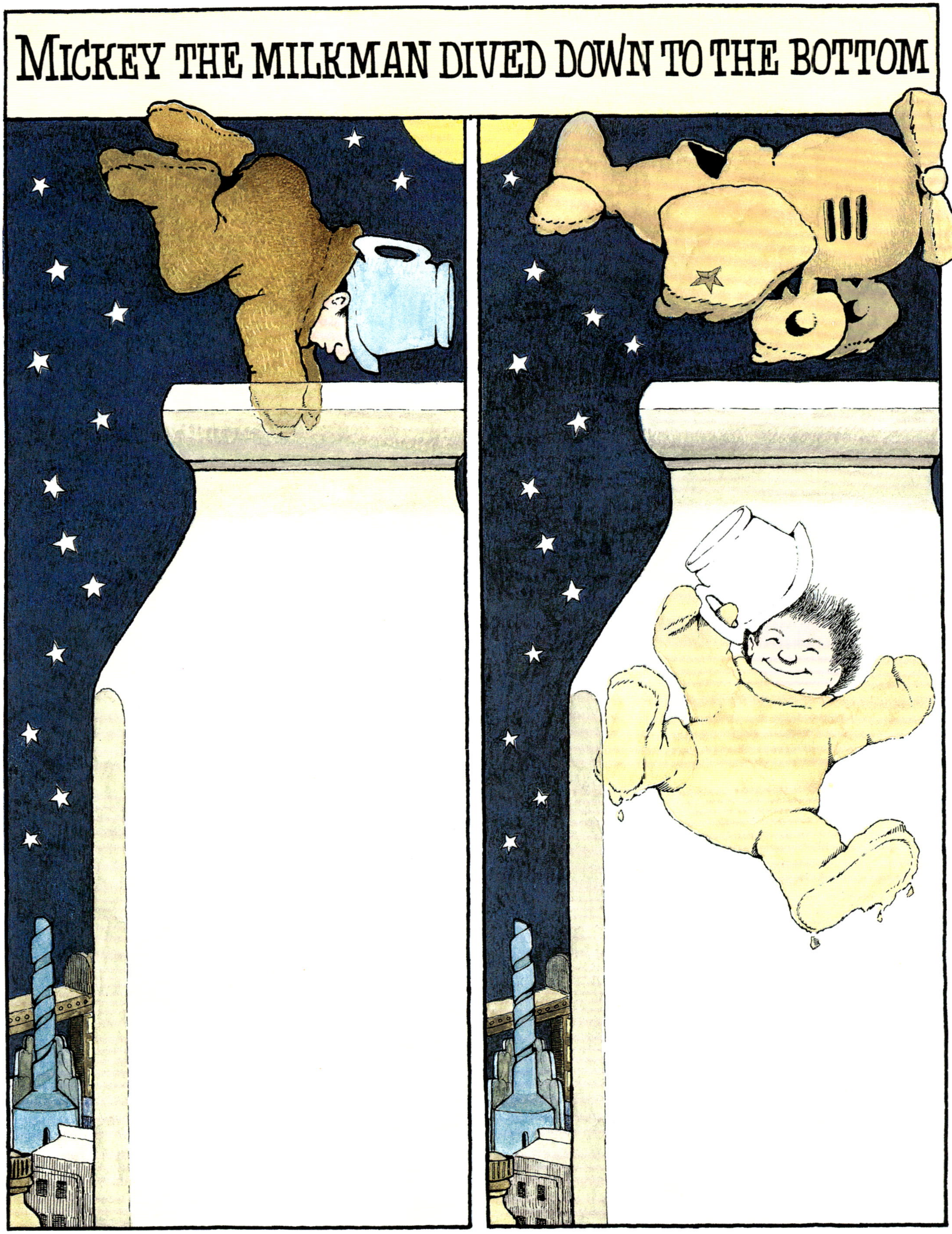

MICKEY THE MILKMAN DIVED DOWN TO THE BOTTOM

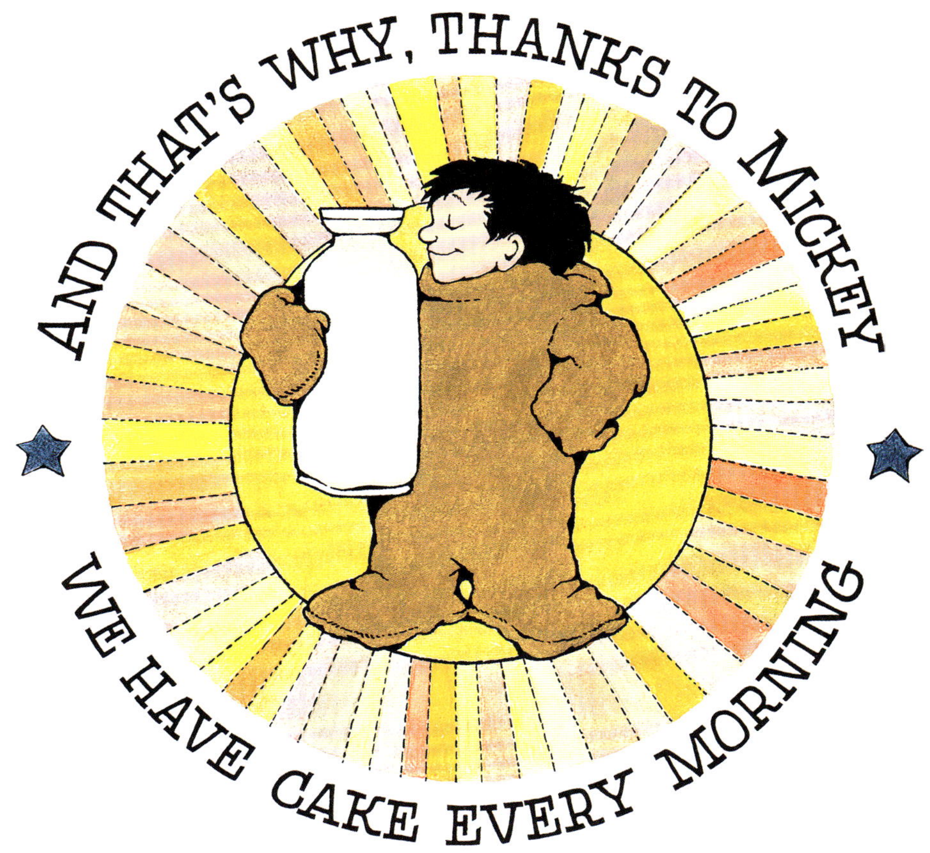

"Mickey's problem is: How do I stay up all night and see what grownups do, and have the fun that is denied me as a child? The fact that there was such an explosion when the book came out, that it could only appear in some libraries after someone painted diapers on the naked Mickey, seems to me grim testimony to our puritanical attitudes."

opposite and above: Maurice Sendak, *In the Night Kitchen*, watercolor and ink on paper as printed in color in Maurice Sendak, *In the Night Kitchen* (New York: Harper & Row, 1970)

The Grimm Brothers, The Juniper Tree and Other Tales from Grimm

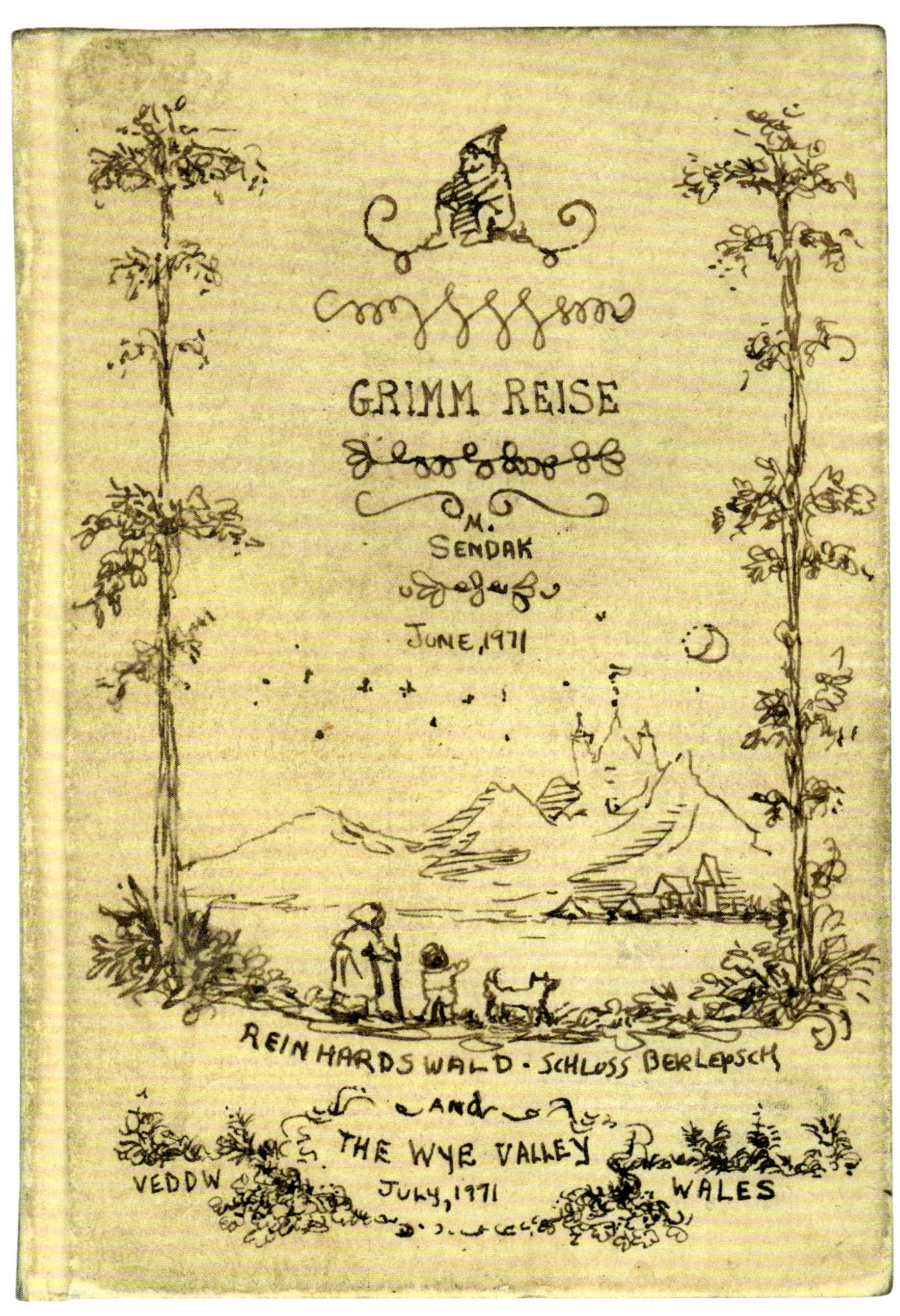

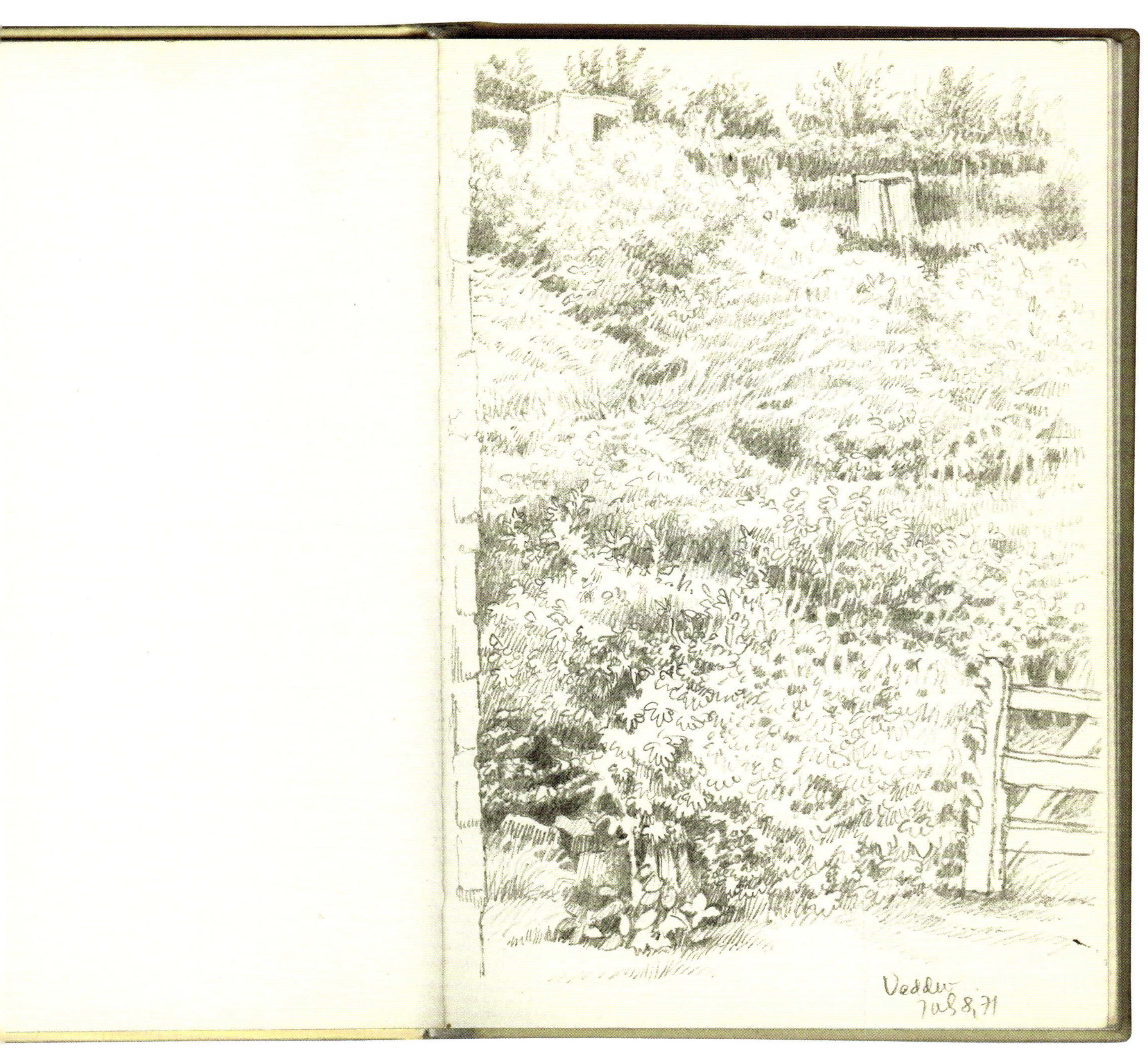

opposite: Maurice Sendak, *Grimm Reise*, travel diary, 1971, sketchbook, 8 × 6 in.; *this page: Veddw*, page from the diary

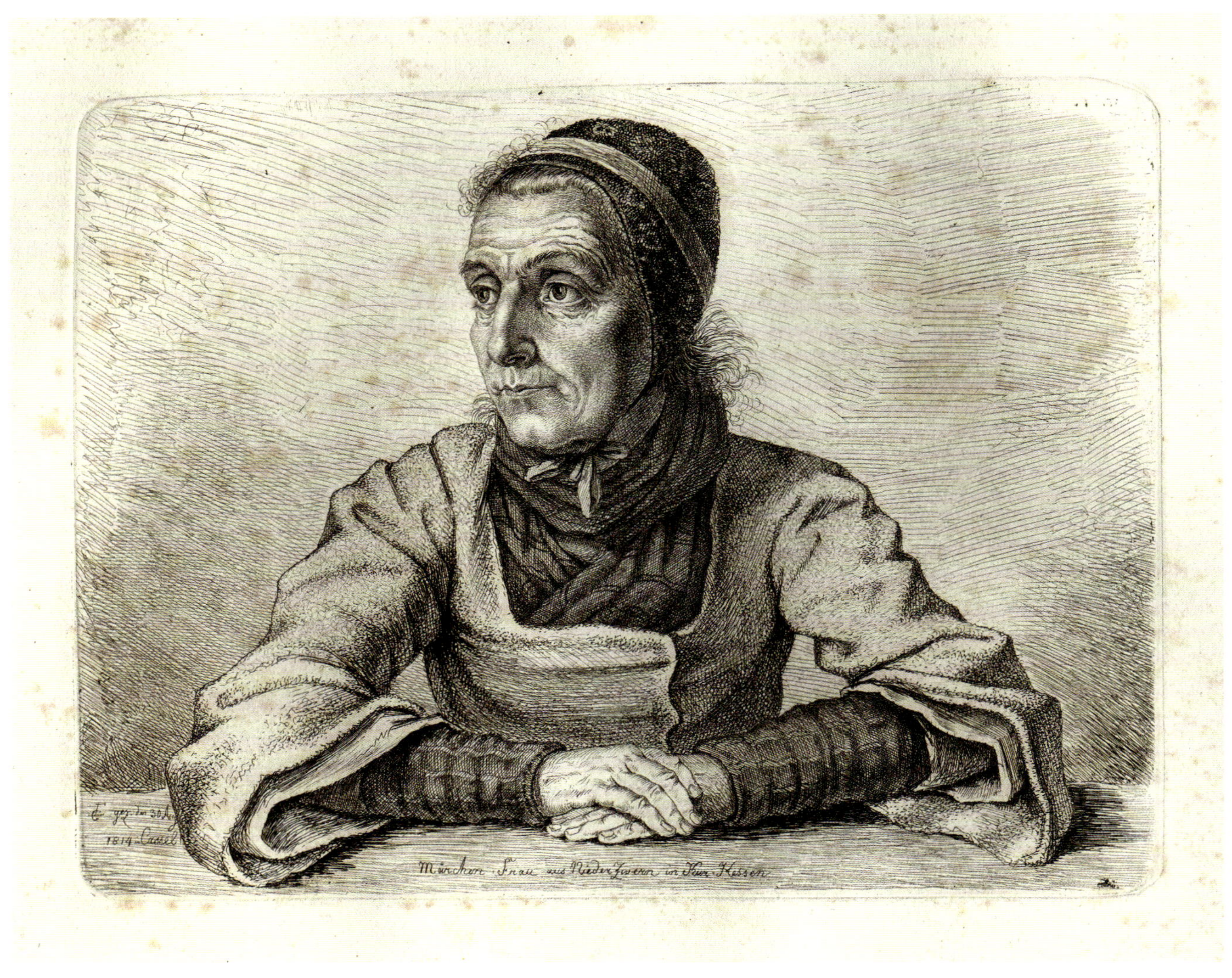

Ludwig Grimm, *Portrait of a Woman*, 1814, etching, 4¾ × 6¼ in.

opposite: Maurice Sendak, "The Devil and His Three Golden Hairs," *The Juniper Tree and Other Tales from Grimm*, 1973, ink on paper, 4½ × 3⅝ in.

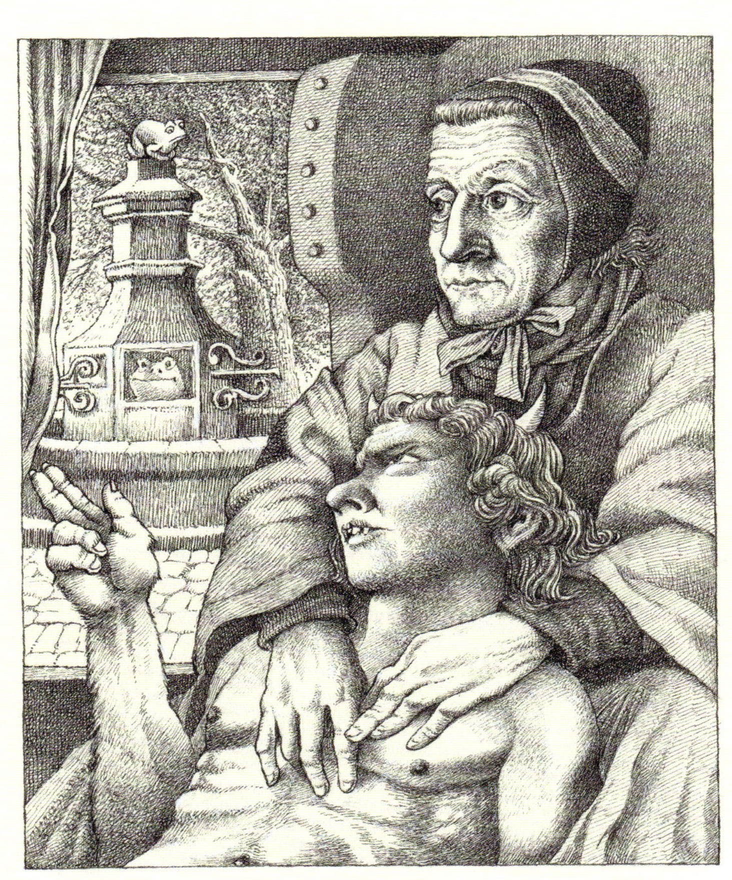

"Clearly the brothers Grimm . . . never bothered their heads about providing so-called healthy or suitable literature for children. How fortunate for us they were only interested in telling a good story!"

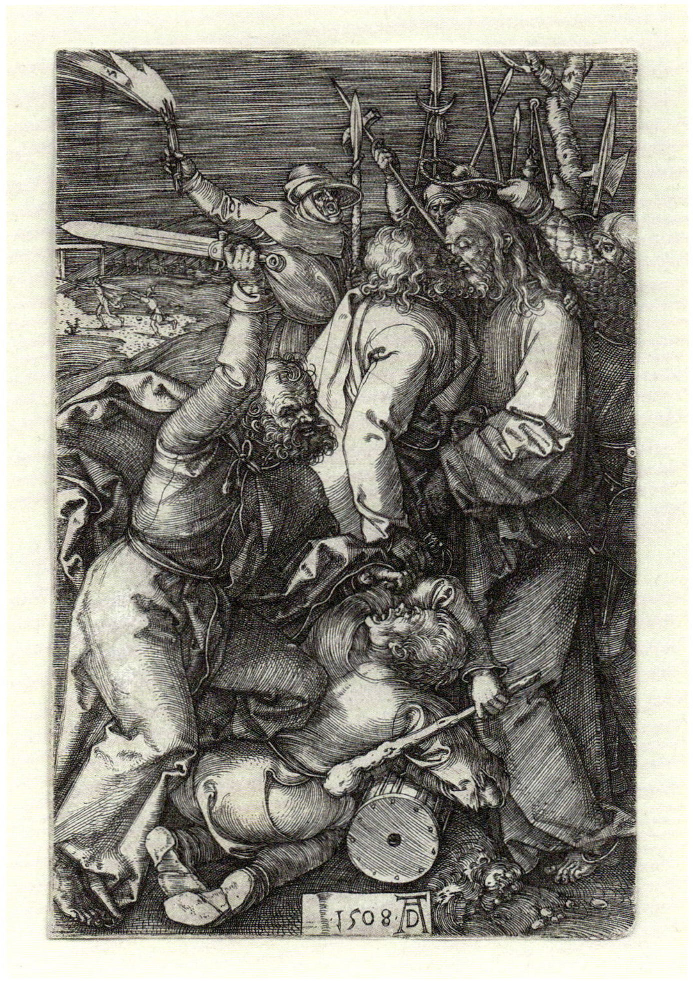

Albrecht Dürer, *The Betrayal of Christ*, 1508, woodcut, 4⅝ × 3 in.

opposite: Maurice Sendak, "Godfather Death," *The Juniper Tree and Other Tales from Grimm*, 1973, ink on paper, 11¼ × 8¼ in.

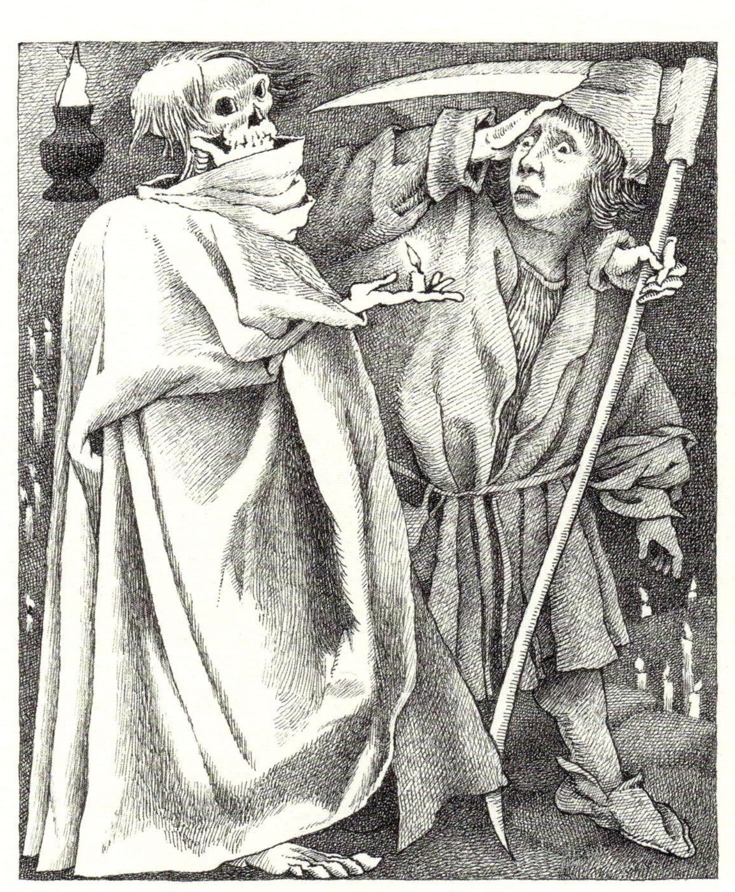

Outside Over There

"Yes, my book jacket is a conscious homage to that painting . . . Look at the fence, look at the baby staring out and clutching part of the flower just the way Runge's baby does. There's no question about that."

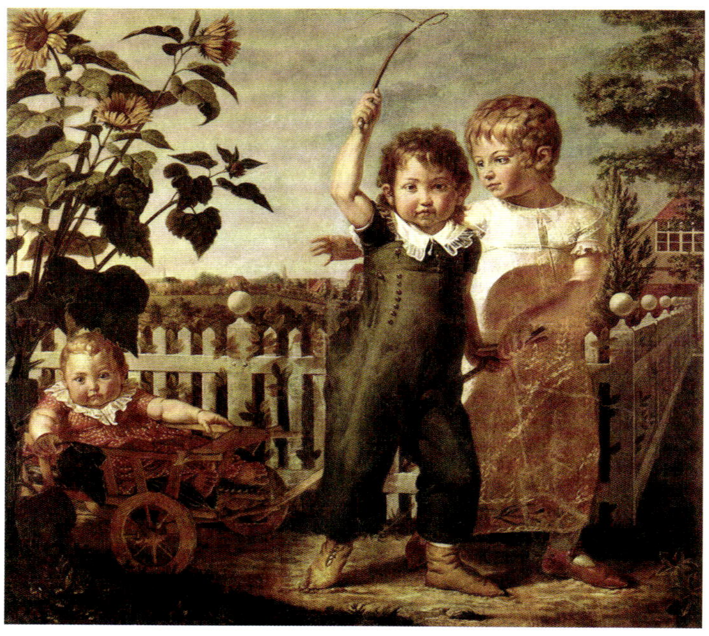

Philipp Otto Runge, *The Hülsenbeck Children*, 1805–6, oil on canvas, 53⅜ × 56½ in., Kunsthalle, Hamburg

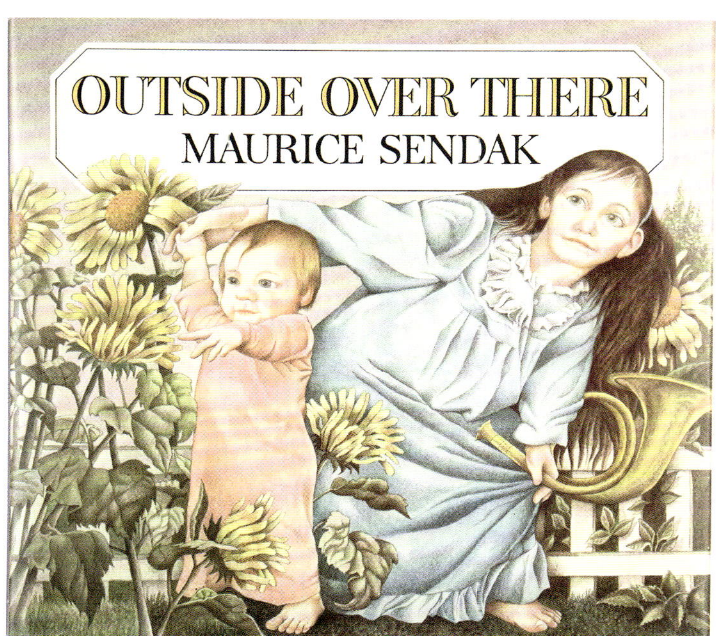

Maurice Sendak, *Outside Over There* (New York: Harper & Row, 1981)

opposite: Maurice Sendak, Dummy for *Outside Over There*, 1977, ink on paper, 3 × 8 in.

IDA PLAYED HER WONDER HORN
TO ROCK THE BABY STILL
BUT NEVER WATCHED!

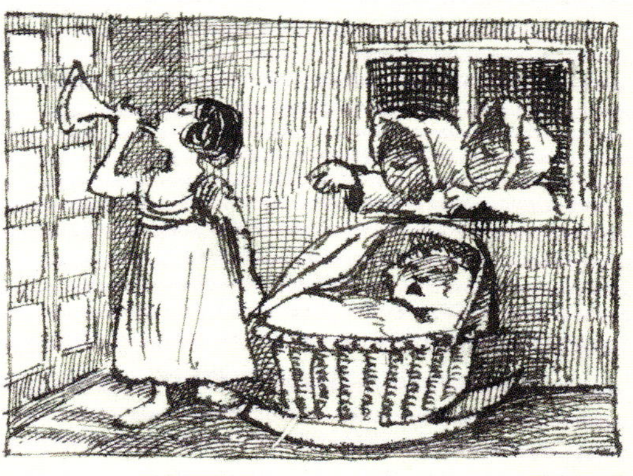

SO THE GOBLINS CAME.
THEY PUSHED THEIR WAY IN
AND PULLED BABY OUT,
LEAVING ANOTHER ALL MADE OF ICE.

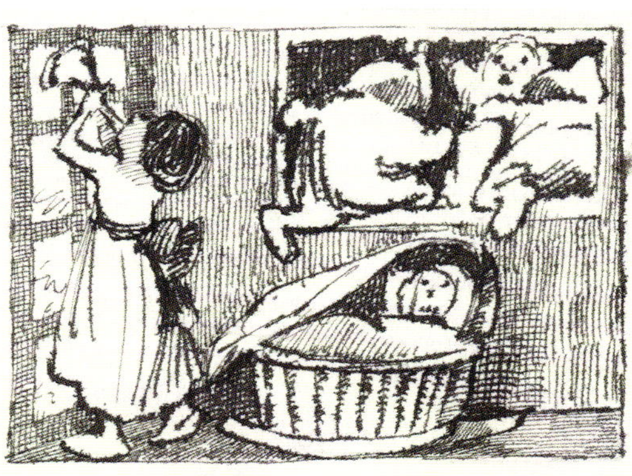

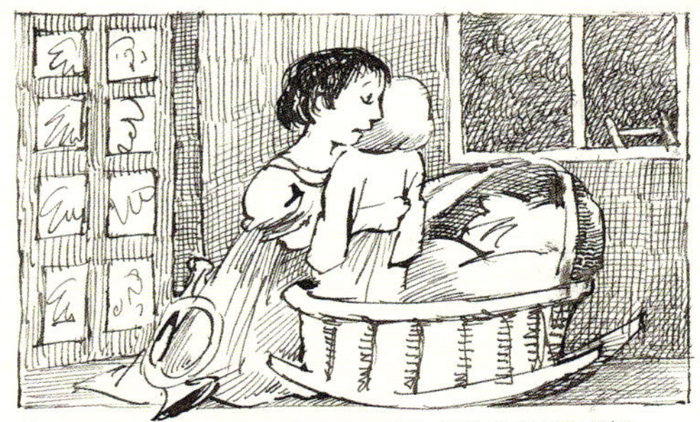

POOR IDA, NEVER KNOWING, HUGGED THE CHANGELING
AND SHE MURMURED, "HOW I LOVE YOU!"

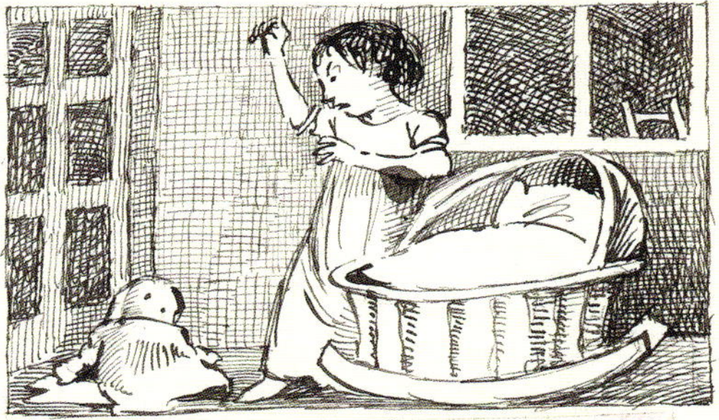

THE ICE-THING ONLY DRIPPED AND STARED,
AND IDA MAD KNEW GOBLINS HAD BEEN THERE.

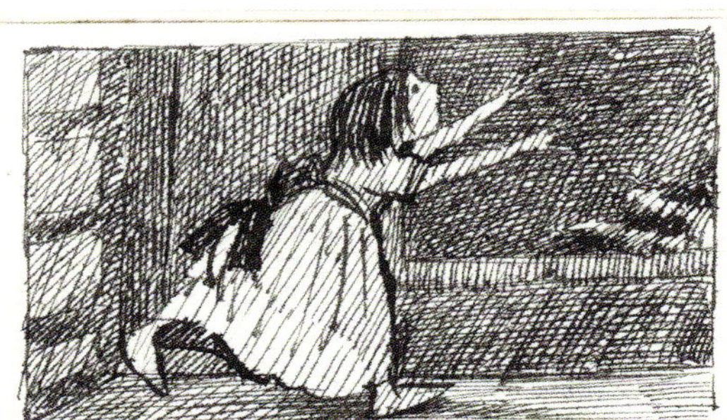

"THEY STOLE MY SISTER AWAY!" SHE CRIED,
TO BE A NASTY GOBLIN'S BRIDE!"
NOW IDA IN A HURRY

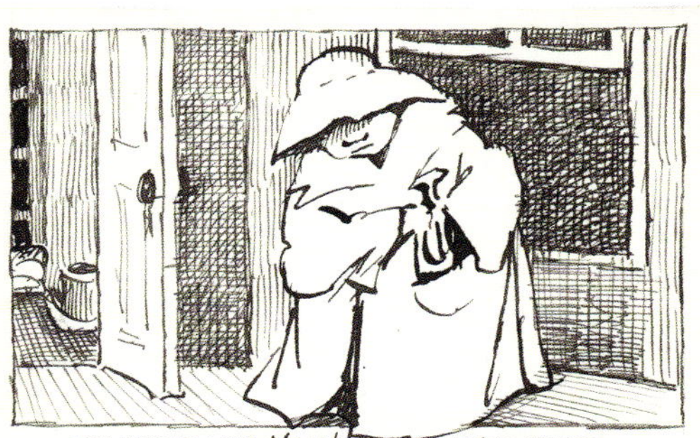

SNATCHED HER MAMA'S YELLOW RAIN-CLOAK,
TUCKED HER HORN SAFE IN A POCKET,
AND MADE A SERIOUS MISTAKE.

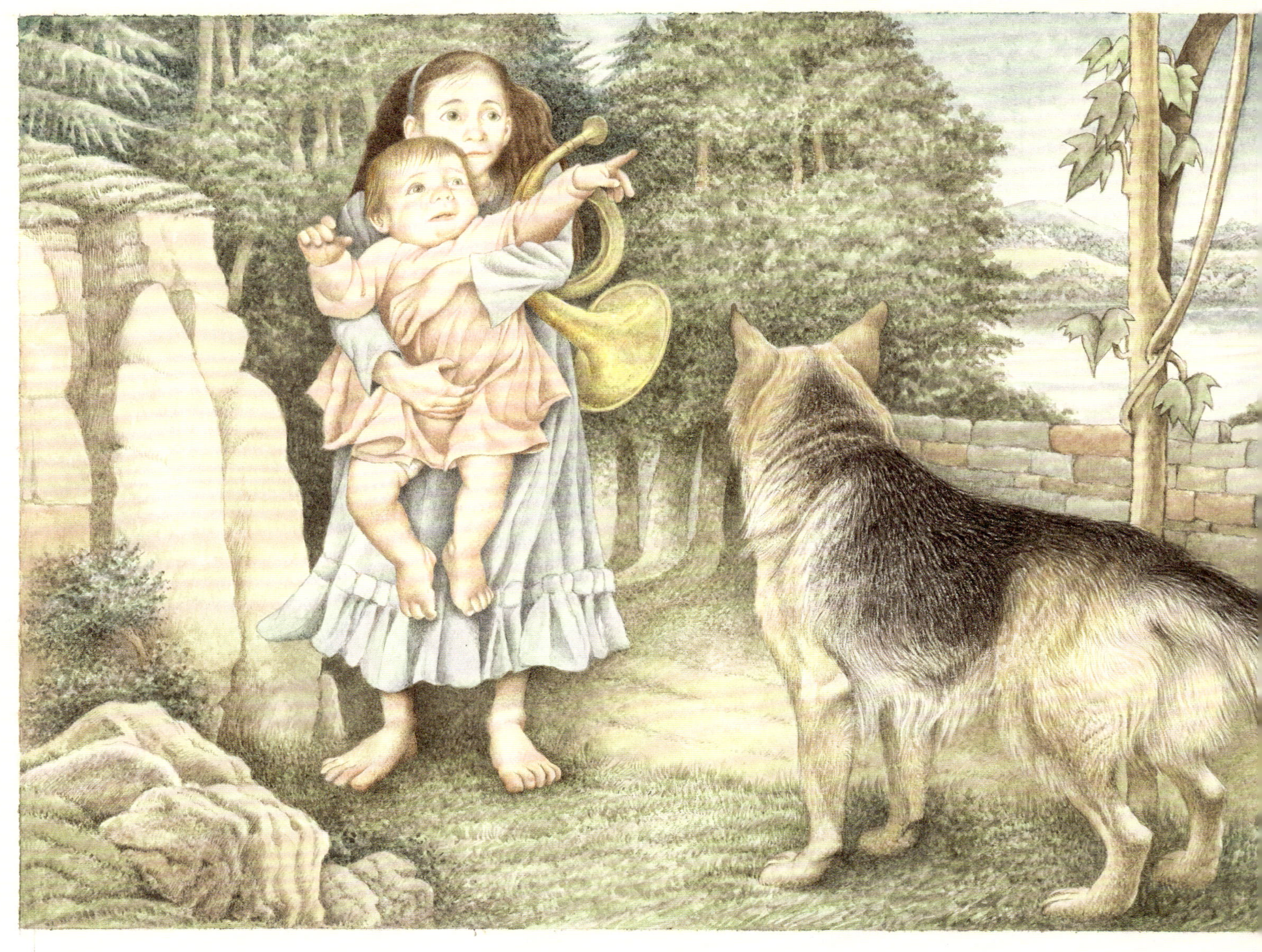

"In fairy tale and fantasy we reconstruct and defuse dreadful moments of childhood. *Outside Over There* became my exorcism of the Lindbergh case. In it, I am the Lindbergh baby and my sister saves me."

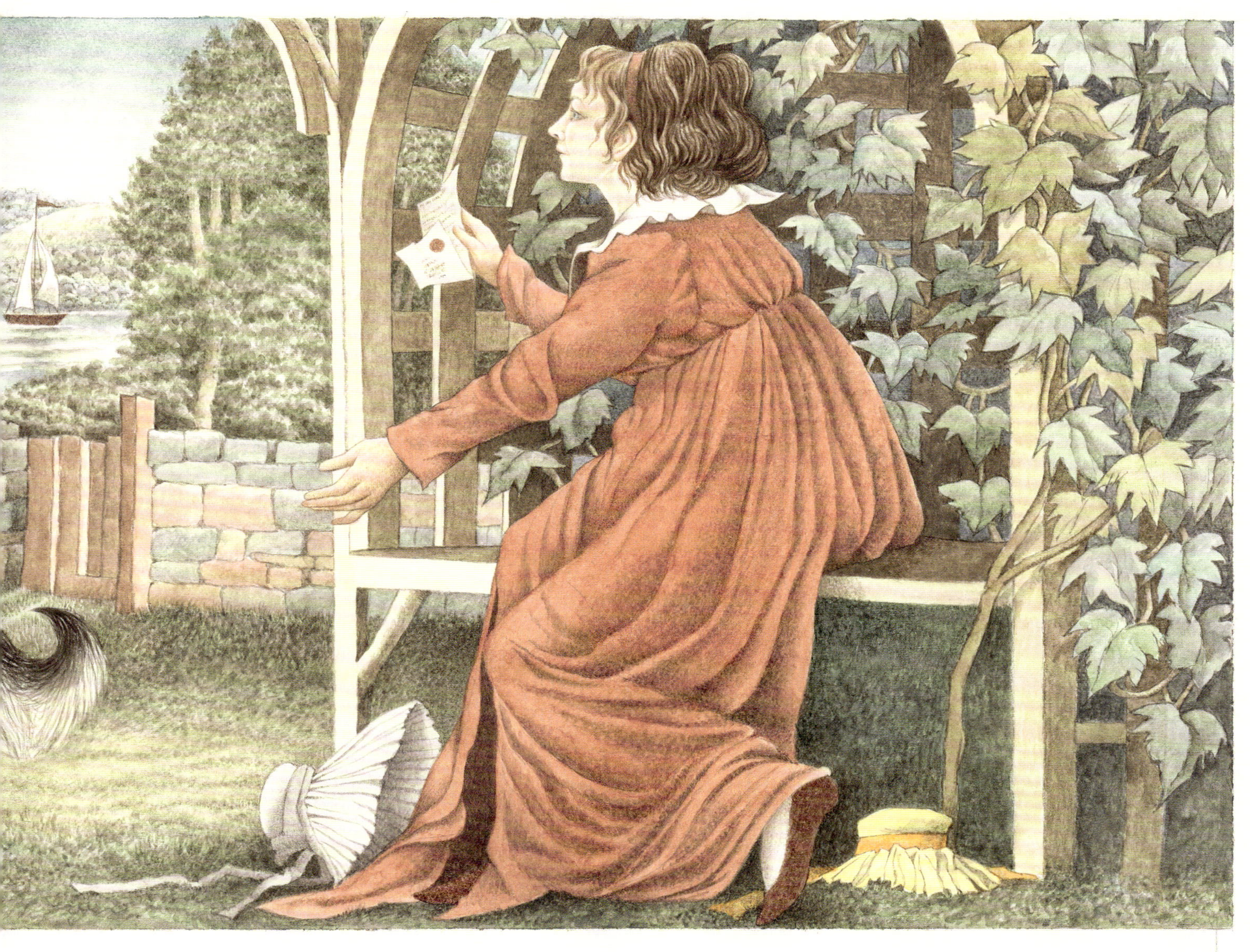

Maurice Sendak, *Outside Over There*, 1978, watercolor on paper, 16 × 19⅞ in.

Dear Mili

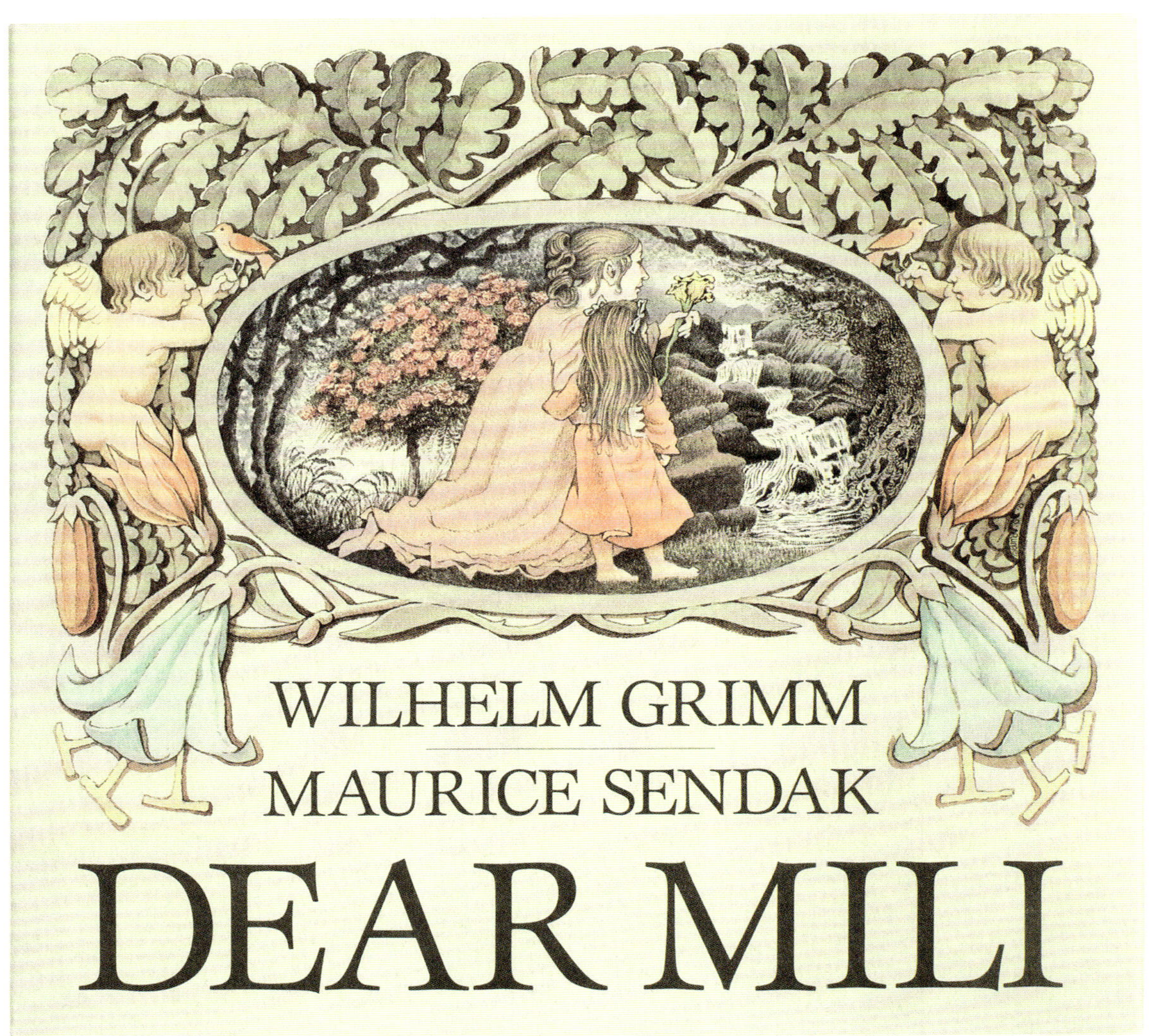

Wilhelm Grimm, *Dear Mili* (New York: Farrar, Straus and Giroux, 1988)

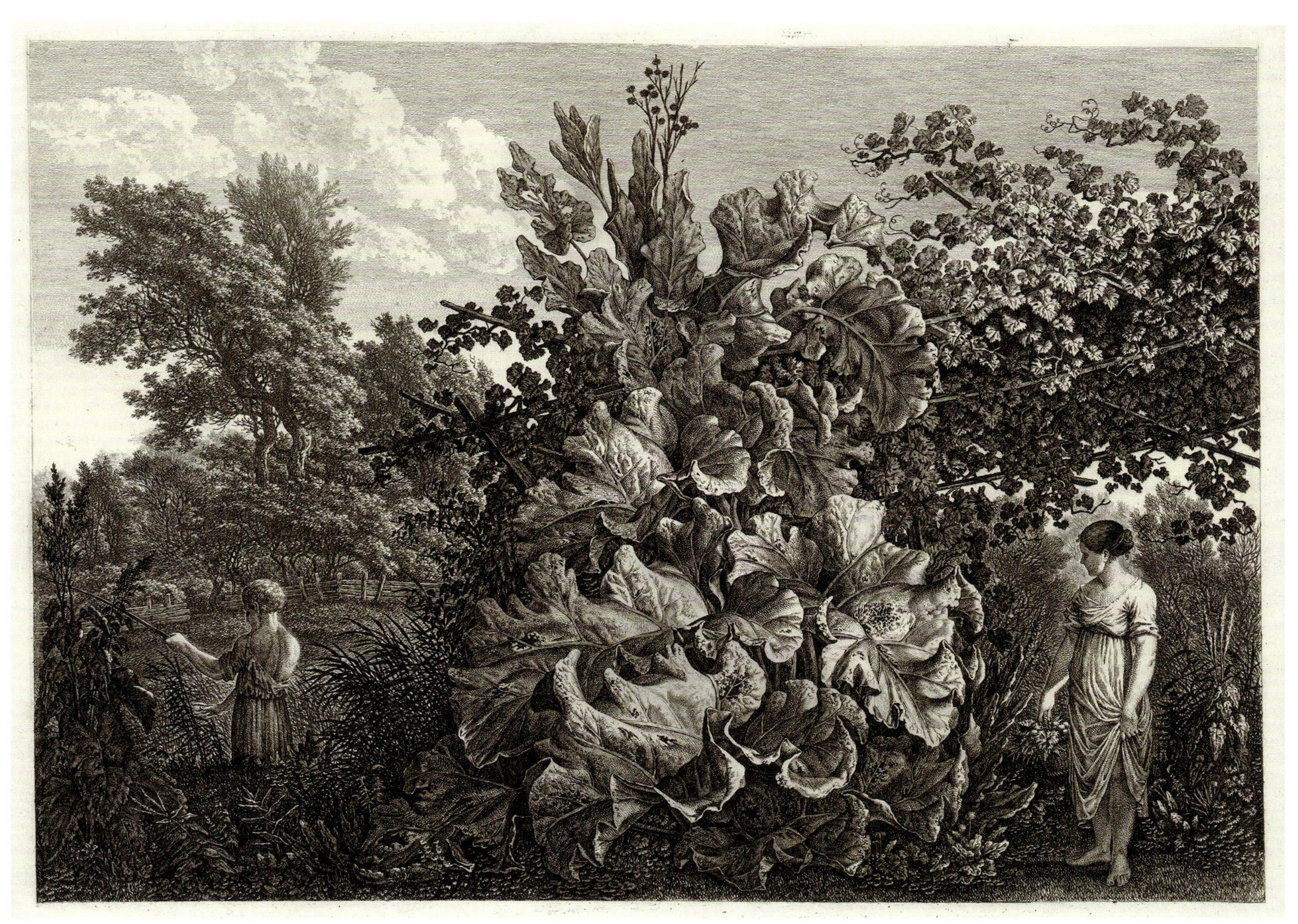

Carl Wilhelm Kolbe, *Large Plant Next to an Arbor with Woman with a Basket*, c. 1820–4, etching, 13⅖ × 17⅘ in.

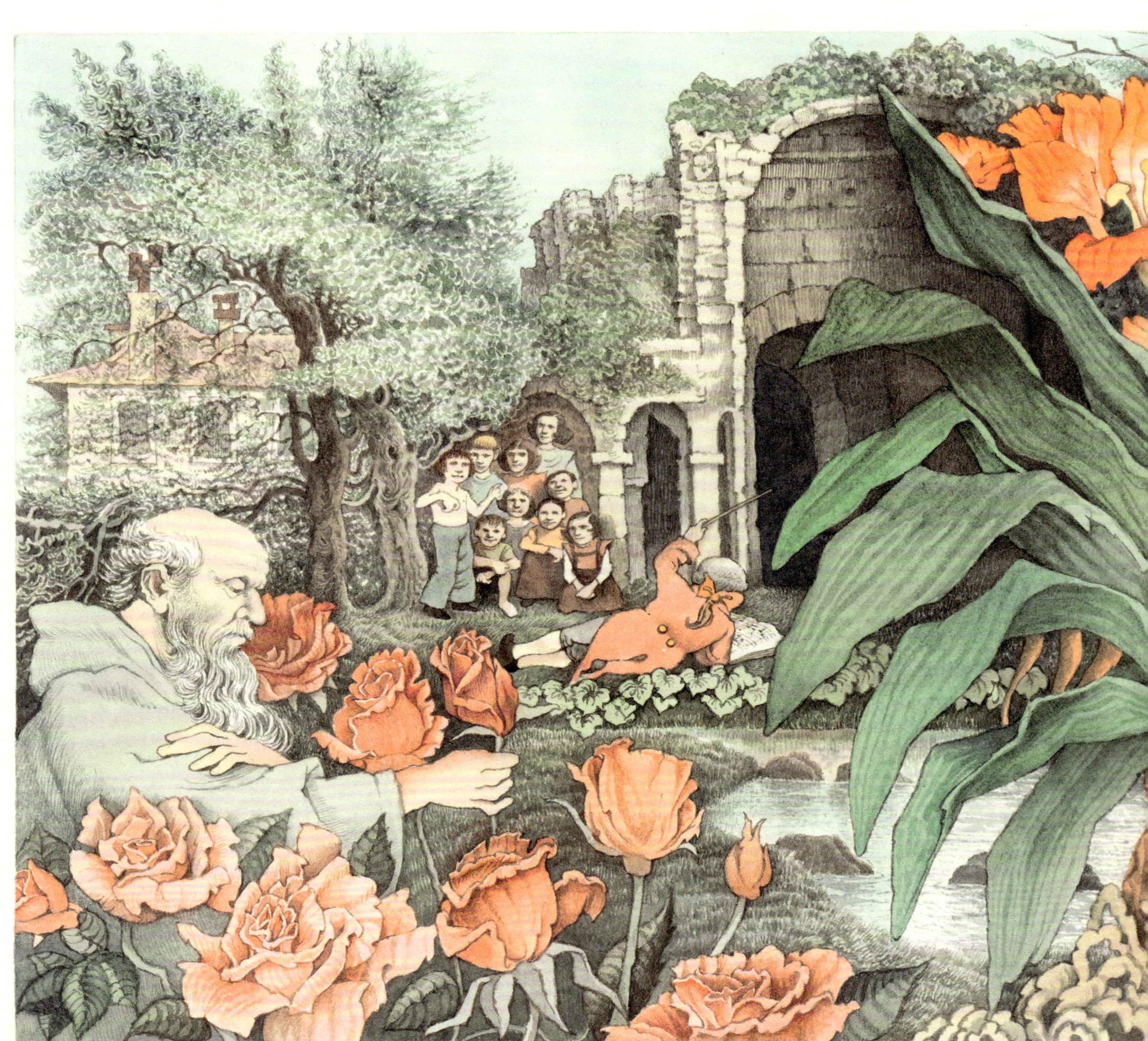

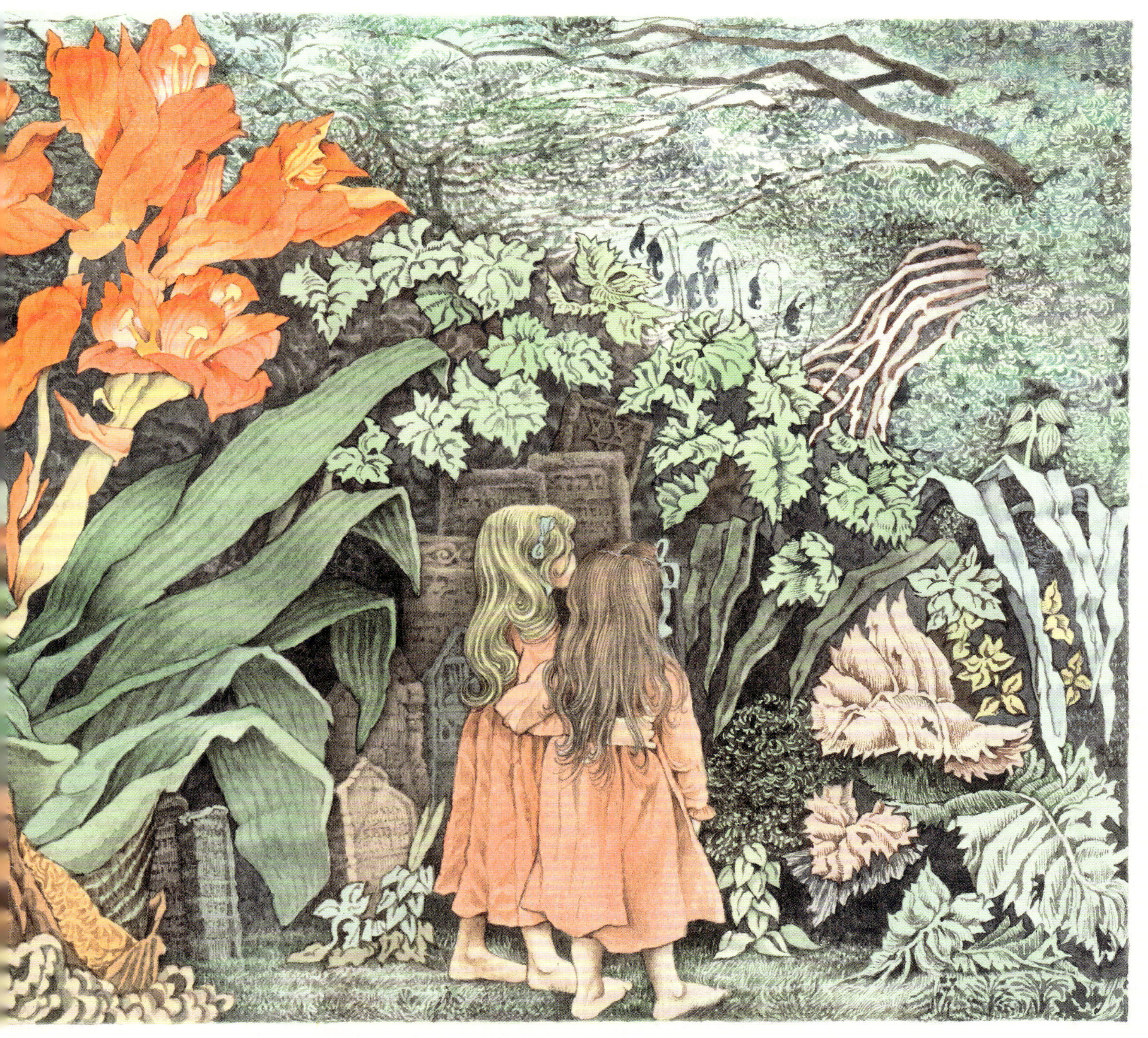

Maurice Sendak, *Dear Mili*, 1985, watercolor on paper, 11 × 22¼ in.

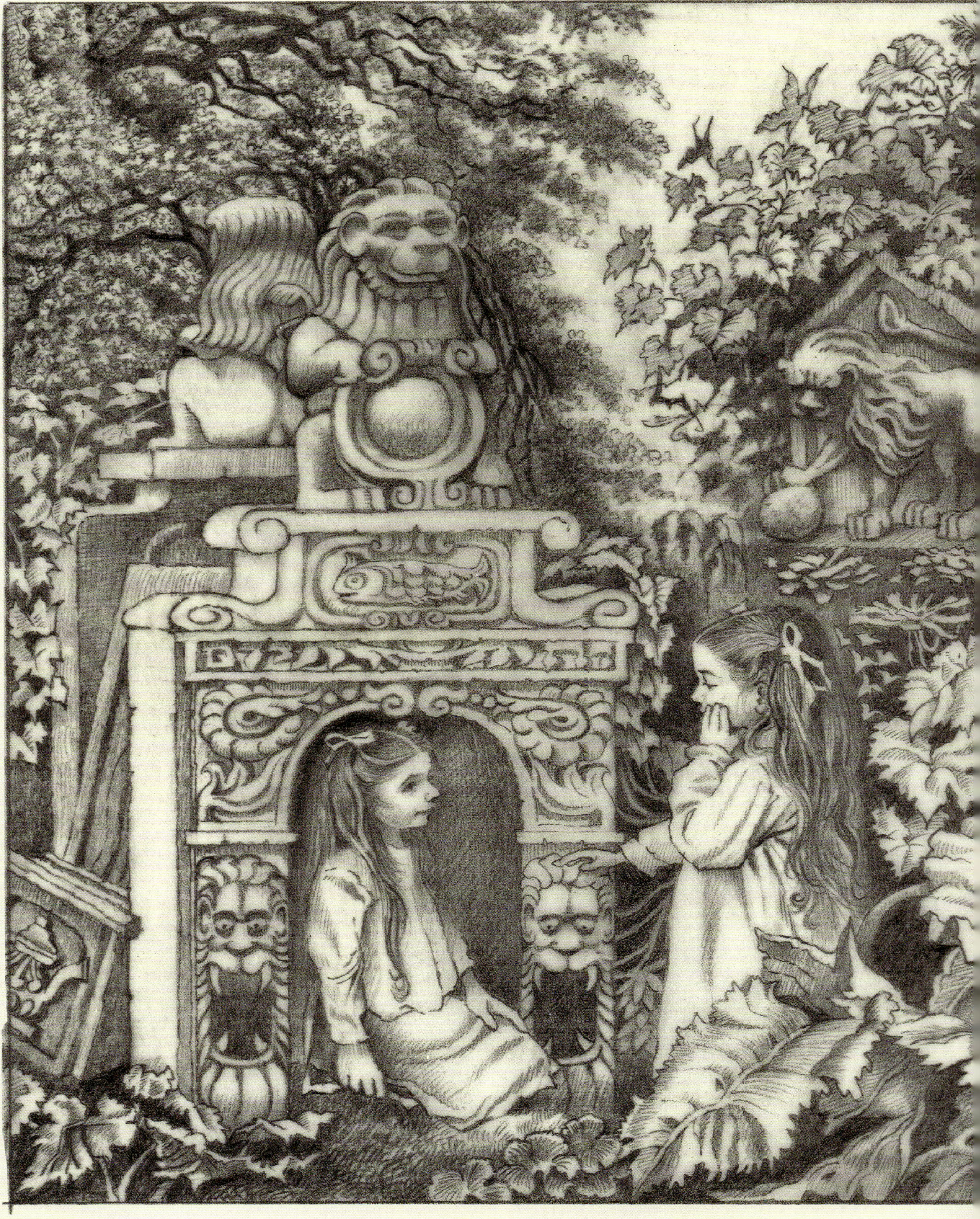

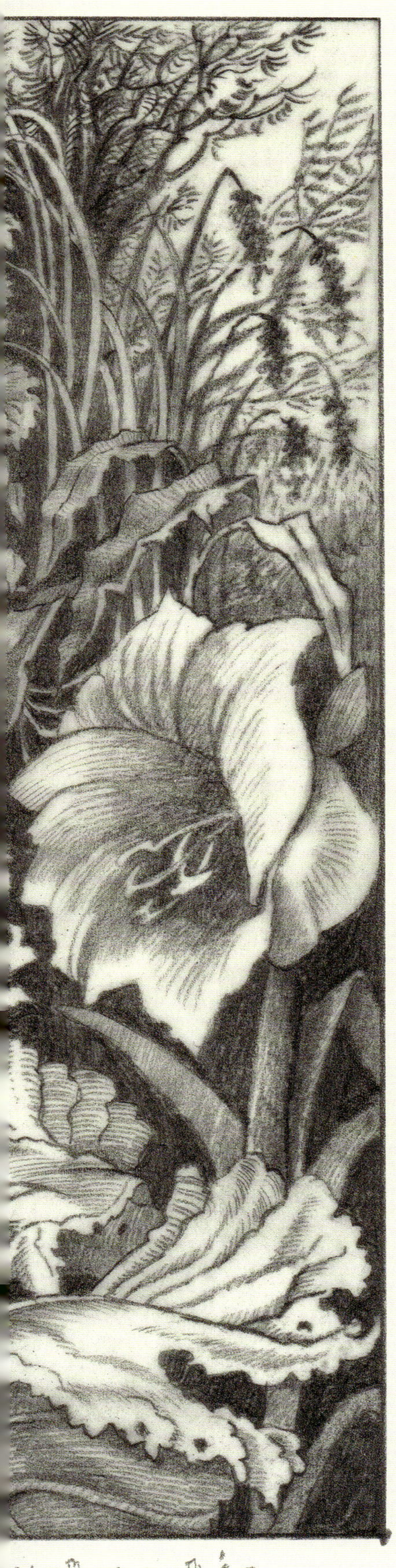

"It was a very simple, pious tale, and yet it hit me at a point in my life where it meant something other than that to me. It was yet another version of all the stories I have written, all the stories that I've read and loved. It has to do with a particular aspect of childhood, which is the incredible, touching loyalty and courage of children, even in the face of demonic forces."

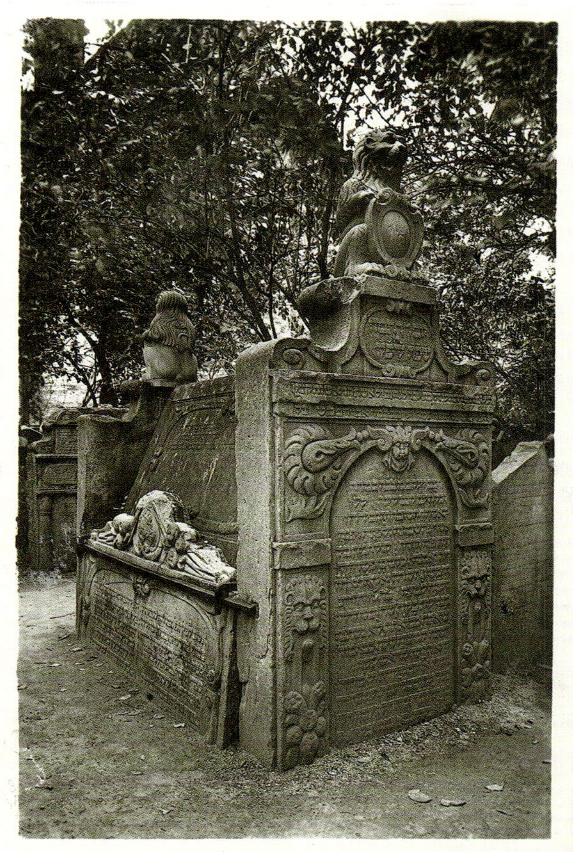

Gravestone, Jewish Cemetery, Prague, c. 1985, postcard

left: Maurice Sendak, Study for *Dear Mili*, 1985, pencil on tracing paper, 7¾ × 10⅛ in.

We Are All in the Dumps with Jack and Guy

"One night on Rodeo Drive . . . I saw the naked feet of a kid sticking out of a cardboard box in front of one of those fucking ostentatious stores, and that was when I saw what Jack and Guy could be: contemporary, political. I'd also been reading about the rounding up in the night by the police of homeless kids in Rio."

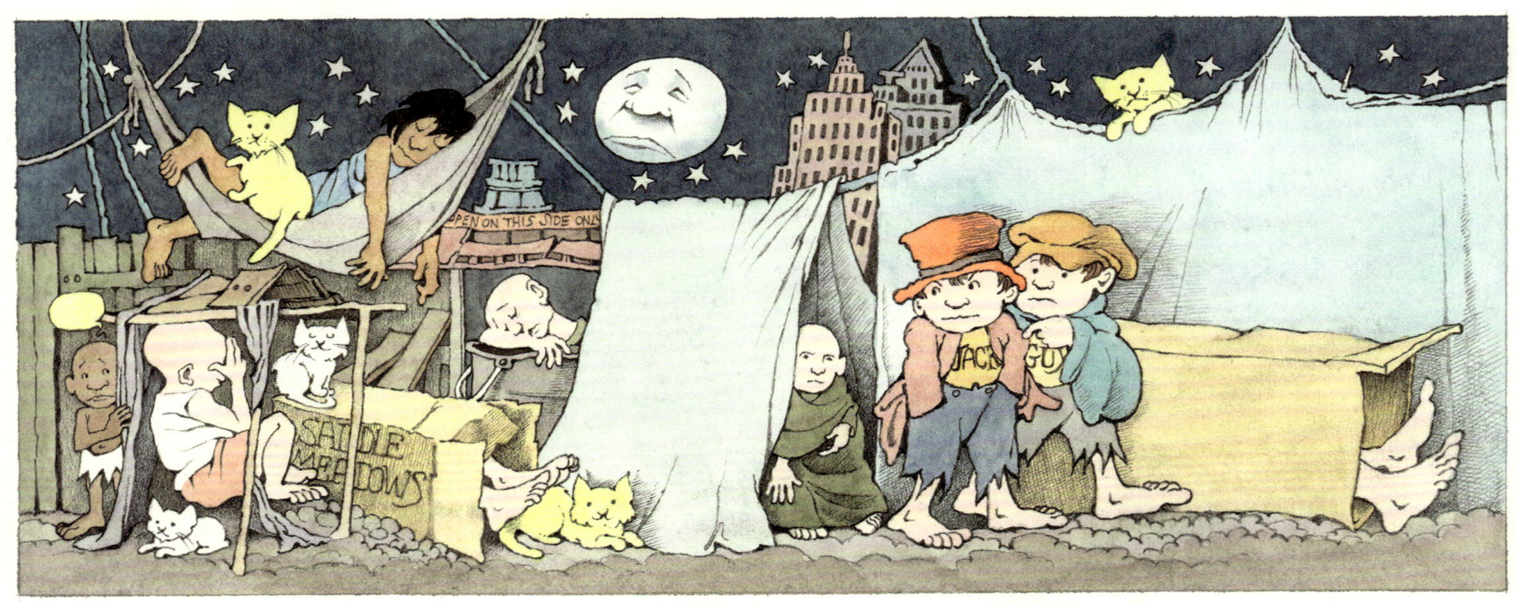

Maurice Sendak, *We Are All in the Dumps with Jack and Guy*, 1992, watercolor and ink on paper, 8½ × 11¼ in.

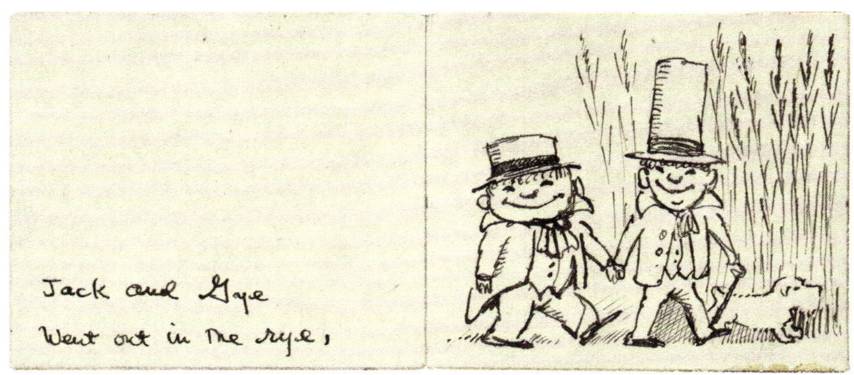

Maurice Sendak, Dummy for *We Are All in the Dumps with Jack and Guy*, 1965, ink and watercolor on paper, 2 × 4½ in.

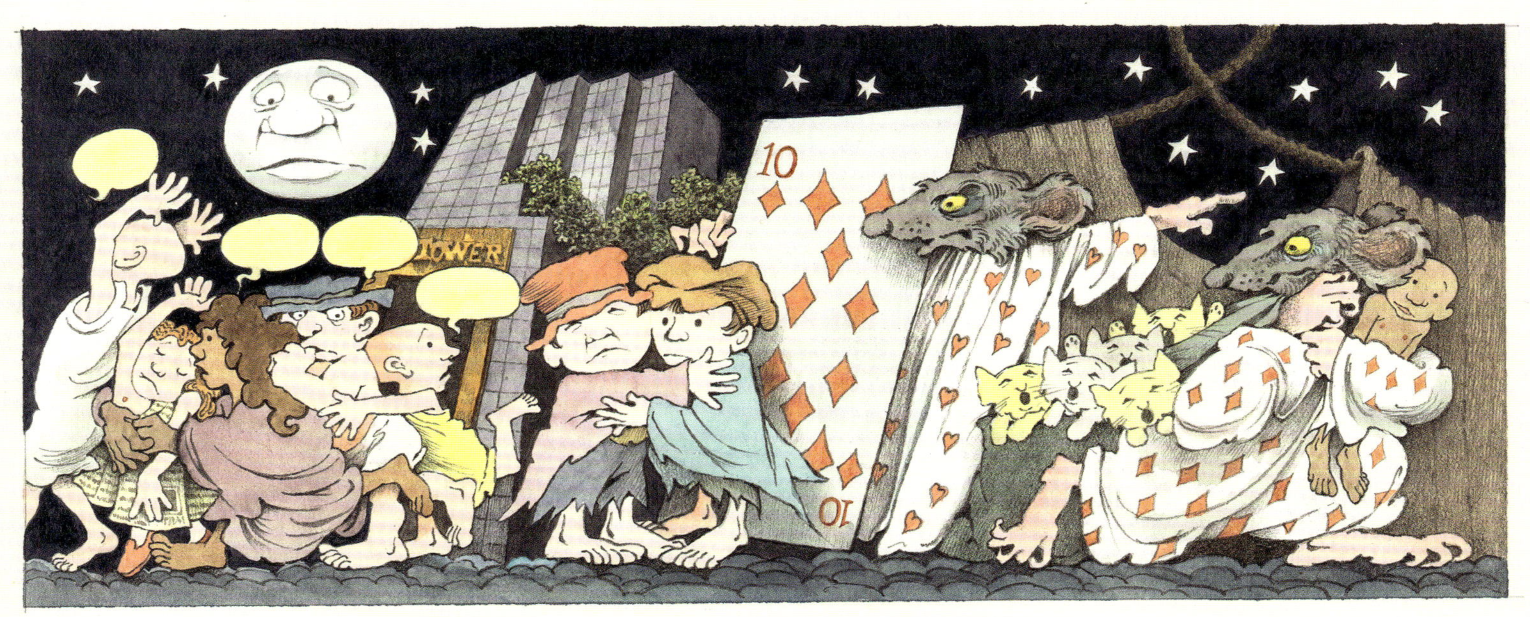

Maurice Sendak, *We Are All in the Dumps with Jack and Guy*, 1992, watercolor and ink on paper, 5½ × 14⅞ in.

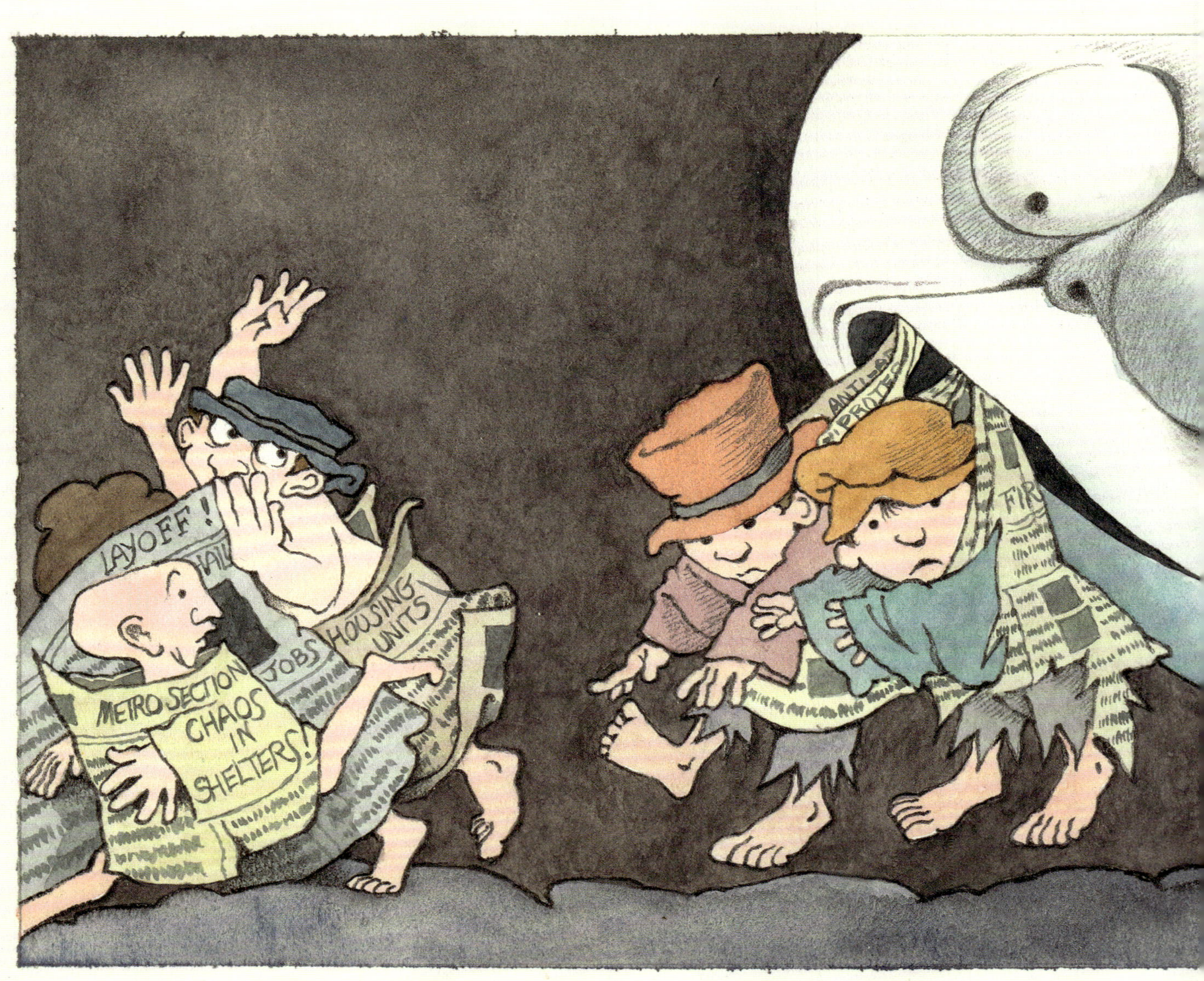
LAYOFF!
JOBS
HOUSING UNITS
METRO SECTION
CHAOS IN SHELTERS!

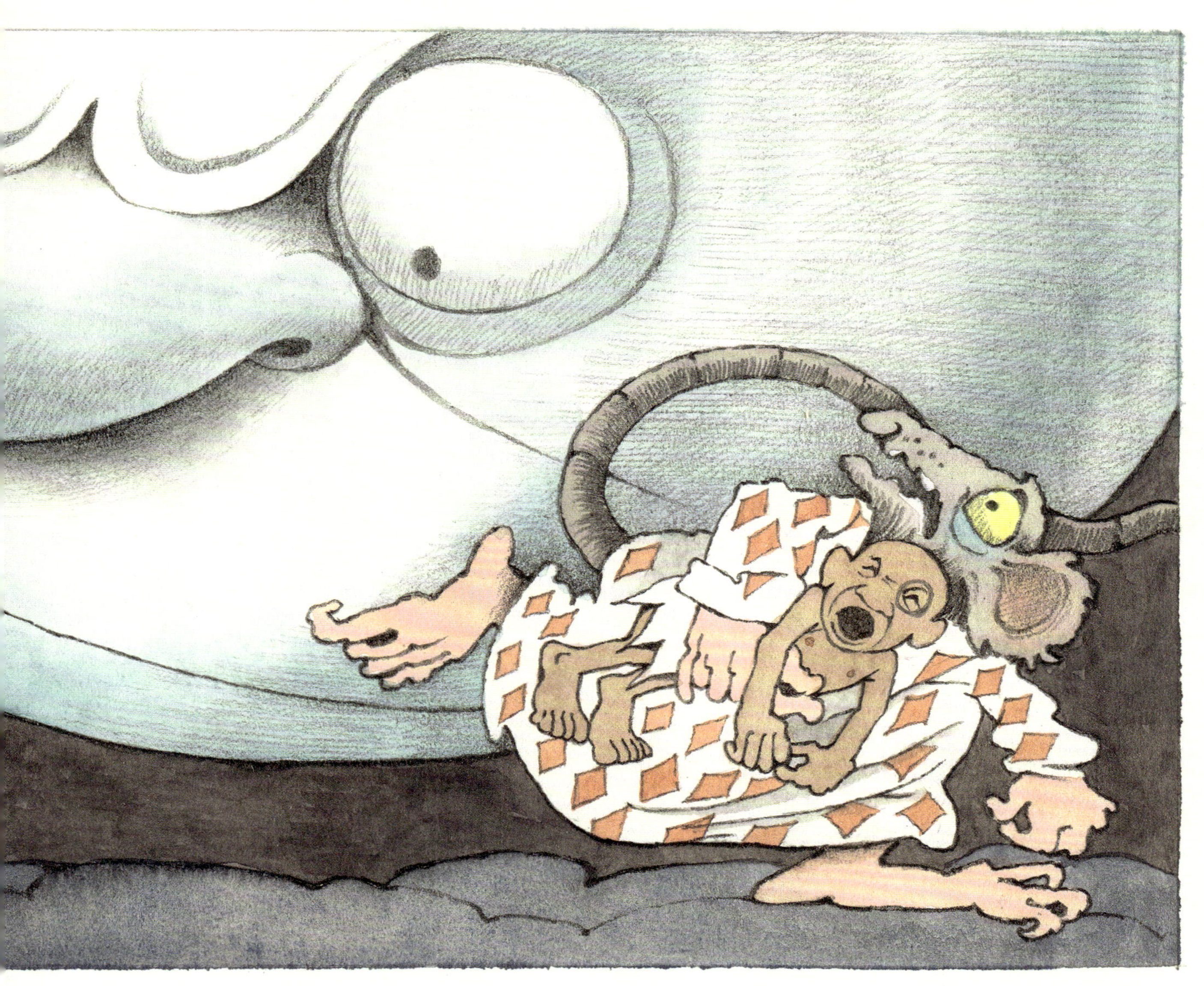

Maurice Sendak, *We Are All in the Dumps with Jack and Guy*, 1993, watercolor on paper, 5½ × 14⅞ in.

CONVERSATION

Arthur Yorinks

The writer and director Arthur Yorinks first met Maurice Sendak in 1970, when he was just seventeen years old. Their forty-year friendship blossomed into a collaboration not only on several picture books, including *Miami Giant* and *Mommy?* but also the creation of *The Night Kitchen Theater* and its productions of *Brundibar*; *It's Alive!* and *Really Rosie.* Yorinks has written a new stage adaptation of *Where the Wild Things Are* for The New Victory Theater and is writing and producing a new animated version of *Really Rosie* for Apple TV +.[1]

LYNN CAPONERA How did you meet?

ARTHUR YORINKS I believe it was the Sunday *New York Times Magazine*, there was an article there on a man named Maurice Sendak, who I had never heard of, because I had no kids' books growing up. I wasn't that interested in what Maurice said about children's books, but he talked a lot about nineteenth-century literature, about writers that I loved, about composers that I loved. Mozart being one of them.

There was something about the whole thing that attracted me to the idea that I was going to meet this guy. And I, in my inimitable insanity, associated that if I met Maurice, I would get out of my parents' house, which I was desperate to do. It made no sense whatsoever, but I said to my friend Les Stoller, "we'll go into the city together, but on the way I'm going to knock on Maurice's door." And he said "What? What the hell are you talking about? You can't do that!" We walked to 9th street . . . And there was the building, and there was his name, but I really honestly don't remember pushing the door button.

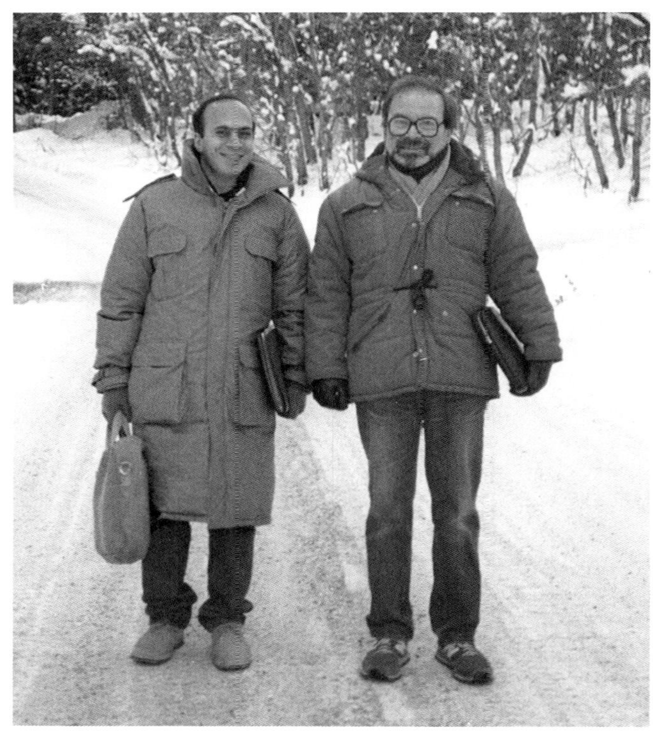

Arthur Yorinks and Maurice Sendak, c. 1987

Still, the wooden door opened, but there was another [screen] door separating us. I said "Maurice?" And he was shocked that I said Maurice. And I was like *The Exorcist*. Words came out of my mouth, but I have no idea exactly what I said. And he, very graciously, said "I'm in the middle of a book"—it was *In the Night Kitchen*—"I'd be happy

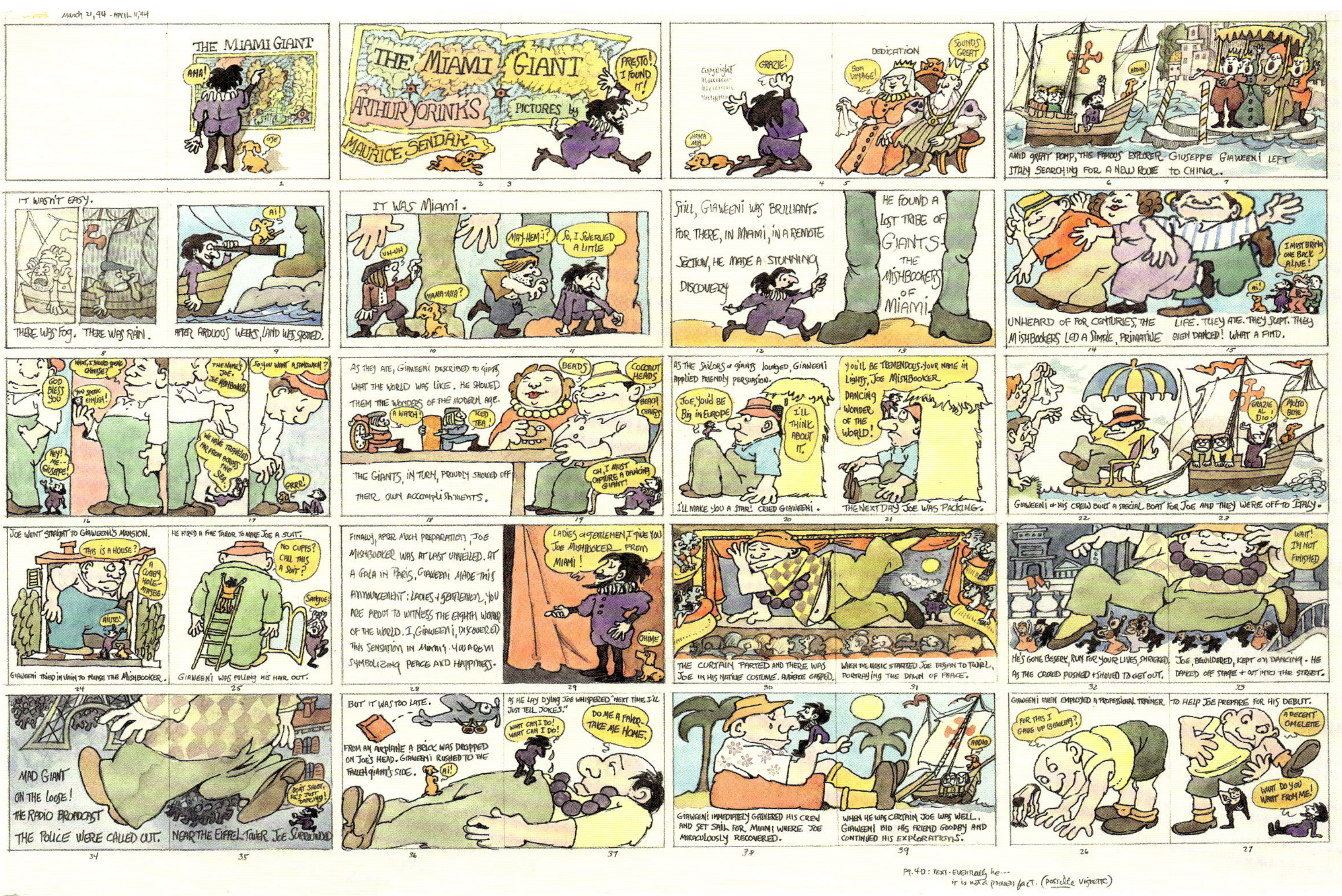

Maurice Sendak, *The Miami Giant*, 1994, watercolor and ink on paper, 11⅜ × 16¾ in.

to speak with you. Why don't you call me on the telephone?" And I said thank you very much. He closed the door and that was that.

Maurice's phone number was in the phone book. And I did a horrible thing. I would call him up; he would answer, and I'd hang up because I would chicken out. And I did this at least two or three times.

So, I'm doing this stupid thing of calling him up with the full intention of hanging up. He answers the phone and just as he answers the phone my dog starts to bark. So now in my own weird insanity, he must know it's me so I can't hang up. "Hello! Who's this?" I told him I'm that kid who, "blah blah blah." And then what ensued was what seemed like a conversation but was more a grilling of me by Maurice. I told him all the books I read. What led me to this, and that I wanted to be a short-story writer. And then he asked, "have you ever read *Winnie the Pooh*?" "What'd you think of it?" While I tried to figure out what to say, my voice blurted out. "I hate that book." There was a slight pause. And he said, "Well come over for lunch on Tuesday."

I went to Ninth Street. He made a tuna fish sandwich. We had a ginger ale. We ate, we talked, we became friends.

I'll tell you one very *Night Kitchen* thing that happened. After that lunch, every so often, I would

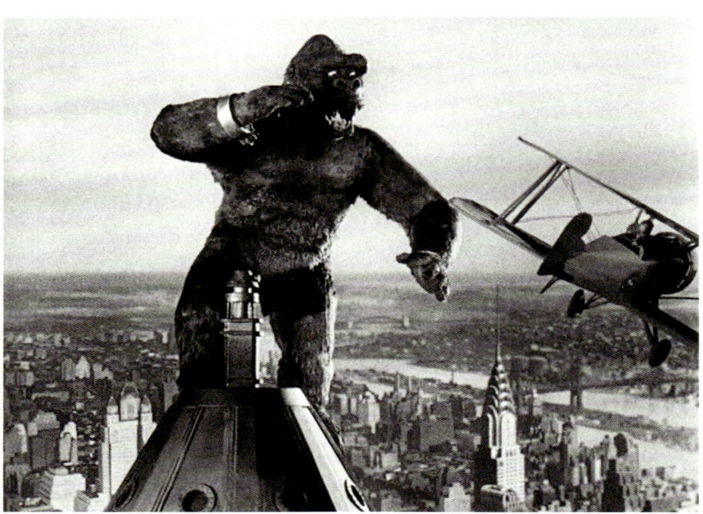

King Kong, 1933

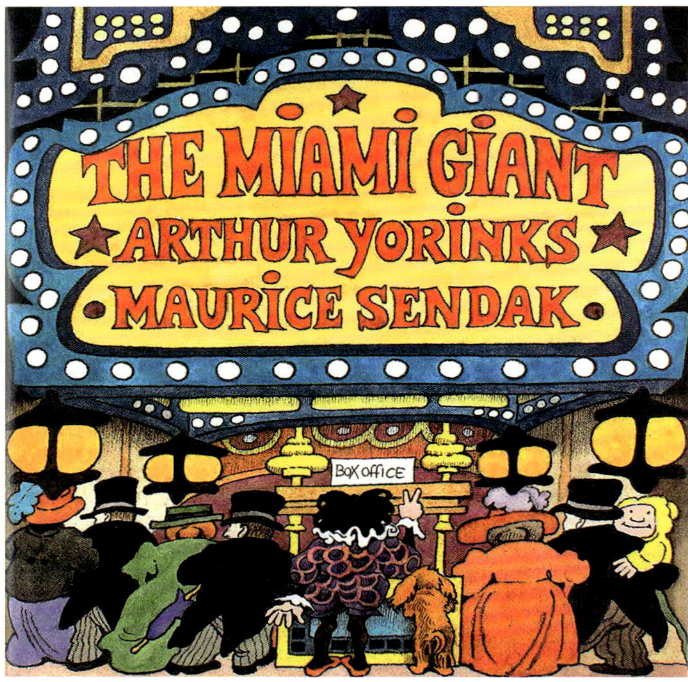

Arthur Yorinks with Pictures by Maurice Sendak, *Miami Giant* (New York: HarperCollins, 1995)

come into the city, and we would take late-night walks. On Fifth Avenue there was a spot where there was a direct shot to the Empire State Building, and it was eleven o'clock at night. It was a full moon. And we looked up, and it was *Night Kitchen*, not the milk bottle, but the Empire State building and that moon. And Maurice was staring at it like he was almost possessed. And he just turned to me and he said, "Look at that!"

New York, in particularly Manhattan, is always Maurice to me. I can't look at the Empire State building, I can't look at buildings lit up at night without remembering Maurice. It was that powerful and I remember thinking to myself, this is exactly like my experience with Edgar Allan Poe: the power of an artist to fundamentally change the way one looks at something forever.

You know people always mistake that I was a student of Maurice's. I was never a student of Maurice's. We met in this very odd way, and we were friends and at some points in time collaborators on a few things. But I must say I hope somewhere I was a teacher to him in some things; in the most basic real-life way there were so many things I did learn from him.

Maurice had a direct connection to what he's feeling and expressing. That direct connection is so unusual and rare among all of us that it is the epitome of charm. Because real charm is not falsehood in my opinion. Real charm is the ability to be yourself in public without a filter. And Maurice was often himself in public without filters. As adults, that's what we find so wonderful about kids.

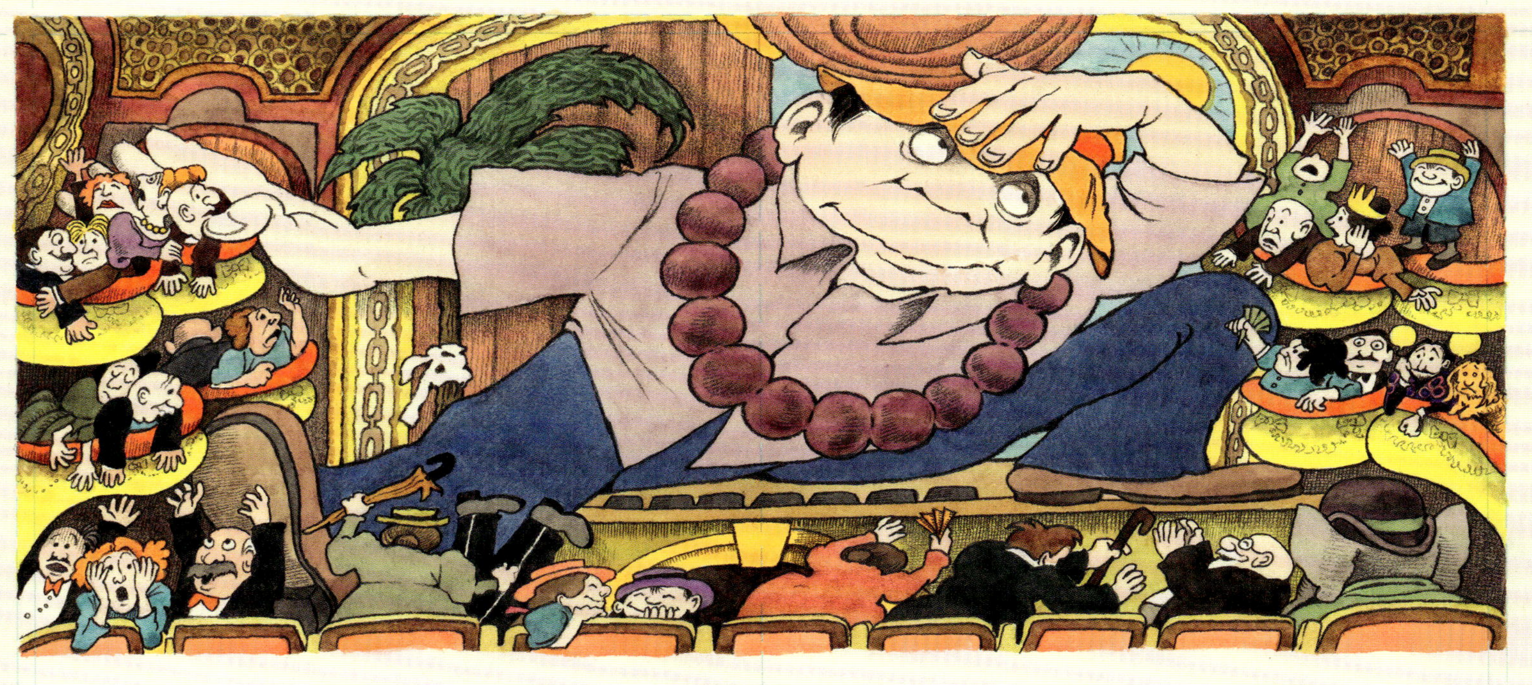

Maurice Sendak, *Miami Giant*, 1994, watercolor and ink on paper, 11 × 14 in.

JONATHAN WEINBERG Talk about your collaboration on *Miami Giant*.

AY There are a lot of references in this book that touched both of us. I mean the *King Kong* movie that we both loved . . . The idea of this crazy tribe being Jewish relatives in Florida. This lost tribe of giants. And in some way this was a sequel to *Where the Wild Things Are*; that these were the Jewish relatives from the *Wild Things*.

So, we did this book. It was not an easy collaboration. A lot of the manuscript became propelled by talk bubbles that Maurice drew; so some of the text no longer physically fitted. And I spent—it feels like a year, but it was probably about a month, six weeks—altering my manuscript, character by character, to fit. The challenge was very difficult. But the fun we had talking about it was sheer joy.

JW When you first met Maurice, was there something that drew you to him right from the beginning? The mythic themes of *Wild Things*? The artist as child?

AY I'll tell you where it collides and collides in the best sense of overlaps. My age-old theme is the search and journey to gain the bravery and courage to be yourself. To find one's identity.

And so, that kind of overlaps with Maurice's kind of theme. Because there's an outsider element to both—the outsider in the child who has to exist in this grown-up world. Maurice's thing was about, in the end, finding a way to be loved. And my thing, in the end, was about finally loving yourself and accepting yourself.

Note

1. Excerpts from interviews with Arthur Yorinks conducted by Lynn Caponera and Jonathan Weinberg in New York City on October 30, 2015, and with Jonathan Weinberg on March 21, 2016.

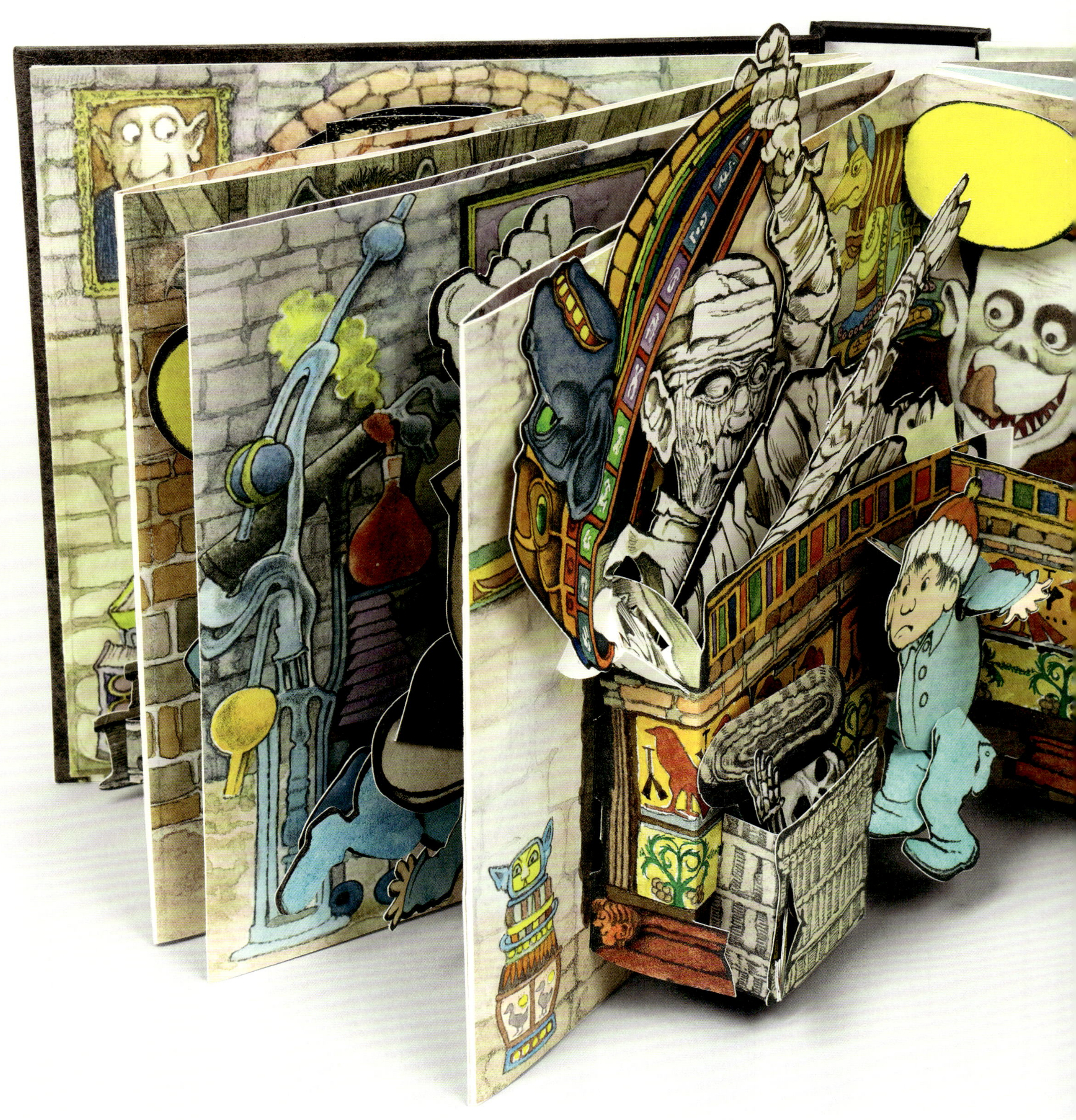

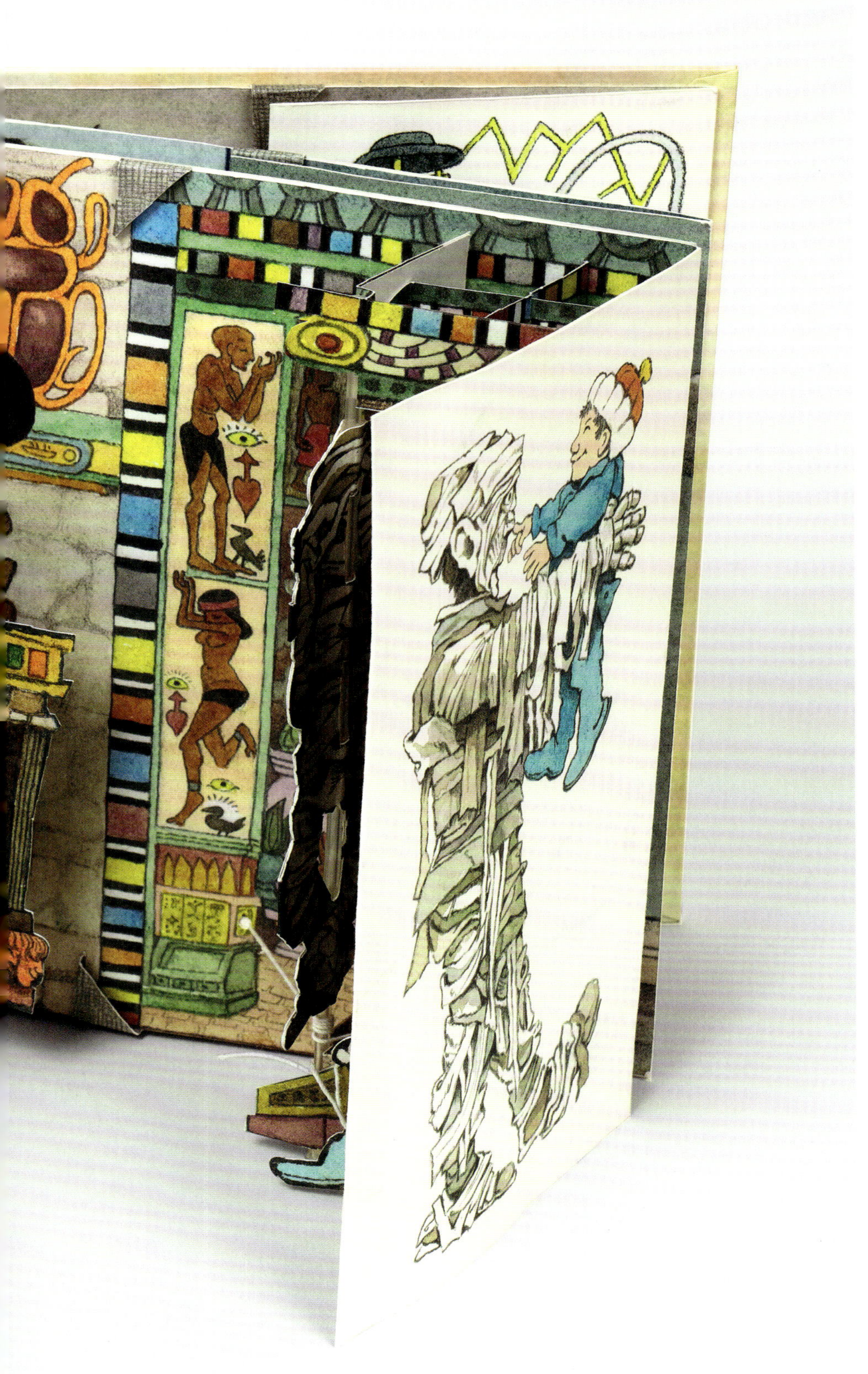

Art by Maurice Sendak, Scenario by Arthur Yorinks, Engineered by Matthew Reinhart, *Mommy?* (New York: Michael di Capua Books/Scholastic, 2006)

CONVERSATION

Carroll and Christina Ballard

Carroll Ballard, the Director of such acclaimed films as *The Black Stallion* and *Never Cry Wolf*, first met Maurice Sendak in Los Angeles in the early 1980s. They worked together when Ballard directed the 1986 film version of Pacific Northwest Ballet's production of *Nutcracker* with sets and costumes by Sendak. They also worked on other projects including a film of *Very Far Away* that never came to fruition.[1]

CARROLL BALLARD (CB) I ran into Maurice over thirty years ago and we hit it off pretty well, both trying to get a film off the ground. And we succeeded in doing *Nutcracker*, which was something he had already totally put together with a ballet company in Seattle. And all I did was come in and film the stage production. And most of the time, we were trying to communicate with Hollywood our ideas for film projects. Without much success, unfortunately.

CHRISTINA BALLARD I grew up in Switzerland. I knew his books. And then we had the meeting in Los Angeles . . . It was lovely to finally see the creator of *The Wild Things*. All *The Little Bear* books. That stuff which we really cherished.

And so it became a friendship. And we had a memorable visit at his house in Ridgefield, Connecticut. With our little daughter Nora. With his dogs. And it was like sort of coming home . . . It was like we had known Maurice for a long time in some ways. But it was more a connection of the heart that was very spontaneous. And we had such good laughs. Maurice had such good jokes. Really. All the time. In the darkest of times. We miss him. A big loss.

LYNN CAPONERA Carroll, didn't he talk to you about making a film out of *Very Far Away*?

CB I read the script and I thought it was the best script that I had ever read. It was the best concept for a movie. I thought it was absolutely sensational.

JONATHAN WEINBERG Why did you think it was so terrific?

CB The concept of it, that this little boy had absorbed the feelings from his family and all the stuff that they had gone through and how he fantasizes in his own mind . . . to me it was just so incredibly creative and I thought it was a great project for a film. Because it broke all the rules and, you know, it worked like gangbusters for me. And I think it could do that in a film. But the powers that be were just terrified. It was too heavy for them.

It was seeing the whole thing through the eyes and the sensibility of a little boy. To me, one of the most powerful elements in film is the point of view, what point of view you see. And we've kind of gotten away from it. The way films are made now, it's all God's point of view. It's all we're watching people, they're talking, they're fighting, they're doing whatever. But we're watching it as observers. We're not in the middle of it. Whereas the way that *Very Far Away* was visualized is that you actually experience it through the eyes of this little boy and his expectations and his hopes and his frustrations.

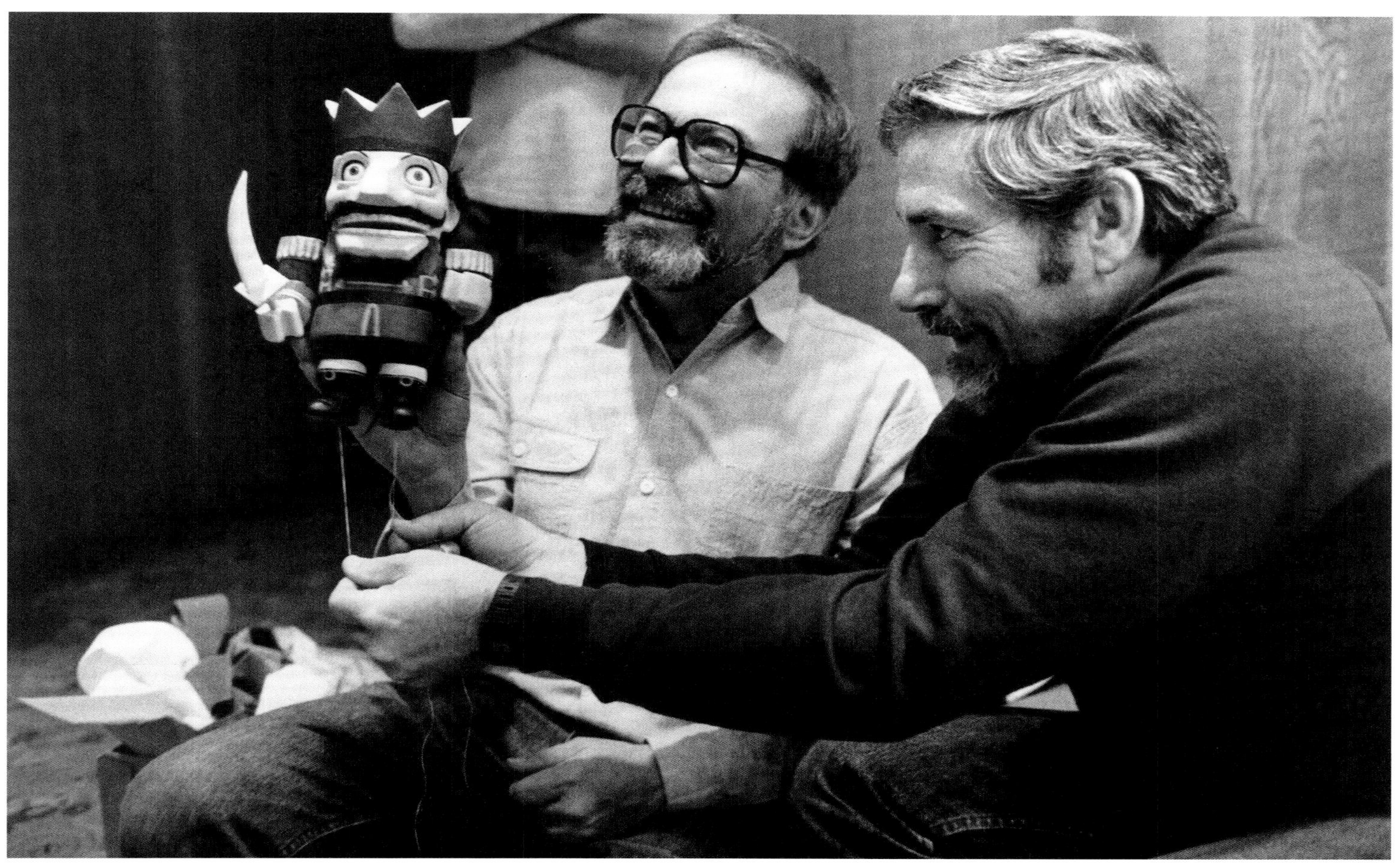

Carroll Ballard and Maurice Sendak during the filming of *Nutcracker*, 1986

ARTHUR YORINKS What was working on *Nutcracker* like? You had a great collaboration with Maurice but there was another person in the room, Kent Stowell, the choreographer?

CB I was struggling, trying to make it into a thing of its own rather than just filming the stage version. Both Maurice and I were arguing to go back to the original story, E.T.A. Hoffman's, "The Hard Nut," which has a lot more horsepower than the ballet, and somehow bring more of "The Hard Nut" into the story, give it a little more weight as a film. But the guys who were [providing] the money were intractable. They thought they could make a cheap Christmas film out of it and make some money. And that was it. They didn't see the potential of what the old "Hard Nut" story really had in it.

LC I remember Maurice specifically commenting on how you brought the sexuality of Clara into it and he really wanted to see that in the staged version, And I wondered, is that clearly what you were going for?

CB Well, I was trying to do whatever I do. You know, give it a little juice.

Maurice had a whole series of children's stories that he would have loved for us to have worked on. But they were similar, in that they all involve children and they reveal their viewpoint through the adventures.

LC You did create this really wonderful friendship between you and Maurice. And I think it even affected the way he created a book. In all the books that he illustrated and wrote, there is this movie sense to them, as if they were framed by a camera.

"The production of the ballet that Kent [Stowell] and I conceived was our effort to embrace Hoffmann—to get back to the gritty, slaphappy German Marchen that never quite explains itself but is fiercely true to a child's experience."

CB Absolutely.

JW Could you talk a bit more about how what you call creating the child's point of view gets translated in the of nuts and bolts of directing a movie?

CB Where do you want to deliver the emotional punch in the story? All right, you see the child's point of view of the bad guy, and how it appears to him. You also see him from the outside too. And you can see it from God's point of view and everything else. But the real punch of it, the real emotional charge that you're trying to build into the scene, is heavily weighted towards how it affected him. We're not just watching some people carrying on in front of a proscenium. We see that he sees the evil in this person's eye. How it affects him. And it's hard to explain because it's actually very complicated and very simple at the same time.

The thing that was so great working with Maurice, the collaboration, was his sense of humor. I mean his sense of humor was so incredibly penetrating. He sized things up in a nutshell. That was the quality that he brought to things, that I couldn't do on my own. It was my weakness and his strength. He was a professor of the foibles of human nature.

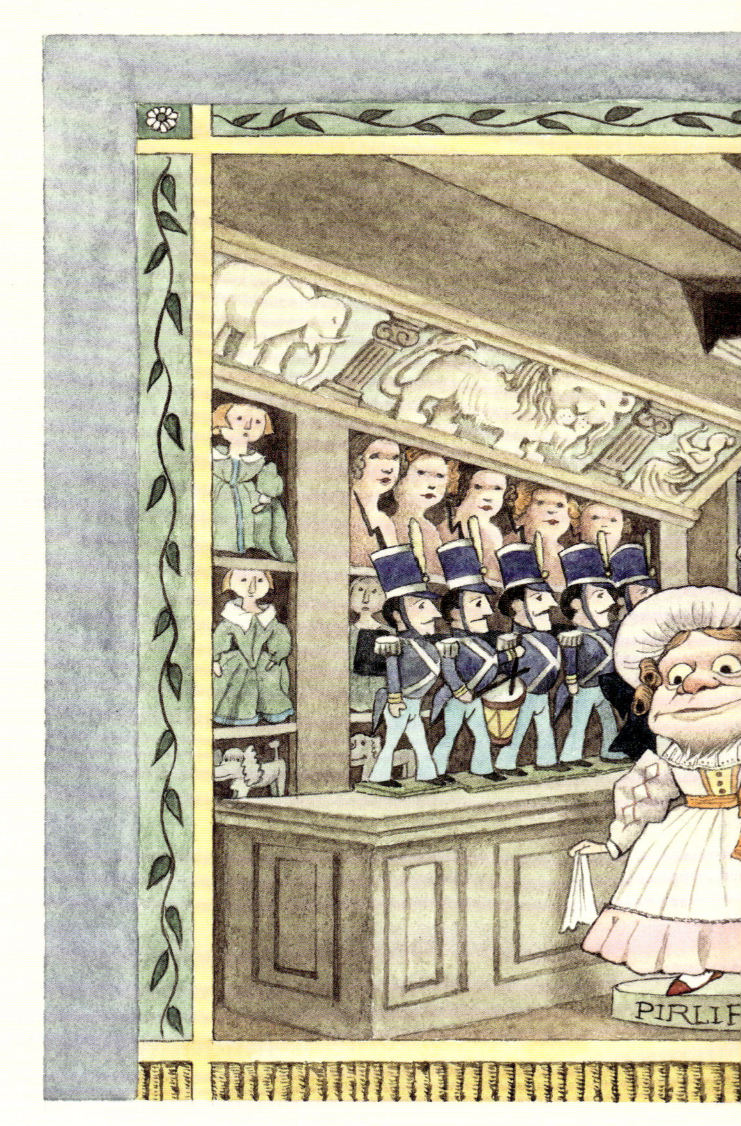

Note

1. Lynn Caponera, Jonathan Weinberg, and Arthur Yorinks interviewed Carroll and Christina Ballard via Zoom on July 8, 2021.

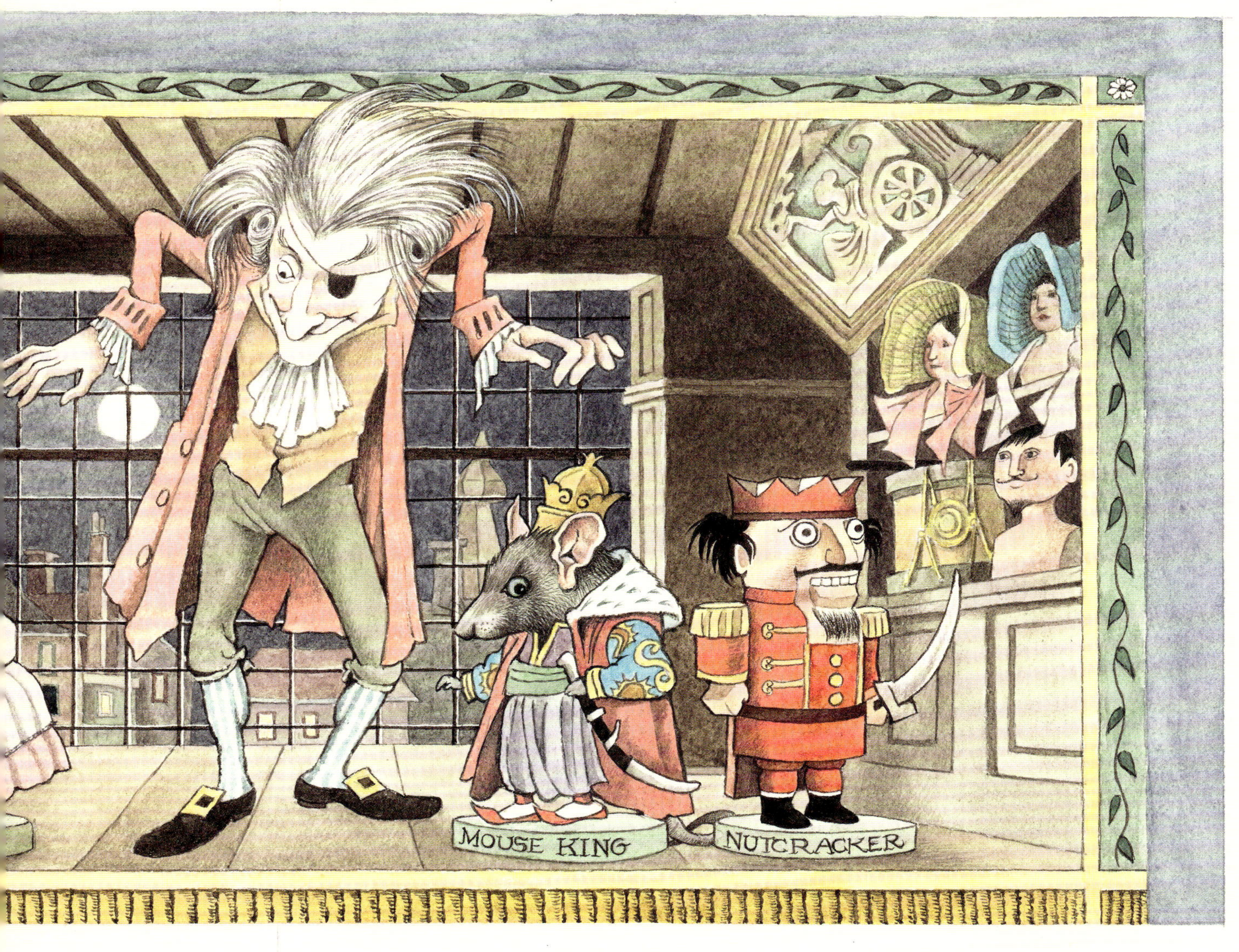

Maurice Sendak, *Design for act curtain, Drosselmeier's Studio*, 1983, watercolor, pen and ink, and graphite pencil, 8½ × 14 13⁄16 in., The Morgan Library & Museum

CONVERSATION

John Dugdale

In 1992 Maurice Sendak commissioned the photographer John Dugdale to stage a series of photographs that he used to create the paintings for Hermann Melville's *Pierre.* The two became close friends, and Sendak was an avid collector of Dugdale's work. It was at the time of the shooting of the *Pierre* photographs that Dugdale first became seriously ill with the complications of HIV, leading to his near-total blindness.[1]

JOHN DUGDALE I met Maurice in Manhattan. He was looking for someone to work with on a photo project. I said why don't you meet me for tea at Anglers and Writers?

At the time I volunteered at a museum, I did nineteenth-century interpretations at Old Bethpage Village on Long Island. I had on nineteenth-century suspenders, a straw hat, farmer's shirt, and broad fall trousers. I thought, "Oh my god I'm going to meet this wonderful illustrator and I didn't have time to change." He got to the restaurant before me, and I walked in and he looked at me and said, "Do you always dress that way?" and that was the first thing he said to me. I sat down and we were instant friends.

In 1992 I had my first bout with pneumonia, and by 93 I had my stroke, and my sight was failing. Jumping forward drastically, one of the things I miss that I treasured were the late-night talks, where I'd say you're my hero in so many ways, and he'd say no you're my hero. They were so mystical, these talks, because I could talk to him in a way that I couldn't with anyone else . . . I could say anything to him.

JONATHAN WEINBERG Maurice really lived in the nineteenth century. It's so appropriate that you would first appear like a dream dressed in nineteenth-century clothes. Was he working on any projects at the time?

JD Ostensibly, he was looking to work on [Melville's] *Pierre*. I had four people, my friend Kay Mehls, my sister Kathleen Dugdale, my partner Darrel Martin, and my good friend Stephen Ashmore. The first thing of course that he wanted them to do was take their clothes off, which wasn't a problem at all. We worked in the front parlor, Maurice became the director, and I was wondering why I felt a little woozy. He stayed here for a week. It turned out the whole time I was taking those pictures, I had a 102.5 fever and pneumonia. But the pictures came out very beautifully.

We had a wonderful time. He sat backwards on an empire chair in the front parlor . . . and he should have had a megaphone and a director's chair and a crop, the way he was yelling . . .

He was so generous, that's one of the things that I really need to say. I went through some awfully difficult times, trying to hold onto my house and keep the studio going when I was deathly ill. I was paralyzed, with a laundry list of issues. Because I was extremely resilient, I had no intention of not finishing what I started, whatever that meant.

Maurice was stunningly intelligent. He helped me allow myself to say that I was an artist, just to him, because I always thought it was corny—I'd always say, "I'm a photographer, not an artist," and

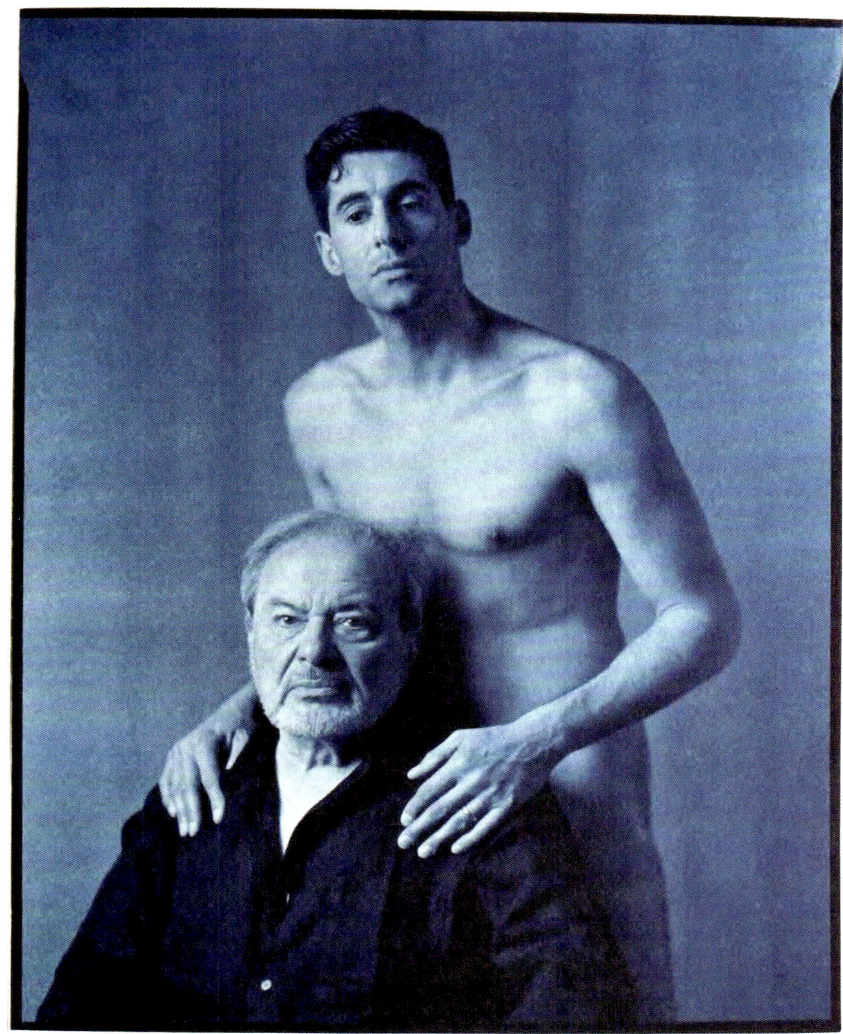

John Dugdale, *Portrait of Maurice Sendak with John Dugdale*, ©copyright John Dugdale

one day I was there by myself, very end of the day, light was going through these wavy glass windows, half way through [Wagner's] ring cycle [was playing,] when Brunhilde is put to sleep by her father and I just started crying. Maurice happened to call and asked, "what's the matter?" and I said, "I'm crying, I have no idea why," and Maurice said, "You don't have to have a reason, you're an artist, of course you're going to cry if you're listening to that by yourself in the winter, watching the sun go down." He just allowed me to be that person that I never let myself be.

I couldn't really read Emily Dickinson. I couldn't grasp it, or it didn't mean anything to me, until after I came out of the hospital, around 1995, when I went and listened to some of it again, not only did I understand it, but it seemed like she wrote it for me. So, we had that in common. He loved her. We went to the family burial plot [and her house], Maurice was extremely excited to be there. It was extraordinary to be there with him, and to stand in front of her desk, near those little books she bound together. It looked like a sparrow with ink had walked across the page. We stood in that spot trying to feel her spirit.

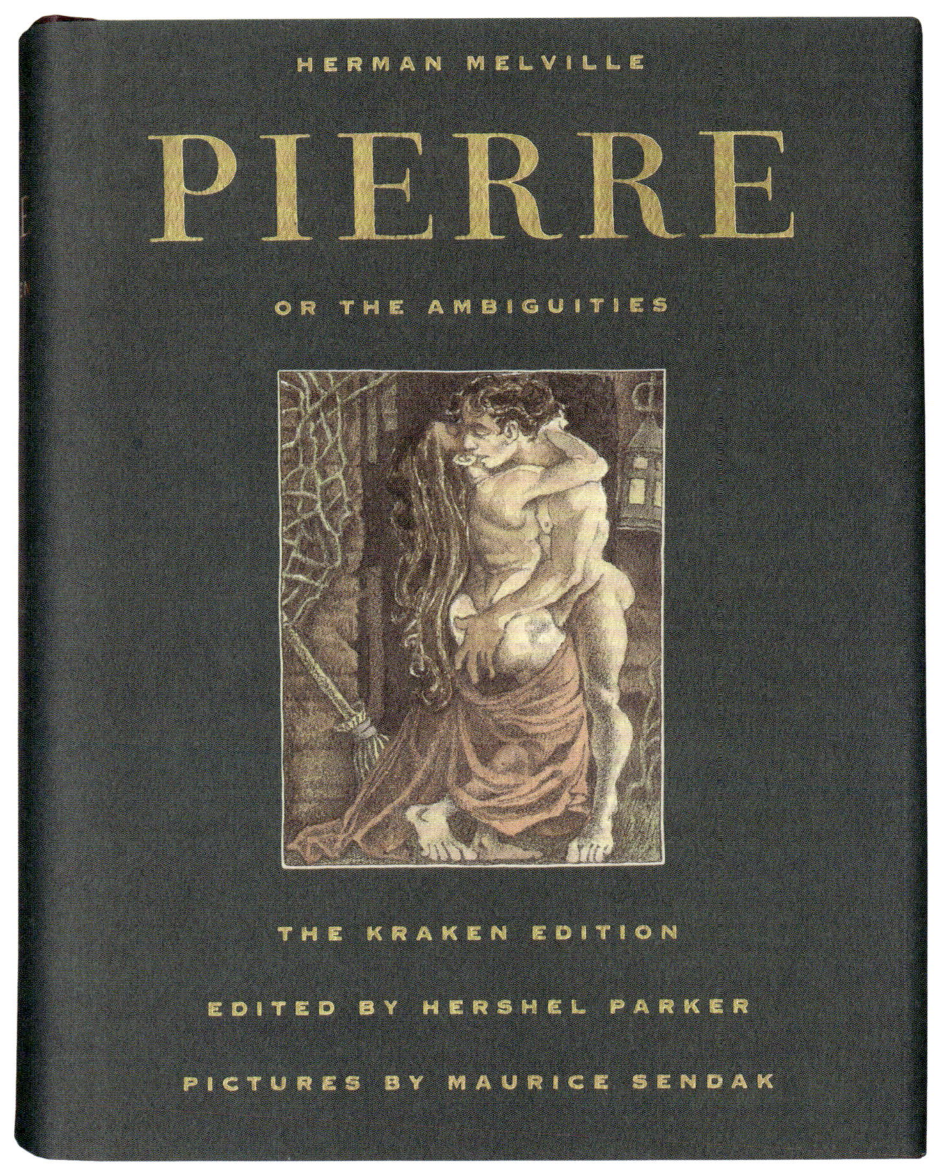

Herman Melville, *Pierre* (Kraken Edition; New York: HarperCollins, 1995), 9 × 6 in.

JW So, Maurice visited you in St. Vincent's. You know Maurice was terrified of hospitals.

JD He walked in; he had a big *Wild Things* doll that he signed the foot. Then he threw himself on top of me on the bed, sobbing. It was so upsetting. I said, "please, please don't cry, you're soaking the bed," and I was stroking the back of his head and I think he came to say goodbye. Then when I got out of the hospital he said, "I don't know how you did it. You're so brave." And I thought, you know it's not really bravery, it's more being stubborn. Because if I really let myself think about what was happening, I probably would have just perished.

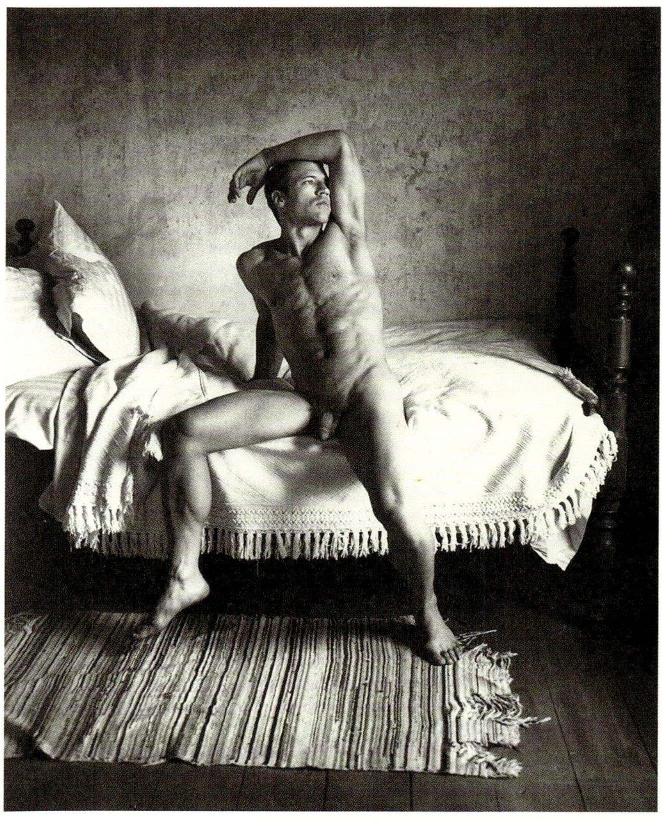

John Dugdale (posed by Maurice Sendak), Stephen Ashmore, *Pierre* Project, 1993 © copyright John Dugdale

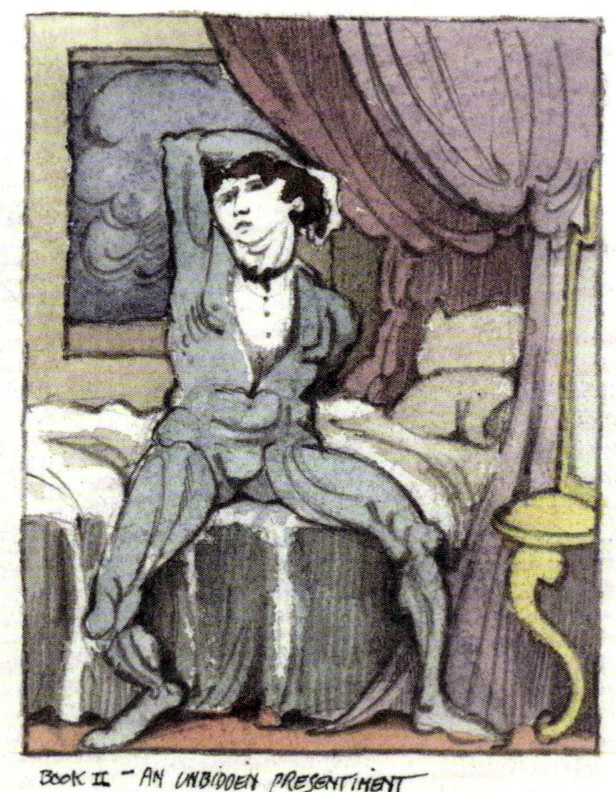

Maurice Sendak, *Pierre: Book II – An Unbidden Presentiment*, detail of studies for *Pierre*, 1993

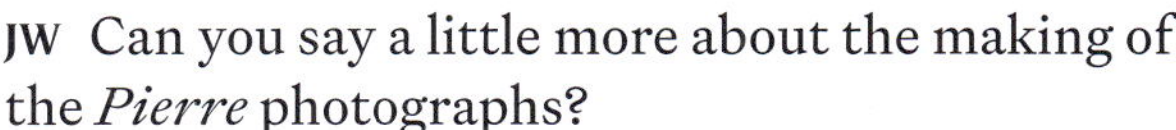

JW Can you say a little more about the making of the *Pierre* photographs?

JD He sat a little away from the action. He did what I learned to do after I came home from the hospital. I described visually what I saw in my mind. He described it to us, to me, and then I took the picture. There was slight interpretation from my point of view, but mostly he was using me to create figure studies.

JW Was it your idea to use your sister?

JD No, though I knew my sister was free with her nudity.

JW But you know *Pierre* is about a brother/sister thing?

JD It's a nice coincidence. I don't think he and I ever mentioned that. He lingered on excessive detail: about which way Darrel's dick was hanging, or where was Stephen going to hug him, or would Stephen stand outside in the field. They were definitely Maurice's pictures, and I am glad. I made some beautiful prints of them through my lab and gave them to Maurice. I can spot the photographs in the drawings.

Note

1. Jonathan Weinberg interviewed John Dugdale over the phone on April 21, 2021.

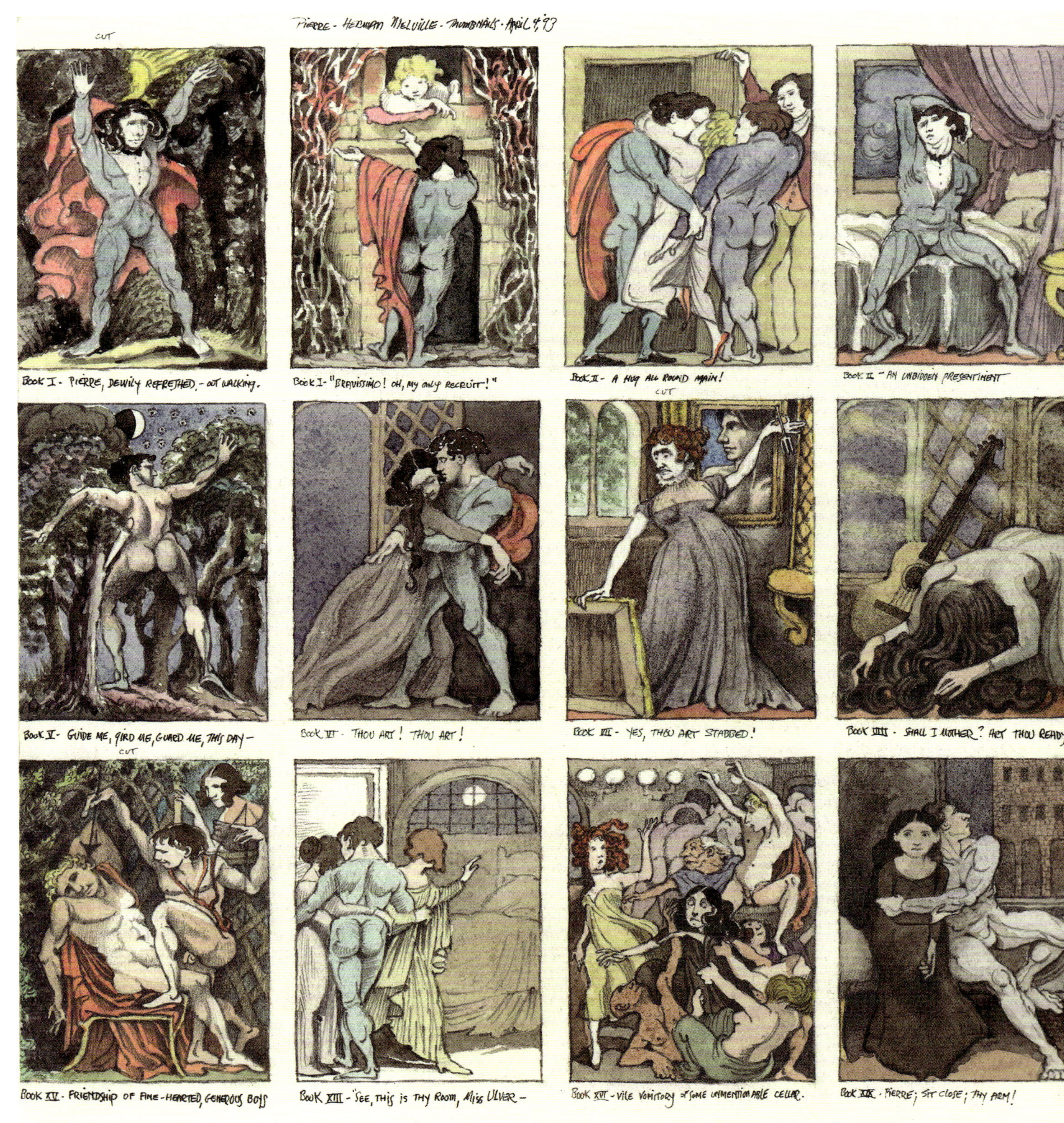

Maurice Sendak, Studies for Melville's *Pierre*, 1993, watercolor and ink on paper, 17 × 22 in.

CUT

CUT

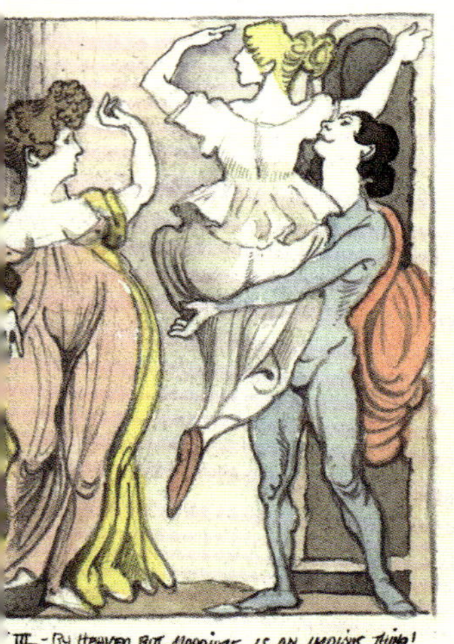
III - By Heaven, but Marriage is an impious thing!

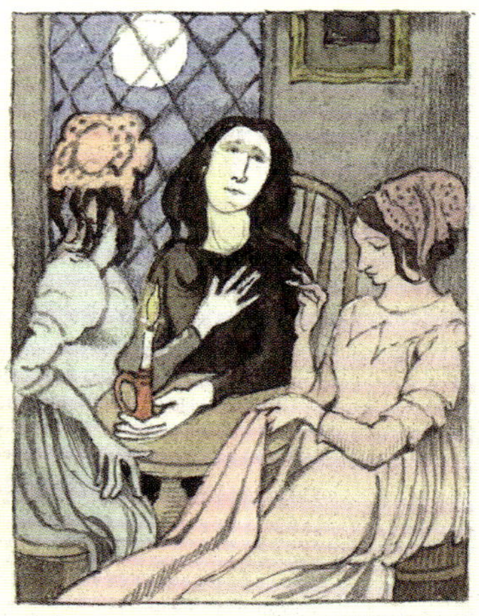
Book III - Her unadorned and modest dress is black

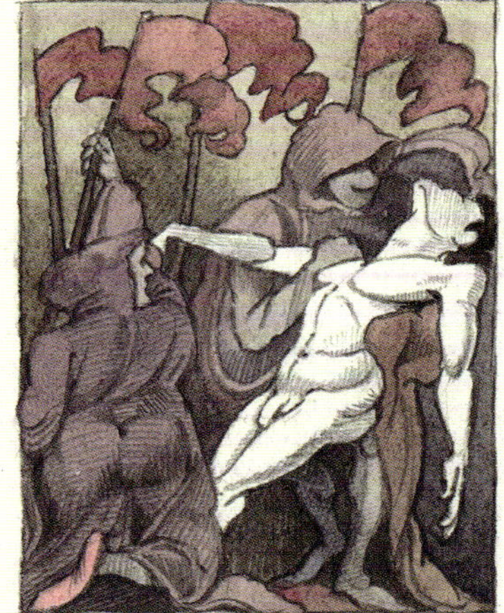
Book III - Phantoms disembarking in his soul

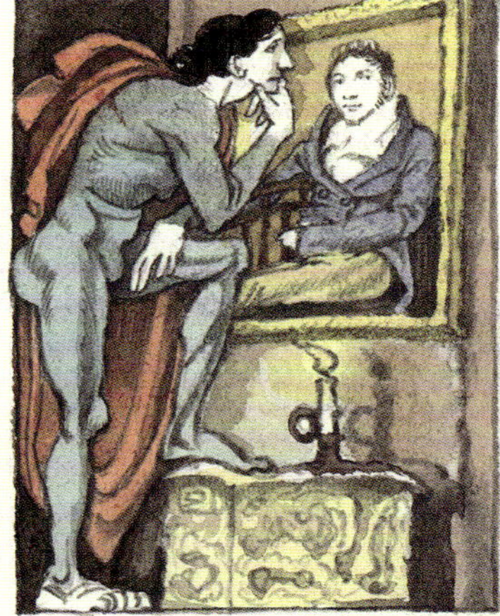
Book III · Youth is hot and temptation strong, Pierre

CUT

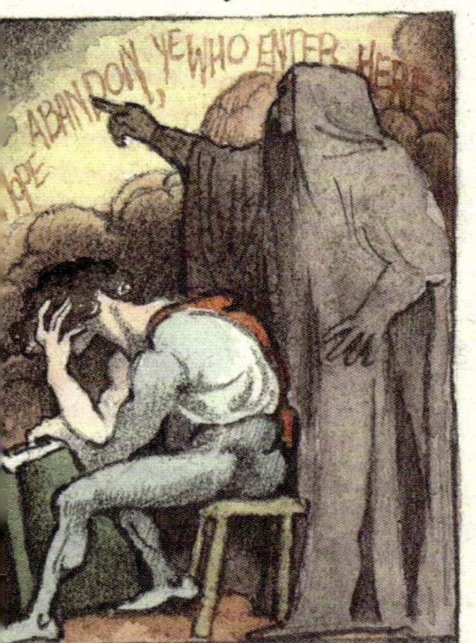

K IX - Dabbling in the vomit of his loathed identity.

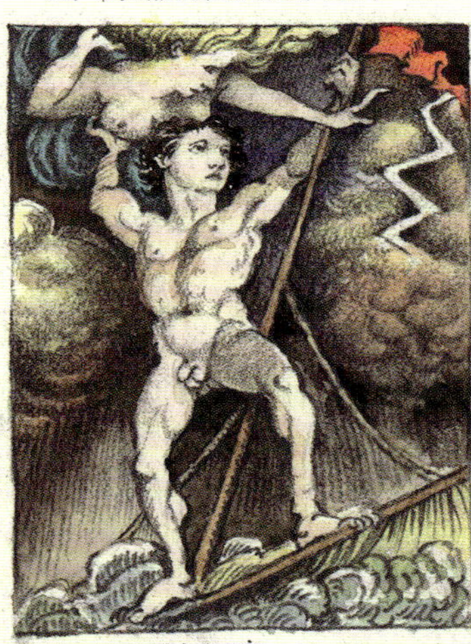
Book X - Self-upbraiding sailor; dreamer -

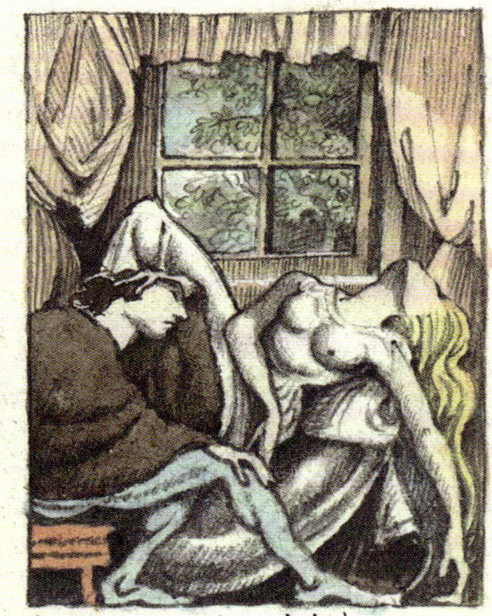
Book XI - So fair a victim!

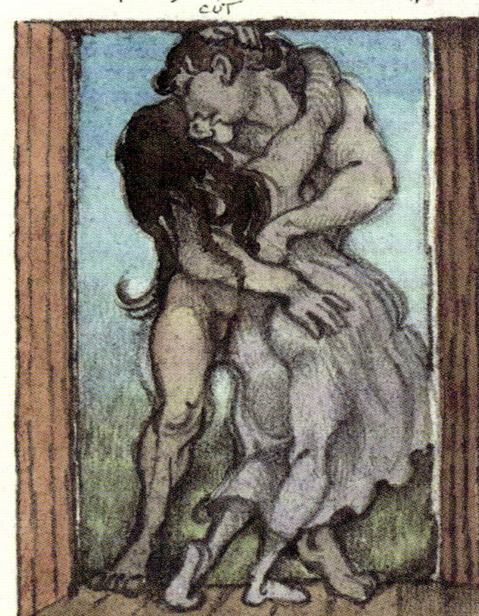
Book XII · His mouth wet her ear; he whispered it.

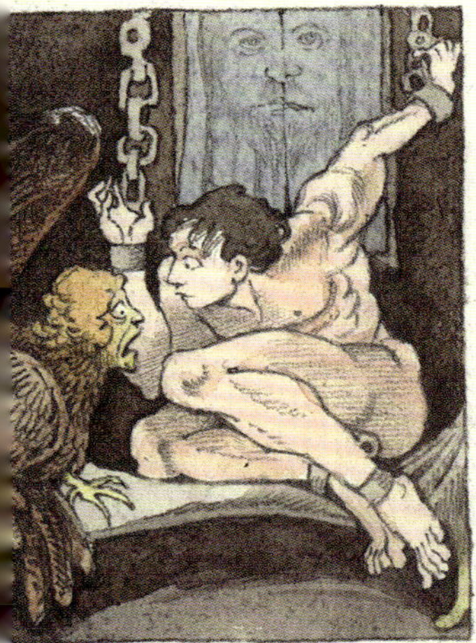
K XXI · Hell-day of an eaten liver forever.

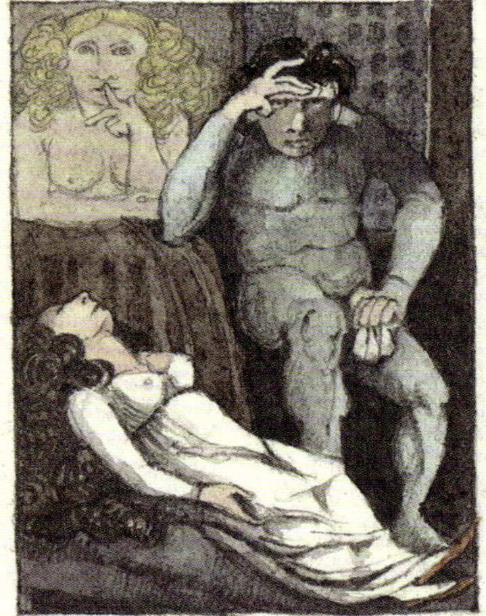
Book XXIII - "The secret is still a secret, Isabel."

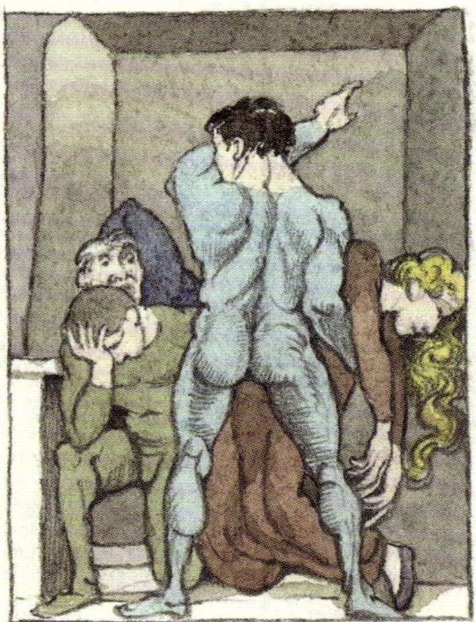
Book XXIII · See; she will faint; let her go, I say!

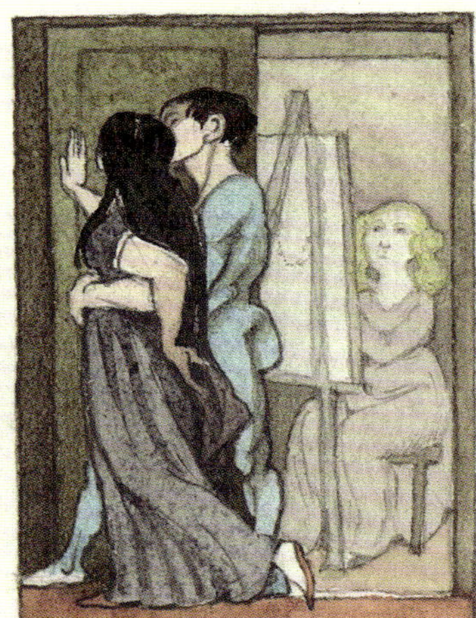
Book XXV - Pierre and Isabel stood locked

CONVERSATION

Twyla Tharp

The acclaimed artist, writer, dancer, and choreographer Twyla Tharp first met Maurice Sendak in the 1980s and they became close friends. Although they discussed and sketched out many ideas for collaborations including an adaption of George MacDonald's *The Princess and the Goblin* they never did create a finished performance piece together. However, in the last years of Sendak's life they spoke on the phone every Sunday morning about art, music, and the creative process.[1]

JONATHAN WEINBERG How did you meet Maurice?

TWYLA THARP I happened to be on one of my rare vacations, having done a very long tour, and Maurice called and said, "hello, I'm Maurice Sendak, would you like to work with me?" I said, "well, hello. Yes, of course. Where shall we begin?" And then we proceeded to speak for at least the next thirty years on this subject: where shall we begin?

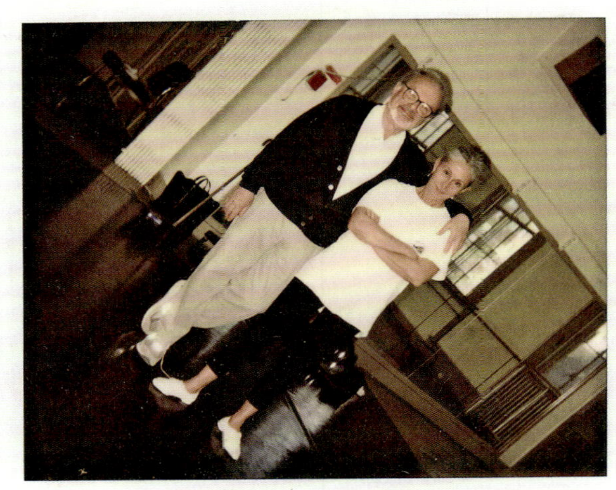

Maurice Sendak and Twyla Tharp, Hunter College, 8 April 1999

One of the last things I remember about him before he went into the hospital was a winter day when I'd come to visit and he was on two canes and it was snowing and he wanted to go to the car. And when I got in, just after the door slammed, he started doing this little jig on his two canes and it was very impressive. When Maurice put his heart in it, he was a really good dancer. And he was always in motion, even when he was on canes, he was still very physically engaged. And obviously, that's one of the things that makes his drawing so effective. He knows what it feels like to be inside a pig, for example, and how a pig would move if it had a good nature to it.

On that phone call that I referenced he said, "well, what do you want to do?" And I said, "well, I don't know, what do you want to do?" And he said, "I don't know, what do you want to do?" And I said, "well, how's about this thing called *The Princess and the Goblin* that was written by a guy named George McDonald?" He said, "yes, that would be a good one."

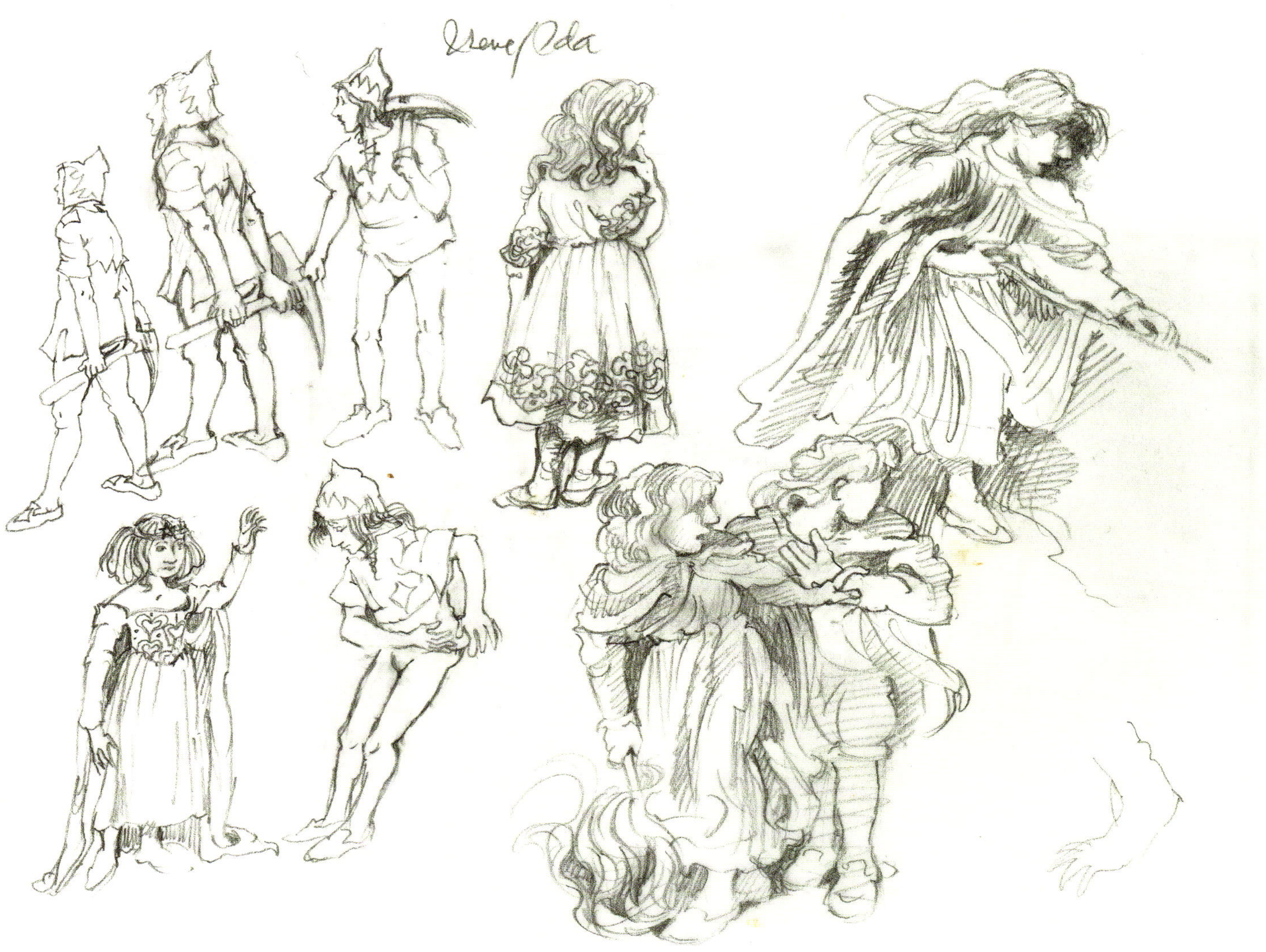

Maurice Sendak, *Irene/Ida, Study for a possible collaboration with Twyla Tharp*, c. 1999, pencil on tracing paper, 12 × 9 in.

Part of the problem is developing what does a goblin look like and what is the underearth cave going to be. You get bogged down in those questions. They're hard to pull out answers from, if you have any kind of information at all about this, because it's replete with all kinds of references. And sorting through that stuff took years and years to try to converse about. I mean, the business of the tender feet, of course, we both loved that a lot—Maurice's drawing of a tender foot with big claws on it and a lot of hair all over it and stuff like that. But that was not necessarily going to produce a ballet. So, we had to sort of work from two ends towards the middle and we never quite achieved it.

The people who say Maurice is like a child have it ass backwards. Children are like Maurice . . . So, he has a strange kind of responsibility to pursue an extreme emotional connection to things that most folk would not undertake. Well, children can be very compulsive, children can be very focused, children can be very disciplined. Children can be unbelievably orderly, anally orderly and morally orderly. And I do think that Maurice had a sense of that kind of dedication to the inner reality that takes you way beyond what people expect to have happen. Another thing, of course, is his closeness to, and intuiting of animals.

LYNN CAPONERA When you were talking about the idea with children being orderly, I think of when you would call every Sunday at 11 am. That was such an important piece of Maurice's life because it was something he could count on always, no matter where you were in the world, we were amazed that you would call at 11 o'clock every Sunday.

TT I'm very happy to hear that because—heaven knows—I got a lot from all that he gave, and thought, and grew, and made, and published, and didn't publish, and having the opportunity to see him living and working in his house. As time went by, seeing him decline so he could no longer be upstairs, so then he was downstairs and then he was in the drawing room. And then pretty soon, he would be living in his drawing chair. But it didn't diminish him. I mean that the diminishment of space and the diminishment of his ability and capacity to move out into the world did not diminish his imagination and his demands on himself. I think that's also extremely important. Obviously, then, he walked and that those walks were incredibly important to him, for many reasons, but certainly not least was the fact that it allowed him to engage this laboratory that was his body. And, if he couldn't read his body, then he probably wouldn't have been able to draw an animated thing. I suspect that's one of the reasons he was so conscientious about walking.

Whenever I came to the house and saw him in the studio, there was always something stuck to the desk one way or the other, a reference, not that he was copying it. I suppose he was imbibing it in a way. I love the story about his favorite piece of fan mail, when the kid wrote him asking "could you please send me your signature." He got Maurice's signature and ate it right up. And that is how Maurice dealt with references.

Maurice obviously had very deep and very committed musical tastes and we talked a lot about music—very knowledgeable and very precise about what he liked—why I liked it.

I think that in some ways our culture does not want artists. It is coming to the conclusion that they're kind of outside the bag and we want to keep all the cats in the bag. And I can well foresee that in the tangible future, the pursuit of an individual discovery or redefinition of what something is, will be both menacing and just a lot of trouble. "Do we really have to bother with this? Couldn't we just cut and paste and move the tail where the ear was before?"

Maurice will always represent a world for the escapee. For those who wish escape he offers great sympathy. What are the percentages of people who really want to escape? Not very great. We might argue they're becoming less and less, and I think they are becoming less and less mostly because of technology. Making a discovery takes a long time. Artificial Intelligence doesn't take a long time, right?

Maurice didn't accelerate time. That was not his way. And I'm sure that that's another thing that perhaps made him feel a little outside, but feeling an outsider was sort of critical to Maurice. I think we could all agree on that.

Note

1. Twyla Tharp in conversation with Lynn Caponera and Jonathan Weinberg via Zoom on August 8, 2021.

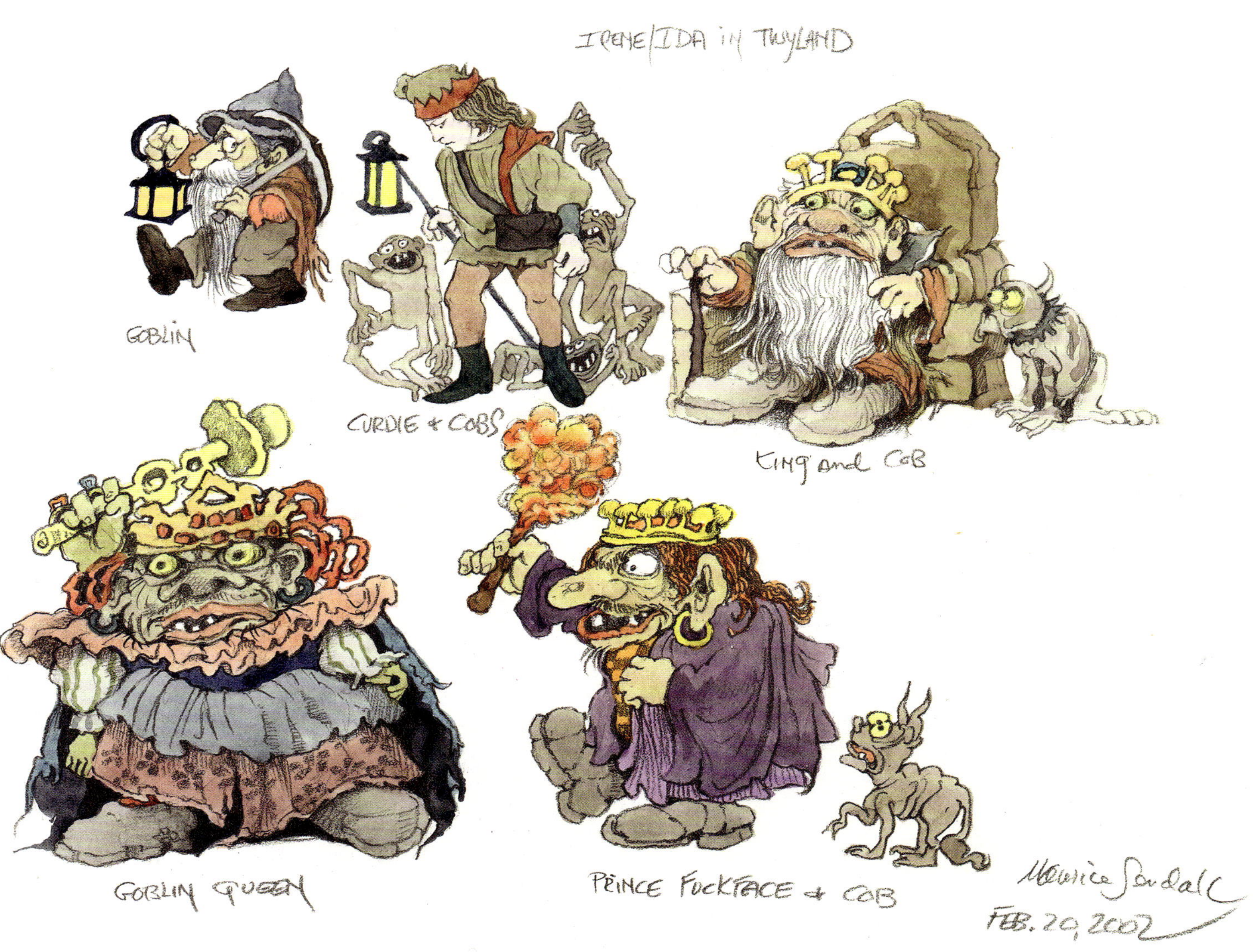

Maurice Sendak, *Irene/Ida in TwyLand*, 2003, watercolor and ink on paper, 10 × 13 in.

CONVERSATION

Spike Jonze

The director Spike Jonze was Maurice Sendak's choice to make the 2009 film of *Where the Wild Things Are*. Jonze was in constant contact with the artist, and Sendak's input, support, and friendship were crucial to the film's production.[1]

JONATHAN WEINBERG When and how did you meet Maurice Sendak?

SPIKE JONZE I met him when I was 25. I'd been making music videos and I got the opportunity to start to talk to movie studios. And the first meeting I went on was at Sony Pictures. And the executive had the *Where the Wild Things Are* book on his desk . . . When I saw that book, it was like an old friend. It turned out that Maurice had a producing deal with John Carls at Sony. And they were working on a movie of *Harold and the Purple Crayon*, which was another book I loved when I was little.

The first time I met Maurice, I was so young, I don't think I fully understood him, or fully got him. I was just in awe of him because I loved him as an artist, and I enjoyed him certainly because he was so enjoyable, so mischievous, and blunt, and direct, and he didn't know how to lie. He couldn't lie if his life depended on it.

The movie ended up falling apart, and the sweet thing was that we stayed in touch . . . I feel like I got closer to him. Every couple of years he would call me and say, "Hey, we're working on *Where the Wild Things Are*, and I'm curious if you want to do it?" And I was always really nervous about it, because

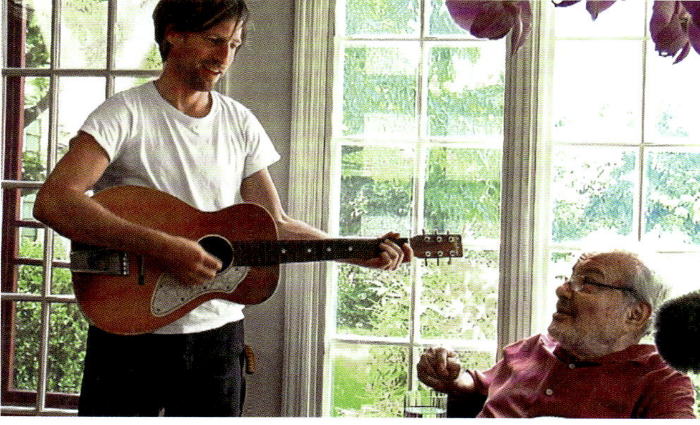

Spike Jonze and Maurice Sendak, c. 2009

I didn't want to add anything inorganic to it, like some made-up plot. It was such a perfect book, and I was worried about adding an awkward, unnecessary extra arm or something.

JW Had Maurice written any scenarios for a *Wild Things* film?

SJ I think the reason he kept coming back to me is because he would have some writers or directors come up with something, or write a script, and he just wouldn't feel it, he wouldn't connect to it.

Over the years, there were three times he asked me about *Wild Things*. The first two times I would go and read the book again and think about it and leave it next to my bed and dream on it. And then after a few weeks, I would have to call and say that I couldn't do it. But the third time, it was probably about six years since he had first asked me, I was in my early thirties. I read the book again, I sat it on my bedside table and I'd read it every night. And it suddenly just hit me, the only thing that really had to be invented was who the wild things were. Let them be these complex characters that are emotionally large, and seductive, and scary, and mysterious. And it was interesting, because at that point I'd gone through life more and was going through a really difficult time personally.

It was out of that, that our friendship really got deep, because he was such a thoughtful, deep human. And he cared so much . . . He was the kind of man that when he loved you, he loved you fully. Everything he felt, he felt fully. Which is why he was a great friend, and why he's a great artist.

When he talked about growing up, he talked about it like it had happened yesterday. His being scared of death as a boy, as a little kid experiencing death for the first time—seeing the kid who got hit by a car in front of his house, hearing about the Lindbergh baby that got kidnapped and was found dead. On some deep level, Maurice felt almost like his life was disposable because of the combination of those things. And I mention that because he had felt that fear of mortality so deeply as a child and he could still tap into that feeling . . . He couldn't help but obsess on it.

That's where a lot of the art came from, that feeling of being at risk as a child, and that's why his work had such a potency because that's a real feeling you have as a kid. And he wrote the feelings of young people honestly and respectfully. The book was obviously very personal to Maurice and he talked about how those wild things were his family—this Brooklyn Jewish immigrant family—and the sort of scariness of them, and their hair coming out of their ears. And their big hands grabbing his face and pinching it. And he always felt it was the scariness of his family and probably his mom in particular.

It wasn't even so much that I was thinking about the scariness, I was just thinking about the feelings I had as a kid. And what really felt scary to me was emotions I didn't understand, both in me and the people around me. The sort of scary, unpredictable, untamable wild emotions in the people I was close to. And the wild emotions inside me as well that I didn't understand and the way that people around me would react to those feelings.

Once I had the idea of who are the wild things were, and their characters, and how they talk . . . they're confusing and complicated, and charming, and seductive . . . it suddenly just came pouring out. I remember calling Maurice telling him the ideas and he was very encouraging, and he said keep going. And so, I kept going.

He basically gave me three rules, "I want you to make it personal. I want you to make it dangerous. And I don't want you to pander to children. And if you do those three things then that's all I care about . . . I completely support anything you do." And that is what I was doing just intuitively . . . I wasn't really making a children's film so much as I was making a very personal film about what it's like to be young.

We worked on it for over five years, in terms of writing it and shooting it. When Warner Brothers saw the edit for the first time, they hated it. And even though they'd read the script, when they saw it—and really, more so—they felt it, it scared them. They did not like the movie. They were like, "Parents aren't going to take their kids. Parents aren't going to like it." And Maurice was like, "We're not making this for parents, we're making this as a film about childhood." It got really intense . . . Maurice had to threaten them, "OK, if you fire Spike, I'm going to the *New York Times* tomorrow and I will let everyone know I don't support this movie. I don't believe in it . . . "

LYNN CAPONERA What was Dave Egger's role in writing the script?

SJ Dave obviously contributed a lot. But also he was as much a mentor as a co-writer—as much a writing teacher as a co-writer. Because it was the first script I'd written. So, we wrote this long, long version, almost stream of conscious, without editing it, and then we went back and pared it down. And as we rewrote it, we kept cutting things out . . . So the novelization basically included all the stuff we never used. Dave's book really wasn't a novelization of the [original picture] book or the movie, it was his own interpretation just as our film was, he went and

"Max is my bravest and therefore my dearest creation.
Like all children, he believes in a flexible world of fantasy and reality,
a world where a child can skip from one to the other and back again
in the sure belief that both really exist."

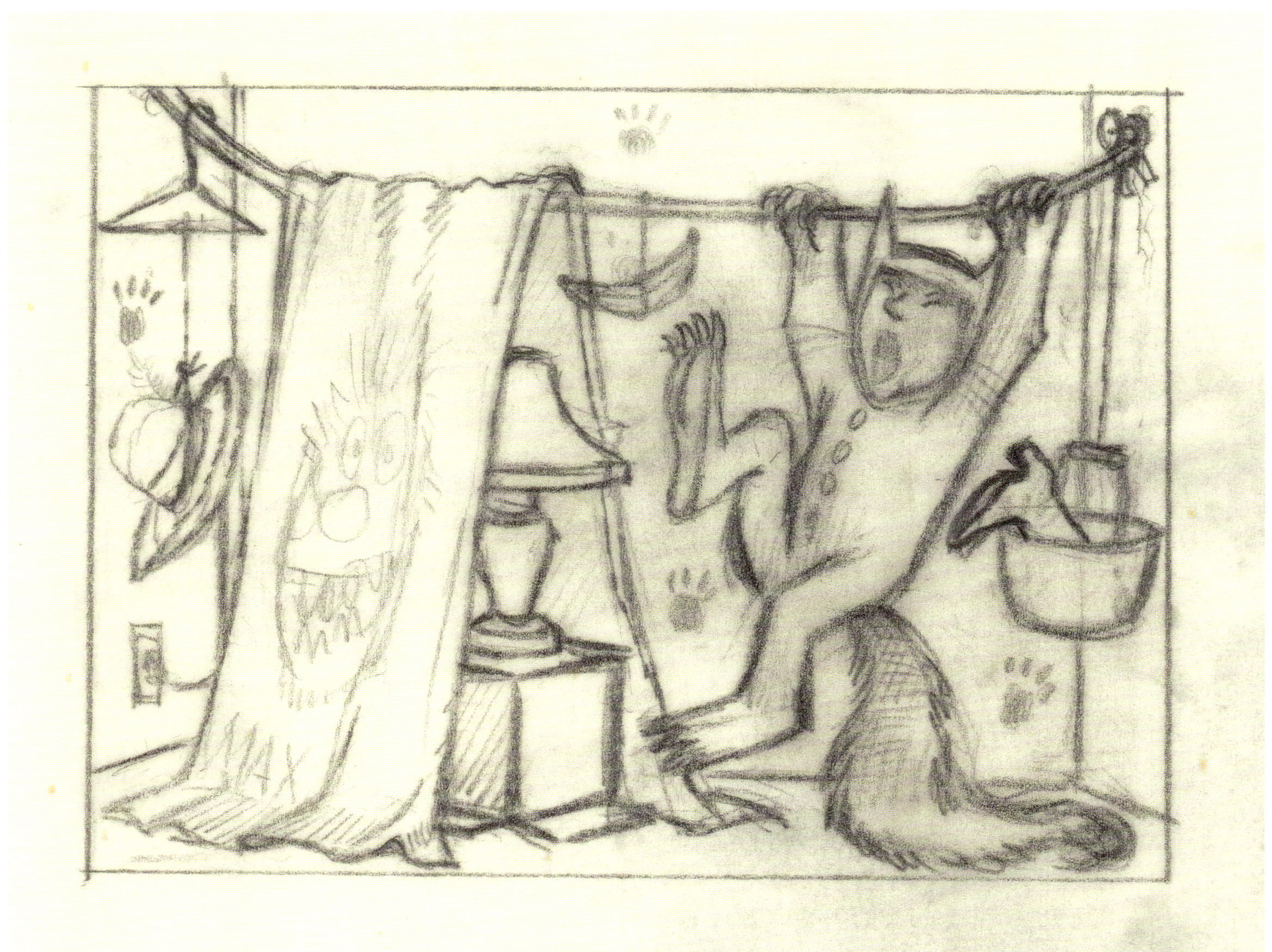

Maurice Sendak, Study for *Where the Wild Things Are*, 1963, pencil on tracing paper, 8⅞ × 11¾ in.

made his version of it, which is so cool. Dave is an amazing person.

We'd come to Connecticut with early designs of the characters, and just sit there with me, and our character designer, Sonny Gerasimowicz, and Maurice, and we'd show him all the stuff, and he'd draw and redraw, and draw over it, and Sonny would draw on it. And we would find the characters together. We were always talking to Maurice, I was always coming to see him. Just like a collaborator: me, him, and Dave; me, him, and Sonny.

It was important for me that everybody [in the cast and crew] connected with him and felt his spirit. Because his spirit is so clear, so powerful, so undeniable, and he was the reason that everyone was there. He was the artist who seeped into our dreams when we were young and that we all grew up on before we even knew what the word "Art" even meant. And so, I wanted everyone on the film to be able to be imbued with Maurice.

Maurice really helped me understand what it meant to be an artist . . . and where you create from. Trusting that, and trusting the subconscious . . . where you're not thinking, where you're coming from feeling. It didn't come from his dreams, but it came from the same place your dreams come from, which is bypassing your brain and bypassing your thinking mind and tapping into . . . play.

He was a huge person. He had deep pain, deep fear, but also deep love and deep mischief. The word "mischief" is in *Wild Things* not by accident—I think it's because it's a defining part of who he was. He was a mischief-maker.

I miss him. What a gift to have a mentor and friend like Maurice. A truly wild, beautiful man who loved fully and I got to be one of the lucky ones who he shined his love on.

Note

1. Spike Jonze in conversation with Lynn Caponera and Jonathan Weinberg via Zoom on October 19, 2021.

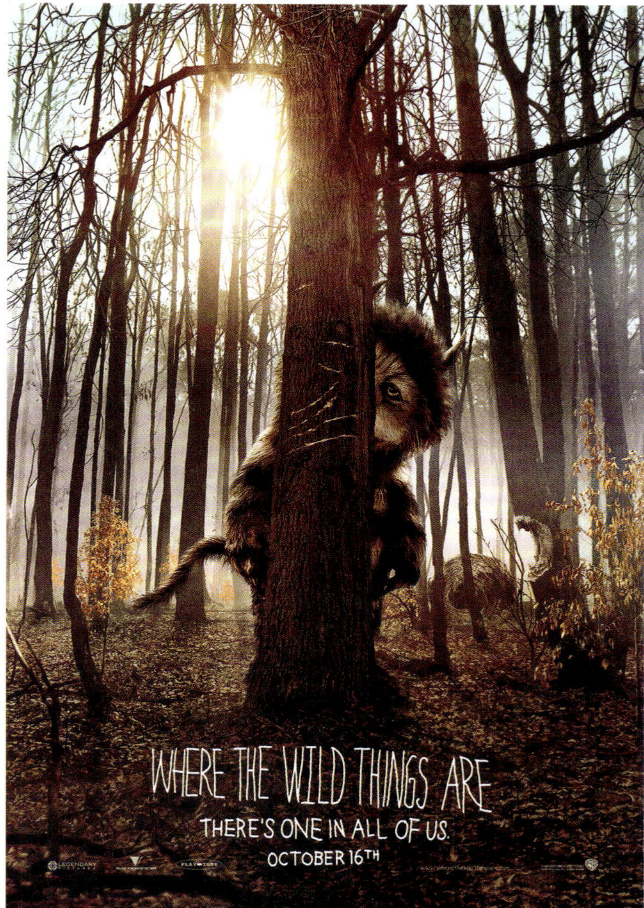

Where the Wild Things Are, directed by Spike Jonze, 2009, poster, 40 × 27 in.

CONVERSATION

Brother Christopher

In the 1980s Maurice Sendak began to visit the New Skete Monastery, drawn by its renown for the breeding of German Shepherds and dog training, and he immediately fell in love with the community, returning regularly over the years to stay with the monks for a few days at a time. He became particularly close with Brother Christopher, the director of the dog-training program. In honor of Sendak's friendship with the center and his love of dogs, the Monastery named its dog training facility after the artist.[1]

BROTHER CHRISTOPHER The community itself sort of fell in love with Maurice, because how can you not fall in love with the guy? I mean he was just a character. Really brilliant, funny, irreverent, unpretentious and yet at the same time very humble, interestingly, and also pretty self-critical too.

LYNN CAPONERA Maurice didn't do things like this. He didn't interrupt work. He didn't leave the house. He didn't get up early, but at the monastery he got up early . . .

BC He attended all the services. Maurice was obviously a curmudgeon. Obviously irreverent and obviously he was iconoclastic in his own spirituality, but to just simply label him as an atheist, it gets it so wrong . . . I can honestly say he was one of the more spiritual individuals that I've had the pleasure of knowing, and I'm saying that as a monk. He was always looking beneath the surface for meaning, for depth and also how these interact with him in terms

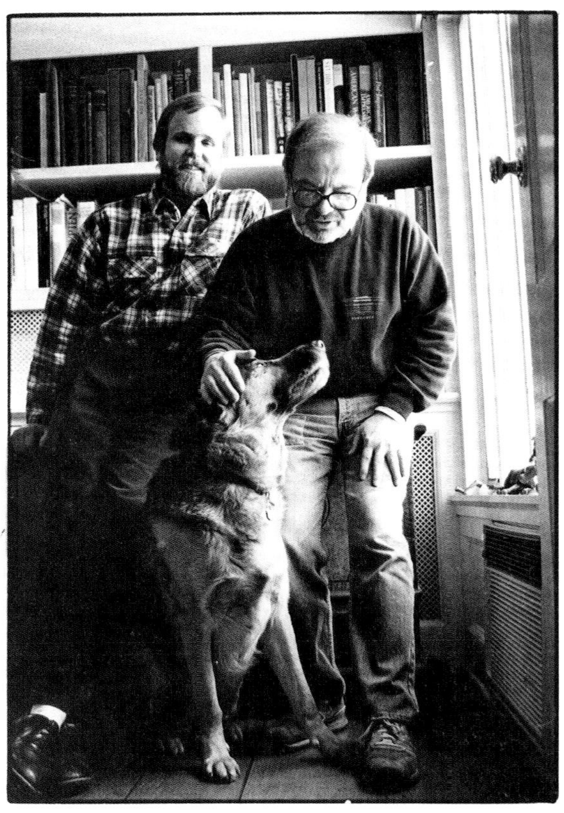

Brother Christopher and Maurice Sendak with Runge, 1991

of self-knowledge, self-understanding and his own development as a human being.

While no doubt he was not traditionally religious . . . I mean he was Jewish to the core but at the same time he certainly wasn't formally observant, going to synagogue. I think that in facing himself there were certain things that didn't really fit into a religious picture, so to speak. Maybe that would be putting it politely.

JONATHAN WEINBERG Well, I'm assuming because he's gay?

BC Yes, and particularly at that time.

JW You used the word irreverent, but it's unusual to hear a monk say it.

BC The stereotypical view of the monk is that they have fled the world, the world is bad, and they have gone into this introspective, ultra-spiritual thing that is disconnected from the earth, from real life. We've chosen the realm of the spirit as opposed to the realm of the flesh.

Well, that doesn't get it at all. We're very traditional on one hand, very deeply committed to our life and to the spiritual vision that animates the whole thing, but at the same time we don't look like we came out of the fourteenth century, with long beards down to the middle of our navels and wearing the black robe all the time. So as a result, ever since the community's inception, we've lived a very serious, but I would think a very modern type of monastic life.

The dogs draw people from all different types of backgrounds. Whether they're getting puppies or bringing dogs here for training, the dogs are the real equalizer, in the sense of piercing through the stereotype and helping people to just simply relax and realize that the community is a pretty human community. Now Maurice picked up on that right away. I think that he, as an artist, saw there was a certain aesthetic beauty to the place that he immediately resonated with.

LC And your lifestyle was really not different from Maurice's lifestyle as an artist?

BC Maurice spent his day in a very structured way. Yeah, it was very quiet and, you know, taking the dogs out, and then reading in his particular space . . .

LC And music.

BC And music, yeah, absolutely; Mozart . . . the whole thing.

He was a person that I think took his relationships and friendships very, very seriously but at the same time there was a real important dimension of solitude that was always present, and you see that in his work. You absolutely realize that he was putting the bucket down deep into the well and bringing up not just simply cold, clear water, he was bringing up precious metals.

JW Several times he would talk about art as his salvation.

BC I think Maurice was extremely sensitive to the mystery of everyday life, both in its challenging senses, as well as its transcendent ones. I say challenging, in that he was obviously very aware of the breadth of his emotional life. He didn't have any qualms saying "I can be an extremely angry person. I can be extremely selfish."

But the point was that he was always growing as a person, always in process, and I think that's where his relationship with his dogs had a real spiritual dimension that most people just didn't have a clue about . . . Here you see this famous artist who is basically saying that on some level the relationships that he had had with his dogs historically had been among the most important relationships in his own personal growth, which is why he had to honor that by placing them in the artwork. They weren't just pretty pictures.

So, getting back to what Maurice saw here: I think he felt that he could trust us to simply let him be himself. I think he also saw that we weren't going to be pretentious, or anything but ourselves . . . I think in his friendships he sensed that there was more than just a friendship. That the friendship was pointing to something beyond itself.

Call it love. Call it that spark of mystery, that Wow! What's this friendship revealing? What is it pointing to? It's pointing beyond itself. I can remember in conversations that I had with him, some of those conversations felt timeless. We'd be talking and all of a sudden two and a half hours had gone by . . .

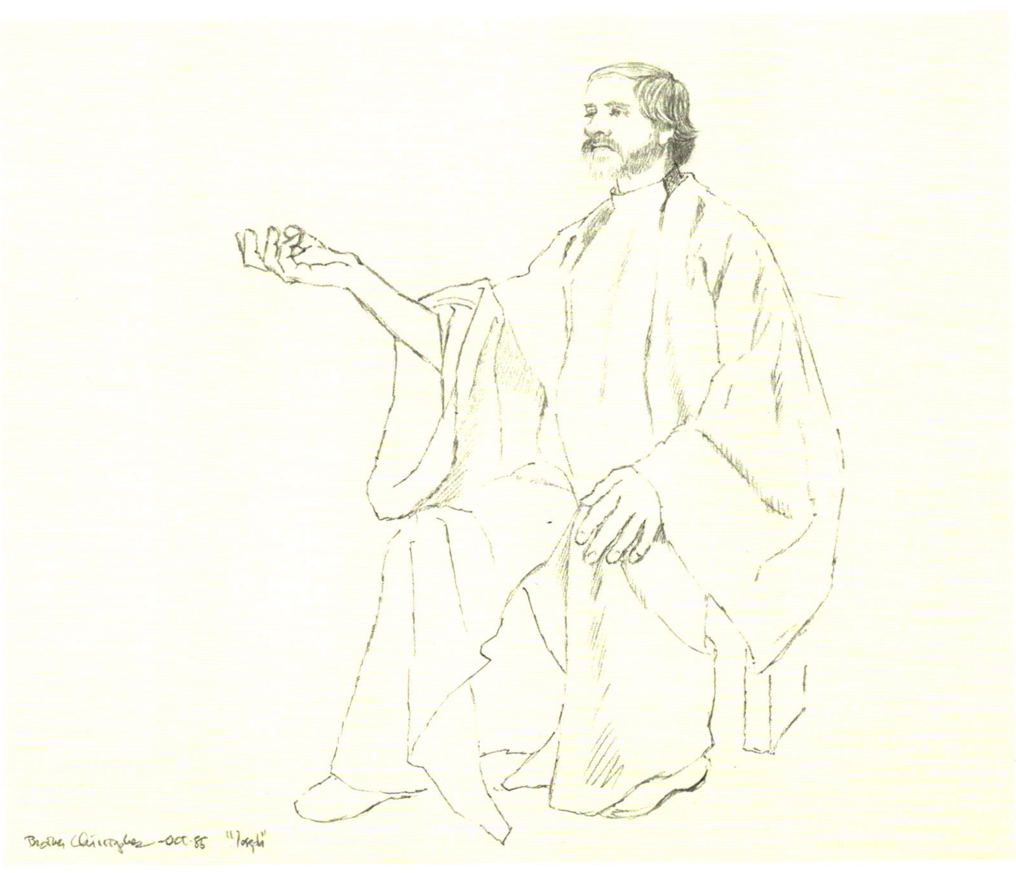

Maurice Sendak, *Brother Christopher, "Joseph,"* Study for *Dear Mili*, 1985, pencil on paper, 9 × 12 in.

I think, you know, what I would say about Maurice is that there were all sorts of gods that Maurice didn't believe in. They were the cruel, sadistic god; the punishing god; the god who was the despot; god the lawgiver; god, do it this way. Maurice didn't have any time for that, but when you peel away all that stuff, the whole question of what he really felt becomes much more of an open question.

LC One of the last full conversations I had with Maurice was in the hospital—it was about six days before he passed—and I had been sleeping in a bed next to him. He looked over and he said, "I just had the most beautiful dream. You were lying out on the bed with a white sheet over you and, in the background, there were clouds and there were hills and there was a German shepherd. Do you think that's heaven?"

I feel terrible because I kind of laughed, because I thought, Maurice talking about heaven? And then I could see his face get tight and I said, "no, I think actually maybe it was heaven, Maurice, tell me more about what was there," and he started going into details. He just said, "I think it is heaven." He said he wasn't afraid, and he was ready. He was really ready to go.

BC At peace?

LC Completely ready to die . . .

BC That's why he was such a beautifully complex individual and you certainly can't nail him down. I know that people in the community were deeply affected by him, in such a good way. For myself I would say it was certainly one of the most unique relationships that I've had the privilege of experiencing.

Note

1. Brother Christopher, Prior of New Skete Monastery, Cambridge, New York, in conversation with Lynn Caponera, Tyler Fallas, Dona Ann McAdams, and Jonathan Weinberg, July 7, 2021.

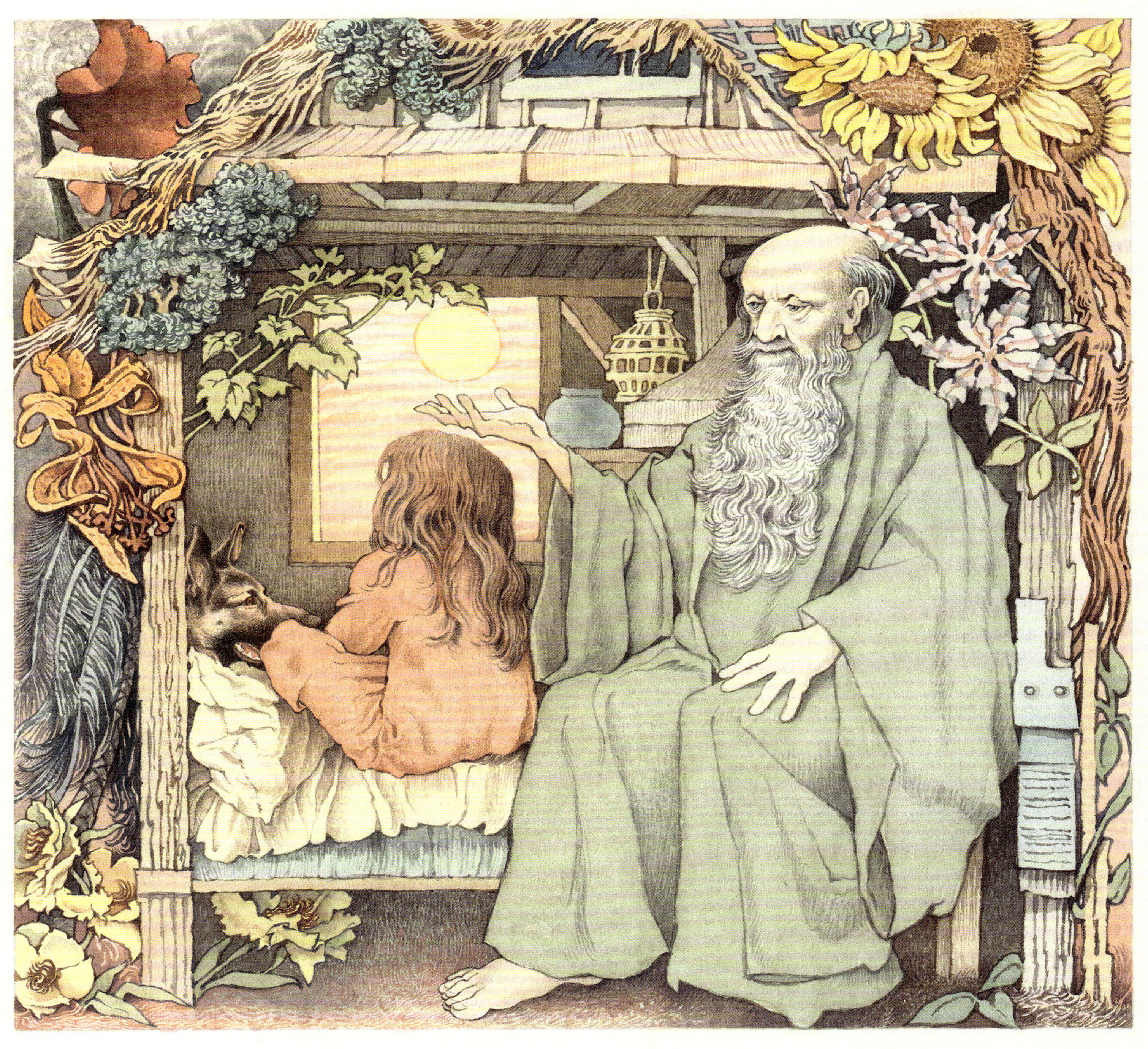

Maurice Sendak, *Dear Mili*, 1987, watercolor on paper, 9⅝ × 10⅛ in.

Interview with Bill Jersey and Terry Strauss, 1994

In 1994, the documentarian Bill Jersey and his associate Terry Strauss interviewed Maurice Sendak for *First Edition*, a public television show hosted by Charlie Rose and Shari Belafonte. At the time Sendak had just completed his book *We Are All in the Dumps with Jack and Guy*.

BILL JERSEY What do you feel is your obligation as an artist?

MAURICE SENDAK I have a kind of fantasy theory, which I can't prove, which is that there is an endowment. It's like a little pot that's filled to a certain degree. And that you spend your whole life taking it out and using it as an artist in the hopes that by the time you die you will have pretty much scraped the bottom of it. In order to do that, you really have to put other things aside. You really have to make sacrifices and choices because you want to get down further into the pot. And any time you do other things, I feel you're basically wasting your time. So, it's a kind of obsession with working, an obsession with getting it out.

And it's really mostly a very narcissistic thing to do work that's so self-satisfying that you can justify your existence on earth by the very work that you do. So it can't be trivial work. It can't be—and I'm a stodgy person. I don't believe in just having fun. I don't know how to do that. I do have fun when I'm working. It just has to be a serious business of achievement—personal achievement. If in that you also are a teacher and useful to other people, well, that's great. But that isn't primary.

BJ I think you said somewhere that you thought of age as being—what was your term? A splendid grace?

MS I feel, beginning in my fifties that life was improving. Anything previous to that was a total nightmare. Something settles in and if you're lucky, because I think it is all mostly a matter of luck, the work begins to thrum in a healthy way, and you can find the sources of it in an easier way. It even improves more so when you get into your sixties. Again, it's a matter of luck because if you don't drop dead and if you don't get carted off to a mental institution or you don't do harm to somebody else, and you manage to have your house working and have subjects to work on, it is a grace period. I think between the fifties and the sixties and more so now it's a grace period of doing exactly what you want to do. Feeling more certain about how you're doing it than you've ever felt before.

It isn't that you think you're perfect or you become a perfectionist. It's just that there isn't that much time to kvetch anymore. There really isn't that much time to be indecisive and ambivalent. And because of that, you thrust yourself forward in your work and you find that all the years of working have paid off. There's a kind of experiential thing that comes into this. You've done it enough times so that there is a polish to what you're doing. And, frankly, there is greater pleasure in what you're doing and less worry about the world and the publishing world, and what are people going to think about it.

BJ In the richness of your world which you have created, with which you have surrounded yourself—the objects, subjects, rooted in other cultures—what's the stuff that turns you on and excites you?

MS Stuff that I can steal from. The stuff in my house is collectibles that are related to the work. Everything is related to the work. The books are related to the work. The pictures on the wall are related to the work. Favorite artists from whom I've been stealing since I was a young man. What I hope is I take them and recook them in such a way that they become me and I think largely that has happened. These are sources of inspiration. So I can come down in the morning and see them and see them all day. And it's one of the pleasures I have allowed myself with a certain success in my life to surround myself with the stuff that turns me on as an artist.

They're all good friends. This room is full of George Stubbs, who's one of my great heroes. It's all work largely from the end of the eighteenth century, which is my favorite. It's the Mozartian time, one of the greatest flurries of artistic activity in history. There's William Blake stuffed into bookcases. There's Stubbs, there's Fuseli, there's Mozart. This keeps me going.

I guess in a sense I'm saying that I reject the world as it is, and I do reject the world as it is. And you could say I'm hiding my head in the sand. I don't think so, because my work is very of the time. But the sources of inspiration are from another period.

BJ Tell us about that transition.

MS We're all living towards the end of the twentieth century and so we're all banged up by that fact. And so we know what's happening all over the world and we know what's happening with scourges like AIDS. And we've all lost best friends and colleagues. I have lost students. To not be afflicted by this, and for the work not to show it means you're dead. And so my work, perforce, has come out politically and made a kind of social gesture. Because I'm angry. I'm angry at the government taking so long to do anything about homeless kids, and AIDS, and just the things we're all angry about. And you finally find there's nothing else to talk about, but that because that's what's on your mind.

BJ You've been accused of presenting to [children] subjects, images, ideas that were too disquieting, too disturbing, too upsetting. To that you say what?

MS It's just so nauseating. That living in the last decade of the twentieth century we could still be so stupid and we could still be so naïve.

BJ As to?

MS As to assume children don't know what's going on. I mean, how can we sort of plump them [down] in front of a television set so they can watch dead Somali babies with flies over their faces and they can watch all kinds of horrible things and that's OK. But then if you tell them an atom of truth in a book, you are breaking a rule and you're breaking a law. And this is so sickening to me that I simply reject it. But it's a battle that's been going on since my career began. And when I unwittingly broke rules, I didn't even think I was breaking rules. I just thought I was telling the most mundane, ordinary truths and they turned out to be alarming truths. But that's because children's books are so ghettoized and specialized, and the assumption is that children are special and ghettoized. In other words, keep them dumb. Assume they're dumb.

Some part of it is touching, because you don't want them to know terrible things. You wish they didn't know terrible things. Kids know largely that their parents wish they didn't know terrible things so they pretend they don't. They don't want to scare their parents. That's the last thing they want to do, until at least they can move away. So in point of fact there is a pretense that goes on about what kids know or don't know. I know from their letters how much they know. I know from their responses to my books how much they know. I have no doubts about what I'm putting in my books that this is familiar territory to children, and it's an enormous relief to them to have somebody telling them—or confirming that they know these things.

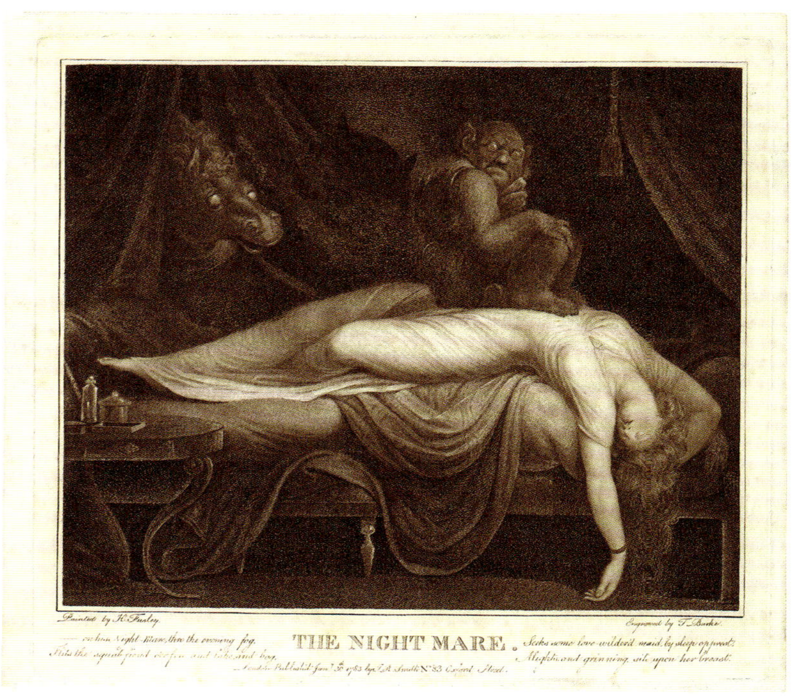

Henry Fuseli (engraved by J. Burke), *The Nightmare*, 1783, mezzotint, 9½ × 10¾ in.

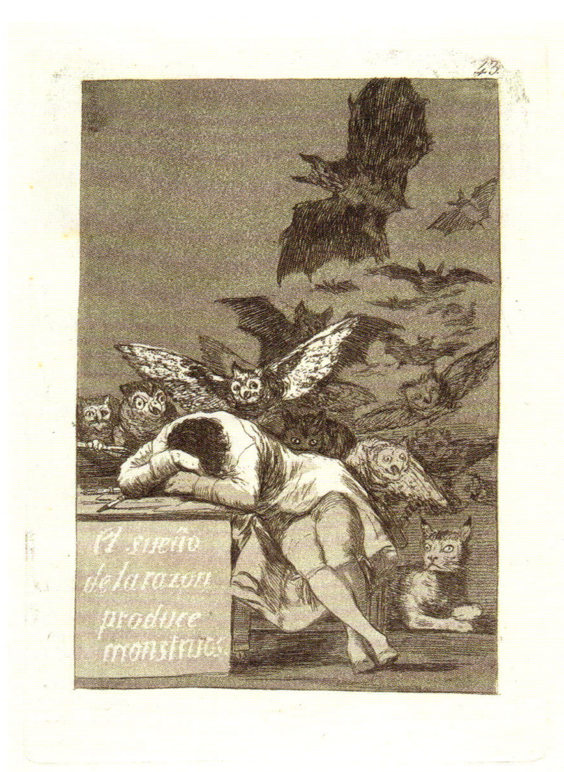

Francesco Goya, *Los Caprichos* No. 43: *The Sleep of Reason Produces Monsters*, 1799, etching and aquatint, 11⅝ × 8¼ in., The Metropolitan Museum of Art, New York

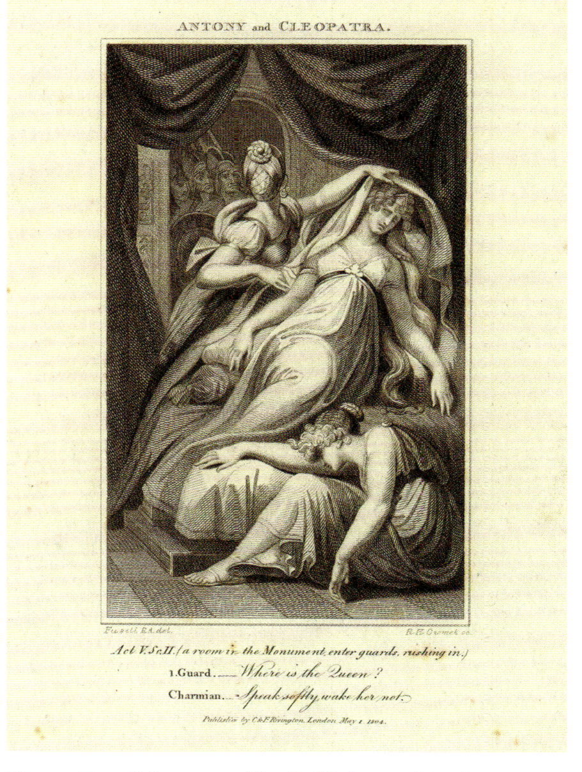

Henry Fuseli (engraved by R.H. Cromek), *Antony and Cleopatra*, 1804, engraving, 11 × 7¼ in.

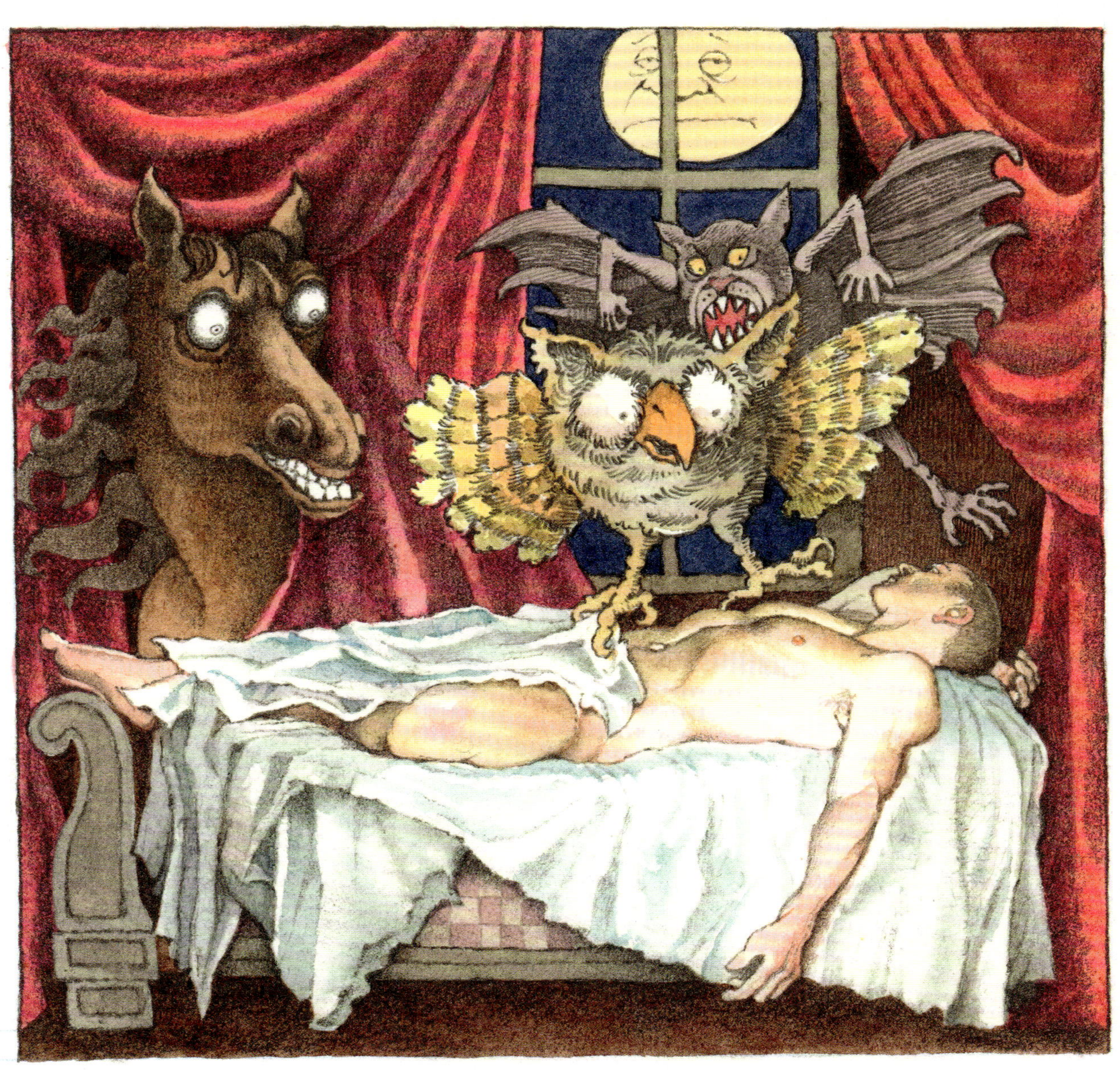

Maurice Sendak, *The Nightmare* (dust jacket for Bill Hayes, *Sleep Demons*), 2002, watercolor and ink on paper, 12 × 10 in.

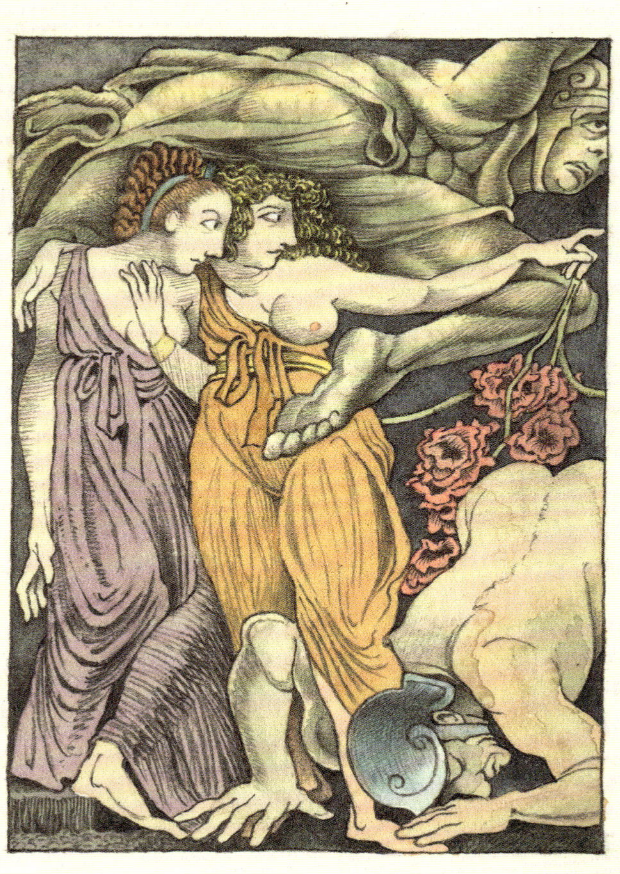

OCT. 17 - 21, '96

SCENE V : TO THROW THAT YOUTH, SO HOTLY COVETED,
TUMBLING INTO THE DUST BEFORE MY FEET.

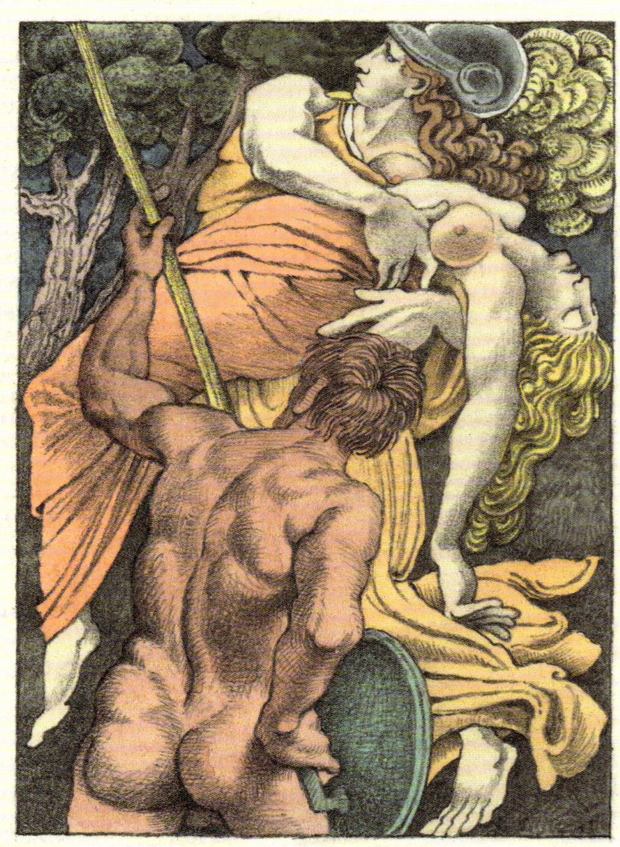

OCT. 27 - OCT. 31, '96 -

SCENE VIII -

AND, TEARING ALL THE ARMOR FROM HIS BREAST
HE FOLLOWS AFTER HER WITH FEARLESS STEP:

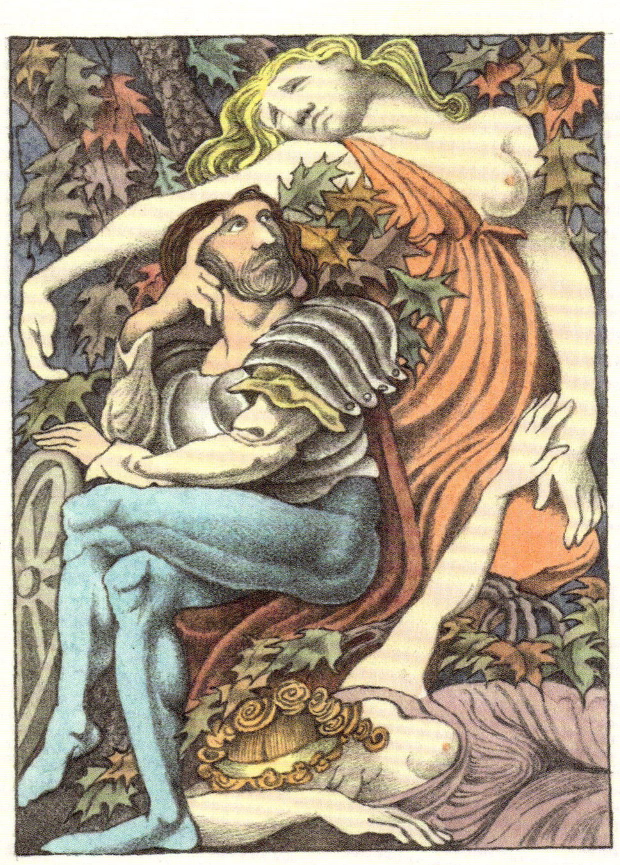

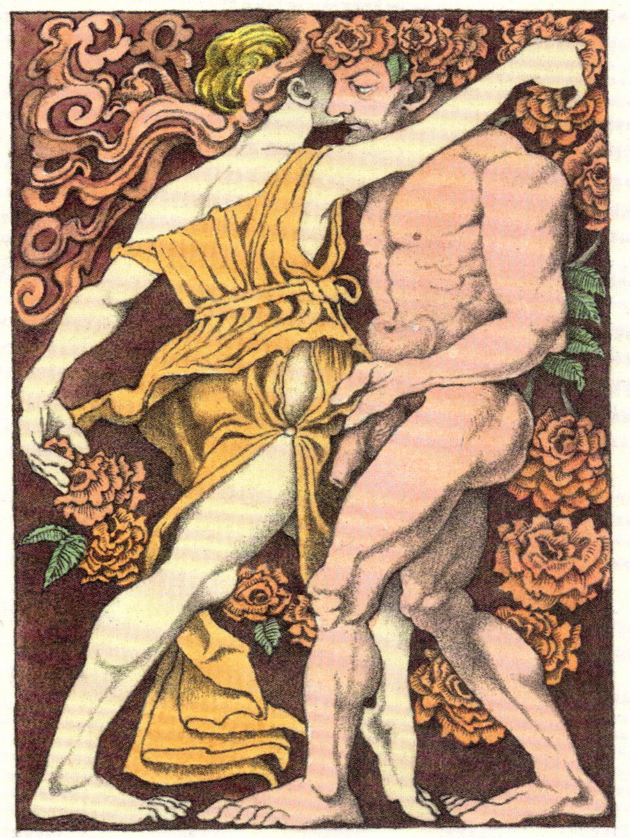

Maurice Sendak, *Penthesilea*, 1997, watercolor and pencil on paper, approximately 8 × 21¾ in.

BJ Tell me about some specifics if you can, responses you've gotten, cards or letters.

MS Thanking me for saying it's all right to hate their brothers and sisters. *Outside Over There* came out in 1980. There was a flurry of letters. Especially from girls because the heroine was a nine-year-old girl. And there are few heroines in children's books who are as muscular and virile as Ida, and as outrageous. And so there were flurries of letters how grateful girls were that they were being allowed in this book to want to get rid of their brothers and sisters. And that they didn't know anybody knew that. They didn't know it was permissible emotionally and psychologically to have this rage.

BJ You were fortunate in having this kind of world you reinforced growing up, weren't you? You had some mentors and teachers.

MS I was lucky because my career began shortly after World War II, when you could begin a career and New York was a welcoming city and publishing was just taking a second breadth. And children's books were a cottage industry that you could experiment in. And in that there was Ursula Nordstrom,[1] who was my editor at Harper's, who thrived on grabbing young people off the street who were uneducated, like me, who never went to college and barely got out of high school. And drilling them and becoming their mentor and teacher and publishing and giving them money. I mean, go find that kind of person.

Then the people I worked with, like Ruth Krauss and Crockett Johnson, and Randall Jarrell, all of whom were considerably older than I was and who took me in. The reason I live in Connecticut is because I always felt if I became successful, I would live in Connecticut because that's where Ruth lived, and Crockett Johnson lived and all the people who basically took me in and taught me roughly. Really handled me roughly. But it was better than art school. I never wanted to go to school. This was a proper school. I was being taught and paid to be an apprentice and getting published all at the same time. What more could you ask?

I began with French fairy tales; Ruth Krauss books came around. I was really lucky with *A Hole Is to Dig*, which was published in 1952, and that was a very successful book. I could quit my job very early on in my career and freelance. Later, in the late fifties, I began illustrating two of my brother's books. He had been my mentor as a child. He was five years my senior and a writer and a reader and a music lover. And partly out of sibling rivalry, I wanted to do everything he did, but partly it turned out I really loved the same things he loved. So that was lucky, too, to have him and my older sister.

It just went on that way right through the fifties. I began to write in 1957 or '58 because Ursula felt I should, and I could. I would never have done it without her encouragement. I thought I was just perfectly happy being an illustrator of other people's books.

BJ That's what I was going to ask you, why write?

MS When you find that you can write, it's the greatest pleasure in the world because, frankly, illustrating is a little easy. It's Polaroid stuff going on in your head. It's a little bit of cheating because you see pictures. All illustrators know that. You see pictures like Polaroid shots. Writing you don't see at all. Writing is arduous and hell. And so I suppose because it's so difficult it becomes a more interesting challenge. And then if you write and illustrate your own book, there's a cohesion, there, that's coming all out of your hot little head. So it's a much more interesting endeavor.

BJ Do you remember your first submission as a writer/illustrator?

MS Yes, yes. It was a book called, *Kenny's Window*, and I gave it to Ursula. It's my first book. I'm very fond of it. It's patches of purple prose. But it has a lot of heart. I was about twenty-six years old. It's a good book.

BJ What did she say?

MS She said it was a good book.

BJ Period?

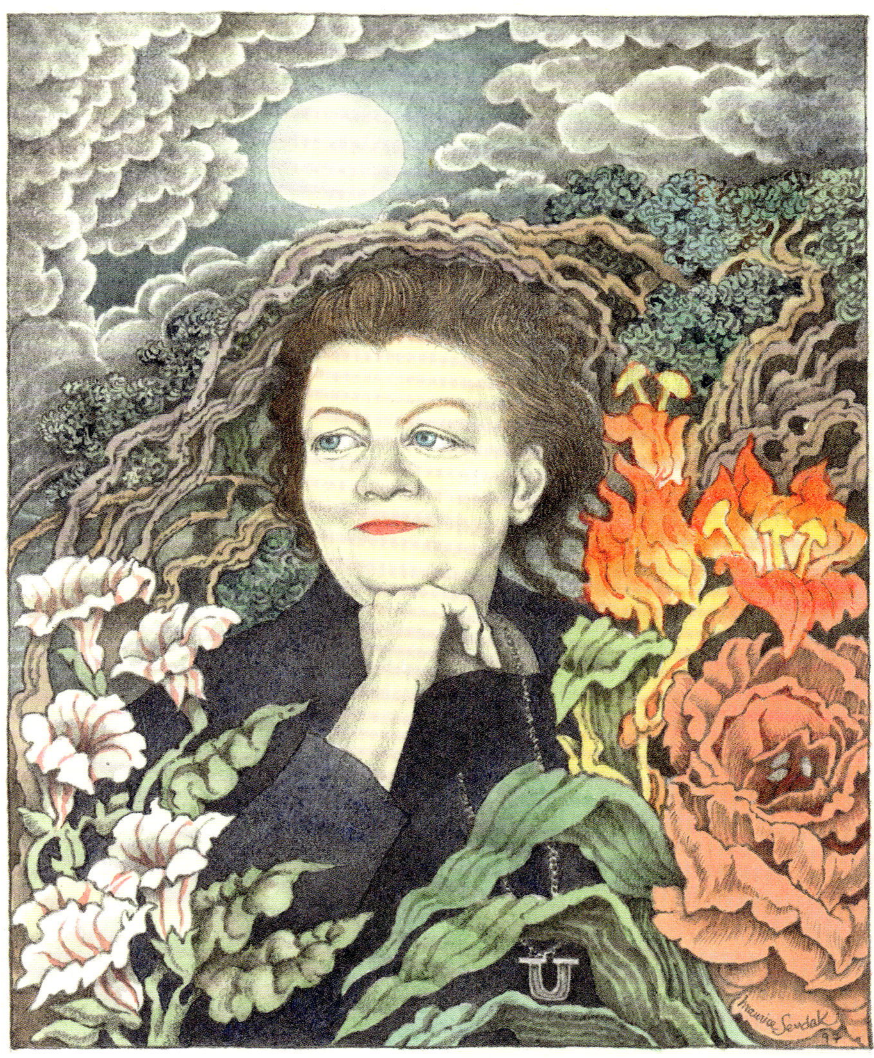

Maurice Sendak, *Ursula Nordstrom*, 1997, watercolor and pen on paper, 10⅞ × 8½ in.

MS After she said it was a good book, she tore it to pieces, and I had to start over again. Everything she told me to do, I did. No, that was a difficult book to finish. It is a very imperfect book. But what I like about it is it's a very eccentric book, idiosyncratic book. So right from the beginning the work was personalized. I wasn't aware of it, but that's what she encouraged. She didn't encourage me to follow the crowd. She encouraged me to be who I was, and she did that with all the young kids. There were like a half a dozen talented people that she was planting all at the same time.

The hero of *Kenny's Window* is a boy who prefers staying in his room and not going outside. At the end of that book there's an implication that he's going to make a shot at it. He's going to go outside and see

"But my projects were mostly through Ursula. She spoon-fed me. . . . I learned how to be a chameleon and change my style and change my look and change my emotional everything to suit the book I'm illustrating. That was a million-buck education."

what it's like. I didn't do that as a child. I never went outside. And it could be rationalized back then that I suffered from all these childhood diseases, which were not unusual. It was typical thirties. No penicillin. You got everything and you stayed sick for a large part of your childhood. And in that I learned to prefer it. I learned to be happy alone, drawing pictures and sometimes my brother or my father would draw pictures with me.

But I learned very early on that I liked isolation very much. I liked being with myself and I like thinking, and reading, and drawing. And that has remained with me for my entire life. Social things are arduous and social things are things you have to do and you do a countdown. In four hours, I'll be home. In six hours I'll be in bed. Six and a half hours I'll have my book. I'm always counting down to get finished with social obligations. I mean, I have friends that I enjoy, so I don't need to sound so overdramatic about it. But essentially the preference is to be alone. Because even if I'm not working, I might work. I might work. If people are around, I can't work.

Music can be in a room with me. I can share my life with music, much better than I can share it with anybody or anything else. And it's also a necessity. Whether it's true or false, I don't know, but the work cannot happen without music. That is the ignition key to the creative work. And why it is that way, I don't know. The best I can puzzle it out is that I always wished I were a musician, a composer. The fantasy that puts me to sleep at night is so trite. I'll share it with you. You're at a concert hall. I'm sure many people have this. And there's a famous pianist playing all the sonatas of Schubert and he croaks right on the stage and the lady runs to the floor and says, "Does anybody here play the piano?" I raise my hand. I've never ever touched the keys. I rush and by magic I play all the Schubert sonatas.

When I draw, I pretend I'm writing songs, Hugo Wolf or Schubert. Everything is mixed up in terms of musical analogy in my graphic work. It is so essential. It's like some of the wiring went wrong *in utero* and I got plugged into the wrong place. I love opera beyond anything, and Mozart beyond anything. And I love musicians and composers better than I love painters.

I think everything I've done is a collaboration with a composer . . . I used to do exercises—drawing exercises. I would have music on the record player, a sonata, or a brief work. And I'd start at the top of the page and I'd have to finish just when that movement finished. That would be my Schubertian or Mozartian or Haydnesque effort. So that each book then is emblematic and becomes very associated with a particular composer. It's too artful to say I sit down and I think, oh, will this by Haydn, or will this be Beethoven? No. It's just an automatic response. I don't think about it. When I was doing *We Are All in the Dumps*, it just was Schubert. I didn't know why. And it was only the piano pieces of Schubert. Just the sonatas, the late sonatas, the posthumous sonatas, the sonatas he never heard performed because he died at thirty-four or thirty-five years old. They were the last things he wrote and I just had them on the record player, over and over and over again. I promise you, they went through my head and into my hand and onto the page. Whatever that means. Of course that didn't happen. It's what I imagined happened. But by imagining it happen, I felt secure in the work that I was doing. That I was with Schubert on this. And that gives you a kind of security. Because you're all alone, in a house, by the drawing table and what's making you work? Your own wish fulfillments and your fantasy needs are making you work, and if they work, great.

It's a curious thing because I'm very cowardly. Actually, I'm afraid of so many things in life. But when I'm working, that's apparently not what happens to me. There's a quote in a letter by Herman Melville and he said, "I love men who dive". He wasn't talking about the Olympics, of course. He was talking about artists, explaining that unless you dove and risked breaking your head on the shoals, then you really weren't an artist at all. You either went all the way deep sea diving, like for white whales, or you were just a boring swimmer. You're just an ordinary artist. There's only one kind of artist to be.

"Herman Melville said that artists have to take a dive, and either you hit your head on a rock and it splits your skull and you die, or, that blow to your head is so inspiring that you come back up and you do the best work you ever did. But—you have to take the dive. And you do not know what the result will be."

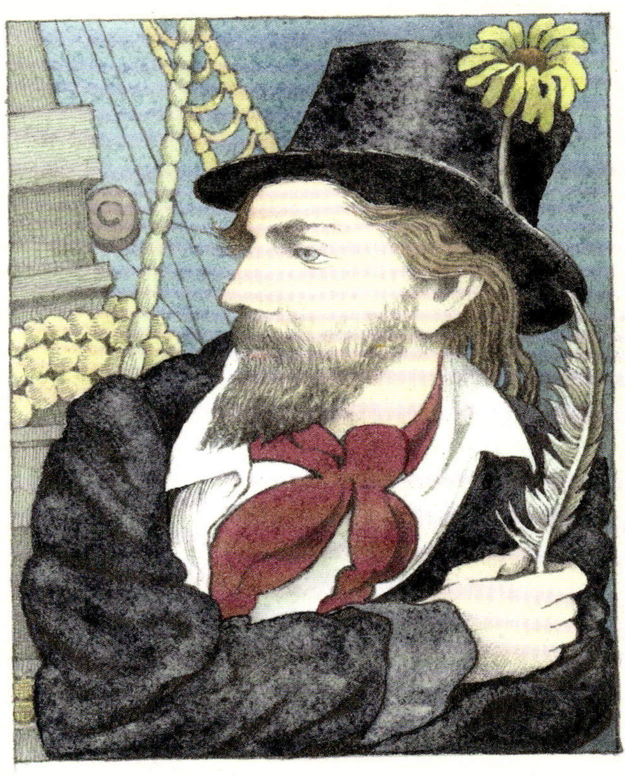

Maurice Sendak, *Herman Melville*, painting for the cover of Hershel Parker, *Herman Melville, a Biography*, volume 1, 1996, watercolor on paper, 8 × 7 in.

And I believe in my own way I have emulated that, I've dived as deep as I can go. Whether I succeeded in coming up with the gold, I don't know, but that has been my purpose, always, to go for the deeper things. So in that sense I'm not a coward. In that sense I'm very brave. And I live with this contradiction in myself. I'm afraid of the snow. But I'm willing to go anywhere in the work of art. And when I'm reading, I'm always reading something that will help me. I'm not interested in light reading and I'm not into the light anything. I'm always reading something that's going to help me find what it is I want to do. And everybody I read is a deep diver. I'm not interested in any other kind of authors.

BJ What do you want for the children who read your books?

MS I want them to feel that they're not being lied to. I want them to feel that here's somebody who respects them. And peculiarly remembers what it was like, how hard it was. Everybody says, "Why do you dwell on the dark side?" I'm perfectly aware that childhood at moments is the happiest time of all. But that's not my subject. Other people have talked about the baby bliss and done it very well. My subject is the other side of the moon of childhood. Because that's the side I remember most. And I address myself to that, because you want to bring comfort, to yourself, because old childhood nightmares still pervade you, no matter how old you are. So you're constantly appeasing that part of you that remains the child. And in so doing you are appeasing and helping and enlightening those real children in the world. Not a lot of people address this and talk to them about it and respect them for it and forgive them for wild and outrageous emotions and thoughts they have.

You know, in *Where the Wild Things Are* Max acts terrible with his mother. And lo and behold she acts terrible to him. A grown woman responds in the same seven-year-old way. The point of it to me was that not only is it forgivable but it's essential. He gets his dinner at the end and there's tranquility and probably two days later the same eruption will occur. But the bottom line is they love each other. And that allows anything to happen in the house without betrayal of that affection. I hope that's what kids get.

BJ What about taking the works of others and incorporating and modifying it as you did?

MS Well, the Grimm fairy tales I think are sort of the bible in terms of children's stories. And that's a paradox because they were not meant to be children's stories. They had no intention that the children read it. They had the same attitude towards kids that this was not for children. But they were the best things in the world for children because they were filled with sex and murder and outrageous behavior and vendetta, and forgiveness and love and you didn't have to be pretty to be smart. You could be the third and ugliest son and you'd make it and your two good-looking brothers would go to hell. Perfect for childhood. And that's how it began.

And then the brothers yielded, finally, and issued an edition of it for children, very grudgingly. They thought it was a putdown that kids liked their stories. So this naivety about children has always been. So, when I approach Grimm, I see these as just a goldmine of material. To go back over and over, and over and over again in terms of essential truths about lives. It's all about siblings. It's all about mothers and fathers.

And kids are victims of such psychotic parents and outrageous behavior, and they have to endure it and live through it. *Hansel and Gretel* is the vortex for children who survive psychotic parents. A mother who wishes them dead. No two ways about it. And lures them to their death. They kill the witch, which is in a sense killing her, and come back alive and forgive their weak and wobbly father. Because children always forgive their parents. It's the only parents they have. It's a myth because most children like Hansel and Gretel do not survive being sent out to the woods. They don't make it. The miracle is these kids come home.

So imagine the joy children have and have had for so long in reading that story. And there are still people who say you shouldn't give it to them. It's too rough. It's too grim. How stupid. They know all about that. They live with it, except for the lucky few.

BJ Mr. Sendak, I'm only ten years old and I read your books and I think they're wonderful and I wish I could be like you. What can I do?

MS Emulate somebody better. Wish to be like me? Work hard, get out of school as fast as you can. If you want to be an artist, avoid school like the plague.

BJ Why?

MS It's a weigh station. It's a postponement of what you have to do. Because you cannot teach an artist how to be an artist. They're wired up or they're not. And all you can do is be a good poppa—encouraging, loving, caring. You can't teach them anything except tricks, technical tricks which they can learn in eight minutes from anybody. So your big job is to nourish them, love them, praise them if they're worthy of the praise. But that's the only thing you can teach an artist. Art school is simply—largely, I think—a waste of time.

BJ Are there things now that aren't being said in the public discourse that need to be said?

MS Everything is not being said about the condition of childhood. About the seriousness of childhood. I mean, we mince about the truth about ourselves. So of course we don't tell anything about children. Does television tell us anything about children? Everything is placation. We placate ourselves. We don't tell ourselves that we're really going to die. We only tell ourselves that there are doctors who keep us living longer, as though we're incapable of dying. As though it isn't necessary that we die. So if we lie to ourselves about such primary issues as death, then goodness knows where the lies end. And children are the tell end of all of that. Because we're protecting them.

BJ Last question from me. Spirituality, religion, god, never directly addressed by you, or is it?

MS I'm an atheist. And I've always been an atheist as far as I've had a working mind. But that's ambiguous, too, you know? And the older I get, the more confused I get about the issue. Because I say things like I have a god. His name is Wolfgang Amadeus Mozart. And sometimes I get a very happy feeling that he is hovering and watching over me. And then I say, "Well, you're a baby. You need to be comforted just like a child and you're tucked in by Mozart every night. That's your fantasy. OK. It's a fantasy." I don't know what it is, anymore. I know that there is something. I would never call it by any of the names that people traditionally call it. I prefer something that is to me incomprehensible that is basically good because Mozart is good.

And when friends died over the past years, young friends of AIDS, I have to imagine they're somewhere. I don't believe in heaven, obviously. And they probably are only in my mind. But I can conjure them up. I have a good mind to conjure the sound of voices not heard for years and faces and I take walks with them. Henry Thoreau was on the road. I bump into him now and then. Herman Melville is all over the house.

TERRY STRAUSS Dreams seem to play such an important role in your books, at least the ones that I am most familiar with.

MS The effect of dreams in my work is nebulous in a curious way. I don't make any connection between my creative work and the dreams I have. I really don't. I don't get ideas. Sometimes I design operas in my dreams. That's a semi-recurring dream, which is very beautiful. So, there's a lot of creative work in the dreams. But mostly they're very childish dreams, like finding a Mickey Mouse toy that I excavate from an old Bensonhurst drugstore. So, it's the childish pleasure dreams. And I've never been able, that I can be aware of, to translate an idea that I had in a dream onto a piece of paper. That was never useful that way.

BJ Never dreamt falling into a milk bottle and saying, "I'm not the milk and the milk's not me"?

MS No. That would have been a nightmare. I would have drowned. I can't even swim.

Note

1. Ursula Nordstrom (1910–1988) was Maurice Sendak's close friend and first editor at Harper & Row. The Sendak books she edited included *A Hole Is to Dig*, *The Nutshell Library*, *Where the Wild Things Are*, and *In the Night Kitchen*.

"If anybody could prove to me that Mozart was God, I would believe in God forever. But I do believe in Mozart as though he were God. If God is someone that's supposed to give you comfort, I think of him and I listen to him when I'm in trouble."

opposite: Maurice Sendak, *The Magic Flute*, 1980, poster, 24 × 17½ in.

following pages: Maurice Sendak, *Mozart*, Painting for the cover of the Glyndebourne Festival Program, 1985, watercolor on paper, 16 × 25 in.

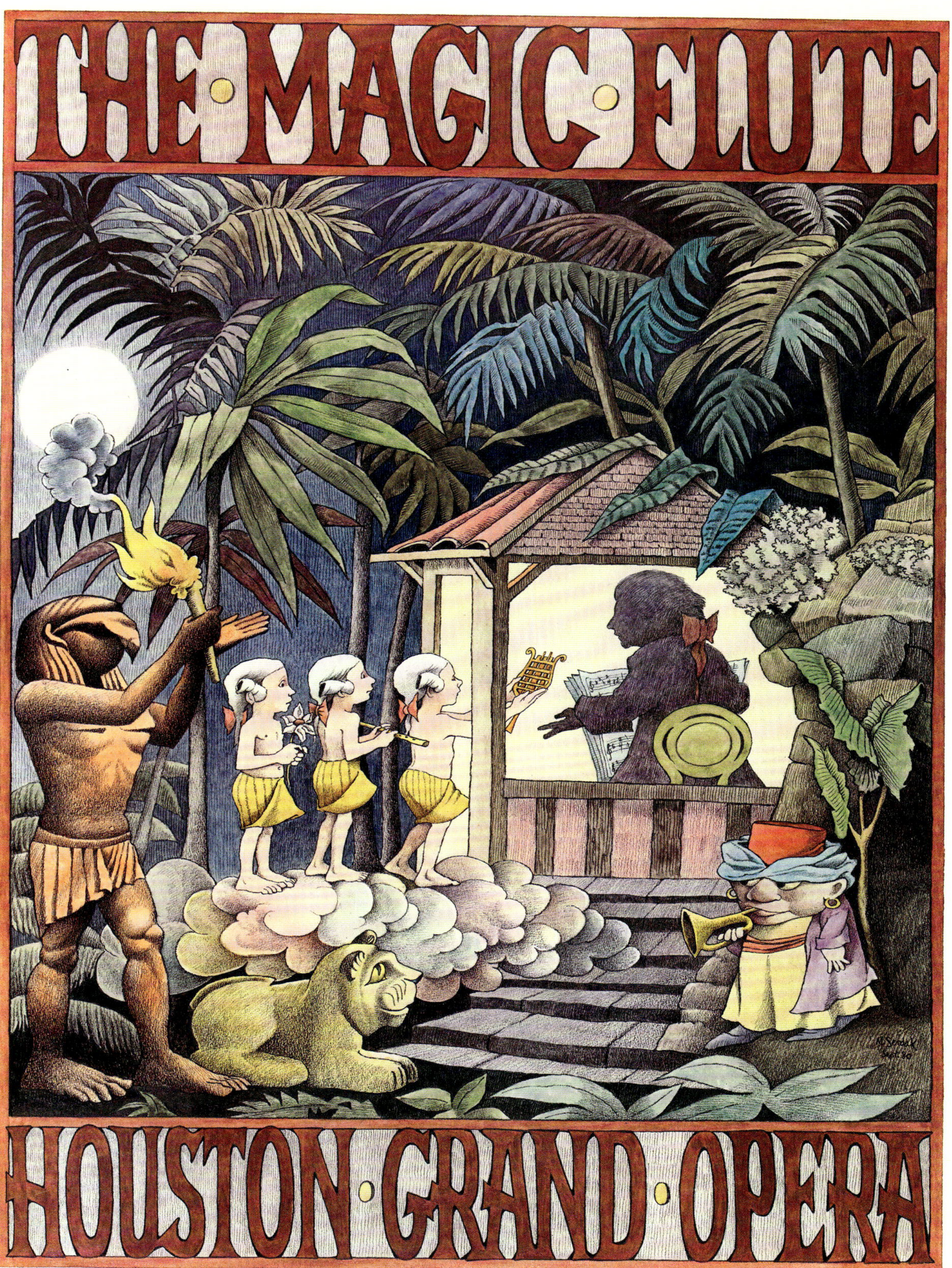
THE MAGIC FLUTE
HOUSTON GRAND OPERA

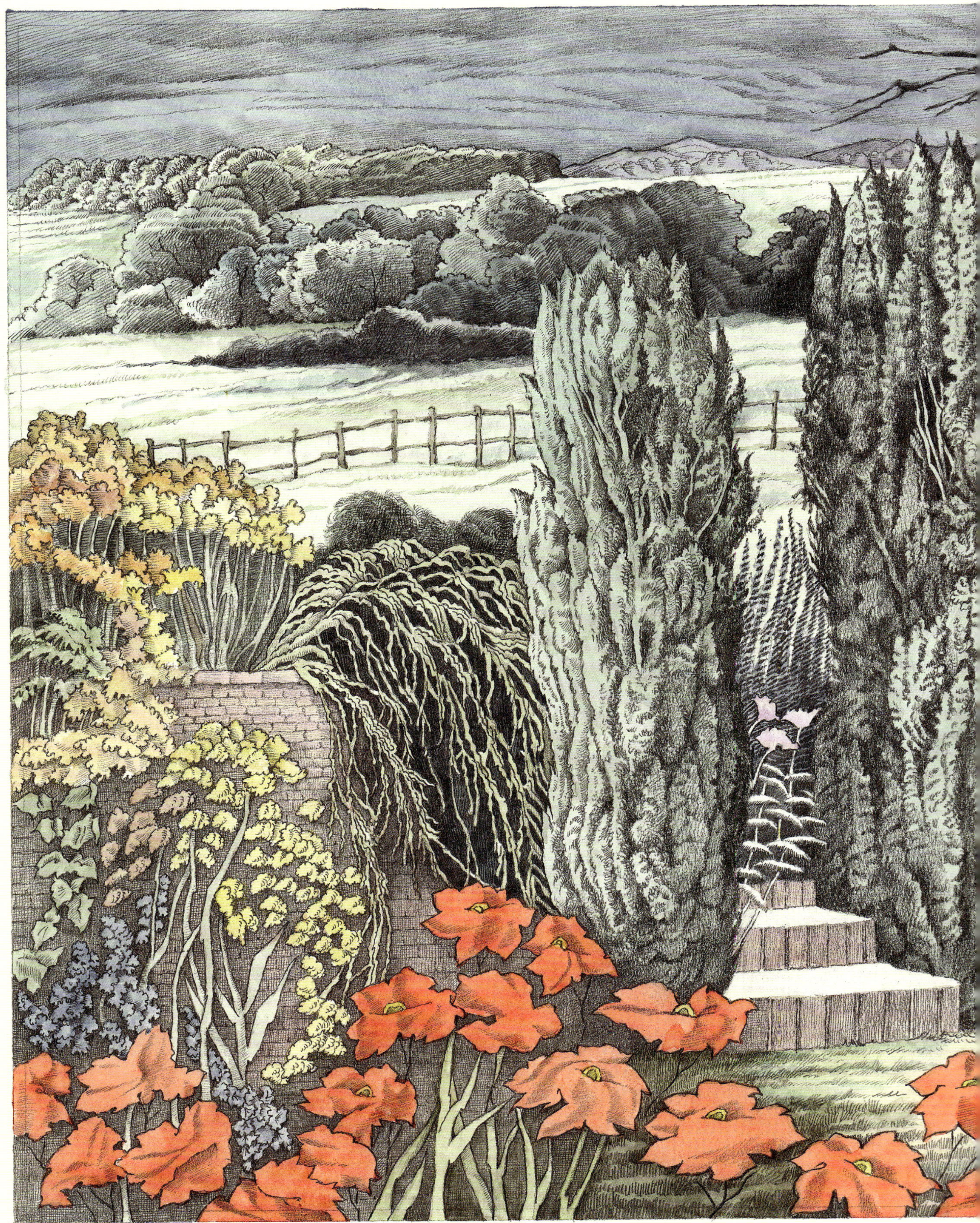

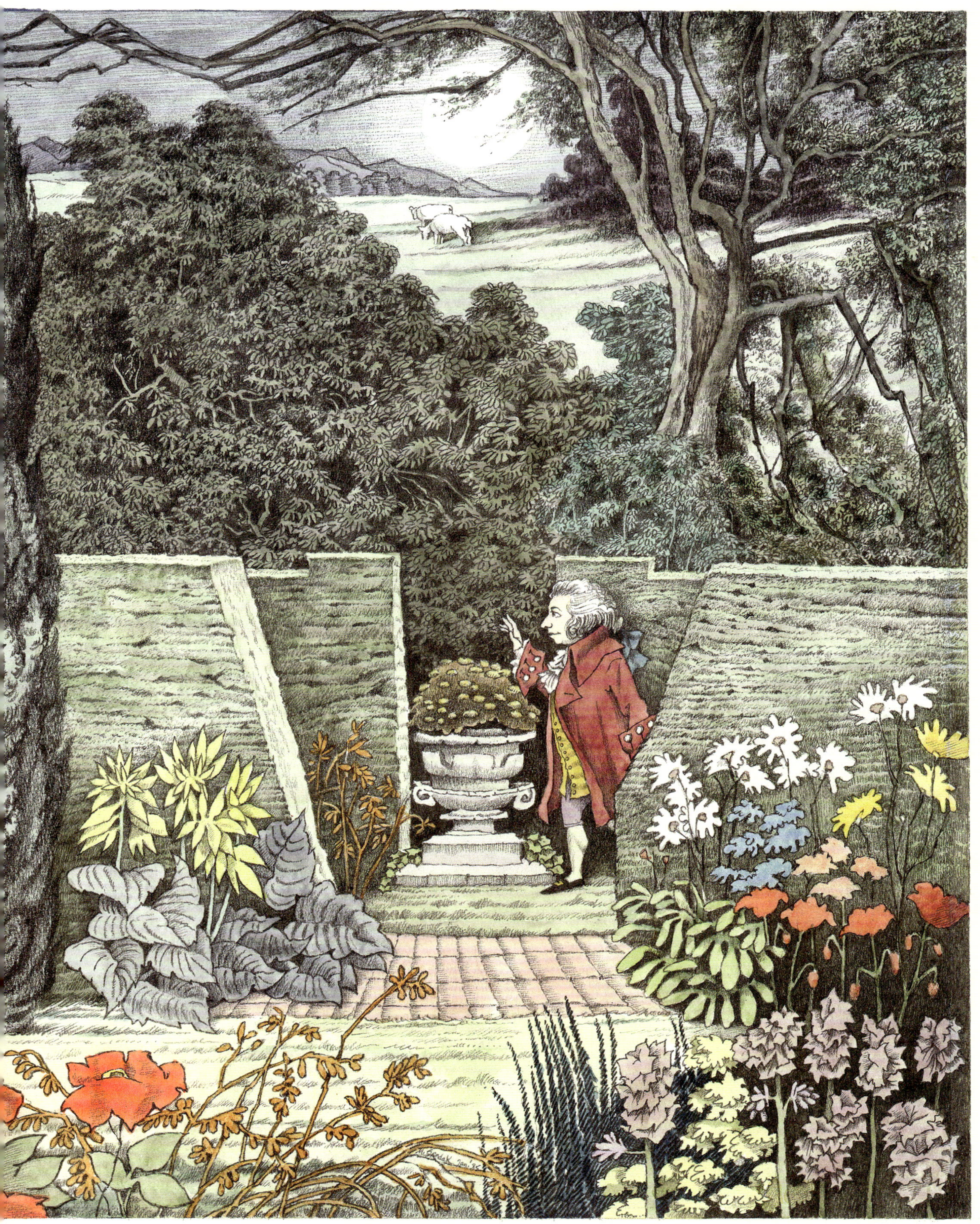

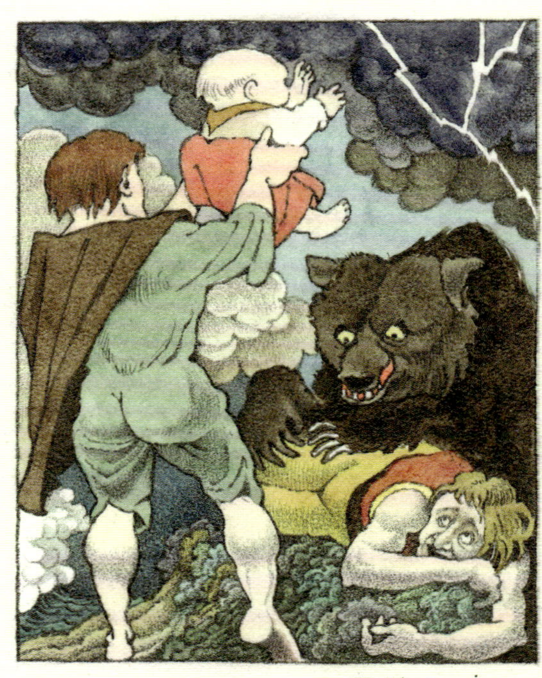

Maurice Sendak, *A Winter's Tale*, CD cover illustration, 1996, watercolor and ink on paper, 8¾ × 7¼ in.

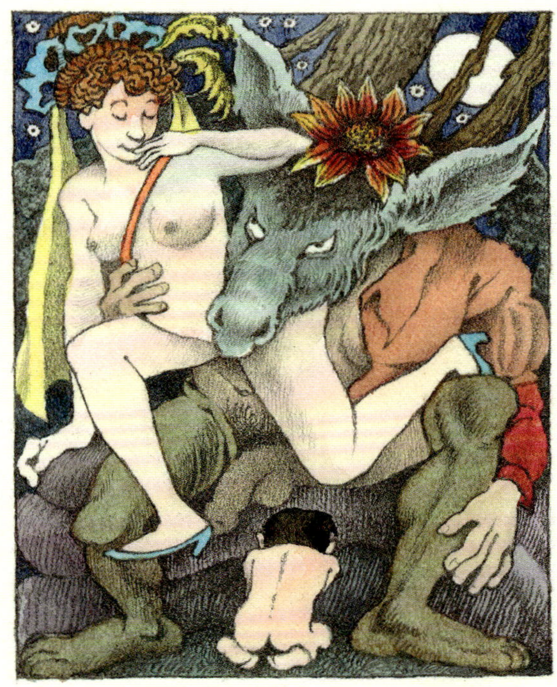

Maurice Sendak, *Midsummer Night's Dream*, CD cover illustration, 1995, watercolor and ink on paper, 8½ × 8½ in.

"My mighty teachers are Emily Dickinson and John Keats, Shakespeare, and Herman Melville . . . I've been reading like my eyes are falling out. But, how many times can you have teachers like that?"

Interview with Jonathan Weinberg, 2003

During Jonathan Weinberg's 2003 fellowship at the New School's Vera List Center for Art and Politics, he interviewed Maurice Sendak at a public event. Sendak has just completed the book of *Brundibar*. As an art historian and practicing artist himself, Weinberg was particularly interested in Sendak's passion for other painters and how he saw his work in relationship to the art world.[1]

MAURICE SENDAK Mantegna's *Descent into Limbo* (p. 23) came into my life in the 1970s. I was about to design my first opera, *The Magic Flute*. I had no experience as an opera designer or stage person at all. This wonderful director in New York, named Frank Corsaro,[2] gave me the job. After you get over the excitement of "I'm going to do *The Magic Flute*"; then comes, "I don't know how to do *The Magic Flute*."

It hit me very quickly that this is where to steal. This is *The Magic Flute*, no question about it. Some of the similarities—immediately, the cave; I love caves. I love openings of caves. The very beginning of the opera is a rocky landscape, and things happen very, very quickly. The young hero comes in. He's being chased by a monster. He freaks out. He falls down the steps of the cave, lands in the cave; and everything takes off in this magic but ultra-realistic world of Mozart and the fate of young people. So, this was my opening scene, basically. It helped me through the whole opera. There was a series of cavern or cave openings. What touches me—this picture, especially—is, I personally have never seen a painting of Christ as seen from the rear.

The sweetness of it—because it's a fearful gesture. You can see his shoulder blades. He doesn't quite know what to do. The wind blowing all around him really reveals the body in a way that is so subtle and makes him so much more human to me. The question is, is he going to do it? Well, of course we know Christ did it. He lunged into that evil-smelling place and saved the prophets.

JONATHAN WEINBERG When you begin a project, you tend to focus on one artist and that becomes a kind of model for that book.

MS Well, part of that is because I can't hold two artists in my head at the same time. And if you're stealing well, you've got to refine it; keep it focused,

JW I want to ask you about the theme of windows in your work. There's a window in *Where the Wild Things Are*. Then there's this terrifying window in *Outside Over There*. And Mickey falling in front of a window in *In the Night Kitchen*. Even the title, *Outside Over There*, sounds like somebody pointing out a window. Windows are like paintings.

MS Yes. But you know, all my titles are pointing titles: *Where the Wild Things Are*, *In the Night Kitchen*, *Outside Over There*—it's telling you to go someplace and find something.

I was one of many 30s children. We were all sick with everything. There were no sulfa drugs. There was nothing, so everybody had everything. I spent a lot of my childhood in bed and kept away from my brother and sister so they wouldn't catch what I had. So, I spent a lot of time in isolation.

The window was the way I saw what was happening . . . I was the only one who liked my grandmother, and she reciprocated. She spoke no English but she was fierce. But I would sit on her lap, and I'd look out the window; and then she made up a game. She would take the window shade and she would bring it all the way down. And then I'd wait breathlessly, and she'd let it go; and it would shoot up . . . it was like a magic show. People came. People went. So, the window was like my cavern.

I was destined to become a book illustrator. The first book I illustrated when I was sixteen was an opera called *Louise* by Gustave Charpentier, not for children of course. Then I thought I would try a children's book, and I chose *The Happy Prince* by Oscar Wilde. I didn't like that, so I did *The Luck of Roaring Camp* by Bret Harte. The main thing is that I always wanted to do books that put together pictures and words, which is what my brother did, too. We were like the two happy kids doing this kind of thing.

But when I went to the Arts Students League it became perfectly clear that I was low man on the totem pole. The painters were upstairs, incredibly depressed, painting rambling, marvelous things. Us commercial whore-like kids were downstairs just going to school to make money.

JW But I think one of the things that's incredible is the way that you were able to do things those contemporary painters weren't supposed to do: like have stories and realistic figures.

MS I never can explain it because I don't feel like I'm doing children's books. I don't set out to do books for children. I don't know how to do that. I don't think anybody knows how to do that.

The point is, I so hated being pigeonholed as a kiddy book illustrator. Whenever I'm introduced, whatever article you read—author/artist, picture-book artist, Maurice Sendak—this long slew of names. God forbid I'm just an artist.

JW Can you talk about the process of collaborating with a writer?

MS the point is to form a relationship with the writer. Now, it's dangerous. Sometimes it didn't work; but I would say the majority of times it did work. If you get to work with the person, and he or she is transformed by what you're putting into it; and it's a back and forth; to me it's what makes the book worth doing, enriching the text. That's the whole point of illustrating—to enrich the text. Primarily it's all about writing. Pictures are there to make you love the writing more.

If the pictures stand up in your face, then you have failed. You have done a portfolio of pictures, which is of no concern to anybody; because they're not integrated into the texture of the writing, which is what book illustration truly is. You're a backseat driver. You come second to the writer; and the best people I've worked with understood that and knew that I understood that. Ruth Krauss, Randall Jarrell—I worked with incredibly marvelous people who got it. Thus, the books we produced are quite good, and they hold up over many, many years; because they're tight like that. Also, then you get the mind of the other person, the intellect of the other person. It's fun to do, but not fun to do all by yourself.

JW Would you talk about *Brundibar* and representing the Holocaust?

MS The more precise it is, to me, the better it is. I don't want an abstraction of it . . . If you read any of the novels of W.G. Sebald, talking about being a Jew, the precision and beauty and presentation—that's it. You tell it like it is, or like you think it is. When you're that great, you do it.

JW In a deep sense, you're a realist.

MS Yes. The reason I watch, *ad nauseum*, births on The Discovery Channel—I love it. People say, oh, you're so morbid. Well, perhaps I am. But in point of fact, I love to see the real thing—see a baby come

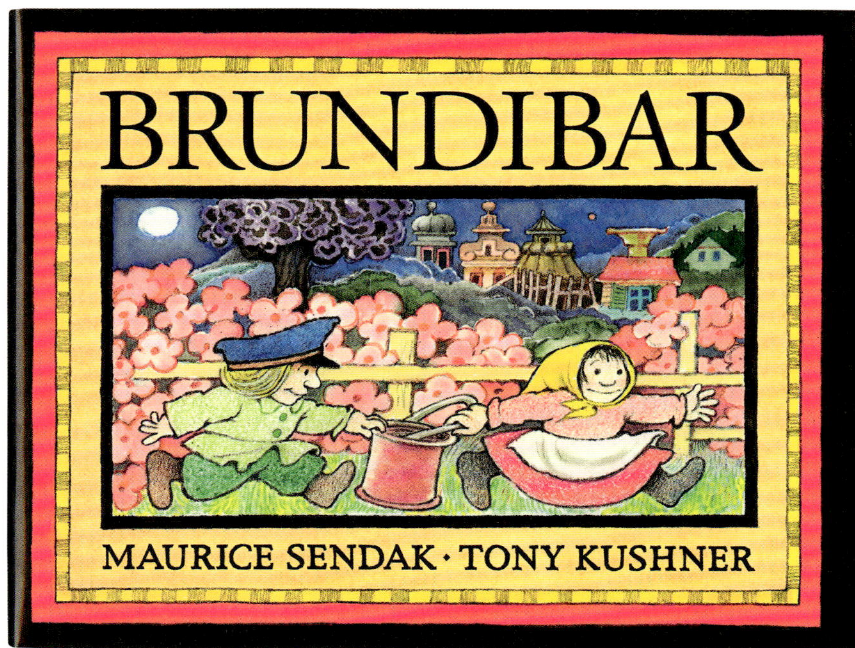

Brundibar. Maurice Sendak and Tony Kushner (New York: Michael di Capua Books/Hyperion Books for Children, 2003)

out, hear all about the mother's stress and distress, the needles. I could do it. I could deliver a child.

I don't want to scare children to death. I really don't want to, but I do want to tell them the truth. In *Brundibar* all the signs of that are there and yet the composition is playful. The colors are bright. It somehow dilutes the expressions on their faces. These are doomed children. Come hell or high water, they're not going to get out of this situation; but they're alive. While they live, they wear bright things. They walk the streets, and they're flying all over the place. Dogs are there.

Brundibar is the hero of this children's opera. He is a hurdy-gurdy player. His name in Czech means the sting of a bee. He rules this little street corner, and these two children are hero and heroine. They need to get money to get milk for their mother. They don't know how to do it. They walk across the town, and the people are rich, obviously; have money stuffed in their pockets, their earlobes, everywhere; but they don't give to the kids. They just don't give to the kids.

So, they think, we can do this, too. They stand on the other street corner and they sing. They're not very good at it at the beginning, and Brundibar hates them, this competition—the two little dumb kids, who are trying to take his place away. He's not going to have it. So, the whole story is about victimization of the children. At the end the animals come in—birds, cats, dogs—and tell the two kids, "Look, you can't do this by yourself; this is a big job. Let's get all the kids."

JW The opera itself was performed in Theresienstadt; a model concentration camp created to fool the outside world about the Final Solution.

MS The librettist Adolf Hoffmeister and the composer Hans Krása were exterminated in Auschwitz, and so were all the children who performed in all these things. It was a huge success, and Red Cross diplomats came. Apparently, they were fooled. Nobody wanted to believe what was coming.

"... if you get to know the work very well, as I have had to, there are elements in the opera that are extremely brave in the face of the circumstances: the tyrant will come down, all bullies will be put away, and we must stick together, brothers and sisters."

JW In an extraordinary way, what *Brundibar* is about is taking that lie and turning it back into the truth. Brundibar is really not just Hitler. He's really the bad artist in a fundamental way. He's the lying fake.

MS The cheater, the bully.

People keep things from children now in the sense that we don't want to frighten them or upset them, yet we all know they sat and watched the towers go down a hundred thousand times.

They're just waiting for you to tell them. They know you're a coward. They know they'll have to find out some other way. Everything I found out that was true was in the backyard in Brooklyn. You played doctor, and you knew the whole *geschichte* right away.

So, I grew up knowing everything—not that my parents felt this way, but there was no way they could hide. You had a radio. Everything that was on the radio I heard.

I heard when the Hindenburg went down. I heard the screams. When the Lindbergh baby was kidnapped, that paralyzed me with fear, I remember—I was only three years old—Mrs. Lindbergh's voice on the radio, weeping, telling the kidnappers that baby had a cold; and could they put camphor on its chest and cover it with a cloth. How do I remember that? But I do. I think it's not a certain thing about me. I think it's a certain thing about children. They have to live. They have to survive. They have to know. We've got to tell them.

Notes

1. Interview conducted at the Vera List Center for Art and Politics, The New School, New York City, October 30, 2003. A longer version of this interview is published in *Art, an Index to (See Also Politics): 25 Years of Vera List Center Fellowships*, edited by Carin Kuoni and Amanda Palmer (New York: Vera List Center for Art and Politics, The New School, 2018), 105–16.

2. Frank Corsaro (1924–2017) was the director for most of Maurice Sendak's opera projects including *The Cunning Little Vixen* and *The Magic Flute*.

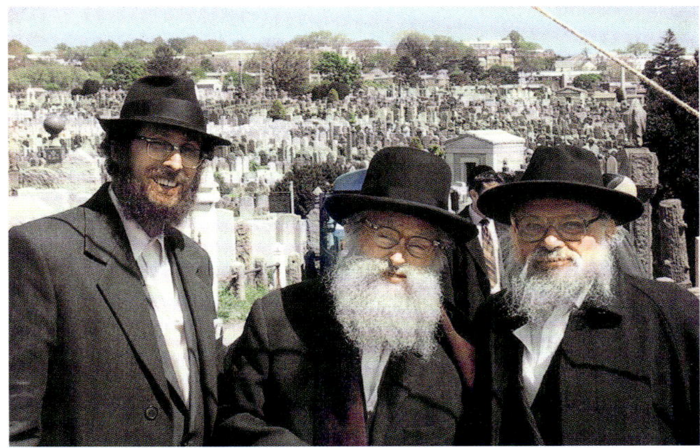

Tony Kushner, Meryl Streep and Maurice Sendak as Three Rabbis, on location, *Angels in America*, 2002

"Tony [Kushner] extrapolated from the libretto into a very gorgeous complex story—the first time he's ever done anything like this. He's amazing. He just adapted it, without any fuss or feathers. Gorgeous, gorgeous funny language."

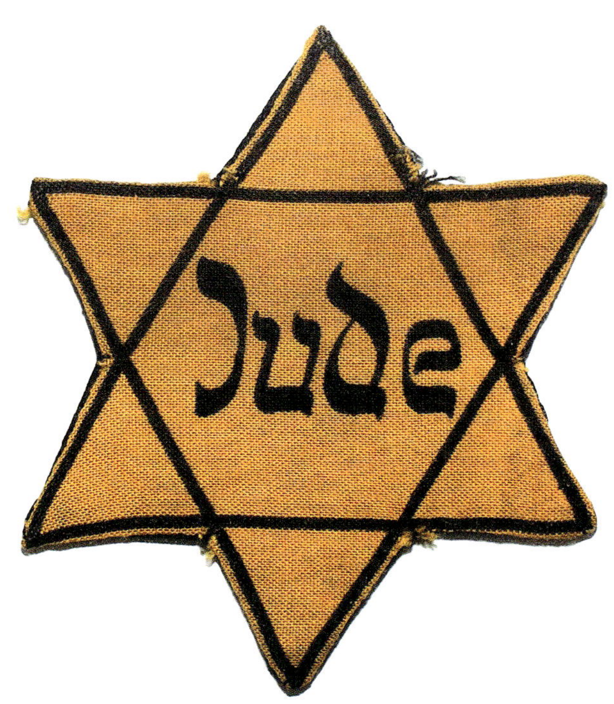

Yellow Badge, c. 1940, 3½ × 3 in.

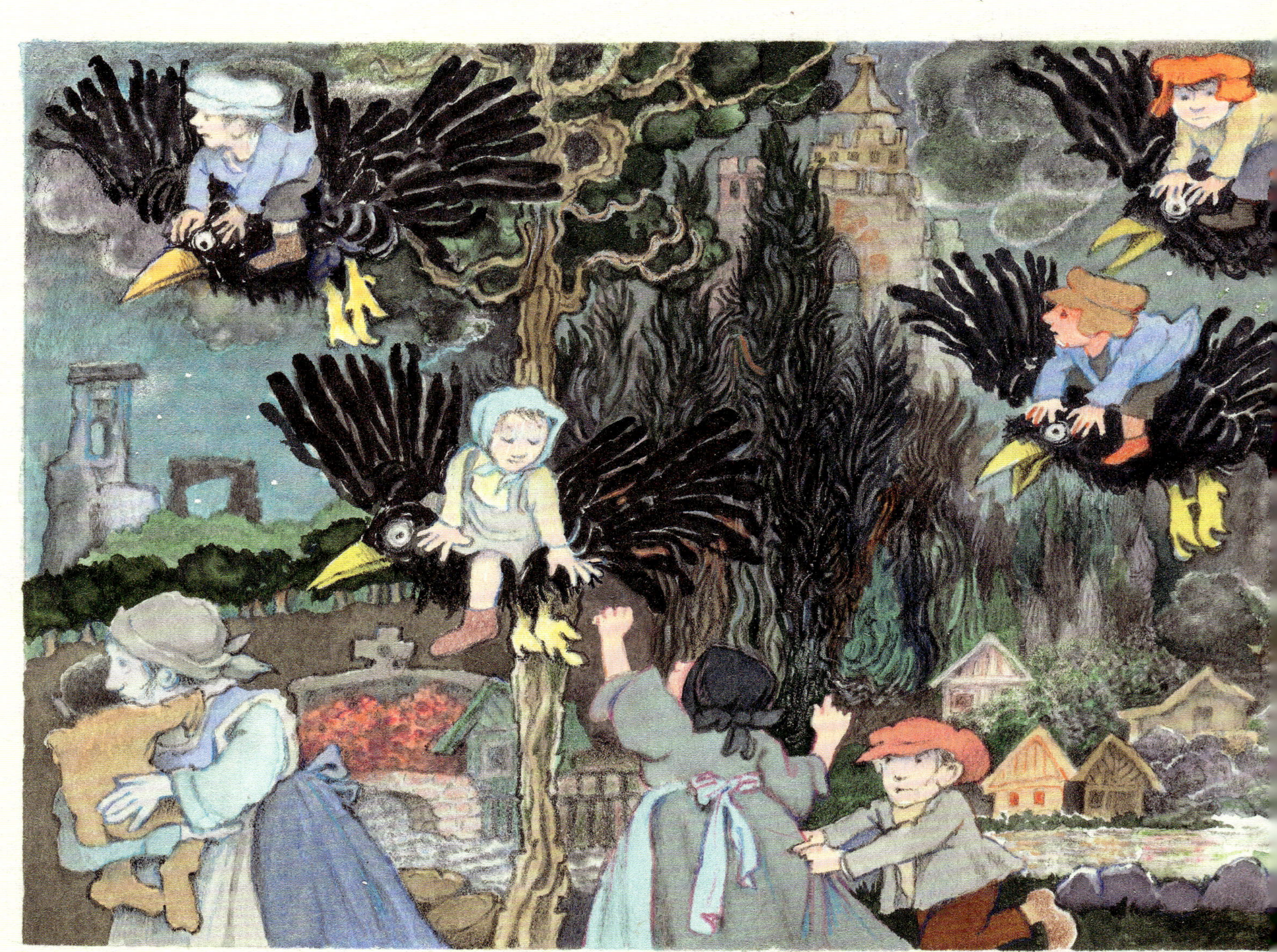

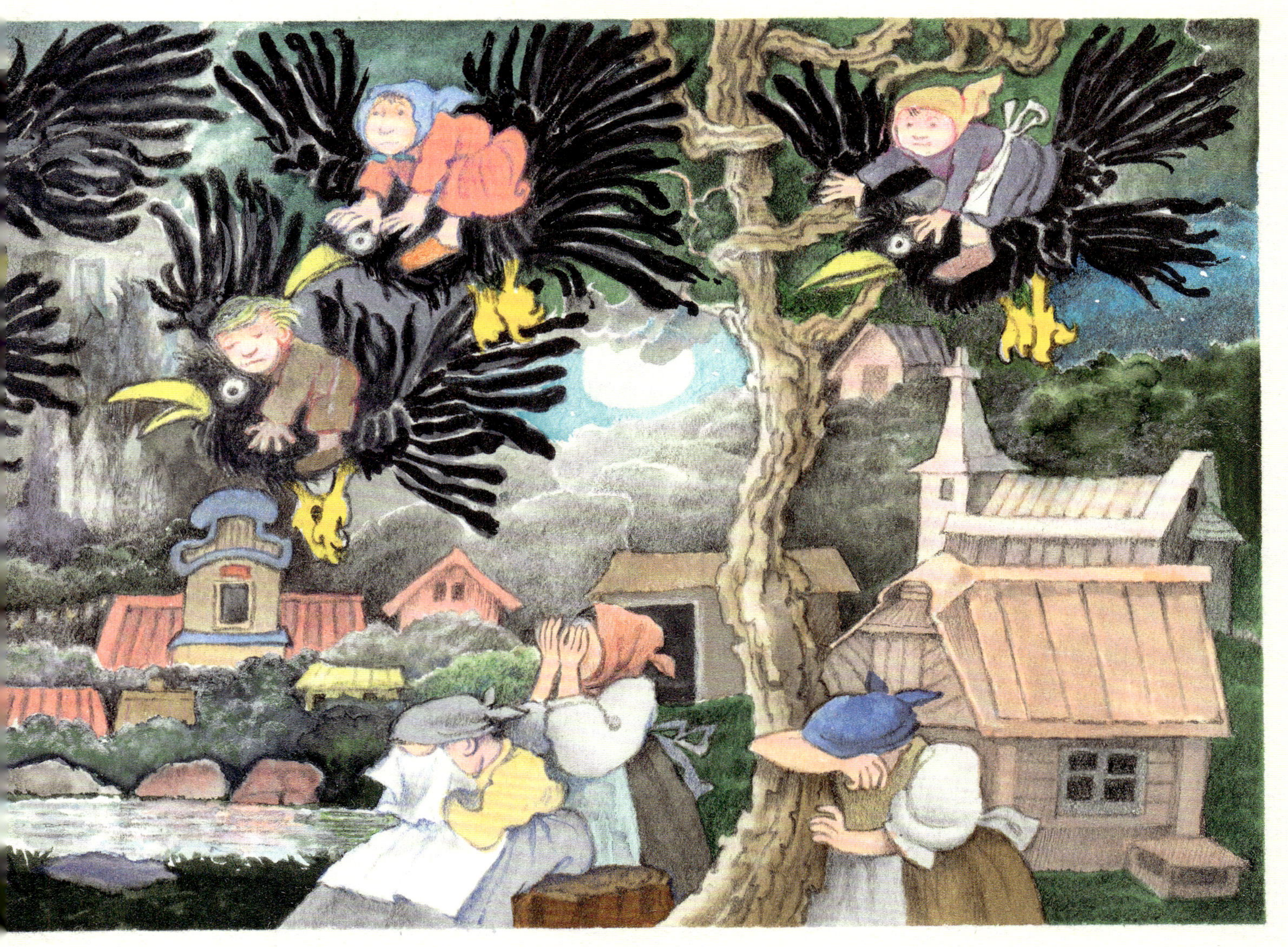

Maurice Sendak, *Brundibar*, 2002, watercolor and crayon on paper, 11½ × 22¼ in.

Bumble-Ardy

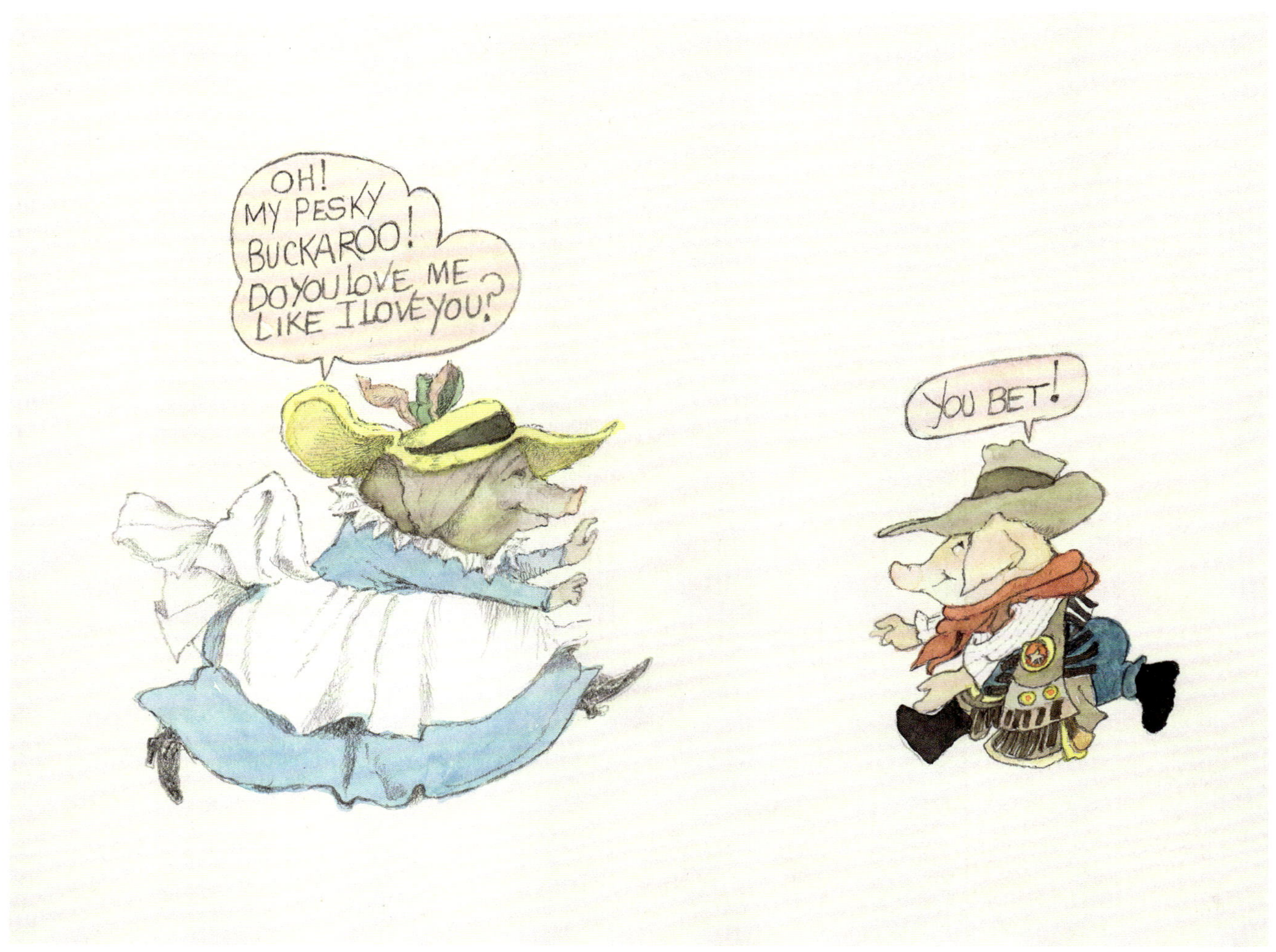

Maurice Sendak, *Bumble-Ardy*, 2011, watercolor and graphite on paper, 10½ × 12⅛ in.

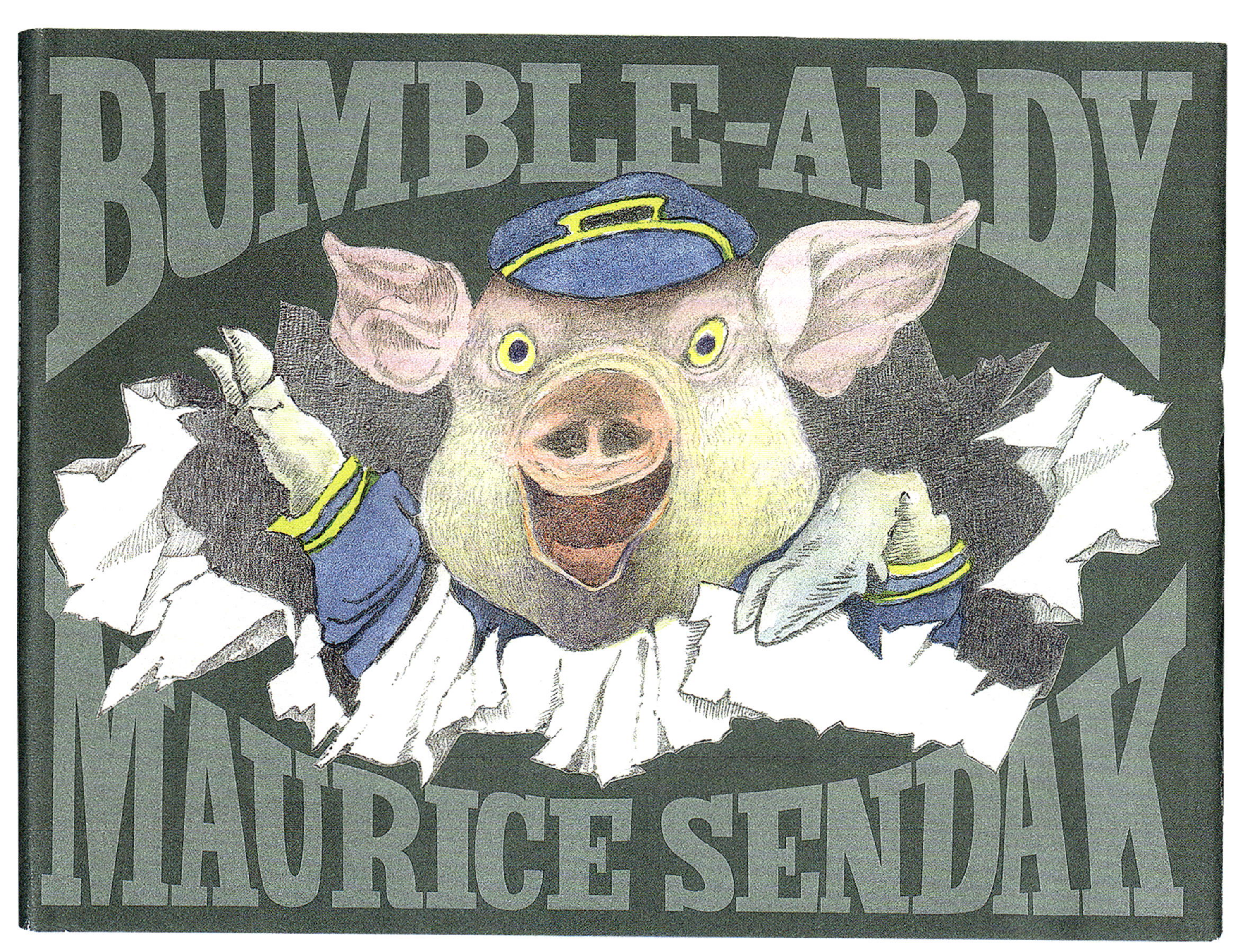

Maurice Sendak, *Bumble-Ardy* (New York: Michael Di Capua Books, HarperCollins, 2011)

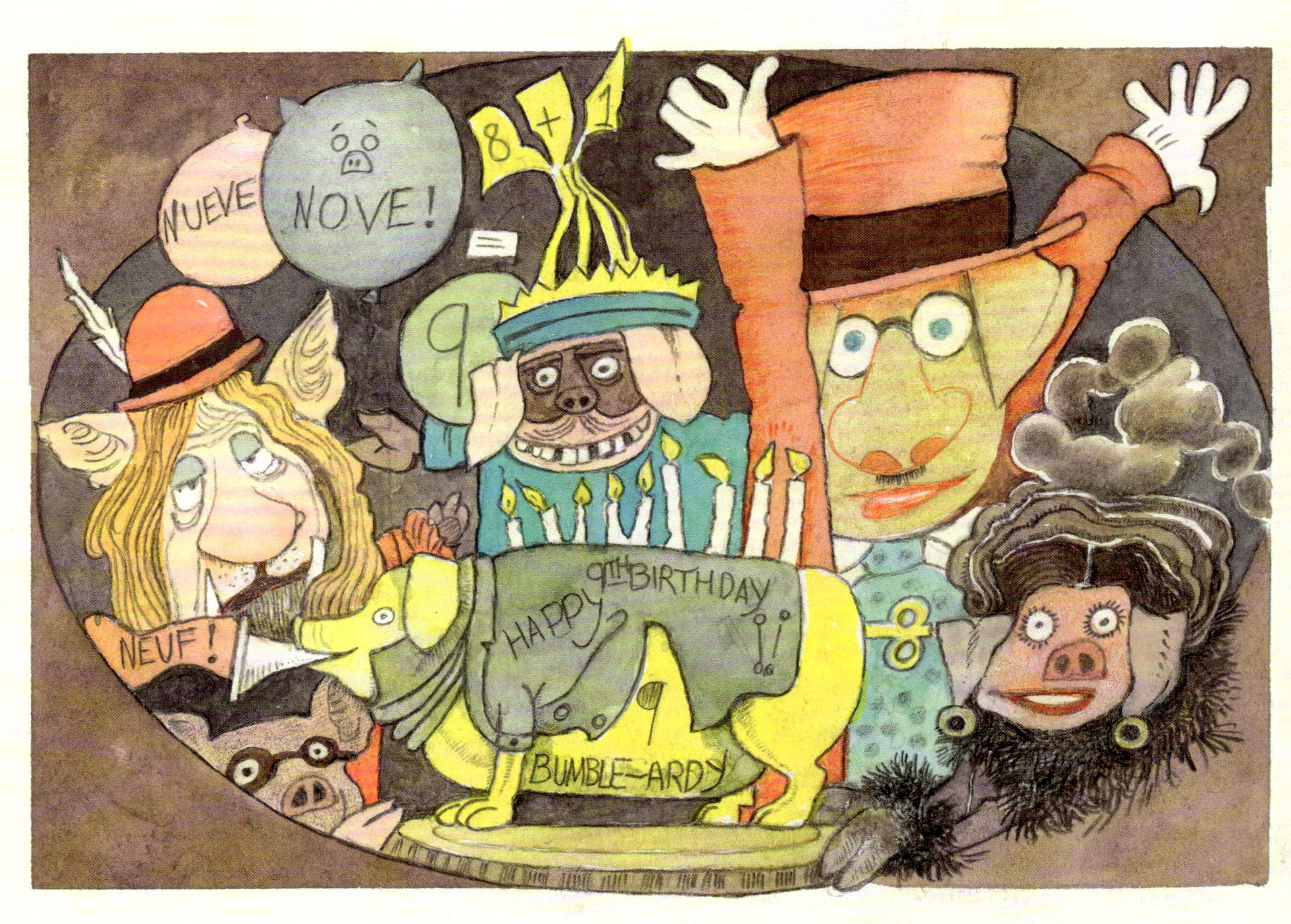

Maurice Sendak, *Bumble-ardy*, watercolor and graphite on paper, 2011, 10½ × 12⅛ in.

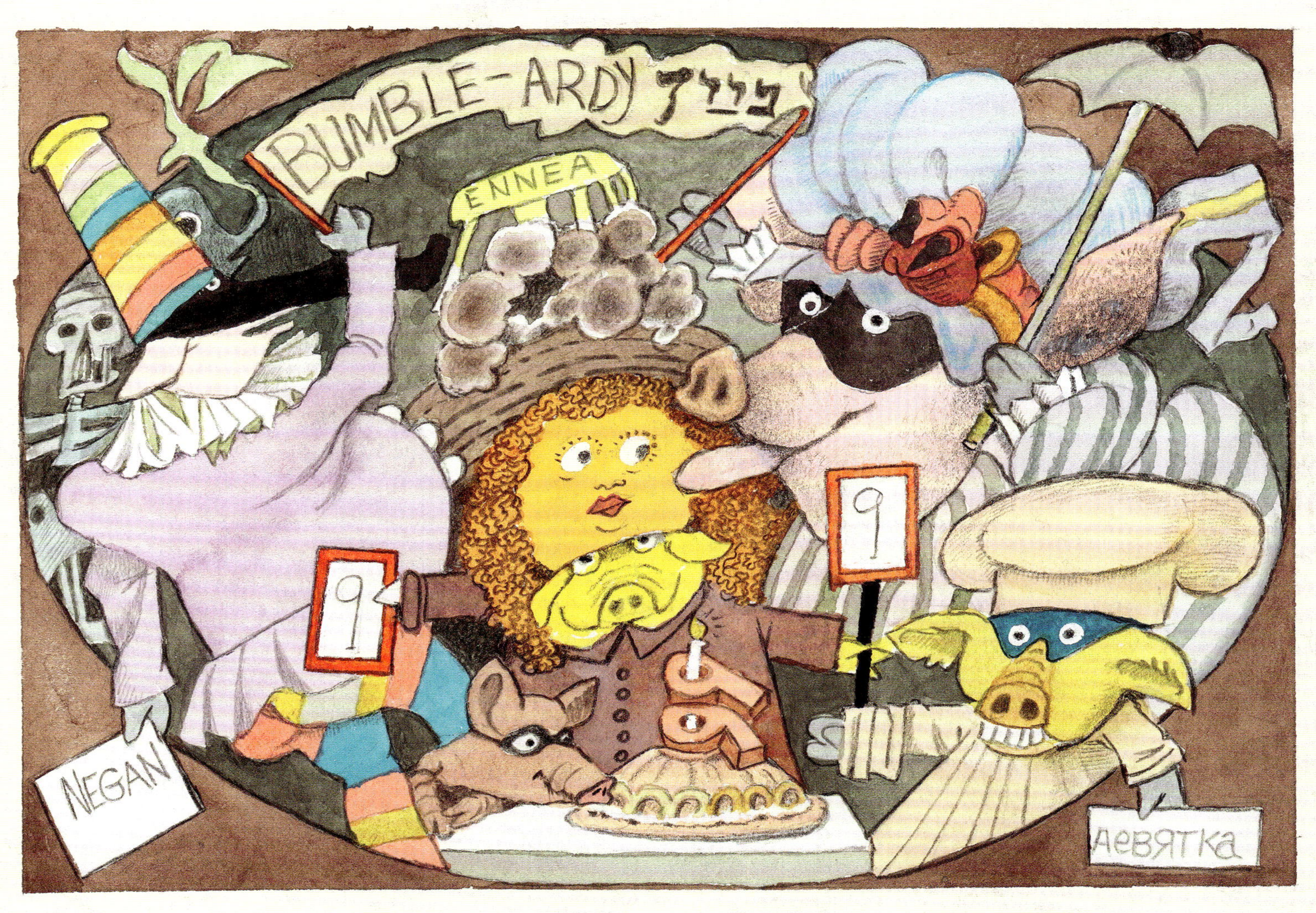

Maurice Sendak, *Bumble-ardy*, watercolor and graphite on paper, 2011, 10½ × 12⅞ in.

CAREER HIGHLIGHTS

June 10, 1928
Maurice Bernard Sendak is born in Brooklyn, New York to Sarah (Sadie) (1895–1968) and Philip Sendak (1896–1970)

1947
Atomics for the Millions, author M.C. Eidinoff and Hyman Ruchus. Ruchus was Sendak's high school Physics teacher and according to the artist, he allowed him to pass the course if he did the pictures for the popular book explaining atomic power

1947–1951
Maurice and his brother, Jack (1923–1995) create mechanical toys that they bring to FAO Schwarz. Maurice Sendak is offered a job as a window designer and through the store's book department is introduced to Ursula Nordstrom, the children's book editor at Harper & Row who hires him to illustrate Marcel Aymé, *The Wonderful Farm*

1952
A Hole Is to Dig, author Ruth Krauss

1954
The Wheel on the School, author Meindert DeJong

1956
Kenny's Window, author Maurice Sendak

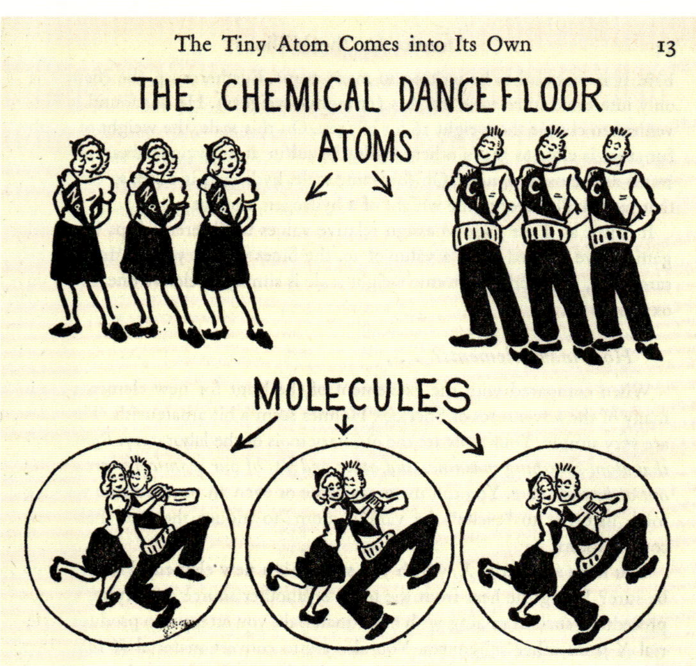

Maurice Sendak, *The Chemical Dance Floor*, illustration on page 13 of *Atomics for the Millions*

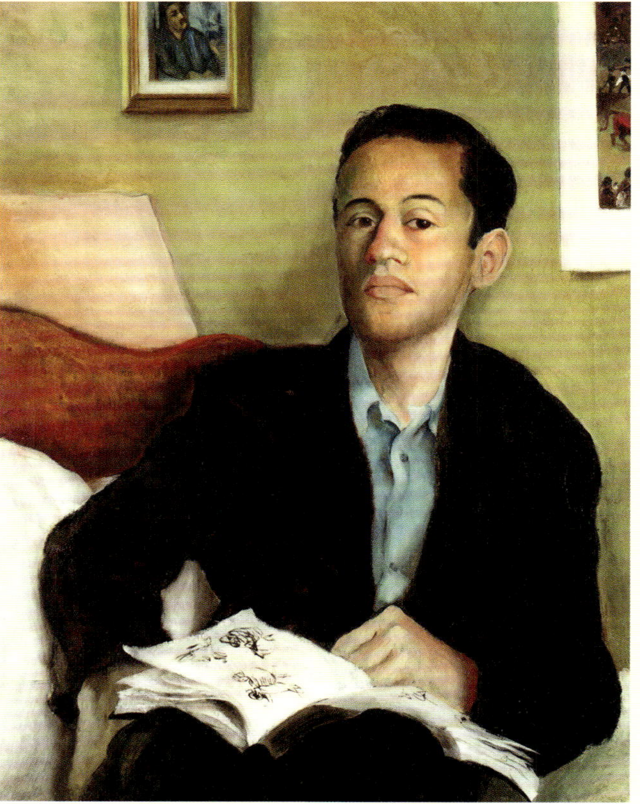

Maurice Sendak, *Jack Sendak*, 1949, oil on canvas, 28 × 22 in.

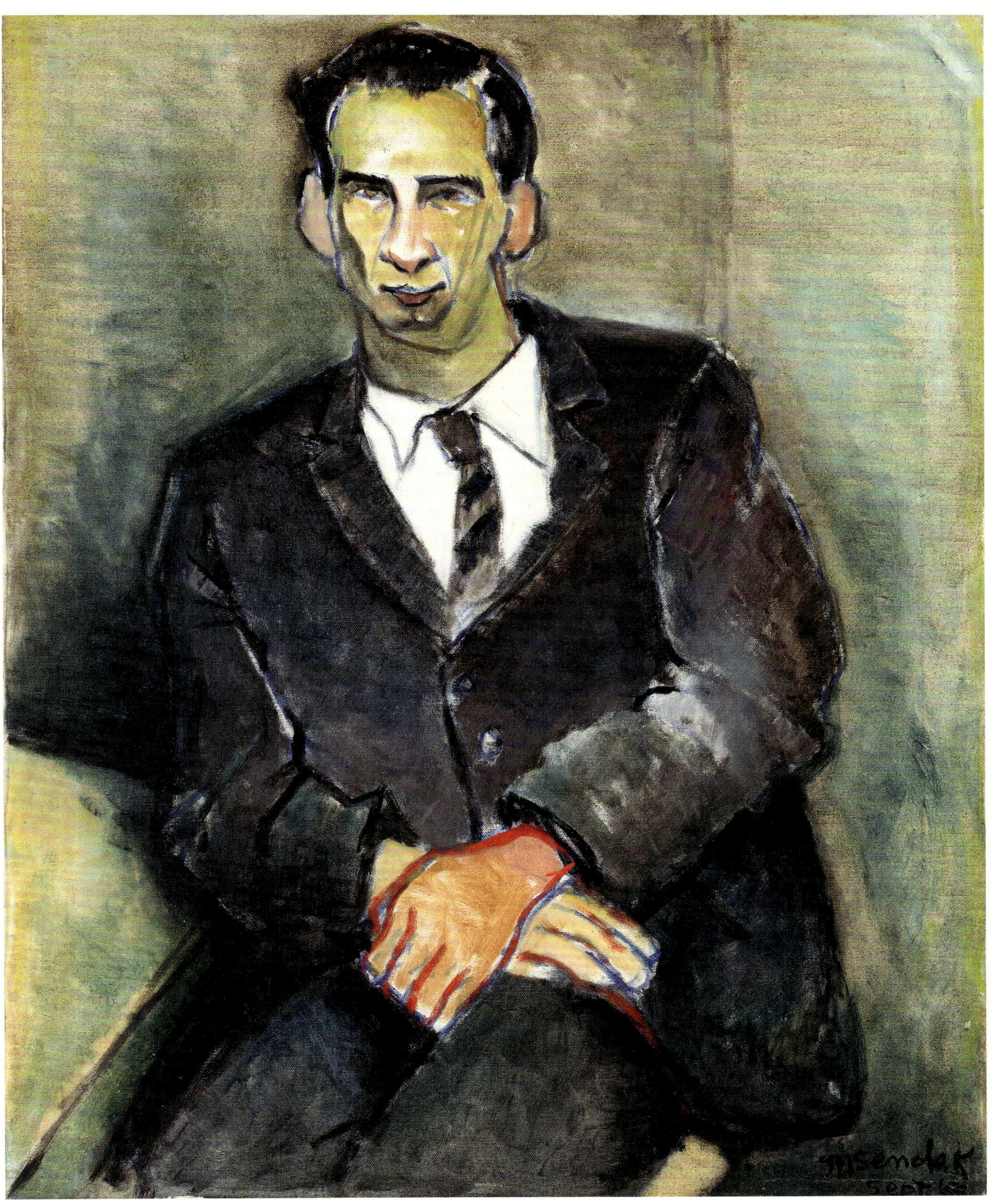

Maurice Sendak, *Eugene Glynn*, 1959, oil on canvas, 30½ × 23¾ in.

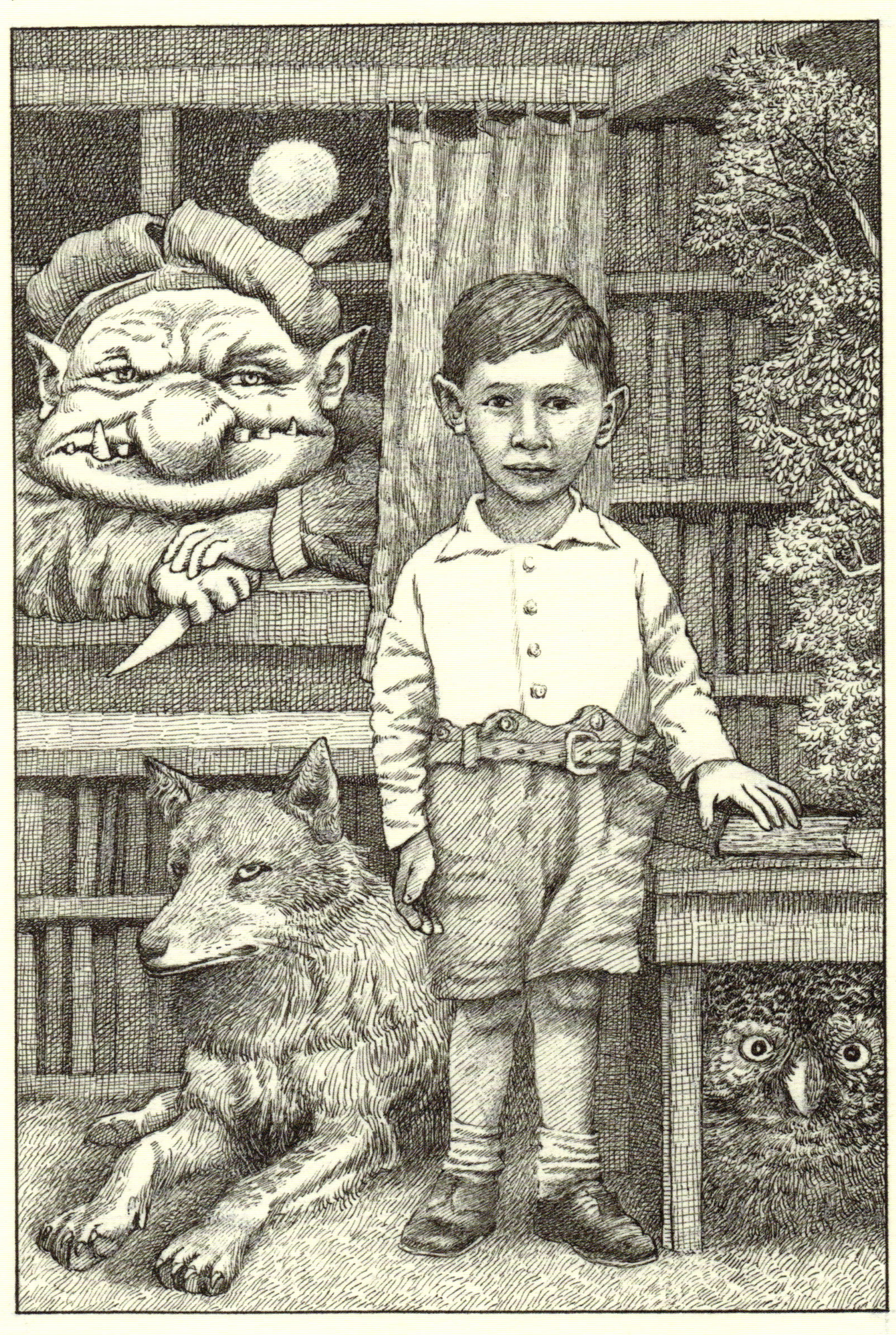

Maurice Sendak, Drawing for the cover of Randall Jarrell, *The Lost World, The Last Poems*, 1967, ink on paper, 8¾ × 7½ in.

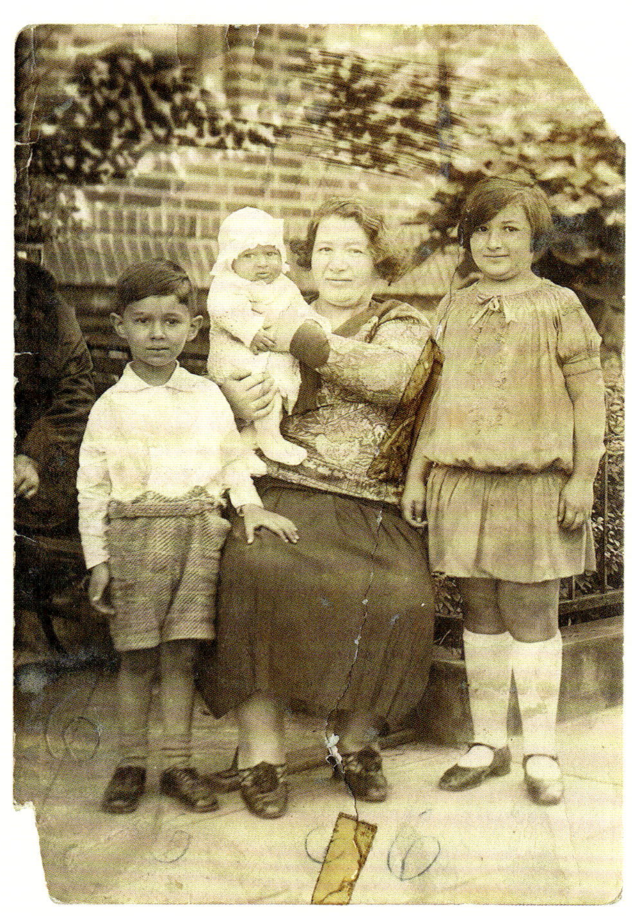

Jack, Maurice, Sarah (Sadie), and Natalie Sendak, 1928

"Often, I am trying to draw the way children feel—
or, rather, the way I imagine they feel. It's the way I know
I felt as a child. And all I have to go on is what I know—
not only about my childhood then, but about
the child I was as he exists now."

following pages: Maurice Sendak, *Fly by Night*, 1976, ink on paper, 7 × 9 in.

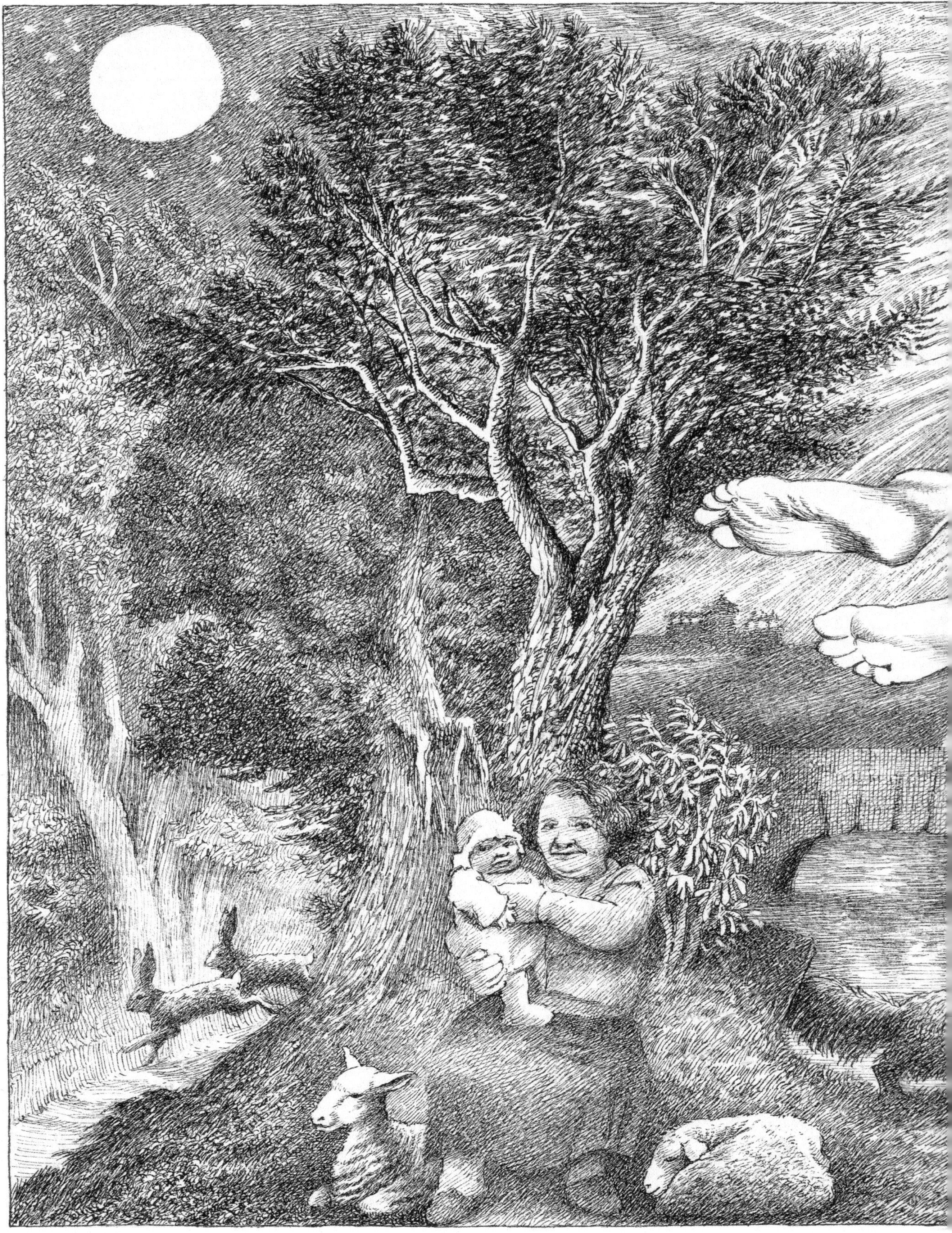

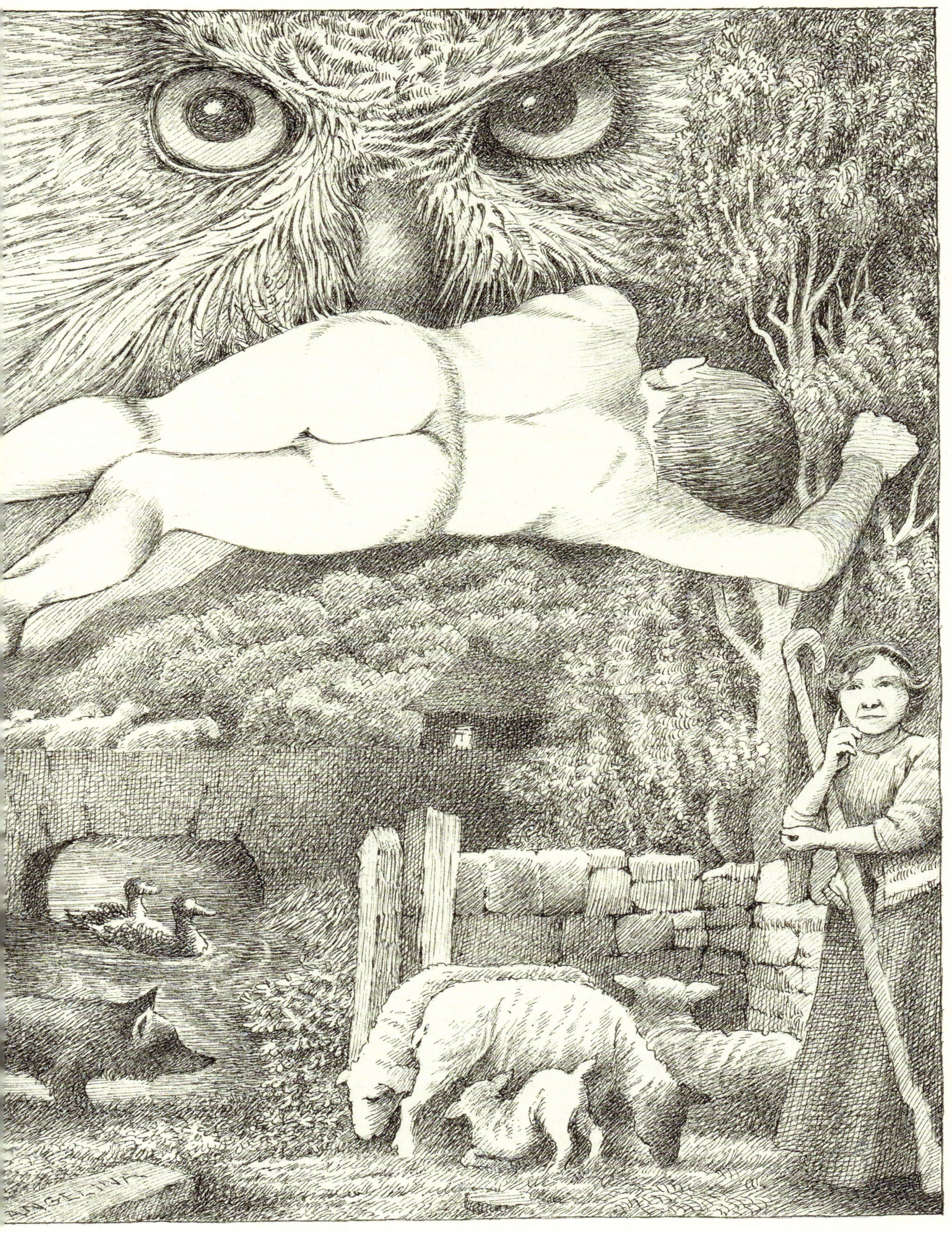

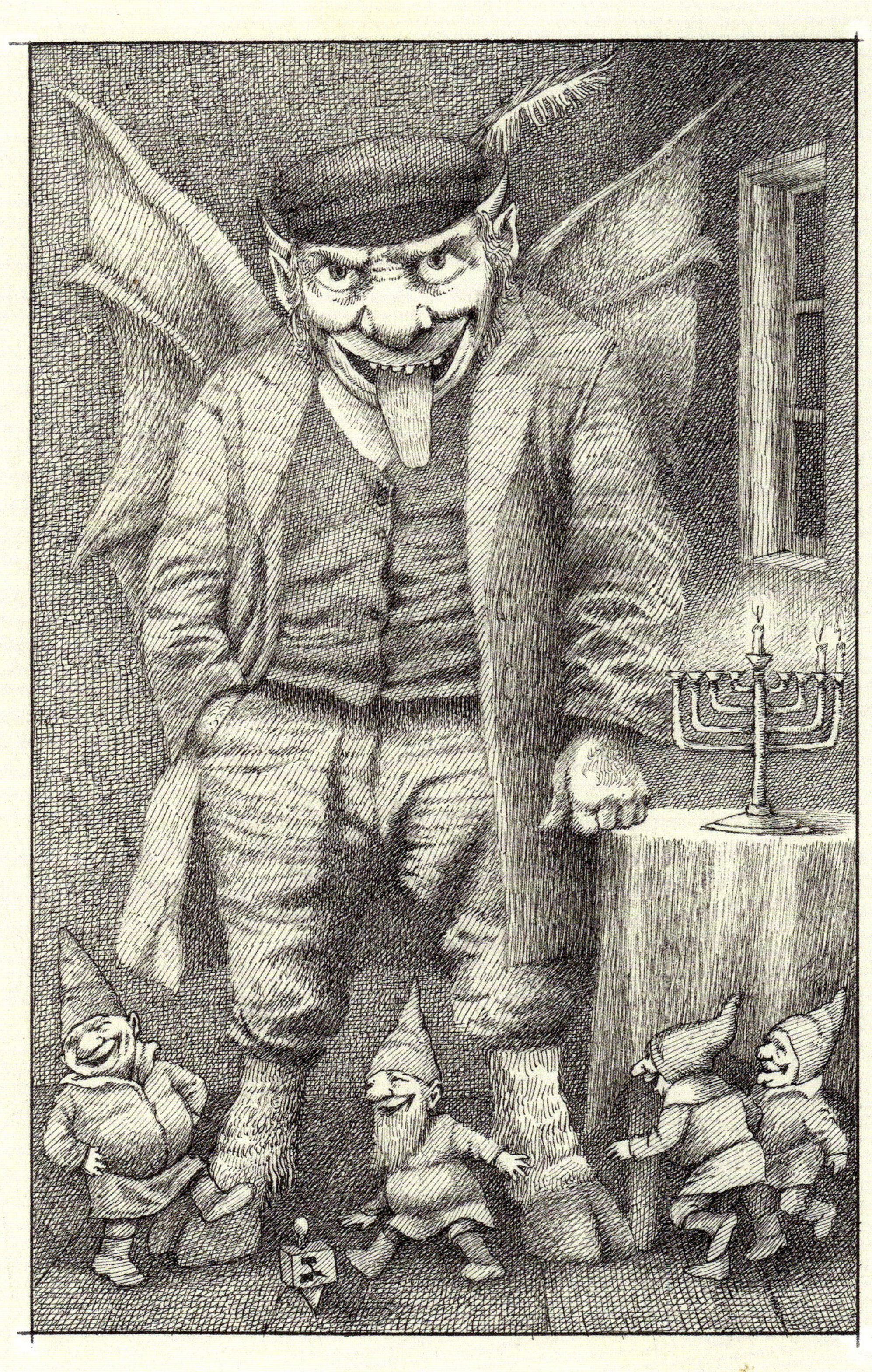

Maurice Sendak, *Grandmother's Tale* from *Zlateh the Goat*, 1966, 9 × 6 in.

"For me, childhood was *shtetl* life transplanted, Brooklyn colored by Old World reverberations and Walt Disney and the occasional trip to the incredibly windowed 'uptown' that was New York-America."

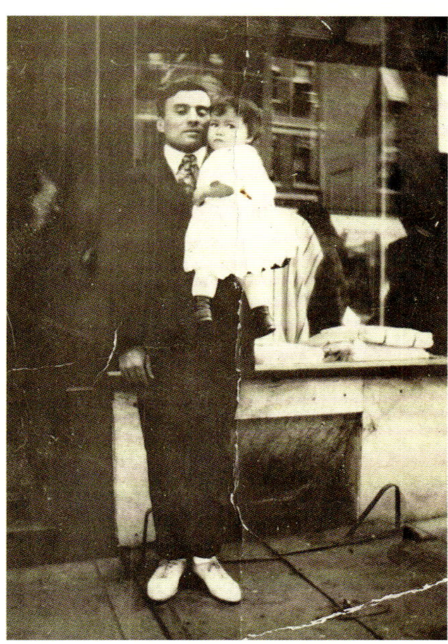

Philip Sendak, the artist's father, and Natalie, his sister, 1920

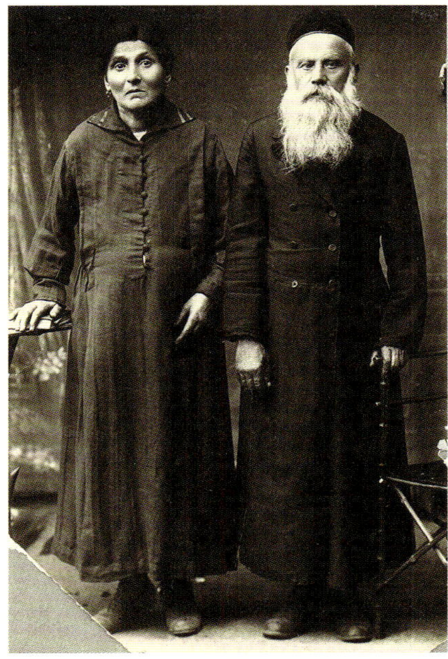

Maurice Sendak's paternal grandparents, n.d.

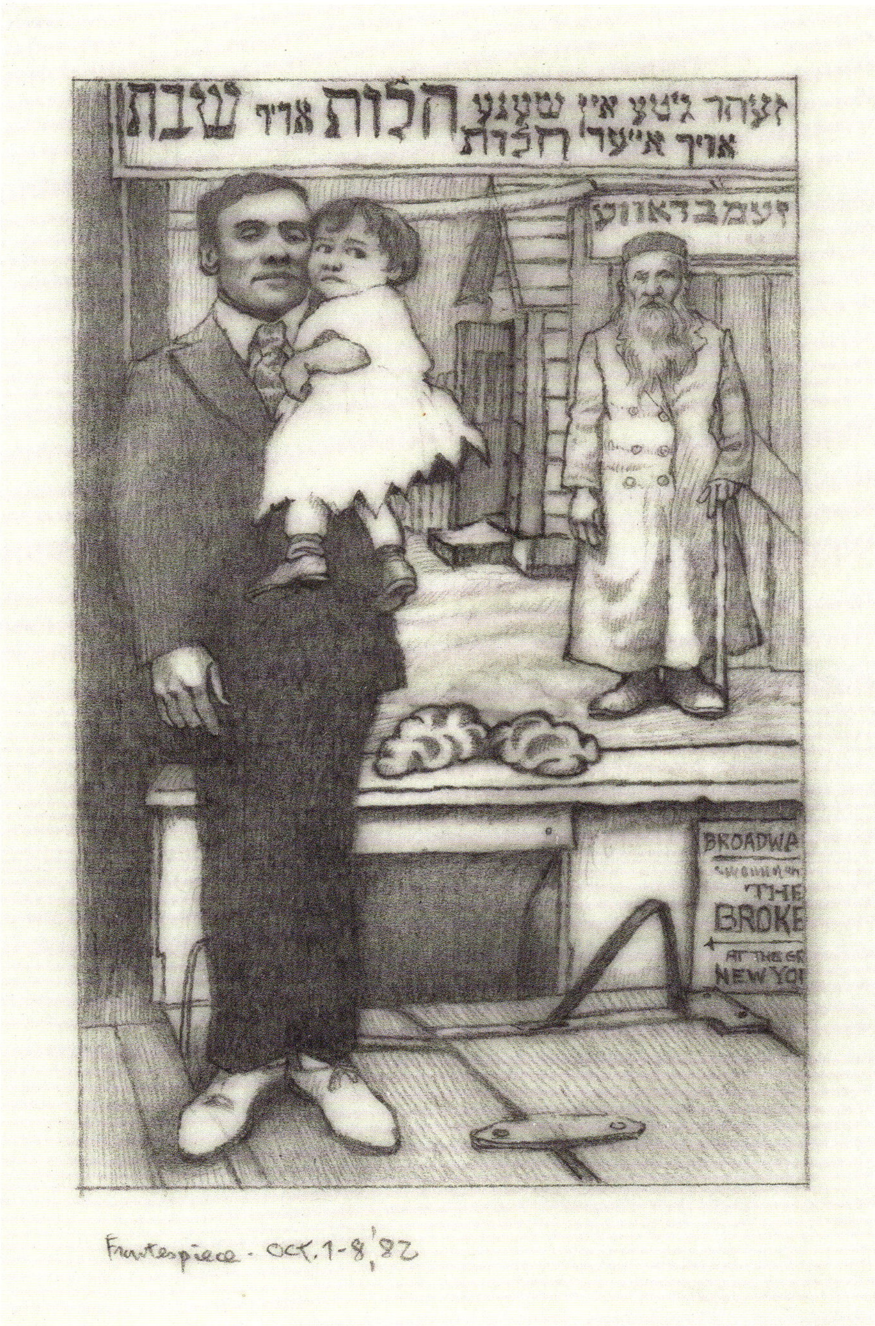

Maurice Sendak, *In Grandpa's House*, 1985, pencil on tracing paper, 11½ × 9 in.

1957
- *Little Bear*, author Else Holmelund Minarik
- *Very Far Away*, author Maurice Sendak

1960
- *The Sign on Rosie's Door*, author Maurice Sendak

1962
- *The Nutshell Library*, author Maurice Sendak

1963
- *Where the Wild Things Are*, author Maurice Sendak

1964
- Caldecott Award for *Where the Wild Things Are*
- *The Bat-Poet*, author Randall Jarrell

1965
- *Hector Protector and As I Went Over the Water*, author Maurice Sendak and Mother Goose

1966
- *Zlateh the Goat and Other Stories*, author Isaac Bashevis Singer

1967
- *Higglety, Pigglety, Pop! or There Must be More to Life*

1970
- *In the Night Kitchen*, author Maurice Sendak
- Hans Christian Andersen Award

1973
- *The Juniper Tree and Other Tales from Grimm*, author the Brothers Grimm, translated by Lore Segal and Randall Jarrell

1975
- *Really Rosie Cartoon* with music by Carole King, libretto, lyrics, and animation by Maurice Sendak

1979
- *Where the Wild Things Are* opera, music by Oliver Knussen, libretto, sets and costumes by Maurice Sendak

1980
- Off-Broadway Production of *Really Rosie*, libretto, lyrics, sets and costumes by Maurice Sendak
- *The Magic Flute* opera, music by Wolfgang Amadeus Mozart, directed by Frank Corsaro, sets and costumes by Maurice Sendak

1981
- *Outside Over There*, author Maurice Sendak
- *The Cunning Little Vixen* opera, music by Leoš Janáček, directed by Frank Corsaro, sets and costumes by Maurice Sendak

1982
- *The Love for Three Oranges* opera, music by Serge Prokofiev, directed by Frank Corsaro, sets and costumes by Maurice Sendak

1983
- *Nutcracker* ballet, music by Pyotr Ilyich Tchaikovsky, choreography by Kent Stowell, sets and costumes by Maurice Sendak

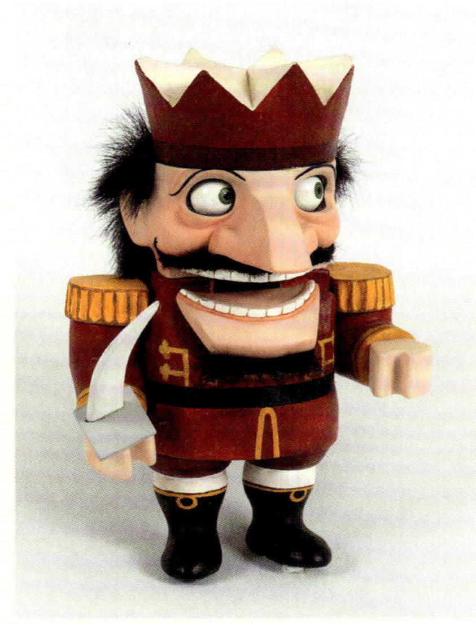

Maurice Sendak, *Nutcracker* from the production of *Nutcracker*, 1983, mixed media, 10 h × 7 ¾ w × 8 d in.

1984
- *Higglety Pigglety Pop!* opera, music by Oliver Knussen, directed by Frank Corsaro, sets and costumes by Maurice Sendak

1986
- *Nutcracker* motion picture, directed by Carroll Ballard, based on the *Nutcracker* ballet production choreographed by Kent Stowell, with sets and costumes by Maurice Sendak
- *The Goose from Cairo* opera, music by Wolfgang Amadeus Mozart, directed by Frank Corsaro, sets and costume by Maurice Sendak

1988
- *Dear Mili*, author Wilhelm Grimm

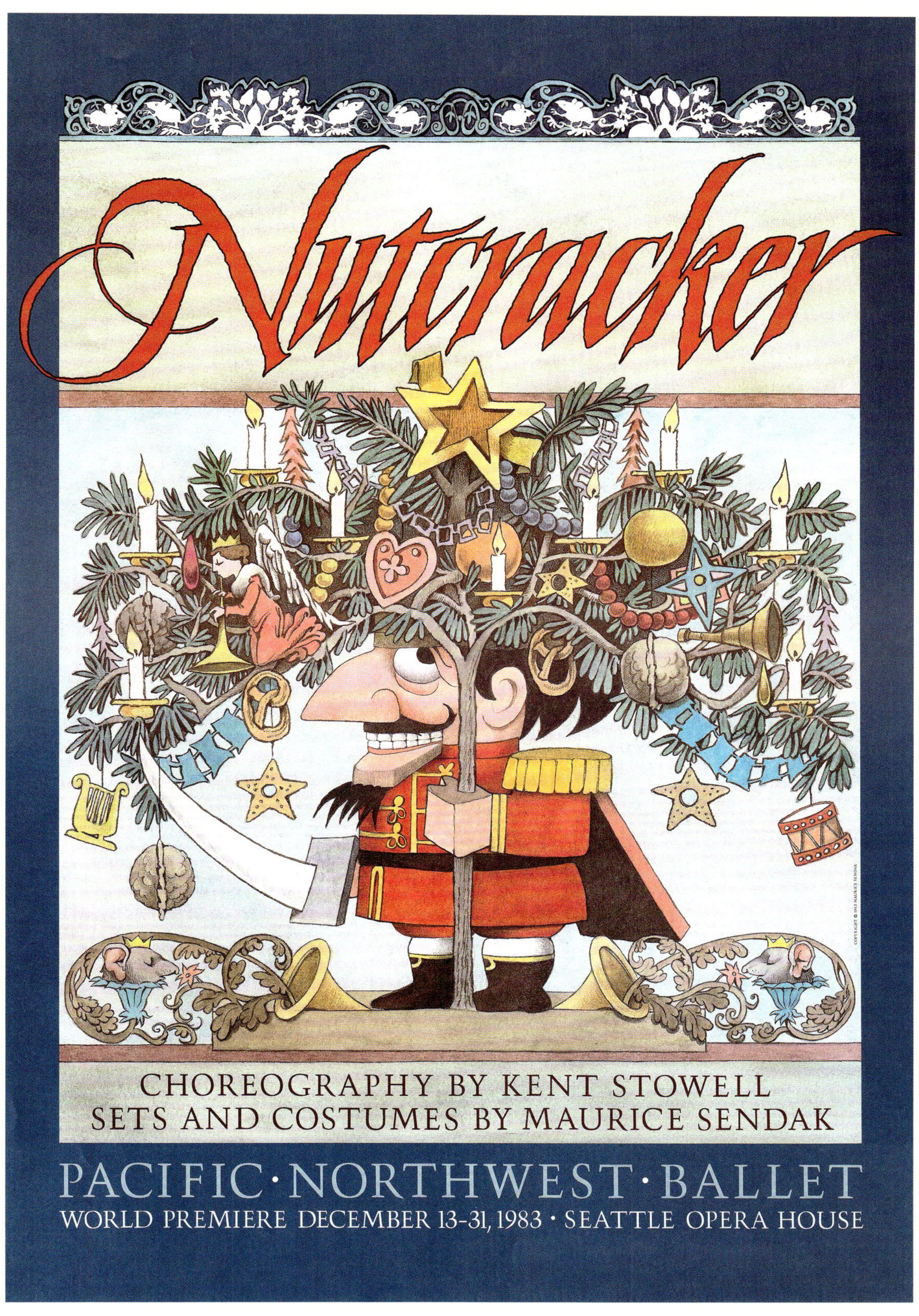

Maurice Sendak, *Nutcracker*, 1983, poster, 26 × 18 in.

1993
❧ *We are All in the Dumps with Jack and Guy*, author Maurice Sendak and Mother Goose

1995
❧ *Pierre, or The Ambiguities*, author Herman Melville
❧ *Miami Giant*, author Arthur Yorinks

1996
❧ National Medal of Arts

1998
❧ Macy's Thanksgiving Day Parade *Wild Thing* Balloon
❧ *Penthesilea*, author Heinrich von Kleist

2003
❧ *Brundibar* opera, music by Hans Krása, libretto by Tony Kushner, direction, sets, and costumes by Maurice Sendak
❧ *Brundibar* book, Tony Kushner, author
❧ Astrid Lindgren Memorial Award

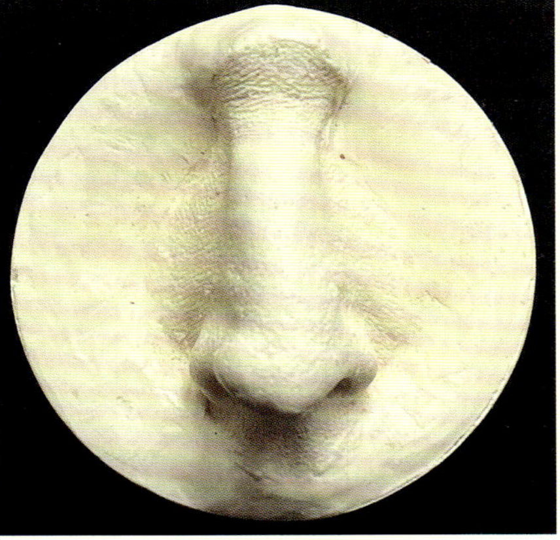

Cast of Tony Kushner's Nose on Maurice Sendak's Ridgefield Studio Desk, plaster 3¾ diameter by 2 in. high

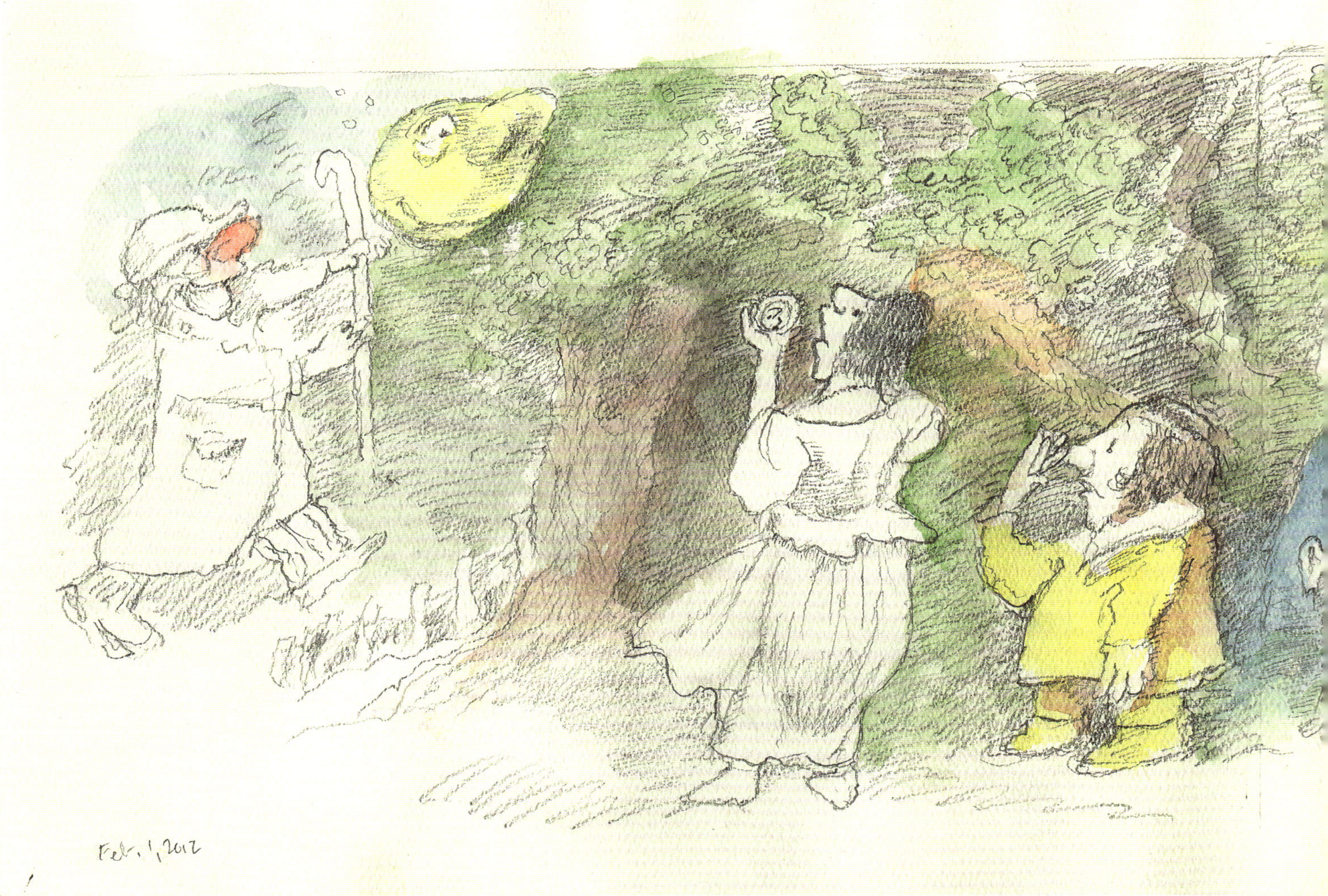

Maurice Sendak, Study for *No Nose*, 2012, watercolor on paper, 7½ × 22 in.

2006
Mommy? Scenario by Arthur Yorinks, Engineered by Michael Reinhart

2009
Where the Wild Things Are motion picture, directed by Spike Jonze, screenplay by Spike Jonze and David Eggers, adapted from Maurice Sendak's book.

2011
Bumble-Ardy, author Maurice Sendak

May 8, 2012
Dies at Danbury Hospital, Connecticut

2013
My Brother's Book, author Maurice Sendak

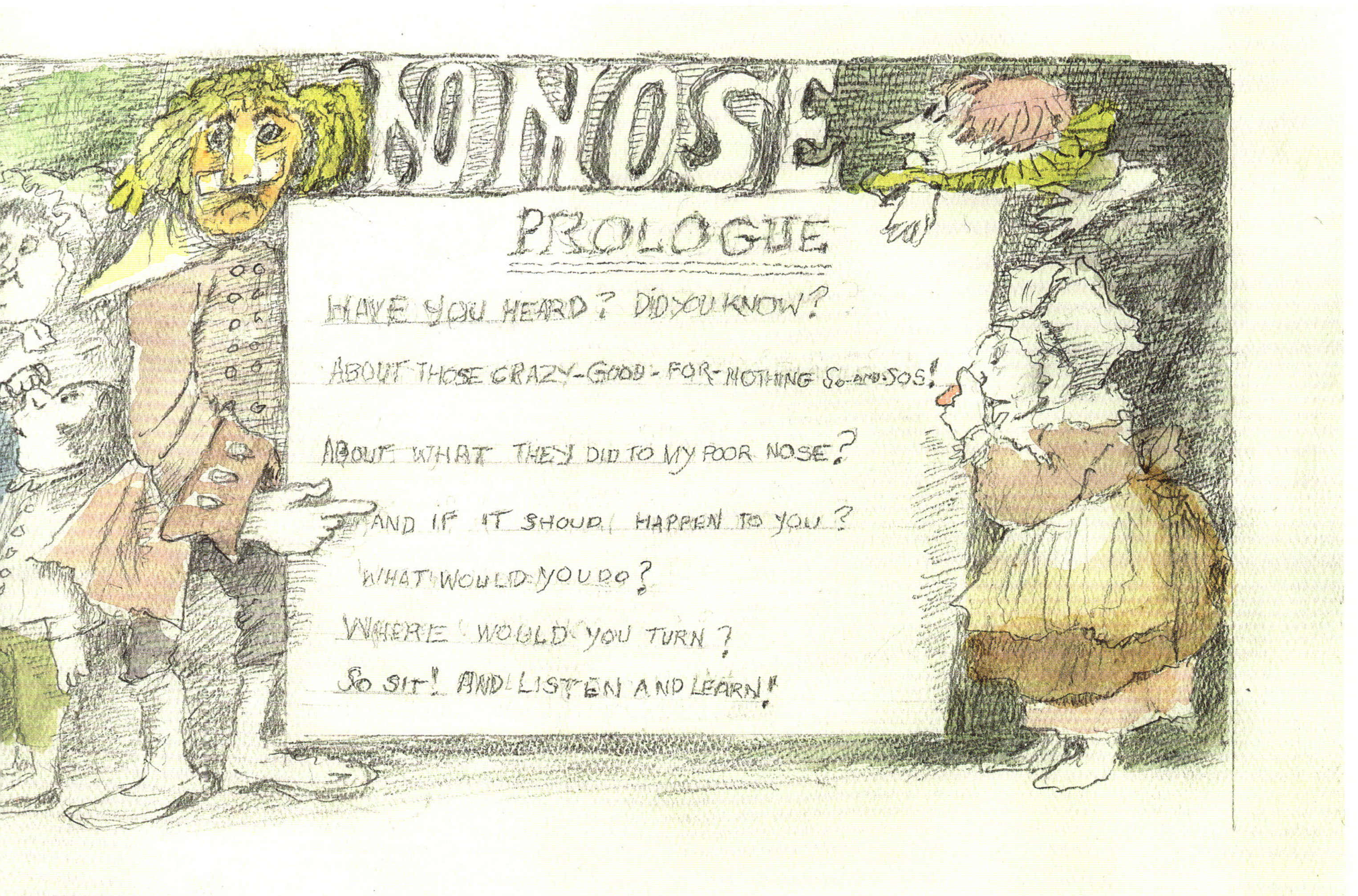

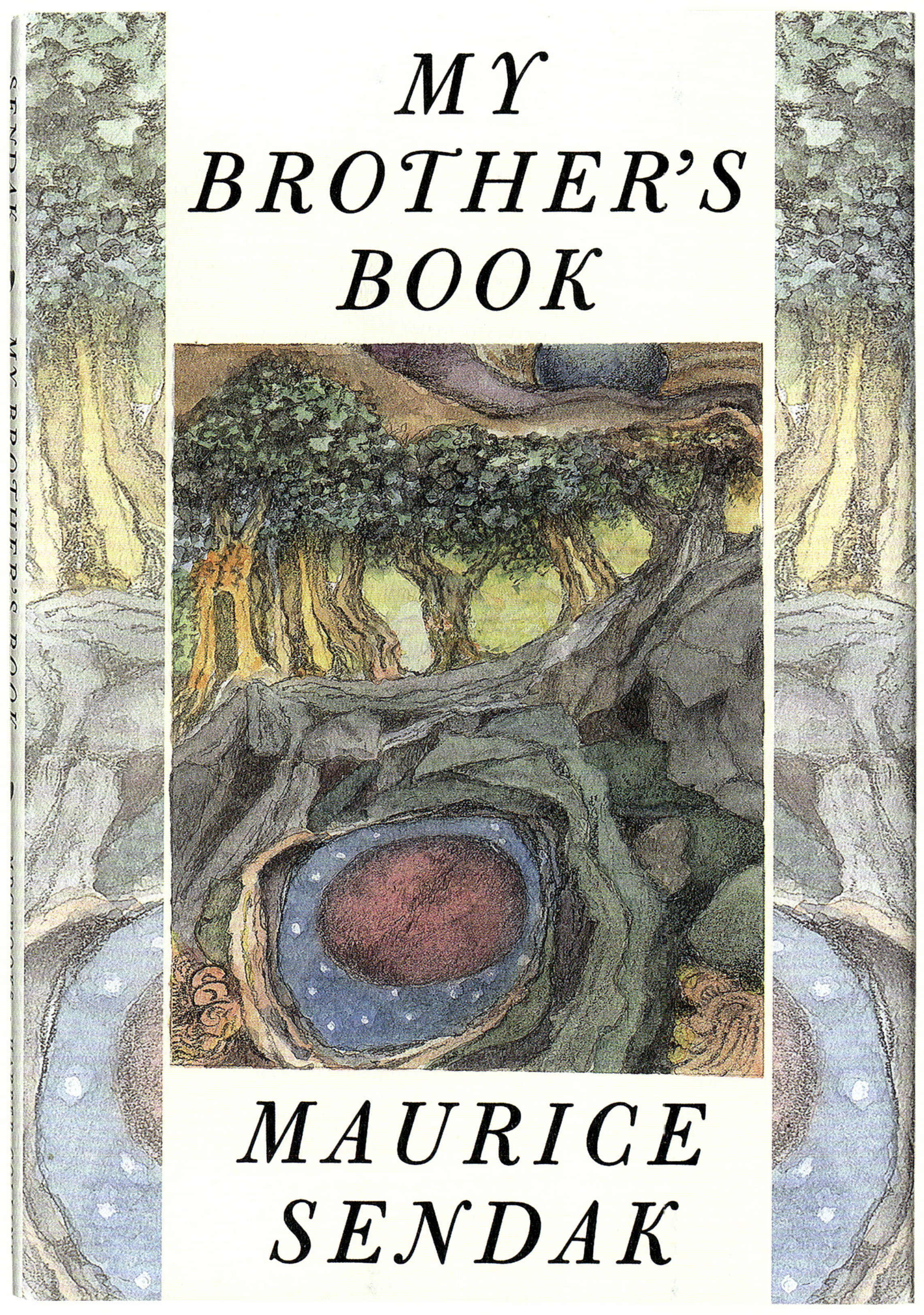

Maurice Sendak, *My Brother's Book* (New York: HarperCollins, 2013)

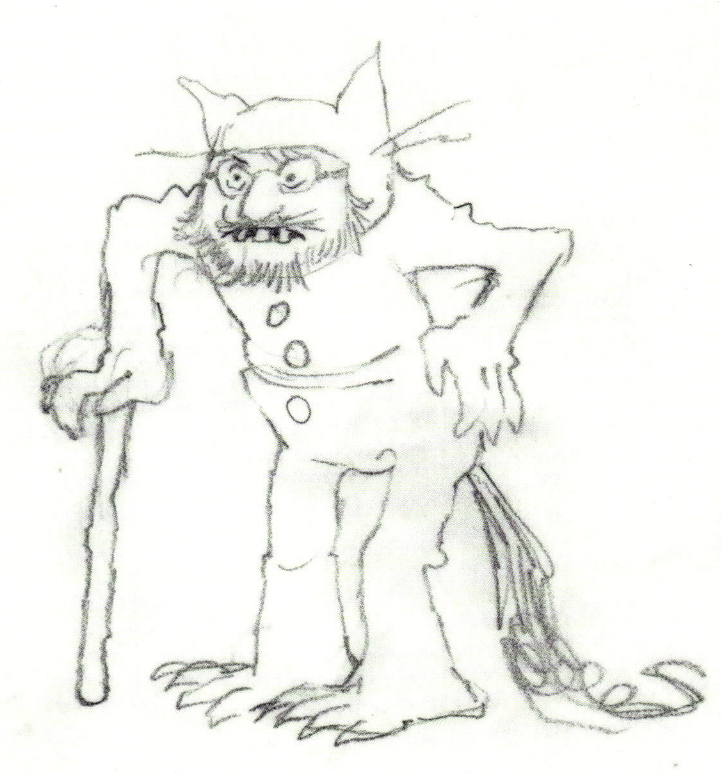

Maurice Sendak, *Self-Portrait in Max Suit*, 2007, pencil on paper, 8 × 8 in., Private Collection

"I've been struggling for over five years to write a memorial to my brother that would not all be revelatory or autobiographical, but would convey what he meant to me. And I did it."

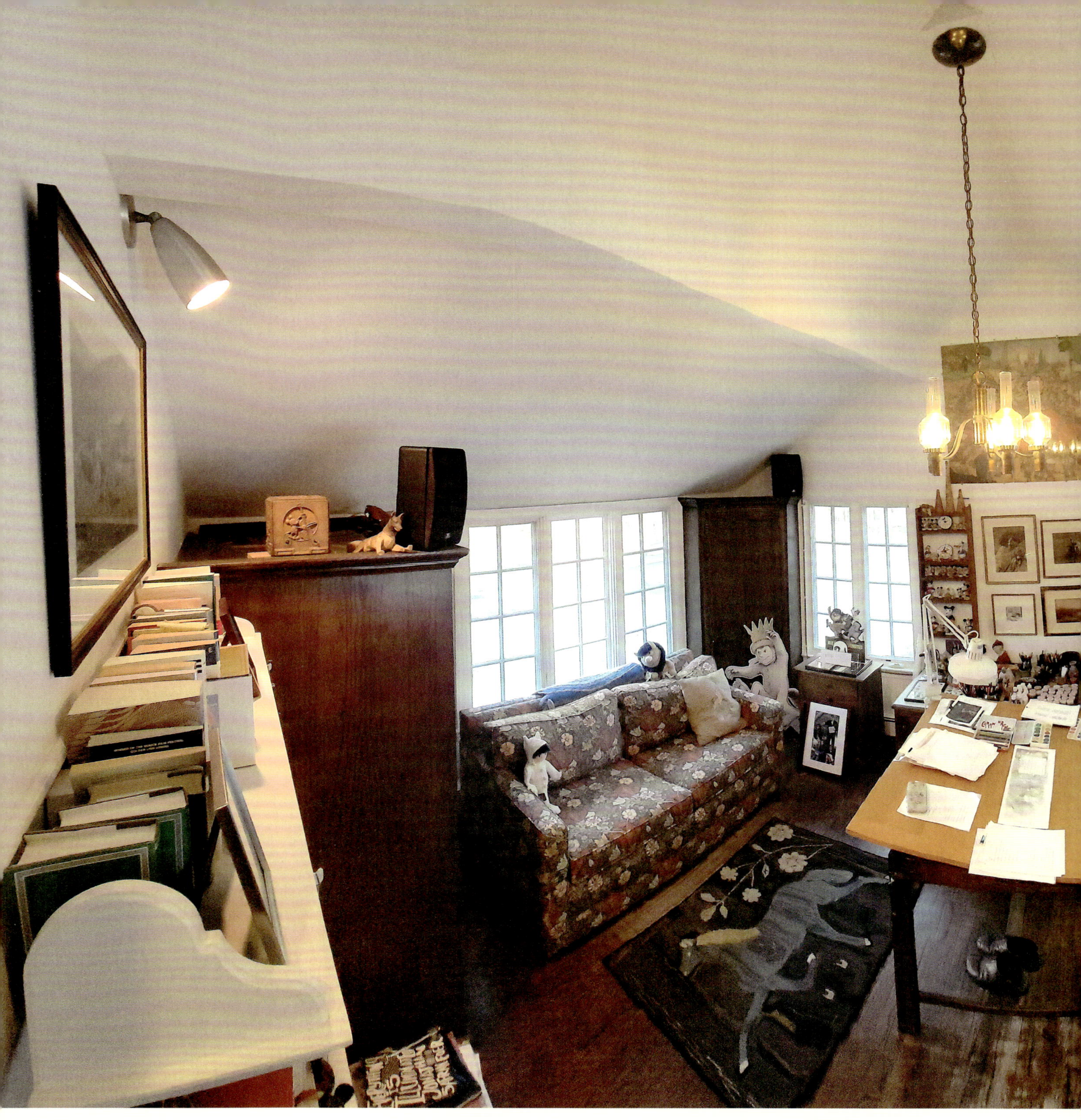

Maurice Sendak's Ridgefield, CT Studio, essentially as it was at his death in 2012 (taken in 2022)

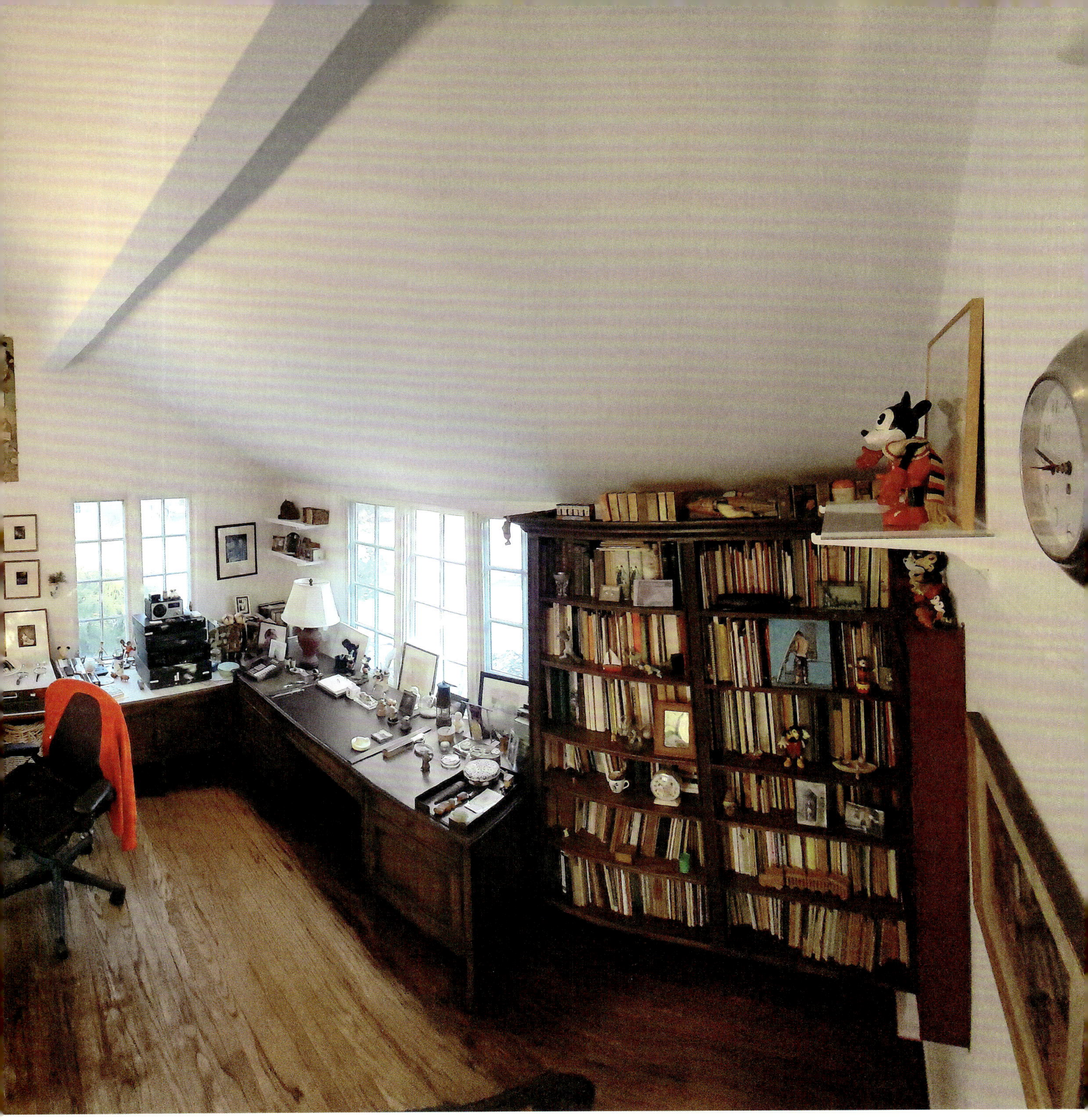

THE MAURICE SENDAK FOUNDATION

The Maurice Sendak Foundation, a not-for-profit charitable organization, is devoted to promoting greater public interest in and understanding of the literary, visual, and performing arts.

The Foundation supports the artistic legacy of Maurice Sendak and nurtures emerging as well as established artists in the fields of children's literature and theater design.

The Foundation also promotes the rights and well-being of children and animals.

The Maurice Sendak Foundation each year supports other not-for-profit organizations whose activities fall within its stated mission. Past recipients include The Good Dog Foundation, P.S. 188 The Maurice Sendak Community School, Yaddo, Portland Opera, and many others.

The Sendak Fellowship, a core Program of The Maurice Sendak Foundation, is a residency that encourages, teaches, and supports artists who tell stories with illustration.

For many years, Maurice Sendak wanted to create an ongoing program for what he had been doing informally his whole career: mentoring promising illustrators. As a young illustrator himself, Sendak was nurtured in the Connecticut home of Ruth Krauss (*A Hole Is to Dig*) and Crockett Johnson (*Harold and the Purple Crayon*). Though Sendak, on occasion, taught illustrating and the art of the picture book in formal educational settings (Parsons School of Design, Yale, etc.), he wanted to create a more intimate setting for passing on his knowledge and artistic wisdom.

In 2009, Maurice Sendak enlisted the help of his long-time assistant, Lynn Caponera, as well as photographer and community activist Dona Ann McAdams to help realize his vision of a residency for illustrators and in 2010 The Sendak Fellowship was founded. Though Sendak was only able to greet and mentor two groups of Fellows before his passing, his legacy carries on.

Once a year, The Sendak Fellowship offers a four-week residency for two to four artists to live and work away from the distractions of their daily routines. It gives artists the opportunity to deeply engage in their work in the relative isolation of a rural setting. While receiving inspiration from each other, the Fellows gain insight from visiting artists and professionals in the field. Much of Maurice's original work is available for viewing by the Fellows, an education in itself. Throughout the Fellowship, guest illustrators and writers lead wide-ranging discussions on publishing, illustrating, writing, and the creative process.

The goal of The Sendak Fellowship, in Maurice's words, is for the Fellows to "... create work that is not vapid or stupid, but *original*; work that excites and incites. Illustration is like dance; it should move like—and to—music."

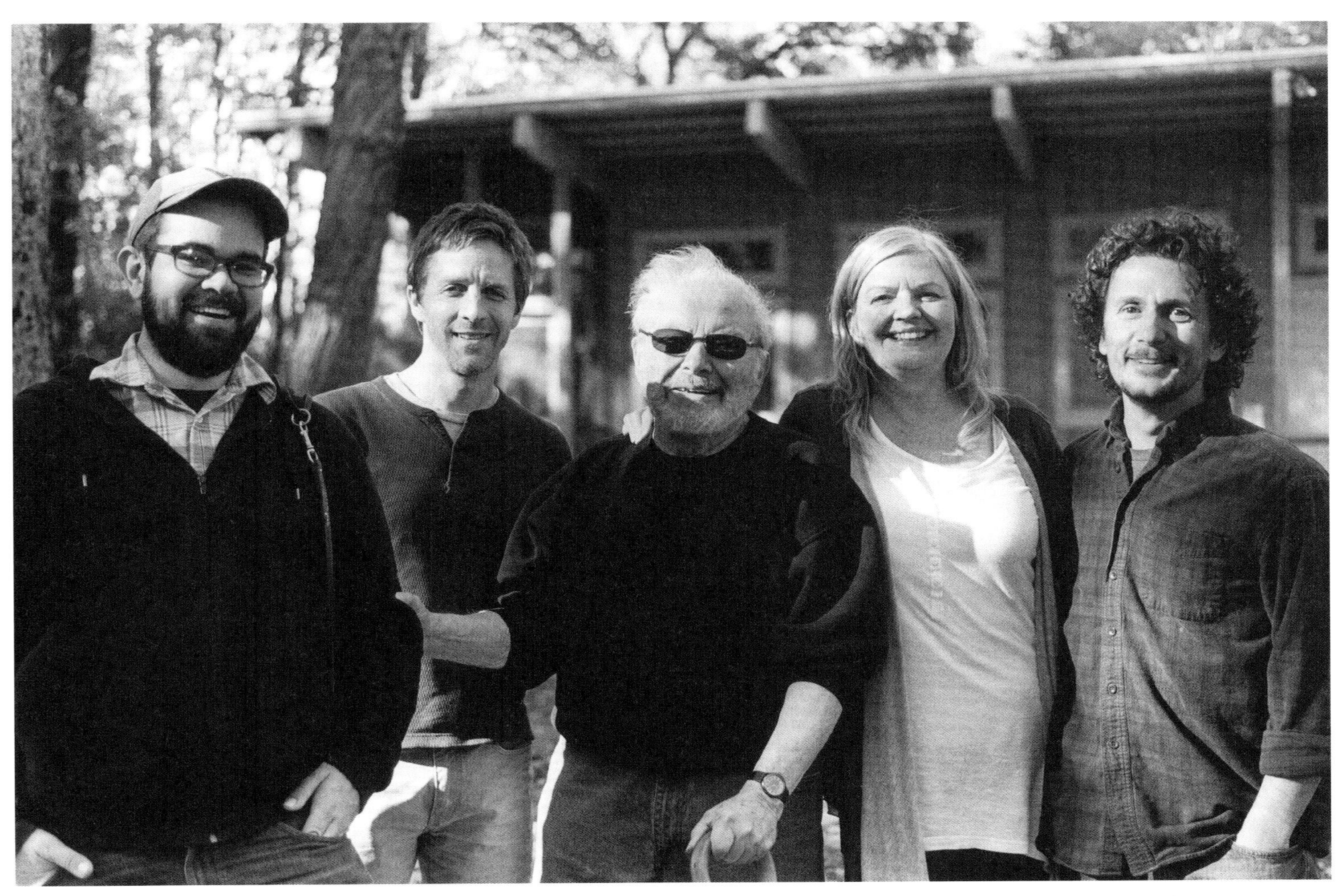

Maurice Sendak with the 2010 Sendak Fellows, Aaron Renier, Paul Schmid, Antoinette Portis and Robert Weinstock, 2010, ©copyright Dona Ann McAdams

CONTRIBUTORS

John Bell, Director, Ballard Institute & Museum of Puppetry, University of Connecticut
Dr. John Bell is a puppeteer and theater historian who began working in puppetry with Bread and Puppet Theater in the 1970s, and continued as a company member for over a decade. He is a founding member of the Brooklyn-based theater company Great Small Works, and the author of many books and articles about puppetry, including "Puppets, Masks, and Performing Objects," "Strings, Hands, Shadows: A Modern Puppet History," and "American Puppet Modernism."

Lynn Caponera, President of the Board and Executive Director of The Maurice Sendak Foundation.
Lynn Caponera met Maurice when he and Dr. Eugene Glynn moved to Ridgefield, CT, in 1971. She spent her childhood at the Sendak / Glynn household helping in the garden, playing with the dogs, and modeling for Maurice for numerous books. At 19 she moved in as caretaker and companion. Over the years she took on a more rigorous role in Maurice's professional and personal life till his death in 2012.

Thomas Crow, Rosalie Solow Professor of Modern Art at the Institute of Fine Arts, New York University
Thomas Crow has authored two influential studies of eighteenth-century French painting: *Painters and Public Life in Eighteenth-Century Paris*, which received the Morey Prize from the College Art Association, and *Emulation: Making Artists for Revolutionary France*. Crow's most recent books are *The Long March of Pop: Art, Design, and Music, 1930–1995*; *No Idols: The Missing Theology of Art*; *Restoration: the Fall of Napoleon in the Course of European Art*; and *The Hidden Mod in Modern Art, London 1956–1969*.

Tyler Fallas, Archivist, The Maurice Sendak Foundation
Tyler Fallas is a writer and archivist who is responsible for cataloging, researching and documenting Maurice Sendak's art collection and work. He has helped to develop The Foundation's presence on social media and further knowledge of Sendak's legacy.

Clara Nguyen, Project Archivist, University of Connecticut Library
Clara was responsible for all activities related to The Maurice Sendak Collection at the University of Connecticut including developing ideas for outreach and educational uses of the collection; and preparing, mounting, and documenting exhibitions in multiple formats and for multiple audiences.

Jonathan Weinberg, artist and Curator of The Maurice Sendak Foundation.
Jonathan Weinberg's books include *Ambition and Love in American Art* and *Pier Groups: Art and Sex along the New York Waterfront.* He was the lead curator of the award-winning exhibition, *Art After Stonewall, 1969–89*. His paintings are in many prominent private and public collections including The Metropolitan Museum of Art, The Belkin Art Gallery, and The Montclair Art Museum.

INDEX OF WORKS

Note: Unless otherwise identified, all works are authored and illustrated or illustrated by Maurice Sendak. Pages with pictures are given in *italics*.

SOURCES

Maurice Sendak's words, quoted throughout the book, were originally published in the following texts

p. 12 Maurice Sendak, *Caldecott & Co.* (New York: Michael di Capua Books, Farrar, Straus and Giroux, 1988), 170

p. 19 Weston Woods Interview, 1965

p. 28 *Caldecott & Co.*, 171

p. 38 Patrick Rodgers, "Selected Sendak: Interviews by the Rosenbach," reprinted in *Conversations with Maurice Sendak*, edited by Peter Kunze (Jackson, Mississippi: University of Mississippi, 2016), 178

p. 42 Stephen Heller, *Innovators of American Illustration* (New York: Van Nostrand Reinhold, 1986) 76

p. 46 *Caldecott & Co.*, 163

p. 50 Heller, 74

p. 67 *Caldecott & Co.*, 78

p. 73 *Caldecott & Co.*, 107–8

p. 74 Hank Nuwer, "Maurice Sendak Q & A," reprinted in *Conversations with Maurice Sendak*, 85

p. 78 Roger Sutton, "An Interview with Maurice Sendak," *The Horn Book*, vol. 79, no. 6, Nov.–Dec. 2003, 689

p. 80 *Caldecott & Co.*, 180

p. 86 *Caldecott & Co.*, 181

p. 88 *Caldecott & Co.*, 154

p. 98 *Caldecott & Co.*, 151

p. 124 *Caldecott & Co.*, 16

p. 130 Selma Lanes, *The Art of Maurice* Sendak (New York: Harry N. Abrams), 1980, 154

p. 142 *Caldecott & Co.*, 208

p. 144 Virginia Haviland, "Questions to an Artist Who Is Also an Author: A Conversation between Maurice Sendak and Virginia Haviland," *Quarterly Journal of the Library of Congress* Vol. 28, no. 4, October 1971, 270

p. 149 *Caldecott & Co.*, 208

p. 154 *Caldecott & Co.*, 158

p. 156 Jonathan Cott, *There's a Mystery There: The Primal Vision of Maurice Sendak* (New York: Knopf Doubleday Publishing Group, 2017) Kindle Edition, 90

p. 158 *Caldecott & Co.*, 210

p. 165 Mervyn Rothstein, "From the Very Busy Sendak, A Book of a Rare Grimm Tale," *The New York Times*, October 19, 1988, C19, 79

p. 166 Tony Kushner, *The Art of Maurice Sendak* (New York: Harry N. Abrams, 2003), 34

p. 178 *Caldecott & Co.*, 202

p. 192 *Caldecott & Co.*, 152

p. 205 Steven Heller, "Maurice Sendak," *Innovators of American Illustration* (New York: Van Nostrand Reinhold, 1986) 74

p. 206 Maurice Sendak, "You Have to Take a Dive," TateShots, https://www.youtube.com/watch?v=xXAjkLUv7dY&t=119s accessed 2 February 2022

p. 210 Heller, 81

p. 214 Philip Nel, "'Don't assume anything': A Conversation with Maurice Sendak," in *Conversations*, 142–3

p. 218 Sutton, 691

p. 219 Sutton, 691

p. 222 Sutton, 691

p. 229 Lanes, 27

p. 233 *Caldecott & Co.*, 170

p. 239 Nel, 142

This book is published in conjunction with the exhibition *Wild Things Are Happening: The Art of Maurice Sendak*, an international touring exhibition organized by the Columbus Museum of Art, 2022–2024.

Columbus Museum of Art
480 East Broad Street
Columbus, OH 43215
columbusmuseum.org

DelMonico Books
available through ARTBOOK | D.A.P.
75 Broad Street, Suite 630
New York, NY 10004
artbook.com
delmonicobooks.com

ISBN: 978-1-63681-052-2

Library of Congress Cataloging-in-Publication control number 2022907334

Designed by Rita Jules, Miko McGinty Inc.
Produced by Miko McGinty
Edited by Sally Salvesen
Type set in Epicene and Rando by Tina Henderson
Prepress by Professional Graphics, Rockford, IL
Printed in Italy by Conti Tipocolor S.r.l., Florence

Jacket: Maurice Sendak, *Where the Wild Things Are*, 1963, watercolor on paper, 9¾ × 11 in.
Cover, front: Detail from Maurice Sendak, *Where the Wild Things Are* (New York: Harper & Row, 1963)
Endpapers: Maurice Sendak, *Where the Wild Things Are*, endpaper, 1963, ink and watercolor on paper, 10 × 22 in.
Frontispiece: Maurice Sendak, Poster Design for *Where the Wild Things Are* and *Higglety Pigglety Pop!* Opera, 1985, watercolor on paper, 33½ × 23½ in.
Page 4: Maurice Sendak, *My Brother's Book*, 2012, watercolor on paper, 11¾ × 8⅞ in.

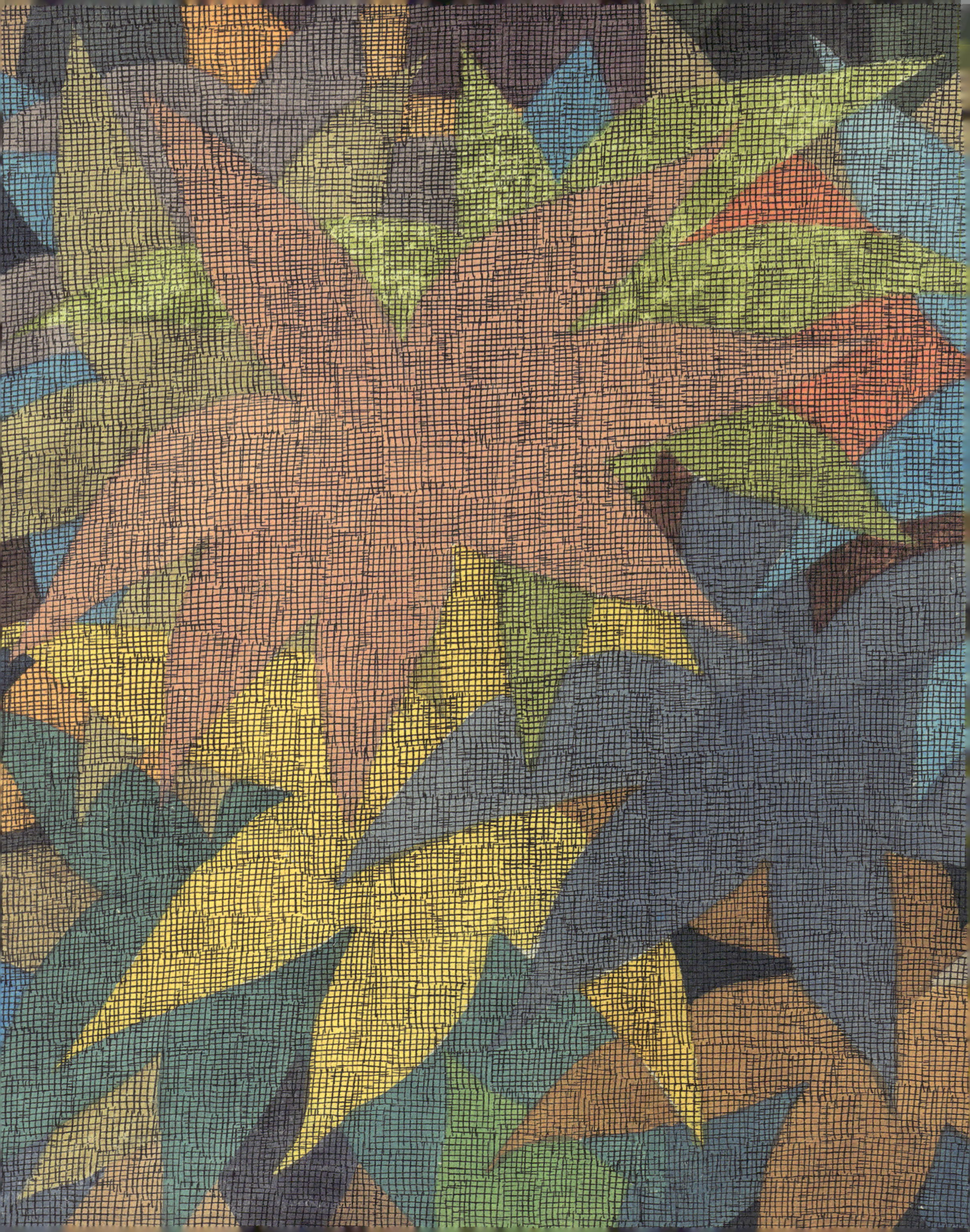